THE
FABULOUS LIFE
OF
SARAH
BERNHARDT

Sarah Bernhardt and Louis Verneuil in *Régine Armand*
(*January 1922*)

Louis Verneuil

———❧———

THE
FABULOUS LIFE
OF
SARAH
BERNHARDT

———❧———

Translated from the French by
ERNEST BOYD

ILLUSTRATED

HARPER & BROTHERS PUBLISHERS

NEW YORK  *LONDON*

THE FABULOUS LIFE OF SARAH BERNHARDT

To Germaine

Contents

Chapter I How I Met Sarah Bernhardt   1

II Childhood, Youth, Beginnings   29

III The Odéon, the War of 1870   62

IV Sarah Bernhardt at the Comédie Française   89

V America, Return, Jacques Damala   125

VI Marriage, Rupture, Apotheosis   158

VII Tours, the Renaissance   188

VIII The Théâtre Sarah Bernhardt   225

IX Last Years   268

Rôles Played by Sarah Bernhardt   297

Important Dates in the Life of Sarah Bernhardt   301

Index   303

Illustrations

Sarah Bernhardt and Louis Verneuil in *Régine Armand*   *Frontispiece*

These illustrations grouped as a separate section, will be found facing page 168

Sarah Bernhardt in *Le Passant*
The Parisian Theatrical World in 1875
Sarah Bernhardt at the Comédie-Française
Sarah Bernhardt on the back of the whale in Boston harbor
The collapse of the bridge over the bay of Saint-Louis, just after the crossing of the "Bernhardt Special"
Sarah Bernhardt as *Théodora*
Sarah Bernhardt in *La Dame aux Camélias*
Sarah Bernhardt and De Max in *Gismonda*
Sarah Bernhardt as *Phèdre*
Sarah Bernhardt as *Hamlet*
Sarah Bernhardt in *L'Aiglon*
Sarah Bernhardt and Coquelin Aîné during the rehearsals of *L'Aiglon* for their American Tour
Sarah Bernhardt and Coquelin Aîné in *Cyrano de Bergerac*
Sarah Bernhardt and Victorien Sardou during the rehearsals of *La Sorcière*
Sarah Bernhardt in her own play *Adrienne Lecouvreur*
Sarah Bernhardt in *La Reine Elisabeth*
Sarah Bernhardt at sixty-nine in *L'Aiglon*
Sarah Bernhardt in *Daniel*

CHAPTER I

How I Met Sarah Bernhardt

THE first time I saw Sarah Bernhardt was in 1904, when I was eleven years old. She was playing at her own theater in Paris *La Sorcière* by Victorien Sardou, the last play he wrote for her and perhaps not one of the best.

I add this qualification reluctantly, because I am a very great admirer of Sardou. Marvelously and ingeniously constructed, his plays are full of invention and extraordinary situations. When it reaches this point, knowledge of the theater amounts to a kind of genius. Although, for more than fifty years and in all his works, he always succeeded in getting the most brilliant casts, it was certainly in Sarah Bernhardt that he had found his most magnificent interpreter. How can one recall, without thinking of her, the great heroines that Sardou created for her and that she alone could bring to life: *La Tosca, Fédora, Théodora, Cléopâtre, Gismonda*?

La Sorcière was not quite in the same vein. True, it had some superb scenes, especially the Inquisition in the fourth act, in which De Max unforgettably personified Cardinal Ximenes, and Sarah Bernhardt, tortured and tormented by the judges and agents of the Holy Office, reached the highest power of tragedy as her terror increased. But the beginning of the play was less remarkable, and the end was more noisy, I think, than really powerful.

Needless to say, at that time I did not notice anything like that. The first act takes place at night. When Sarah Bernhardt entered, as the striking figure of Zoraya, the Moor, violently lit by a shaft of moonlight, her left arm full of wild flowers, freshly cut on the hillside with the silver sickle which she held in her right hand, I felt as if a supernatural being had suddenly appeared. When she spoke I was seized by a kind of ecstasy. From the beginning to the end of the performance I was positively fascinated. When, at the end of the fifth act, I saw her dying, carried to the stake by the archers, where the howling mob wanted to see the sorceress burned, a great sadness suddenly came over me, not at seeing her die, but because thus early ended a spectacle so beautiful that I should certainly never see another so magnificent.

Sarah Bernhardt was then sixty. Of course, child as I was, I did not suspect it and naïvely thought her the most beautiful and youngest woman in the world. But this illusion was not so very absurd, for, in fact, she was extraordinary for her age. Even in the front row of the orchestra, when she played *La Sorcière*, nobody would have thought her more than thirty-five to forty.

That play was far from being suitable for children, and my father would undoubtedly have preferred to take me to see her play a classic or even *L'Aiglon*. But early in December, 1903, a few days before the opening of *La Sorcière*, Sarah Bernhardt was seriously ill. Once again it was rumored that her life was in danger and that she would probably be ordered to take a very long rest. As a matter of fact, such rumors had been circulating periodically for more than thirty years. Even before the war of 1870, at the time when Sarah Bernhardt created the part of Coppée's *Le Passant*, it was currently said that she was consumptive and that it was sad to think she would obviously die young.

As the years passed, these apprehensions naturally diminished. But there came a time when those who were alarmed about her health became worried about her age. While, contrary to the legend, it gradually became certain that her lungs were completely intact, people began to fear earlier for her than for any other woman the weight of her years. Shortly after she did *L'Aiglon*, it was already being said: "Obviously a woman is by no means old at sixty. But think of the career she has lived through. She made her debut at eighteen, and how she has worked since then . . . tours in every part of the world . . . theater managements . . . productions of tremendous spectacles . . . money troubles . . . sleepless nights . . . enough to kill a much younger and stronger person."

Thus, for nearly fifty years, the imminent death was expected of this woman who lived for seventy-eight years and a half.

Moreover, it was just as absurd to believe that her life was prematurely threatened by old age as formerly to have imagined the threat of illness. She had no rival for endurance and energy, and it was only a *fifth* attack of uremia in 1923—her right leg having been amputated eight years earlier—which overcame her physical resistance, whose power, until then, bordered on the miraculous.

Nevertheless, in 1904, it was whispered that she could play only as a result of constant care; that she received injections at each intermission, her doctor remaining in the wings every night during the entire performance; and that *La Sorcière* might well be the last play in which she would ever be seen.

Was this gossip the result of a real indisposition, or had her manager hit upon this elementary stunt, so often used elsewhere, to draw bigger crowds of her adoring public? I honestly don't think so. At that time, and for a long time to come, Sarah Bernhardt was in the full splendor of her glory. Her effect upon the crowd was enormous. For box-office purposes there was really no need to have recourse to those little tricks employed by second-raters.

However that may be, my father was deeply impressed by this alarming news. He had applauded Sarah Bernhardt at the dawn of her fame, had seen her with Mounet Sully at the Comédie Française in *Hernani*, in 1877, and since then had seen her in almost all her roles. If she was really going to die any day, or even retire from the stage, he would never have forgiven himself for not having offered me at least one chance of seeing someone whom, like nine tenths of the French of the period, he considered the greatest artist of all times and all countries. He little knew that this performance of *La Sorcière* would subsequently have such a direct and decisive influence on my life.

If I have always been drawn by the theater; if, as far back as my childhood's memories, I have never thought of any profession other than that of a dramatist; if, at school while not yet a senior, I began presumptuously to write tragedies; and if, filled with impatience, I had my first play produced at a theater in Paris at the age of eighteen —it was assuredly my frantic admiration for Sarah Bernhardt, the cult I made of her from the day I saw her, the feeling which she alone gave me that the theater could be much more than an art—a mission—and could attain to heights of beauty inaccessible to the uninitiated, which transformed my vocation into an exclusive and overwhelming passion such that, for thirty years, I have lived, so to speak, only for the theater.

Furthermore, I had never approached Sarah Bernhardt when she thus imperiously showed me my path through life. It was not until

1919, when I was twenty-six and my professional activity was already considerable, that I was introduced to her, and she first spoke to me. It is true, my long patience was rewarded. From that day until her death—that is, during almost the last four years of her life—I practically never left her. First I very quickly became a familiar friend of her home and her theater. Then, early in 1921, I became legally and religiously attached to her by the closest and most direct family bonds. But I had not waited until then to make her—as did so many others —the idol of my life and the unique object of all my adoration.

From 1904 to 1914 I really believe I saw Sarah Bernhardt act on an average of twelve to fifteen times a year and, of course, several times in the same part. Very soon my assiduity and some small presents had got me into the good graces of the woman at the box office and, even if I arrived at the last minute before the curtain rose, she would arrange to keep me one of my favorite *strapontins*, in the orchestra, to the left or right, on one of the side aisles nearest the stage. In this obscure corner I spent the finest nights in the theater of my entire life.

Phèdre, L'Aiglon, and *La Dame aux Camélias,* of course, are my outstanding memories of Sarah Bernhardt at that time. But I also saw her, unforgettable, in many other plays, especially *La Samaritaine,* by Edmond Rostand; *Les Bouffons,* by Miguel Zamacoïs; *Lucrèce Borgia* and *Angelo,* by Victor Hugo; *Le Procès de Jeanne d'Arc,* by Emile Moreau; *La Belle au Bois Dormant* and *La Beffa,* by Jean Richepin; *La Vierge d'Avila,* by Catulle Mendès; *La Femme de Claude,* by Dumas *fils; Fédora* and *La Tosca,* by Sardou; *Lorenzaccio,* by Musset; and finally *Jeanne Doré,* by Tristan Bernard, which she created in December, 1913. In this part of a simple, provincial bookseller, wearing a plain black serge dress, she was as powerful and as beautiful as when she played the most gorgeous queen or some mysterious heroine of legend.

I also had five or six large albums entirely filled with photographs of Sarah Bernhardt, at every age and in all her roles. I had every one of the hundreds of picture postcards of her and every program of the plays in which I had seen her. Even the walls of my room were actually covered with her pictures. A tiny head of her was pasted in the case of my watch and I had a larger one in my pocketbook.

Needless to say, this veneration did not imply the slightest trace of love, even respectful, distant, and hopeless. In the first place, I was a youngster and she was a grandmother. When I was twenty-one,

Sarah Bernhardt was seventy. Above all, she seemed to me a being so supernatural, so superhuman, so beyond this life, that I could not even imagine anyone feeling for her anything but the most humble admiration, a kneeling devotion.

Those who were not alive in her day or who never saw her act will perhaps shrug their shoulders slightly and think that my tenderness and gratitude, added to my great intimacy with her, tend to make me exaggerate my enthusiasm somewhat. I hope that the pages of this book, in which the essential facts of her life are faithfully related, will render any subsequent incredulity impossible. On the other hand, how many authors I could cite, among the world's most illustrious, who have expressed themselves about her in terms much more frenzied than those I employ. Suffice it to recall some striking words of Jules Renard.

If I choose Jules Renard, it is precisely because he was neither a poet nor in any way lyric, as is well known. Conciseness was his fixed idea, simplicity his pride. He had the most restrained, the least expansive, of styles; he was extremely discreet in his use of epithets and was willing to admit that enthusiasm was unknown to him a priori. In the matter of praise, two dry, clear lines of Jules Renard are equal to two dithyrambic pages of Catulle Mendès. Thus, speaking of Sarah Bernhardt, Jules Renard expressed himself in his admirable *Journal* in 1896:

"Imagine the ugliest of men. Nobody loves him. He knows it and is resigned. But sometimes he thinks: 'Ah, if I could only live for a while in a little corner near Sarah! I should believe I was the most beloved of men. I should ask nothing of other women. The others are very nice, very pretty, but Sarah is genius.'

"In the crowd waiting at the door of her theater, there are rich people whose only importance is that they admire her, and there are beggars who are equal to the greatest on earth, because they are going to see Sarah pass. There may even be a criminal, a man abandoned by all, who has abandoned himself, who will be arrested as soon as She has passed. But he says: 'Now I don't mind dying. I have seen Sarah before I die. Sarah is genius.' "

It would seem to me difficult to carry hyperbole further than this.

I may add that no more than I, no more than the vast majority, great or mediocre, famous or obscure, who made the same cult of her, did Jules Renard mingle the slightest love with the idolatry which she inspired in him. During that same year in his *Journal*, a few pages later, is this charming and significant phrase: "At a sign from Sarah Bernhardt I would follow her to the ends of the earth . . . with my wife."

Early in 1915 the operation which had been feared for years was decided upon as absolutely necessary. At a hospital in Bordeaux her right leg was amputated a little above the knee. With smiling courage she went through this terrible ordeal, and from that day Sarah Bernhardt never walked another step.

Numerous legends have circulated about this subject. It was said that the reason why, in her later years, Sarah Bernhardt always appeared on the stage without moving, seated or lying down, was because she did not wish to limp in public, as her artificial leg obliged her to lean on a walking stick, thus rendering her movements difficult and ungraceful. It was said that, despite her age, she herself adjusted her artificial leg every morning and detached it at night unassisted, as she would not allow anyone to help her at this task.

All that is absurd, for one very good reason. Never at any time during the eight years between her operation and her death did Sarah Bernhardt wear an artificial leg. People were often astonished when I gave them this information.

"But, how did she walk then? On crutches?" they asked naïvely.

"Did she hop?" the irreverent would add.

Neither. She did not walk. She never walked.

How, then, did she move about?

She was carried, always and invariably carried.

The day after her operation, a kind of folding chair was made for her. It was narrow and took up very little space. At the sides, on a level with the seat, were two wooden shafts about six feet long, which folded when the chair did. On a very much smaller scale, with just a back and, of course, no doors nor roof, it was like a seventeenth-century sedan chair. As a matter of fact, she called it "my chair." Its total weight was not more than six and a half pounds. Two people, one in front and one behind—her valet, her companion, the manager of the theater, a couple of scene shifters or friends (how often have I helped myself!)—would get between the shafts, raise them, and thus carry her from one place to another.

In the morning, when she awoke or, rather, when she wanted to get up, the chair was brought and unfolded beside her bed. With the help of her hands and her one leg she sat down on it, and was carried to the bathroom where she dressed—sitting down, of course. In the same way she was taken from her bathroom to her little drawing room or to the dining room. When she went out from the dining room to her car, with its specially constructed body, the doors being unusually wide to admit "the chair," Sarah Bernhardt settled back in the seat, while her attendant, seated beside the chauffeur, held the folded chair in front of him during the drive. On her arrival at the theater or elsewhere, the chair was again set up inside the car, and the chauffeur and the attendant carried Sarah Bernhardt to her dressing room or to the people whom she was visiting. As may be imagined, she regularly passed between two rows of curiosity seekers or admirers lined up on the sidewalk.

It was under these extraordinary conditions that Sarah Bernhardt made her last tour in the United States, during which she appeared as a music-hall "turn." She never walked, and she played only short one-acters or a scene from some one of her former triumphs: the fifth act of *La Dame aux Camélias*, for example, in which she could remain lying down throughout, or the prison scene from *Le Procès de Jeanne d'Arc*.

This tour lasted eighteen months, from the end of 1916 to the beginning of 1918. Her last performance in New York took place on January 14, 1918, at Keith's Riverside Theater, in an act entitled *Du Théâtre au Champ d'Honneur*, in which she played a young French soldier mortally wounded and dying in a trench.

She returned to France a few months before the Armistice, extremely tired by the long journey, and for a long time she was not seen on any stage or in any public place. Later she told me that during this American tour she had been seized by a deep melancholy, which she felt was shared by the public, because she could no longer go on except under those unimpressive conditions, for fifteen minutes, and in some unimportant trifle, or in fragments of great plays which she once played in their entirety, and that on her return, heartsick, she had decided never to act again in Paris.

However, after more than a year's silence, she yielded to the pressing offers of a great music hall, the Alhambra, in the Place de la République, and in the autumn of 1919 she agreed to appear for two weeks in one of the short acts—they would be called sketches nowadays—which she had played in the United States: *Vitrail,* by René Fauchois.

I hesitated a great deal before going to this play. Five years had elapsed since her last performances in *Jeanne Doré* at the Théâtre Sarah Bernhardt. Naturally I knew about her operation and that she could not walk. Was I not going to be terribly disillusioned at seeing her reduced to such a plight, she who for fifteen years had been for me the incarnation of Art and Beauty in their purest and most complete expression? Despite everything, I could not resist the desire to see her once more, perhaps for the last time—as everyone feared even as far back as *La Sorcière.* With a vague pang in my heart I went to the Alhambra.

I went back again the same night!

Obviously she had changed. Now she no longer looked young. But her voice was still just as beautiful and, above all, I found unchanged her astonishing aura of poetry. Her sovereign charm was intact and, as soon as she began to speak, the same inexplicable but customary thrill of wonder, I could plainly see, seized the two thousand spectators who crowded the house, the Alhambra, packed from floor to ceiling. Old and mutilated, tragically and implacably condemned to sit still, Sarah Bernhardt was still Sarah Bernhardt, true to her motto: *Quand même!*[1]

Once again I was disturbed and delighted. At last, after this long silence, we were going to see Sarah Bernhardt again. But, I thought, never again in a music hall, between jugglers, dancers, and a trained monkey, in surroundings so shocking and so completely unworthy of her. Certainly she would reappear in great parts, written, of course, to suit her present circumstances, but in real plays, at the Théâtre Sarah Bernhardt, which, I fondly imagined, must be arranging a play for her return.

I made inquiries. I was totally mistaken. Her theater, the management of which she had left entirely to her son and her manager, Victor Ullmann, did not anticipate any further performances by Sarah Bernhardt. Besides, they said, how could one think of her return since she could not perform in any of the plays in her repertory?

I was astounded. How could this be? Sarah Bernhardt was still in possession of almost all her faculties. Without tiring herself in the least, she was now playing twice a day at the Alhambra. Granted, she

---

[1] "In spite of everything" or words to that effect. *Trans.*

could not walk; but her memory seemed to be infallible and, in any case, her genius, her tremendous personality, and her magic were practically as powerful as in her heyday. Why had no writer, none of the authors for whom she had created successes in the past and who, seeing her constantly, knew today that she was still capable of acting— why had they not thought of giving her an opportunity? Rostand and Sardou were dead, it is true. But how many others could or should have had this idea, which became irresistible if one just looked at her for five minutes on the stage.

I soon ceased to be indignant and began to think things over, with the result that, two days later, I made an appointment with her son, Maurice Bernhardt. I knew him slightly, as I now knew more or less everybody in the theater. Moreover, at the time, I had had some ten plays produced in Paris, two or three of which—*La Charrette Anglaise, Monsieur Beverley, Le Traité d'Auteuil*—ran for many weeks. I felt that I could make the proposal which had taken me to his office, without seeming ridiculous.

Maurice Bernhardt was then nearly fifty-five. Tall, slim, with fine features, he had undoubtedly been one of the handsomest men of his generation. But *paralysis agitans*, which had attacked him in 1914 and had since been gradually increasing, had aged him prematurely. At first only the little finger of his right hand was affected. Soon this constant tremor spread to all the fingers, then to his hand, and now to his forearm. Henceforth, night and day, he did not know what it was to be still. As early as 1919 he had to hold his right hand with his left in order to write.

He listened to me in amazement and then he said: "Write a play for my mother? Don't you realize that she can't walk?"

"Well, the character won't walk."

"And that she is seventy-five?"

"I saw her at the Alhambra three days ago. She is marvelous. Besides, Sarah Bernhardt has been ageless for years."

"She can play an act running a quarter of an hour for several days. But she could never learn three or four acts and play them for months."

"In the first place, it is not a question of three or four acts. Even played by her, I do not think that a motionless character would be bearable for a whole evening. The character I have in mind for her would appear only in the last two acts of a four-act play. That is, she would be on the stage only for an hour and a quarter at most."

"So you believe you would be able to . . ."

"Let me try, at least."

Utterly unconvinced, I admit, and certain that I was either dreaming or crazy, Maurice Bernhardt replied: "Very well." Whereupon I immediately started to write.

If he had been more encouraging, more interested in my idea, I would have begged him to ask his mother to see me. Then, to save a lot of possibly useless work, if the play happened not to please her, I could have outlined the scenario to Sarah Bernhardt before writing it. But I knew how passionately devoted she was to her son and the influence he had with her in consequence. His attitude showed me that he would talk to her about my project without enthusiasm. Therefore, my only chance was to submit to her a completed play which would attract her so much that she would want to play in it as soon as possible.

A few weeks later I finished the play which I had described in general outline to Maurice Bernhardt. It was called *Daniel* after the part which I had written for Sarah Bernhardt. During the first two acts she was constantly mentioned, like *L'Arlésienne*, without ever appearing. When the curtain rose on the third act, Daniel finally appeared, confined to an armchair by sickness, and played the entire act, which was very long, without leaving the stage. In the fourth, last and very short act, Daniel lay dying.

About the end of November, 1919, I read the play to Sarah Bernhardt. I shall never forget that first interview with her.

While I was working I had not seen Maurice Bernhardt again, but I had met Victor Ullmann, his partner, several times. Being a shrewd businessman, he realized that if her part were cleverly built up the return of the "boss" was sure to bring in large receipts. He, at different times, had warmly encouraged me and had spoken of me and my play enthusiastically to Sarah Bernhardt, although he had never seen a word of it.

Consequently she was well disposed toward me in advance when she received me early one afternoon, about half past two, at her house in the Boulevard Péreire, on the second floor, in the room which she mostly used, leading to the bedroom. It was a small drawing room—a sort of boudoir with a bathroom—where a huge wood fire crackled in the tall chimney piece eight or nine months of the year. She was alone with her companion, Jeanne de Gournay, whom she immediately asked to leave the room. At my request Ullmann had advised Maurice Bernhardt not to interfere and, after I had read the four acts to his mother, without any other audience, to ask her to make whatever decision she pleased on her own account, without consulting anyone. If she liked the play and felt capable of acting in it, she herself was the best judge.

Dressed in a flowing gown of white satin, Sarah Bernhardt was seated in a large armchair by the fireside. She received me with a charming smile and extended her white hand, so spiritual and expressive, the nails very convex, its movements still incomparably graceful.

I was deeply moved. At last, after fifteen years of silent and distant admiration, I was being received by Sarah Bernhardt in her own house! I was seated three feet away from her and, to open our initial conversation, I was going to read her a play specially written for her! It must be admitted that there was a great deal to make me feel nervous. As a matter of fact, I have rarely felt so frightened as I did then.

It was not that I was afraid of the effect my reading might produce on her. Somehow I felt intuitively that she would like *Daniel*. What actually upset me was meeting this legendary, this fabulous, woman about whom Europe and America had been talking for forty years, in all the newspapers, in every language, commenting upon her slightest gesture. Here I was, talking familiarly with the prodigious artist who, ever since my childhood, had given me the most indescribable happiness; in short, finding myself suddenly in the presence of one who was indisputably the greatest personality in the entire world at that time.

I may add that my case was not exceptional. Later, when I was constantly close to Sarah Bernhardt, I had occasion to introduce or to see introduced innumerable people, among them distinguished personages, important politicians, or famous artists from every country. I swear that, for more than three years, I have never seen anyone, man or woman, young or old, obscure or famous, speak to Sarah Bernhardt for the first time and not succumb at once to an uncontrollable emotion, which was usually barely concealed.

She is the only person I have ever met who inevitably produced this extraordinary impression on all people who had not previously met her. For the last thirty years, I believe, I have been in contact with the greatest figures in contemporary Europe. I have personally known—some more, some less—Mounet Sully, Anatole France, Rodin, Bartet, Saint-Saëns, Massenet, de Porto-Riche, Réjane, Coquelin, Rostand, D'Annunzio, Poincaré, Clemenceau, Briand, Foch . . . How many others? None of them was so impressive, none had such an astonishing hold on his listeners, as Sarah Bernhardt.

She was aware of this, and often deliberately employed this exceptional gift to make it extremely embarrassing for intruders and people asking for favors. On the other hand, when she wanted to, she was just as capable of putting the most nervous visitor at his ease.

That is what she did for me with infinite good grace that day. At the end of fifteen minutes, having almost recovered my assurance, I was able to begin reading without my voice choking. She listened almost without moving, her eyes fixed on mine. After the first, and then after the second, act, she aked: "Are you quite sure you don't want a glass of water? Some lemonade? Would you mind throwing a log on the fire?" That was all. Not a word of approval, however vague or halfhearted. I was beginning to lose confidence. However, I started resolutely on the third act—"her" act, the best, as I thought; the act, in any case, for the sake of which I had written the play. And when I reached the "big scene," I was intensely happy to notice that Sarah Bernhardt was crying.

During the few pages of the fourth act her emotion was the same. When, for the last time, I said "Curtain" and closed my manuscript, she held out her hand to me without speaking. In one movement I was on my knee before her. She gently kissed my forehead and murmured in all simplicity: "Thanks."

Obviously this gratitude was not addressed either to the play or to the part. Could she be moved by anything so slight, she who had created the purest masterpieces, had interpreted Shakespeare, Racine, Victor Hugo, and Rostand? What touched her was the possibilities I offered her, the opportunity, as she suddenly realized, to continue to act, in spite of her infirmity, and for as long as she had strength enough. I have said that she did not want to appear in a music hall again, nor play in those little sketches, which were so misrepresentative and "showed her off" rather than permitted her really to enter into a part. But the alternative was inactivity, retirement, and, what was more serious, straitened circumstances.

Sarah Bernhardt was poor. In the course of her long career she had made fortunes. No lyrical, no dramatic, artist had achieved such financial successes as she, but she had saved nothing. She had always lived in regal style, throwing incredible sums to the winds. When I brought her *Daniel*, as I learned later, she was in the greatest difficulties. Pawnbrokers, moneylenders, notes renewed or protested, this admirable woman had been through all that. Many countries in Europe felt it a duty and an honor to help their national figures in case of need. France had not thought of such a thing.

That is precisely why, from the first day, Sarah Bernhardt devoted to me that affection which was manifested in so many ways and never failed. Just when she believed that she could no longer earn her living, I provided her with the means of raising receipts until the end of her days. Not with *Daniel* alone, of course, but in all the other parts for which this prepared the way. The method and, if I may so express myself, the suitable length of a motionless part having been indicated, other plays of this kind would necessarily be offered to her and, contrary to the prophecies of all around her, would enable her to enjoy a second career.

As a matter of fact, at her theater they were so convinced that she would never act again that a well-filled program had been drawn up for the current season. Plays had been accepted and stars engaged. Three or four plays were awaiting their turn, all of which had to be put on before the summer of 1920. Thus, when Sarah Bernhardt told her son and Ullmann that she would play *Daniel*, they had to warn me, despite their obvious desire to bill her name, that the play could not be produced until the following October.

Ten months' wait! I was horribly disappointed, but Sarah Bernhardt was not in the least put out. "The time will pass quickly," she said. "You will come to see me often. You will go through my part with me. We'll have time to get together a perfect cast, to have magnificent sets made." At seventy-five she postponed the creation of a part to the following year with the utmost calm and, generally speaking, she formed many projects which were to materialize even much later.

However, now that she had in her possession a play that was ready and needed only an available house in order to be produced, her inactivity, which was due to no disability of her own, suddenly weighed upon her more than before. Her own theater was not available; but obviously she could have played *Daniel* immediately in any other house, which would have been only too happy to receive her. But she could not bring herself to confer the glamour of her name on another management; to compete with the Théâtre Sarah Bernhardt, especially with her own son. Besides, Paris would not have understood why an event which promised to be her return—after the war, her operation, and prolonged absence from the stage—should not take place at the theater to which she gave her name, in 1899, and a vogue which had made it one of the most sought-out theaters in the capital for twenty years.

As her impatience grew, she wondered if she could not find a part in some classical play in which she could act, as in *Daniel*, without moving; or a part, at least, in which she could come on or go off stage, carried on a litter or palanquin. She went over all the French tragedies of the seventeenth century, even those of Voltaire, the works of Shakespeare, and she glanced through Sophocles, Euripides, and Aeschylus. It turned out that, with a few modifications and some careful cutting, several parts could be so adapted as to be played without walking. First she thought of playing Agrippina in *Britannicus*. But the part is very long and is spread over four acts of the play, thereby necessitating frequent entrances and exits. That was the chief stumbling block. The fact of being carried onto the stage, permissible in itself for the mother of Nero, would have been tolerable to the audience once or twice. By the third time this clumsy device might have provoked smiles. And all her life Sarah Bernhardt was extremely sensitive to the slightest trace of ridicule. So she reluctantly chose *Athalie*.

Just as she profoundly admired the work of Racine, up to and particularly *Phèdre*, so his last two tragedies, written after a long silence and only for the edification of Madame de Maintenon's pupils, seemed to her inferior. Some fifteen years earlier, for a few classical Thursdays, she had amused herself by producing *Esther*, reproducing exactly the performance at the Ecole de Saint-Cyr, all the parts being played by women, Sarah Bernhardt herself playing Assuérus. But this had been for her much more a relaxation, a game, than a genuine revival performed with love and conviction. I may add that *Athalie*, in particular, had always seemed to her a mortal bore. But it had one essential advantage: the character appears only twice, in the second and fifth acts. Going to and coming from the temple, the queen could be carried quite naturally by her guards, on a sort of throne.

One day in February, 1920, I received a telephone call from her companion, asking me to come to see Sarah Bernhardt. I have not explained, for it goes without saying, that after the reading of *Daniel* I had had occasion to see her again several times and more and more frequently. Rarely a week passed that she did not do me the honor of receiving me, at least once or twice, at tea or in the evening after dinner, even at lunch, when she had about ten guests every day. She always received me with extreme friendliness and good grace.

That day, when nobody yet knew of her project, she said: "Just imagine, I should like to play *Athalie*." Then, bursting immediately into her slight, silvery laugh, she continued: "No. Let me tell the truth. I just want to act, and the only part I can find is *Athalie*. Before deciding, I wanted to know what you thought of the idea."

I protested that Sarah Bernhardt really did not have to consult anybody and especially me. . . .

Smiling at my misunderstanding, she interrupted: "That is not the question. I promised to make my return in your play. *Daniel* can't be produced before October. Very well. Like you, I will wait, and I'll not do any other play anywhere regularly; that is, uninterruptedly, at night, with a dress rehearsal and invitations to the press. That's agreed. I have *Athalie* in mind only for eight or ten isolated performances, not consecutively, at the rate of two matinees a week, Thursdays and Saturdays. But, all the same, I'll be doing a play before yours. If you don't like that, say so, frankly. I'll postpone the project and give *Athalie* next season, after I have created *Daniel*. You decide."

Obviously, my only reply was to thank her for allowing me and all of Paris to see her as soon as possible in a part which she had never played before.

Under the conditions outlined—that is, only at classical matinees, while her theater continued at night to carry out its program—Sarah Bernhardt played *Athalie* early in April, 1920. She was absolutely extraordinary in the part, in the sense that she positively *created* the character, giving it a reality not only different but exactly the reverse of that given for two hundred years by all the most celebrated actresses in the part.

Athalie has always been portrayed as an impressive queen, harsh, almost brutal, talking in loud tones and spreading terror about her. I remember Sarah Bernhardt lucidly explaining why that is absurd.

"What? Here is a woman who treacherously comes to see what is happening in the temple; that is, in the camp of her enemies. She is not going to scold and shout, thereby putting everyone on his guard. If she has the slightest intelligence, she will first try to reassure those who are watching her and, by an exaggerated pretense of sweetness, gain their confidence.

"This seems to me particularly important," she added, "in the famous scene with little Joas. At the Comédie Française I have seen several famous actresses, especially Madame Segond Weber, begin her interrogation in a hollow tone of voice, frowning, and with threats on her lips. Observing such an attitude, the child will obviously be frightened, burst into tears, and run away at top speed, refusing to answer this virago who—and she will deserve it—will not find out anything she wanted to know."

What subtlety, what power, what truth, on the other hand, in Sarah Bernhardt's interpretation when, blonde and smiling, she beckoned to the little boy to come to her, caressed his hair, kissed his forehead, and in her sweetest voice, with its melodious and persuasive intonations, questioned him: "What is your name? . . . Your father? . . . Have you no parents?" I can still hear her with delight and I shall always hear her.

Early in the summer of 1920 Sarah Bernhardt departed for Belle Isle, where she had spent her vacations for years. She had very kindly offered to have me there for a few days. But, in July and August, with Gaby Morlay, I was touring the casinos in my latest comedy, *Mademoiselle ma Mère,* in which we had opened that February in Paris. I had to refuse Sarah Bernhardt's invitation, and how I regretted it!

In order to allow her to rest at Belle Isle until the end of September, her son, Ullmann, and I had set the opening of *Daniel* for the beginning of November. So we began rehearsing about October 1.

What those rehearsals were like, how the play was produced, why I wrote a man's part for Sarah Bernhardt, who were the other members of the cast, how the opening performance of *Daniel* was received, on November 9, 1920; the repeated ovations which greeted her return to the theater; the run of the play, first in Paris and then everywhere she played it for two years—I could not describe all that briefly here. This is just an introductory chapter, whose only purpose is to furnish my references, so to speak, to establish clearly in the reader's mind how I came to know Sarah Bernhardt much better than any other living writer. Others, in fact, may have known her longer. During her last years none was in such constant and close relations with her as I.

I shall return in detail to *Daniel* in the last chapter of this book, when, having told the story of her young life and her entire career, as I heard it from her own lips, I retrace the period of which I was a personal and daily witness.

It was after her return from Belle Isle, and because of my play, that my intimacy with Sarah Bernhardt quite naturally became greater and greater. During the entire month of October, almost every day, I arrived at her house about eleven o'clock. I made her rehearse her part, she kept me to lunch, and took me in her car to the theater, where rehearsals were held from half past one to half past five.

From November on, when the play was being performed, Sarah Bernhardt was in her dressing room every day about six o'clock. First, she rested on a sofa for half an hour; then she had a light dinner, after which she made up. At least every other evening I reached the theater shortly before her and hardly left her until the play was over. On Sundays, between performances, she kept me in her dressing room for dinner, and she usually had her family with her and a few close friends; that is, Maurice Bernhardt, his wife, and his two daughters; Ullmann; sometimes a member of the cast—Arquillière or Marcelle Géniat, for example—and almost every week Louise Abbéma, the oldest and most faithful friend of Sarah Bernhardt, and one of her two official portrait painters. The other, Georges Clairin, had died in September, 1919.

At the beginning of January I went to London, where *Daniel*, translated into English by Mrs. Sybil Harris, was produced by Gilbert Miller at the St. James's Theatre. The cast included Lyn Harding, Alexandra Carlisle, C. Aubrey Smith, and Claude Rains in Sarah Bernhardt's part. I wanted to be present at the final rehearsals and the opening night, which was January 15, 1921. Two days later I returned to Paris.

Having reached this stage in my story, I must interrupt myself in order to quote, without comment, a news item which, with slight variations, appeared simultaneously in all the Paris papers of March 10, 1921:

"At noon yesterday, at the Church of Saint François de Sales, the marriage took place of Monsieur Louis Collin du Bocage, known as Louis Verneuil, dramatist, to Mademoiselle Lysiane Bernhardt.

"The bride is the younger daughter of Maurice Bernhardt and the granddaughter of Madame Sarah Bernhardt.

"Witnesses for Mademoiselle Bernhardt were Messrs. Henri Lavedan and Arthur Meyer; for Monsieur Verneuil, Messrs. Robert de Flers and Georges Berr.

"Notables of the theater, literature, and the press filed into the sacristy to offer their respectful congratulations to the great artist who, eleven years ago, in the same church, was present at the marriage of the elder of her granddaughters, Mademoiselle Simone Bernhardt, who is now Madame Edgar Gross."

From that day my life was identified, so to speak, with that of Sarah Bernhardt. I did not live with her—at least, in Paris—but until her death I did not let a day pass without seeing her. I accompanied her every time she traveled, especially on the five or six tours which she continued to make during those two years, despite her age.

First it was London, where, on April 4, 1921, she played *Daniel* with the entire company from Paris. Three months after it had been performed in English at the St. James's, it was produced in French at the Prince's Theatre. Then it was Spain, where, in May, Sarah Bernhardt played *Daniel* in Madrid and Barcelona. Then came the annual rest at Belle Isle, where I spent the summer of 1921, from July 15 to September 15.

The property of Sarah Bernhardt at Belle Isle also had its story. Thirty-five years earlier, when she was looking for some isolated place where she could spend her vacations quietly, she had been enchanted to discover, one hour by sea from the French coast, embarking at Quiberon, this almost desert island, whose only vegetation was furze and tamarisks, and where, hidden on the lonely moors, there were only two villages: Sauzon and Le Palais.

For two thousand francs Sarah Bernhardt had bought from the military authorities an old coast-guard fort which was no longer in use, situated at the extreme point of the island a few yards from the shore, and had arranged it as a country cottage. She lived then alone, with the companion of her first years in the theater, Madame Guérard, and her son, who was still a very young man at the time. Consequently, a large combined dining and living room, three bedrooms, and a kitchen were quite enough. All around the fort the moors stretching beyond the horizons constituted a park, wild but immense.

Some years later Maurice married, and Sarah Bernhardt had a little four-room villa built, about a hundred and fifty feet from the fort, so that he and his wife could move in and they could all enjoy quiet and independence. Maurice had one daughter, then another, who first had a nurse and then a governess. Forming a triangle with the fort and the villa, Sarah Bernhardt had another villa built for the use of the children, their governess, and the servants, whose number had increased as the family grew.

Her two best friends, Georges Clairin and Louise Abbéma, having gradually become more and more intimate with Sarah Bernhardt, were now almost part of her family. They did not spend just a few days each summer at Belle Isle, as they used to, but two or three months. They had to be properly housed; so she built a third villa for them, with a huge studio on the second floor. At the same time, knowing that numerous other friends would also come in increasing numbers to spend part of their vacation with her regularly, and as she never knew where or how to put them up, she added a fourth villa, this time with six rooms. Now she had finished with builders once and for all!

Thus, about 1905, Sarah Bernhardt's property on Belle Isle consisted of five buildings—the fort and its subsequent annexes—grouped a few yards from one another in an irregular circle. All over that point of the island there were no intruders, no noise—just this miniature village. The construction, decorating, and furnishing of these five buildings cost her something over a million francs. But this was of secondary importance. Money had never meant anything to her. The main fact was that she was delighted with the arrangement which she had patiently planned and finally achieved, suiting her own taste and the convenience of everybody.

However, on arriving at Belle Isle the following summer, Sarah Bernhardt saw with horror that, on a little hill some fifteen hundred feet from her, during the previous winter, someone had built a huge structure, now almost completed, which was a hundred and fifty feet long by thirty-five or thirty-six broad!

By that time everyone in France knew that Belle Isle was the summer retreat of Sarah Bernhardt, and it had become the goal of growing crowds of excursionists. A Breton hotelkeeper had had the idea of opening a twenty-room hotel for trippers in proximity to the celebrated fort. Horrified, Sarah Bernhardt immediately entered into a deal with him and bought the hotel on the spot. Naturally he took advantage of the situation to demand an astronomical figure, out of all proportion to the value of the building. Obviously he had built it solely in order to resell it to Sarah Bernhardt, whose immediate reaction he had foreseen. Be that as it may, in order to get rid of him, she paid. And, so that the same thing could not happen again, she also bought—as she should have done long before—all the surrounding ground, over an immense area, acres and acres, as far as the eye could see.

Her first idea was to take down this hideous hotel, but she changed her mind. It was still in the process of construction. She would complete it according to her own plans and, leaving the fort and the four villas, which had the disadvantage on rainy days of being rather far from one another, she would live in it herself, with her entire family and her friends, reunited henceforth under one and the same roof. The ex-hotel became a country house and was named the Manoir de Penhoët, after a small port in the neighborhood.

This program was completed the following summer. Everyone moved permanently into the house, while the unfurnished and deserted old residences and Clairin's studio became places to walk to or to take shelter in when a storm came on. Thus, having very prudently paid two thousand francs for the first house when she settled on the isle, after building and furnishing the house, laying out the park, and cutting cement steps in the rocks leading down to the sea, Sarah Bernhardt had sunk a little over four million francs in Belle Isle.

It was thus that I spent the summer of 1921 at the Manoir de Penhoët, the only building that had been inhabited for ten or twelve years. My room, hung with green *toile de Jouy*, was on the ground floor, with two windows overlooking the sea, and was separated from the main hall by a narrow vestibule, from which a small stone staircase of a few steps led directly into the park.

As usual, the guests were numerous. First, there was the family: Maurice Bernhardt and his second wife, Marcelle; Simone Gross and her two children, then aged eight and ten years; Jeanne de Gournay, the faithful companion of Sarah Bernhardt during her last years; and Dr. Marot, her personal physician, who came to see her every morning in Paris and always accompanied her when she left town. There were also Louise Abbéma; Denise Hellmann, a friend of Lysiane's; Jacqueline Bernhardt, a distant young cousin; and Maurice Perronnet, Sarah Bernhardt's godson and secretary of her theater. Reynaldo Hahn came to spend a few days, likewise the writer Marcel Boulenger. Others were Victor Ullmann and his daughter, Alice Dufrène, the actress, and another young actress called Violaine, a vague family connection—I cannot recall them all. We never sat down at table fewer than twelve or fifteen.

In the morning, after breakfast, which we all ate together in the dining room, we went upstairs about nine o'clock to Sarah Bernhardt's room. She received us while still in bed, gladly and with kindness. To receive in her home those whom she loved was always her greatest pleasure. After fifteen minutes or so, they retired one by one and, until lunch time, scattered according to their favorite amusements—tennis, fishing, shooting, walking, boating, and so forth—as people usually do. Everybody had been coming to Belle Isle for years. It had become a habit with them to spend a month or two at Sarah Bernhardt's. They had forgotten how exceptionally lucky they were. But this was my first summer there. I had not become blasé— and I never did.

When all the other guests had left the room, I used to say to her: "Great,[2] I hope I'm not disturbing you?" (Nobody ever called her "Grandmother." That was a word she did not like. Her grandchildren, her daughter-in-law, her great-grandchildren, her entire family except her son, who called her "Mother," always called her "Great.") She would smile: "Why, dear, of course not." Then I installed myself at the foot of the bed and, five times a week, at least, I spent the whole morning with her. She sent me away only on her correspondence days; that is, when she dictated about fifty letters in two hours to the unfortunate Jeanne de Gournay, who, not knowing shorthand, toiled in vain to write as quickly as Sarah Bernhardt spoke. Then she often became irritated and called me back to act as her secretary. I spent the other mornings listening to her and asking her a thousand questions, the number and variety of which amused her. I got her to describe her career, her early successes, the parts she created, her tours,

---

[2] English in the text. *Trans.*

the celebrities of the previous century whom she had frequented, and the innumerable adventures she had lived through in the course of her prodigious existence, which had begun professionally sixty-one years earlier. Born in October, 1844, Sarah Bernhardt had entered the Conservatoire in October, 1860, at the age of sixteen.

Those wonderful mornings, which were repeated the following summer, remain among the richest hours of my life.

Suddenly she would look at the little clock at her bedside and cry: "Half past twelve! I'll never be ready for lunch. Be off with you at once!"

In joyful and pretended anger she would throw all her pillows at me, one by one, as I walked to the door. As a matter of fact, she often did not appear in the dining room until almost half past one. Everyone was waiting for her.

As soon as she entered the door and was seated in her chair, she would say: "Louis got me chatting again. If everything is overcooked, it's his fault. He is a nuisance. I'll never keep him in my room again in the morning."

And the next day I remained just as long as the day before.

Toward September 15, Sarah Bernhardt returned to Paris, where she was expected at her theater for rehearsals. As she anticipated, after *Daniel* other plays were brought to her in which she did not have to walk. Among these she took one in verse, *La Gloire,* by Maurice, the son of Edmond Rostand. It opened at her theater on October 19, 1921.

By the end of November, while playing *La Gloire* every night, she began rehearsing the second play which I wrote for her, *Régine Armand,* which was her last part. Encouraged by her incredibly good health, in this dramatic comedy in four acts I ventured to have her appear in three acts, all except the first. She opened in *Régine Armand* at the Théâtre des Galeries-Saint-Hubert in Brussels on January 12, 1922. Since Christmas she had given a few performances at the same theater of *Athalie, Daniel* and *La Gloire.* Thus, at the age of seventy-seven, in the space of three weeks she performed in four plays in Brussels, one of them being an original new part.

During the latter part of January, all February, March, and the beginning of April, she went on a long tour with my two plays, in Belgium, Holland, Switzerland, and all over France, always accompanied by me. We played a different town every day or every two days, with two performances on Sundays. I still wonder how she was capable of such a strain, repeated daily. After a few weeks we were all exhausted. Only Sarah Bernhardt was the first to rise, the last to go to bed, and she appeared every morning as fresh and as rested as during her vacation.

It was on April 20, 1922, after having played the part nearly a hundred times in the provinces and abroad, that she gave her first performance of *Régine Armand* in Paris. That was her last public dress rehearsal, her last triumph.

The summer of 1922 saw us all back at Belle Isle, and my mornings in Sarah Bernhardt's room were even better employed than the previous summer. She had thought of writing an "Art of Diction," and dictated two chapters to me; but nothing more, unfortunately. As this slow and detailed work took up a lot of her time, she often asked me to come also in the afternoon from four to seven. Then I found her in a kind of enormous kiosk which she had built at the end of the park, on a height perpendicular to the sea, where she liked to be alone. Sarah Bernhardt always adored light, sun and space, broad horizons. As the conversation frequently reverted to her memories, whose diversity dazzled me, I begged her to finish her *Mémoires*, of which only the first part had been published—stopping in 1881, after her first tour in America. The book is deliberately very incomplete, for it deals only with her career and strictly avoids all her private, sentimental, and intimate life. Yet, even if she related it in the same spirit, obviously the second part of her life must be the more interesting. Therefore, almost every day I returned to the charge.

"There's plenty of time," she used to say. "I'll do that when I'm eighty."

However, as a result of my insistence, I obtained a promise from her that, as soon as next summer came around, she would dictate the end of her *Mémoires* to me. So I did not press her any further. Next year, why not? Like everyone else about her, I had gradually become accustomed to thinking that time meant nothing to her, that she would be always there.

Nevertheless, she did not spend a good summer, doubtless because of the fatigue of a winter of overwork. Consider that she had played, almost without a break, from October, 1921, to June, 1922, and in the same season had created two new parts and gone on a long tour.

During the whole of September, especially, she felt weak, low-spirited, and constantly tired. This irritated her intensely; she would not admit that she was ill. One fine day she decided that it was Belle Isle which did not suit her. There were so many worries, even to get there, the interminable journey, the sea crossing—the business of traveling was in itself exhausting. Then the keen air, which was very good for her when she was young, must now be extremely bad for her. Moreover, what could be more stupid than to have a place so far from Paris that she could spend only two months of the year there? In short, here was the typical Sarah Bernhardt: Having come to Belle Isle regularly every summer since 1887, she suddenly discovered that the place was utterly uninhabitable. At the end of September, with the suddenness characteristic of all her important decisions, she put her property up for sale, and said a final farewell to the Manoir de Penhoët.

Returning to Paris, she went from one extreme to the other and bought a piece of property at Garches, fifteen minutes by car from her house in the Boulevard Péreire.

"That, at least, is a country house I can use," she declared with satisfaction. "As soon as it will be ready, I will go there every Sunday. I shall live there as soon as the weather will be fine and spend six months of the year. And there we'll finish my *Mémoires*," she said to me. "I'll expect you at Garches in May at the latest. And you shan't leave until we have finished."

Alas! She did not finish her *Mémoires*, and she never lived in her house at Garches.

At the end of October, 1922, she went off with *Daniel* and *Régine Armand* on a six weeks' tour of the south of France and Italy, beginning at Marseilles. Eight days later she had a motor accident between Nice and Mentone. Sarah Bernhardt was not hurt, but her car was badly damaged and was useless for weeks. They looked everywhere for another with doors wide enough to admit her chair, but in vain. As I have explained, her car had a special body; so she had to continue her tour by train. What additional fatigue this meant and what excessive annoyances! Every day, instead of setting out in her car at her own hour, and driving directly from her hotel in one town to her hotel in another, she had to follow timetables, and leave sometimes at seven in the morning only to arrive, after two or three changes of train, at five in the evening, in order to appear at eight o'clock. At each station she had to be lifted in her chair into the carriage, which was often very high, her porters climbing three or four steps with great precautions and then carrying her down at the next station. The daily complications can be imagined. We begged her to stop, to return to Paris, to postpone the completion of her tour until spring. She would not hear of it. She had been announced; the public counted upon her. As long as she had strength, she would play wherever she was expected. After appearing in Genoa, Pisa, Rome, Naples, Florence, Bologna, Venice, Verona, and Milan, she ended this frightful circuit at Turin, where she played *Régine Armand* on November 29 and *Daniel* on November 30. This was her last performance, the last time in her life that she appeared in public.

The next day, utterly exhausted, she returned to Paris to rehearse a new play by Sacha Guitry, *Un Sujet de Roman,* in which she was to open at Christmas with Lucien Guitry, at the Théâtre Edouard VII. She had three weeks in which to learn her lines and create her part. In an incredible burst of energy, she succeeded. But on December 23, the very day of the public dress rehearsal, her strength began to fail. About five o'clock, when she was already in her dressing room, she suddenly felt her whole body enveloped in an icy chill, which she knew only too well. It was an attack of uremia, her fourth. She was rushed home and the performance was canceled.

But the play was not postponed. Realizing at once that Sarah Bernhardt was very seriously ill, the author decided that it was useless to wait for her recovery. The following day he sent out a call for another actress, and the first performance of *Un Sujet de Roman* took place on January 4, 1923, with Lucien Guitry and Henriette Roggers (Madame Claude Farrère) in the part written for Sarah Bernhardt.

For nearly a month her condition was critical, and the last week of 1923, especially, kept us in a state of continual anxiety. Maurice Bernhardt, Marcelle, Lysiane, and I took turns at spending the night in the room next to hers. Then, about the middle of January, she got better or appeared to do so, at least. She came down again to the dining room for her meals, and soon her circle of intimates was grouped around her once more.

In February she began again to make plans. Work was progressing on her house in Garches. She went there several times to spur on the contractors and workmen. As she had said, she was determined to move in on May 1 at the latest. Until then she still and always wanted to act. As her doctors forbade her to go on another tour, she began to study the role of Cleopatra in Corneille's *Rodogune*. This was also a part which she could play seated or when carried, and was all the better because, though she appeared in three acts, she had only one entrance and one exit. Cleopatra is on stage when the curtain rises on the second act, when it falls on the fourth, and during the whole of the last act. Sarah Bernhardt was wild with delight at the material possibilities of this part, which she proposed to play at classical matinees at Easter, 1923, as she had played *Athalie* three years earlier.

Furthermore, because she was urgently in need of money, as usual, she agreed to make a movie (silent, of course) called *La Voyante*. She played the episodic part of a soothsayer. Louis Mercanton was the director, and Mary Marquet had the leading role. As she was too tired to go to the studio every day, she asked them to make the movie at her house, which was very large—particularly the ground floor, which included an immense hall, studio, drawing room. There the sets were erected of the scenes which she was to play in *La Voyante*, all the lighting apparatus, the background shots, and other accessories having been brought into her hall, which was transformed into a veritable movie studio.

Toward March 15 she appeared before the camera two or three times. Then, on March 21, she had another attack of uremia—the fifth. She could not fight it. For four days her condition very rapidly grew worse. On the day of March 25 she went into a coma and, on Monday, March 26, 1923, about 8:00 P.M., she died without recovering consciousness.

The French government considered giving Sarah Bernhardt a national funeral. But several ministers were away and the Cabinet could not come to a binding decision. Then the City of Paris took the initiative in providing for her funeral. She who had contributed so much to the splendor of the capital was buried with municipal honors. They were unforgettable.

Maurice Bernhardt, whose neuritis was getting much worse,[3] could not attend to anything, and it was I who went to the City Hall and, on behalf of the family, arranged everything with Monsieur Aucoc, the syndic of the City Council. Behind the hearse, in front of the

---

[3] Maurice Bernhardt died December 22, 1928, on the anniversary of his birth. He was exactly sixty-four years old. *Author's note.*

carriages reserved for officials and relatives, five enormous cars for wreaths had been provided, solely to carry flowers. They were quite insufficient, and heaps of sheaves and hundreds of wreaths, for which there was no room, lay pell-mell in the mortuary chapel and the church.

The day of the funeral, from eight in the morning, from one end of the route of the procession to the other, from the Boulevard Péreire to Saint François de Sales, and from Saint François de Sales to Père Lachaise cemetery, an immense crowd had assembled on both sidewalks along the street, and waited six and seven deep. Traffic in Paris was practically suspended for half the day. Maurice, who was unable to cover the long distance on foot, had to share the carriage with his wife and daughters; so the chief pallbearers were Edgar Gross and myself, as the two nearest male relatives of Sarah Bernhardt.

For three hours, to the slow step of the caparisoned horses, an interminable procession, including the most distinguished names in the theater, literature, and politics, all of whom insisted on escorting Sarah Bernhardt to her final resting place, marched between two solid, compact hedges formed by hundreds of thousands of Parisians, grave, moved, and upset. The greater number were weeping and, as the coffin passed, many knelt on the sidewalks and on the pavement of the streets.

The emptiness I felt after the disappearance of Sarah Bernhardt was immense. For nearly three years, since the first rehearsals of *Daniel*, all my time, so to speak, had been devoted to her. Suddenly I was deprived of the only object, of the very reason, for all my activity. It took me months to make a new life for myself, which she could no longer fill.

At least, I had innumerable memories of her, both moving and picturesque, exciting and infinitely funny at times—a host of anecdotes and facts, many little known or not at all. The pages which follow will be filled only by these memories. I was personally present at everything subsequent to 1919. Everything prior to that was related to me by Sarah Bernhardt herself, in the course of our long, familiar conversations. It seems to me it would be difficult to invoke a better authority. That is why I thought I could write this book.

As I begin the story which follows, I cannot omit this opportunity of paying my sincere and friendly homage to the piety with which Lysiane has devoted herself to the cult of her grandmother.

By the summer of 1923 our divorce permitted her to resume the name of Bernhardt, which must have been a great source of joy and pride to her. Thanks to her attentive devotion, the fervor of innumerable faithful admirers of the illustrious artist is intelligently and regularly sustained. On every occasion her memory is honored. Every anniversary is piously celebrated.

In the name of all who have loved and admired Sarah Bernhardt, I thank Lysiane for helping us to remember. . . .

CHAPTER II

Childhood, Youth, Beginnings

SARAH BERNHARDT was born in Paris, at 5 Rue de l'Ecole de Médecine, on October 23, 1844.

There have been many controversies about the date and place of her birth. It was said that she was born in Brittany or Normandy. It was said that she was German, or at least was born in Frankfort. It was said that she was Algerian, Jewish, Dutch, Hungarian, and even American! On her first tour in the United States, in 1880, some half dozen Bernhardts claimed to be her father, one at Philadelphia being particularly insistent. Why and how could such disagreements occur over a definite event which was registered legally at the time, could easily be verified, and therefore could not logically give rise to any discussion?

There are several explanations. First, because Sarah Bernhardt's parents were not married—though as soon as she was born, her father recognized her and gave her his name. But as he never lived with her mother, traveled constantly, and died young, in 1857, very few people ever met him. Secondly, because her mother was not French, did not arrive in Paris until a year or so before the birth of Sarah, her eldest daughter, and afterward had two other daughters by two different fathers, both born far from Paris and possibly abroad. Finally, by a peculiar coincidence, the father's name, Bernhardt, and the mother's name, Van Hard, were very similar. This similarity gave rise to the suggestion that, the child of an unknown father, she had taken her mother's name and then changed it from Van Hard to Bernhardt, which thus became merely a pseudonym. This completely unfounded fable was the reason for so many extraordinary legends and, for thirty years, gave an excuse to fools, crackpots, and certain admirers more ambitious than others to pretend to be the father of the distinguished artist.

It may be admitted that Sarah Bernhardt, who never underrated the importance of publicity, probably never did anything necessary to put an end to these debates, whose frequency and intensity wrapped her origin in a mystery well calculated to increase the curiosity of the crowd. She also was not displeased perhaps at having seven or eight towns fighting for the honor of having given her birth, just as with the divine Homer.

Sarah's mother, Julie Van Hard, was born at Rotterdam, Holland, in 1823. Her parents, Gustave and Lisa, were both Dutch and in modest circumstances. Her Jewish mother was a dressmaker. Her father was a bookkeeper, a Catholic and a very pious one. They had six daughters, of whom Julie was the third. As their parents could never agree as to which religion they should be brought up in, they all grew up without following any religion whatever. The relatively early death of Gustave Van Hard left Lisa alone with her six children, the last three of whom were still quite small. As she could not bring them up with her slender resources, she had to let the older children shift for themselves.

Thus, at the age of fourteen, Julie went off to Hanover, having found a job as a minor assistant in a German dressmaking establishment. Afterward she went to Berlin and then Frankfort, where in 1843 she was a salesgirl with a fashionable milliner. There she made the acquaintance of a French consular agent who, on returning to Paris, took her with him. But he soon tired of her and left her. She was twenty years old; spoke very bad French; and found herself penniless on the streets of Paris, where she knew nobody. However, she found a job at a milliner's on the Left Bank.

On Christmas eve, 1843, in a café in the Latin Quarter, she made the acquaintance of a young law student, Edouard Bernhardt. The latter, a Frenchman from Havre, was temporarily in Paris following his law courses at the university. Julie was very pretty, despite her poor little dress and her humble position. Edouard Bernhardt soon fell so much in love with her that he took her away from the shop where she worked and set her up in a little apartment, 5 Rue de l'Ecole de Médecine, where Sarah Bernhardt was born the following October.

During the summer of 1844, as the university was closed, Edouard had to return to Havre and his family. In September his father, who was in an important export business, created a position for him and he did not return to Paris. Gradually and without a violent break, his idyl with Julie came to an end. However, as soon as he heard that the young dressmaker had a daughter who was undoubtedly his, he immediately appeared and formally recognized her. As long as he lived and as far as his means allowed, he shared in the expenses of her education and upbringing. When he died, he left to little Sarah in his will a modest income, the capital of which was to be paid to her on her majority.

Sarah Bernhardt knew her father very slightly. He not only lived in Havre but was constantly traveling all over the world on business for his father. He even went as far off as China, and he died in Italy. Whenever he happened to be in Paris he used to come and see his daughter, either in school or in the convent, and he would take her out once or twice and then disappear for months.

Meanwhile Julie Van Hard's good fortune had turned in her favor. The birth of Sarah seemed to have brought her luck. Two or three months later she met a surgeon called Baron Larrey, the son of the chief medical officer in the armies of Napoleon I. She became his mistress and, leaving her little lodgings, took an attractive apartment in a more central and more fashionable neighborhood, 6 Rue de la Chaussée d'Antin. But she seldom lived there. Baron Larrey was constantly called on consultations in all parts of Europe, or he traveled for his own amusement, and, being very much in love with the young woman, he always took her with him.

As she had continued to correspond with her sisters, Julie told them of the sudden and surprising improvement in her position. Two of them, Anna and Mathilde, were peacefully married in Holland, and a third in Martinique. Rosine and Henriette, the two elder girls, had been vegetating, leading in one country or another an existence very much like that of Julie before she met Baron Larrey. They immediately hastened to Paris, that wonderful city where one made such rapid success. If Julie had succeeded, why should they not be equally fortunate? After all, if luck was slow in coming for a while, their sister might always help them just a little.

As a matter of fact, Julie did not have to look after them. They were both pretty and, as soon as they were introduced to the fashionable and frivolous society in which their sister now moved, they were both rapidly "settled" and, in their turn, were more or less generously kept. The eldest, Henriette, soon married a gentleman of means called Félicien Faure and led a respectable life. Rosine and Julie remained the two who never settled down.

As for little Sarah, since her father was always away on business and her mother traveling for pleasure, she had been put to nurse with an honest Breton peasant near Quimperlé. But at that time it was quite an undertaking to get to Brittany. Whenever the whim seized her to kiss her child, Julie Van Hard wasted a lot of time. In order to be less inconvenienced, she brought back the child and the nurse and installed them at Neuilly. There she could fulfill her maternal duties in two hours' round trip, and when she was too busy she would ask her sister Rosine to go and see little Sarah instead.

In due course the nurse, who was a widow, was asked in marriage by an honest fellow who was a concierge in Paris, at 65 Rue de Provence. Having given him her hand, and preparing to go and live with him, she went to Julie Van Hard to ask her to take back her child, who was now four years old. But the door was shut. Julie had gone away again with Baron Larrey and was in Poland, or Portugal, or somewhere else. The nurse went to Rosine's, but she was also traveling with some one of her lovers. Not knowing what to do, and not knowing how to write, the good nurse took the child with her and for months Sarah Bernhardt lived in the concierge's quarters!

They were situated on the mezzanine floor, above the porte-cochère, and the only light that came to the suite was through a little round window looking out on the street. There was one room which served as a bedroom and kitchen, and Sarah Bernhardt's little bed stood in a dark corner separated by a curtain from that of the "young married couple." Accustomed to the fresh air of Brittany and then of Neuilly, the child felt atrociously unhappy. She spent the melancholy days playing in the courtyard of the house or in the gutter with other little boys and girls of her age, the children of the neighborhood concierges. She awaited the day when somehow some member of the family would remember her existence and come to get her.

Lo and behold, one morning she saw a young and beautiful lady, accompanied by an elegant gentleman, getting out of a carriage with two horses and stopping at the house next door. She recognized her immediately and shouted: "Aunt Rosine! Aunt Rosine!" It was Julie's sister who stopped and looked in disgusted surprise at this little urchin with wild hair, a checked apron, frighteningly dirty, her clothes stained from head to foot. Then she suddenly cried: "Why, it's little Sarah!"

Apologizing to the gentleman with her, she entered with the child and asked for explanations, which were immediately forthcoming. Fifteen minutes later the young woman left, promising to discover where Julie was and write to her. But in despair Sarah clung to her and sobbed: "Take me with you, Auntie, take me with you!"

Rosine pleaded with her. She had not the faintest desire to take this dirty child in her smart carriage and, above all, to introduce her to her companion. She asked the nurse to keep the little girl, whom the good woman took in her arms to carry upstairs. But the imperious and self-willed nature of Sarah, who was then only five, suddenly revealed itself. Furious with rage, she jumped through the little window to rejoin her aunt and crashed on the sidewalk. Fortunately the mezzanine was not very high, nine feet at the most. Nevertheless, her arm was knocked out of joint and her kneecap broken. The terrified Rosine was compelled to take the child with her and to call doctors and surgeons in great haste. A few days later Julie came home and took the child to live with her. She kept her two years, but in charge of a servant.

Her manner of life was not suited to the constant presence of little Sarah under her roof. Julie was now twenty-eight and was becoming more and more fashionable and more beautiful. Her success was constantly increasing. She was now at the top of her vogue. In order to keep her, the indulgent Baron Larrey now had to let her go out and be seen with many other admirers. Many of the latter would have been disappointed to learn that their young and seductive friend was the mother of a child of seven.

Another important event occurred: Julie was pregnant. A few months later she would bring a second child into the world. Who was the father? No one ever knew exactly. It was certainly a man for whom she had a strong liking, because this second daughter, Jeanne, was always her favorite. It was, therefore, in order to get rid of a child who was too old and to concentrate whatever time she had on the child about to be born, that Julie decided to send Sarah to a boarding school.

About the end of 1851 she settled her in the school of a certain Madame Fressard, situated at 18 Rue Boileau, Auteuil. There Sarah remained for two years, feeling happy and working industriously, and she had nice children as companions, some of whom remained her friends for a very long time. One of them in particular, Clotilde, became the wife of a politician named Pierre Merlou, who was for some time Minister of Finance at the beginning of the century. She came regularly to all the first nights at the Théâtre Sarah Bernhardt, and she never failed, during the intermission, to go backstage and greet the woman who, fifty years before, had been a fellow pupil at Madame Fressard's boarding school.

Between Sarah's parents there soon arose the usual disagreement concerning the education of a child whose father and mother are not living together. On his first visits to his daughter, Edouard Bernhardt had approved of Madame Fressard's establishment. Then, one fine day, he came to the conclusion that the studies there were not sufficiently advanced. The school was classed as a preparatory one for very small girls, and the children were given no religious instruction—a fact which had escaped Julie Van Hard but which appeared to him perfectly outrageous. Finally, after a long exchange of letters and probably some interviews with Julie, he insisted that Sarah should be taken away from this school and sent to a convent, where her education would in future be directed by nuns.

This fact is the most convincing reply to those who assert that the father of Sarah Bernhardt was a Jew. If he had been, he would not have insisted so much on educating his daughter at a convent, where, moreover, as the child of Jewish parents and consequently Jewish herself, she would not have been admitted.

Her maternal grandmother, Lisa Van Hard, was undoubtedly Jewish. She died at a ripe old age in Paris, about 1880, and many of Sarah's friends knew her. But she was her only Jewish relative. The Bernhardts from Havre are still in existence, and, in spite of the way their name is spelled, they are a recognized Christian family.

One morning in September, at the beginning of the school year 1853–54, Sarah Bernhardt entered the convent of Grandchamps, at Versailles, just beside the Satory Barracks. Her mother had brought her to Madame Fressard's and her father took her to the convent, where he handed her over to the Superior, Mother Sainte Sophie. Two days later, filled with remorse at having allowed her daughter to be shut up in an institution which she had not even visited, Julie Van Hard hastened to the convent and, during an entire afternoon, examined it conscientiously: the classes, the dormitories, the refectory, the chapel. She was so delighted that, later on, she sent her second child, Jeanne, there—but not for very long—and also, for two years, her third daughter, Régina, Sarah's other sister, who was born in 1854 and died at the age of twenty.

Sarah Bernhardt remained at the convent until 1859. No remarkable event occurred during those six studious years, in the course of which she acquired a solid and extensive education which she never lost, thanks to her astonishing memory. Of this period only one incident needs to be recalled. In June, 1856, Sarah made her first communion. Being very pious at that age, she prepared for this important ceremony with great solemnity. Among the hundred little girls of her age who, like her, were going to communion for the first time, she displayed a mystic ardor which was particularly edifying.

A few weeks before the event, the priest who directed the retreat of the communicants asked each of them for her baptismal certificate. Sarah at once wrote to her mother asking her to send it. Then Julie Van Hard suddenly discovered that her daughter had none, and for a very good reason. It should be remembered that, when Sarah was born, Julie had only been a few months in Paris; had very little money, no knowledge of the world, and no religion. In a word, she had completely forgotten to have the child baptized, and perhaps she did not even know that this was generally the custom. Edouard Bernhardt, arriving posthaste from Havre and returning the same way, had recognized the little girl but had not troubled about her christening, as he was convinced that her mother had thought of that.

Sarah had now been living for nearly three years with the nuns, but she was not yet a Catholic in the strict sense of the word. This lamentable omission had to be repaired at the first possible opportunity. On May 21, 1856, at the age of eleven and a half, in the church of Grandchamps, she was baptized by the chaplain of the convent: "Sarah, Rosine, Marie, Henriette, born in Paris in the twelfth district, October 23, 1844, daughter of M. Edouard Bernhardt, residing in Havre, 2, Rue des Arcades, and Mme. Julie Van Hard, residing in Paris, 265, Rue Saint Honoré. Godfather, M. Régis Lavolée, 65, Rue de la Chaussée d'Antin, Paris; godmother, Mme. Anna Van Hard Van Bruck, aunt of the child."

Such is the exact text of the baptismal certificate, which Sarah Bernhardt kept until her death.

Early the following year, in the course of one of his many journeys,

Edouard Bernhardt died at Pisa, after a brief illness. Now Sarah had only her mother, who was always distant in every sense of the word and who left her for another two years in the convent. In June, 1859, Julie Van Hard began to miss her second daughter, Jeanne, unbearably, and decided to have her with her henceforth. She did not, however, dare to take her away from the convent while leaving her eldest daughter, who was nearly fifteen and had almost completed her studies.

At this date, therefore, Sarah left the convent and, after spending a summer with her uncle and aunt Faure at Cauterets, returned to her mother's home, a large and luxurious apartment at 265 Rue Saint Honoré.

In all the glory of her thirty-six years and in the marvelous development of her beauty, Julie Van Hard had now become a real personality. Having always kept a slight Dutch accent, she pronounced her own name in the German fashion: Youlie. Finding this less commonplace than Julie, almost all her friends called her Youle. They formed a little court about her, fervent and joyful, and almost every evening there were brilliant gatherings in the beautiful apartment in the Rue Saint Honoré. Among her close friends were General de Polhes, the godfather, or perhaps the father, of her third daughter, Régina; Fleury the painter, Doctor Monod; Régis Lavolée, Sarah's godfather; Adolphe Meydieu, the godfather of Jeanne; Rossini, the celebrated composer of *The Barber of Seville*; the Faure household, which consisted of the elder sister, Henriette, and her husband; her other sister, Rosine, always escorted by a new lover; and good old Baron Larrey, now sadly reduced to the status of a friend of the house where he had once been the master. There also came, towering over everybody in rank and stature, and received with profound respect, the Duc de Morny, the stepbrother of the Emperor Napoleon III and one of the three or four most important people in France at that time. He was one of the most constant visitors at the Rue Saint Honoré for a very special reason.

Youle, it happens, was the last passion of the famous Duc de Morny. During the last seven years of his life he showered her with favors and, carrying over to the daughters some of the affection which he felt for their mother, he opened to Sarah the doors of the Conservatoire and then the Comédie Française, and gave generous dowries to Jeanne and Régina. He died in 1865, aged fifty-four, leaving a nice fortune to Julie, which enabled her from that time on to put an end to her gallant adventures.

Yet this brilliant existence did not suit Sarah and she was not happy with her mother, possibly because the latter showed too clearly her preference for Jeanne. Perhaps also because she could not stand idleness, which was contrary to her active and enterprising nature. In any case, every day she escaped from her mother's apartment and went to a sweet and quiet young woman on the floor above, who had become a friend of Julie's and for whom young Sarah had conceived a violent affection. Her name was Madame Guérard and she was the wife of a historian, a good man but not very talented. She was widowed early in life and, having no money, a few years later became the private secretary and companion of Sarah Bernhardt. For nearly thirty years she always accompanied her everywhere. Her death, in 1890, was the greatest loss that Sarah Bernhardt had ever sustained.

In contrast to the luxurious and gay apartment of Julie, the modest and restful home of the Guérards seemed to Sarah a sort of refuge. For hours she would sit beside her great friend and, gazing into the future, would form the maddest and most contradictory plans. "With you, my little lady" [this was what she called Madame Guérard], "I can dream out loud," she used to say.

She most frequently dreamed of returning to the convent, but not as a pupil—as a nun! She was repelled by life, and especially life as she saw it around her. Not one of the men appealed to her, although some were already paying court to her, two or three even having asked her hand in marriage. At the age of fifteen she had no object, no desire, and no ambition of any sort. Nothing interested her, or—what is worse—everything bored her. Whenever her mother gave a large dinner party, which was very often, she invented numerous pretexts for not being present. She would have preferred that her place should not be set at the table, if company was expected. Sometimes, either because there would have been thirteen without her or because some important personage, brought by the Duc de Morny, wanted to make Sarah's acquaintance, Julie insisted that she should be present and make herself agreeable to the guests. Then, a few minutes before sitting down at table, she would upset an ink bottle on her dress or pretend that she had sprained her ankle. Anything, no matter what, provided she could escape from these boring proceedings.

This attitude, this wild character, may seem surprising. Later on, the entire life of Sarah Bernhardt proved not only that she did not dislike crowded parties but, on the contrary, that she detested solitude. She liked to be constantly surrounded by friends, whether they were intimate or not. But, in this case, it was she who chose them; she was the person they came to see. She was the center of attraction, the only object of interest and admiration to everybody present. She was not particularly vain, but she did not like it very much when the people around her were concerned with anybody or anything but herself.

It was this attitude which was becoming vaguely evident so early. In 1860 Julie, who was then at the height of her perfect beauty, attracted all the admiration. It was logical, therefore, that little Sarah, who was thin and uncoquettish, with her flowing curly hair always in disorder, usually sulky and difficult to handle, should be treated as a negligible quantity. Julie neither did anything to show off her daughter nor tried to win her by tenderness.

Julie said very little, was slow and graceful in her movements and of average intelligence; but, thanks to her natural feminine cleverness, she had succeeded very well in life—that is to say, she had met and held successively several wealthy men of good social position, who had kept her. She looked in surprise and discouragement at this girl, whose beauty was not then evident; who was turbulent, nervous, and restless, always fighting against everything and everyone, capable of violence that was noisy and in bad taste; and who paid no attention to either her appearance or her manners. Without rhyme or reason, or at least for the most trifling reasons, she would go from the wildest enthusiasm to the deepest despair, with shocking exaggeration.

At first Julie tried to reason with her, to make her "normal"; but soon she gave this up. Gently stroking the silken hair of the younger sister, Jeanne, who was so playful, affectionate, and easy to get on with, she would declare, with a sigh, that Sarah was decidedly an incomprehensible child. In fact, Julie never understood the character, nature, or even, later on, the talent of her daughter. She died in 1876, at the age of fifty-three, well after Sarah's first great successes, but she never realized in the slightest that she had given birth to a very great artist. She found her eccentric, disconcerting, unusual, and, above all, somewhat tiresome. That is all that Julie Van Hard ever saw in Sarah Bernhardt!

At home the constant clash of these two profoundly different natures became more and more brutal every day. After a few months Sarah's boredom had almost become hypochondria, and Julie, always so calm, felt her impatience gradually turning into exasperation. The Duc de Morny quickly noticed this and decided, out of his love for his mistress, that she should be freed as soon as possible from the perpetual worry of her eldest daughter.

But what could be done with Sarah? Her father was dead. Neither of her aunts wanted to have her. At the age of fifteen and a half, she was too old to be sent to boarding school again and too young to live alone even with a governess. The only remedy was to find something for her to do.

One evening after dinner when, by some miracle, the only other guest was Madame Guérard, the Duc de Morny said carelessly: "If my name were Sarah, I know very well what I would do."

The little girl, as usual, was lost in reverie. She started up. "Well what would you do?"

"I would try to enter the Conservatoire."

There was a long silence after this unexpected suggestion. Julie, Sarah, Madame Guérard, and little Jeanne, who was then nine years old, looked at one another. The Duc de Morny had not informed his mistress in advance of his idea, which had suddenly occurred to him and in the most logical fashion. Having completed her studies without preparing for any special career, Sarah was not equipped to take up any profession worthy of her mother's position. Moreover, women doctors or lawyers were very rare in France eighty years ago. In general, except as dressmakers and milliners, women did not work. Looking for an agreeable profession for Julie's daughter, one which would absorb her energies and did not require any particular previous knowledge, the Duc had thought of the one possible place: the theater.

Sarah reflected: "I don't like your idea very much, Monseigneur."

"Really? And why not?"

It was Julie who answered in her gentle voice: "Because she is too thin for an actress."

Touched to the quick, Sarah immediately protested: "That is not what I meant at all. I have seen Rachel."

"How could that be? She died before you came out of the convent."

"I have seen pictures of her. She wasn't very stout either. I do not believe that the success of an actress depends essentially on her weight."

The Duc de Morny smiled. "Quite right. Well, then, what are your objections, my child?"

Sarah was silent for a moment. When the conversation began, Morny's proposal had seemed stupid to her. She had gone to the theater only four or five times, and had not been particularly amused. As for the stage as a profession, she had not the faintest idea what it was like or what it implied. She knew that one learned parts by heart and recited them on the stage, but the preparatory studies, the rehearsals, the mounting of a play—her ideas about all that were as vague as about the work of a chemist or a civil engineer. Her only definite impression was that she could see a world and a manner of existence which did not attract her in the least or, to be more exact, did not seem in the least interesting. She was about to reply to this effect, but once again her mother had annoyed her and almost defied her. Well, she would accept the challenge. They would see whether she was as thin as all that! The theater? Very well. Let it be the theater! After all, why not? On one condition, however: that there must be a lot of hard work. If she suddenly agreed to take up a career which five minutes earlier had seemed perfectly intolerable to her, it was because this decision would result in her being busy from morning till night; that is to say, keep her away from her mother's receptions and unpleasant comments.

The Duc de Morny laughingly reassured her: "I believe that the comedy classes at the Conservatoire are held only twice a week, but during the rest of the time you will have to learn your parts. Besides, in the theater as elsewhere, one cannot succeed without working hard."

This information definitely decided young Sarah, who, the very next day, searched in her schoolbooks for the tragedies of Racine and Corneille, in which she immediately began to learn all the parts, male and female, without distinction. Some days later her godfather, Régis Lavolée, and Adolphe Meydieu, Jeanne's godfather, who were both highly amused by Sarah's sudden resolutions, agreed to choose with a little more discernment the parts which, they thought, she should study at first. It was these two respectable citizens, with no experience of the theater, guided only by their instinct as subscribers to the Comédie Française, who were the first teachers of Sarah Bernhardt.

All true artists, it is said, have been attracted from earliest childhood to their art by an irresistible vocation. That is true in principle.

But if there is an exception to this rule, it will be admitted that Sarah Bernhardt was one.

At the age of almost sixteen years she had never thought of acting. In order to take her off her mother's hands, who did not like her, one of the latter's lovers said one fine day: "Why not try and make an actress of her?" In order to get away from her mother, whose life as a kept woman shocked her, Sarah replied: "All right, let us try." It is hard to believe that this is exactly how was decided the career of a woman who was destined to become the greatest artist in the world.

With great conviction, in deadly earnest, as in all things which she undertook in the course of her life, Sarah prepared for her entrance examination at the Institut National de Déclamation. This zeal was more or less superfluous. On returning from his summer vacation, in 1860, the Duc de Morny had gone to see the director of the Conservatoire, who was Auber, the celebrated composer of *Fra Diavolo* and *Le Domino Noir*. Although he was then nearly eighty and his fame was great, the distinguished musician was extremely flattered by the fact that the Emperor's brother had taken the trouble to come and see him instead of summoning him to the Tuileries. This meant that, whatever her qualifications—or even if she had none—young Sarah Bernhardt was admitted in advance. How could one not admit a candidate who was warmly recommended by the Duc de Morny in person, and who, as was soon discovered, was the daughter of his mistress?

At the beginning of October, 1860, at the yearly examination, Sarah Bernhardt thus presented herself under these very favorable conditions to the jury on admissions to the Conservatoire. In addition to Auber, these consisted chiefly of Beauvallet, Samson, Régnier, Provost, Bressant—five of the most important members of the Comédie Française—and Augustine, the elder of the two Brohan sisters who, in the roles of coquettes, had a very striking career.

M. Meydieu, who suspected nothing, had made Sarah study the part of Phèdre. Then it was thought that perhaps she was rather young and inexperienced for such a part, and Aricie was substituted. Then, after profound reflection, they set her to learn the part of Chimène in *Le Cid*. But neither her two mentors nor Madame Guérard were satisfied with all that. Sarah scarcely looked her sixteen years, she was so blonde and frail, and she had nothing of a great tragic heroine. So there was a radical change and she studied Agnès in *L'Ecole des Femmes*, by Molière. On the list of candidates she had put her name down for the famous scene in the second act with Arnolphe, "The little cat is dead." . . .

On the day of the examination at the Conservatoire, accompanied by Madame Guérard, she awaited her turn, greatly excited, in the room reserved for candidates, where young men and women had been filing past for an hour onto the famous little stage.

Five minutes before her name was called, the usher came to her and said: "Have you got someone to give you your cues?"

"My cues?"

"Yes, your partner, the young man who answers you in the part of Arnolphe? Who is he? Where is he?"

Sarah turned pale and so did Madame Guérard. Nobody had thought of a partner! When Meydieu, Lavolée, or Madame Guérard went over Agnès with her, one of them read the other part. They had completely forgotten that on the day of the examination an actor would be needed to play that part on the stage with her. This shows with what inexperience, with what naïveté, Sarah Bernhardt had been prepared for her examination. What was to be done? Should they look among all the candidates present for one who knew Arnolphe to rehearse the scene with her? It was too risky and would take too long, as Sarah was about to be called any moment.

Resolutely she decided: "Oh, well, it can't be helped. I'll recite a fable!"

And when her turn came she was announced to the astonished jury: "Mademoiselle Sarah Bernhardt . . . in *Les Deux Pigeons*, by La Fontaine."

The thunderous Beauvallet turned toward Auber and murmured: "Is this a joke? This is not a kindergarten!"

By way of a reply Auber quickly scribbled some words on a sheet of paper, which he passed on to him and his other colleagues. When they read the name of the Duc de Morny, who was not only all-powerful but extremely well liked at the Théâtre Français, they all became attentive and well disposed immediately. Without hearing the bell ring for her to stop, Sarah recited her fable nicely from beginning to end. When she had finished, Auber made a discreet gesture of applause and gave her a little friendly and encouraging sign. An hour later she was told that out of the hundred or two hundred candidates who had presented themselves, she was among the fifteen or twenty who had been admitted.

Sarah Bernhardt remained at the Conservatoire for two years. She spent the first in the class of Provost, a fine actor and, particularly, a remarkable teacher. He enjoyed great prestige because he had been Rachel's teacher. The advice of this excellent man, whom she adored, was extremely valuable to Sarah Bernhardt. He taught her the first principles of an art of which, up to the day of her examination, she knew absolutely nothing, and aroused in her that passionate love of the theater which, for more than sixty years, was to be her only reason for existence.

He succeeded so well in making an excellent pupil out of this naïve apprentice, in making almost an actress, that at the contest at the end of the year she distinguished herself in the most unexpected fashion, without owing anything this time to her influential protector.

In July, 1861, she obtained a second prize for tragedy in Voltaire's *Zaïre*, and honorable mention for comedy in *La Fausse Agnès*. At the age of seventeen this was a nice result, seeing that she had never learned two lines of verse by heart ten months earlier. It was a great encouragement to Sarah, and with enthusiasm she began her second year at the Conservatoire—at the end of which a first prize seemed certain.

Unfortunately, in January, 1862, Provost fell seriously ill and had to give up his classes. Sarah went to the class taught by Samson, in whom she had much less confidence and who did not understand her and directed her badly. In spite of her protests, at the end of the year he forced her to offer two old plays of Casimir Delavigne, a childhood friend of Samson's, for whom he had a cult and an admiration which were quite inexplicable, since Delavigne had been dead for twenty years and was already old-fashioned.

In July, 1862, therefore, Sarah Bernhardt competed in a tragic part in *La Fille du Cid*, by Delavigne, a very mediocre drama, written in 1839, and in a comedy part in a worse and even mustier play, *L'Ecole des Vieillards,* which had once been a success—but that was in 1823. She did not get any prize. Because of the good reports she had earned during the course of the scholastic year she was cited for her second prize in tragedy of the year before. It was a terrible disappointment for her and an intense humiliation when, on returning home, she had to announce this pitiful result to her mother.

Julie sighed. "I knew that would happen! You will never get anywhere in life, my poor child!"

For weeks Sarah was desperate. She wanted to kill herself, to return to the convent, to disappear forever. The Duc de Morny took pity on her and again intervened, this time with Camille Doucet. The latter was a not very successful dramatist, but a sweet, kindly man who stood well at court. The following year he was appointed Director General of the Beaux Arts and, later, perpetual secretary of the Académie Française. At this time he already had considerable influence in the state theaters. He went to see Edouard Thierry, the general manager of the Théâtre Français, and, despite her mediocre record, obtained an engagement for Sarah Bernhardt at the Comédie Française.

There she made her debut on September 1, 1862, in the part of Iphigénie in the tragedy of Racine. She was excessively nervous and, paralyzed by stage fright, made an absolutely insignificant appearance. Next day, in *L'Opinion Nationale*, Francisque Sarcey, the eminent critic who for forty years made and unmade, as he pleased, the reputations of the most distinguished French writers and actors of the nineteenth century, wrote:

"Mademoiselle Bernhardt, who made her debut yesterday in *Iphigénie*, is a tall and pretty young person with a willowy waist and a very agreeable physiognomy. The upper part of the face, particularly, is remarkably beautiful. She holds herself well and pronounces her words perfectly distinctly. That is all that can be said of her at the moment."

The custom of "three debuts" in succession was then an unchangeable tradition, although it has since been gradually relaxed at the Comédie Française. So, on September 5, Sarah Bernhardt made her second debut in *Valérie*, a drama by Scribe and Mélesville, first produced at the Théâtre Français, in 1822, and rarely revived. It had recently been put back into the repertory on the occasion of the death of Scribe, which had occurred the year before. In honor of the distinguished dramatist, who had brought them so many successful plays, the Comédie Française revived in 1861 and 1862 most of those which had been first staged there.

In *Valérie*, which is a good part, Sarah succeeded no better in attracting attention, and her third debut, on September 11, in the part of Henriette in *Les Femmes Savantes* of Molière, was equally dull.

That evening inspired Sarcey to write a remarkable article, in which he showed not only how little effect Sarah produced but also that the distinguished company of that theater, even then, was being subjected to the kind of criticism of which it has always and regularly been the object ever since. He wrote:

"The performance was very poor and arouses sad reflections. The fact that Mademoiselle Bernhardt is inadequate is not very important. She is making her debut, and it is perfectly natural that among these beginners there should be some who do not succeed. Many must be tried before a good one is found. But what is sad is that the actors supporting her are not much better than she is. And they are members of the permanent company! The only difference between them and their young colleague was that they had more experience on the stage. They are today what Mademoiselle Bernhardt may become in twenty years, if she stays at the Comédie Française."

Far from staying there, she very quickly left that great theater.

In the course of the last months of 1862, Sarah Bernhardt played several parts in repertory, particularly Hippolyte in *L'Etourdi*, by Molière, all without any success, and therefore without any pleasure. As we know, she disliked being overlooked; and that was exactly what happened to her during her first period at the Comédie Française. Sharing the opinion of Sarcey, the general manager and the committee regarded her as a very ordinary member of the company, without any talents or any future, who, being incapable of attracting any attention, would gradually reach the time when she would get her pension, without ever having played other than third-rate parts. A very unimportant instance was to decide otherwise. It occurred on January 15, 1863.

Every year, on that date, at the Théâtre Français, the birthday of Molière is celebrated by closing the show with what is called the "Ceremony." The bust of the immortal author of *Le Misanthrope* is placed in the center of the stage; all the members of the company, junior and senior, enter two by two and place palm leaves in front of it. They then line up on both sides and listen to lines written for the occasion, which are recited by one of the most important members of the company.

That evening, as she was about to take part in the Ceremony, Sarah Bernhardt came down the staircase leading from the dressing rooms to the greenroom and then onto the stage, holding by the hand her little sister Régina, who was scarcely nine years old and whom she had brought, as she occasionally did, to keep her company in her dressing room while the play was going on. In front of them an important member of the company, Madame Nathalie, was walking solemnly. She was a pompous actress of mediocre talent who, despite her stoutness and her approaching age of fifty, still had admirers in high places. Inadvertently little Régina stood on Nathalie's train and she almost fell. With one hand she held on to the banisters while with the other she sharply pushed away the child, who fell against the wall. Blood immediately appeared on her forehead.

"Nasty beast!" Sarah cried furiously, giving Nathalie two loud slaps on her flabby cheeks.

There was noise and confusion, and the stout actress fainted. People rushed up to her. The Ceremony was delayed for ten minutes. Next day Sarah was summoned to the general manager's office. Monsieur Thierry ordered her to apologize to Madame Nathalie in his presence and in that of three of the oldest members of the company.

"After that," he added in glacial tones, "the Committee will decide whether you should pay a fine or hand in your resignation."

Her successive disappointments at the Conservatoire and the Théâtre Français had not softened Sarah's character, whose violence and impetuosity were never calmed by anything. The notion of apologizing to this mean woman who had hurt her little sister drove her into an indescribable rage.

"The Committee will not have to make any decision," she replied to Edouard Thierry, "for I am leaving. I guessed what you were going to ask me and, in reply, I have brought my contract. Here it is!"

Taking her contract from her bag, she tore it into eight pieces and threw it in the face of the astounded manager. She slammed the door behind her as she left his office.

This violent break with the famous theater where she had the unheard-of luck to be admitted as a favor did not render Sarah's life easy with her mother. Now it was not only the sighs of resignation and the disdainful lassitude of Julie which she had to bear but also the bad temper and severe reproaches of all the friends of the house: Meydieu and Lavolée, hurt in their pride as "teachers"; her aunts, who at least knew how to arrange their own lives. Distant but courteous, the Duc de Morny said nothing. He had lost interest in this terrible child. Only Madame Guérard still had all her old affection for her.

Furthermore, the reasons for her departure from the Théâtre Français became known all over Paris, and Sarah was everywhere considered as a young actress who really had too little talent to indulge in such tantrums. She could not get an engagement as no theater would accept her. This enforced inactivity soon had logical results. Hitherto she had devoted herself exclusively to work, spending two extremely studious years at the Conservatoire, then at the Théâtre Français, forcing herself vainly but diligently to play as best she could the parts given to her. Since as an actress she was not wanted anywhere, as a woman she might have more success. She was almost nineteen, her features had become finer, and her personality was more distinct. One could detect a strange and singular beauty which was soon to be recognized as hers. She set herself to enhancing this beauty. She, who had never thought of such things, began to take care of her appearance, to choose pretty clothes, to try to attract and to please. Naturally, her mother encouraged this new departure. If Julie was never tender with her daughter, she was always very generous and she paid her bills without even looking at them. She was satisfied to see that at last Sarah seemed to wish to become a little civilized.

From this time dates the beginning of the love life of Sarah Bernhardt, if those are the words to describe the period when she ceased to be a young girl. What could happen to a little actress without a job, pretty, well dressed, and living in a circle where morals were free and easy, where the aunt was a demi-mondaine and the mother a kept woman? Her father was dead and the only person to look after her was Madame Guérard, who was very sweet and honest but loved her far too much ever to reproach her with anything. Her idleness was bound to lead her to go out with young men and, sooner or later, to give in to the one who was most pressing. It is in this banal fashion that Sarah Bernhardt came to know love. Her first lovers, whom she accepted without joy and left without regret, were perfectly anonymous and aroused in her nothing but friendly indifference.

It was precisely the complete absence of emotion in such an existence which very soon disgusted her. Sarah's nature, generous, excitable, ardent, and always inclined to exaggerate, ever demanded super-human tasks professionally and great passions sentimentally. These little adventures, which led nowhere and were without interest, could not satisfy her.

In spite of so many rebuffs and refusals, she made a supreme effort to force her way into the theater. At the beginning of 1864, thanks to a friend of her godfather, Monsieur de Gerbois, she obtained an interview and then an engagement, at one hundred and twenty-five francs a month, from Montigny, who left a considerable reputation as manager of the Gymnase.

Her first appearance at this theater took place in March, 1864, in a play called *La Maison sans Enfants* by Dumanoir. Sacrificing her vacation, in the middle of summer, she created, on July 16, 1864, a rather nice part in *Le Démon du Jeu*, a play by Théodore Barrière and Crisafulli, which had a great success. In spite of the warm weather the play ran for three months, until the last new play which was to appear at the Gymnase that year, *Un Mari qui lance sa Femme,* a comedy by Eugène Labiche and Raymond Deslandes.

In this play Montigny had given her a minor part of a Slavic princess, slight, vague, and elusive, constantly eating sandwiches and dancing on every possible occasion. It is obvious how little Sarah Bernhardt was suited to such a part, even when very young. On the night of the opening she could not possibly have been duller and more awkward.

The next morning in her boudoir, while she nonchalantly polished her nails, Julie said to her in the presence of the Duc de Morny: "Goodness, my poor child, you were certainly ridiculous as a Russian princess! I was ashamed when I noticed in the theater people who knew you were my daughter."

This failure, with which she was taunted most cruelly, plunged poor Sarah into the depths of despair. She was now twenty, and four years after her admission to the Conservatoire she had got no further. She would not continue to play for another day a part which brought such sarcastic remarks upon her. That very evening, having made her preparations during that day, she left for Spain, after writing a letter of apology to Montigny which ended with these words: "Have pity on a poor little crazy girl!"

Some twenty years later Victorien Sardou told Sarah Bernhardt that he happened to be in Montigny's office at the Gymnase when, about four o'clock, a letter was handed him from the young actress, telling him that she would not play that evening. He read it, swore, and called his director, so that he could get an understudy immediately, and then sat down greatly disturbed.

Sardou questioned him: "What has happened?"

"It's that young fool who has already run away from the Comédie Française," Montigny muttered. "I engaged her—I don't know why— and now she is also leaving the Gymnase, without so much as a word of warning."

"Oh, yes, that little blonde with the curls," said Sardou. "What's her name? Sarah something or other?"

"Bernhardt, but it doesn't matter. After two such mistakes, if she gets another engagement in Paris I'm ready to eat my hat! To leave a play the day after the opening! Did you ever hear of such a thing? And just read this letter!"

Sardou read Sarah's letter, which was absurd, disconnected, alternately angry and despairing. She was indignant at the part she had been forced to play but begged Montigny to forgive her—all this in the wildest disorder, in which there was, however, a certain eloquence.

Sardou put the letter down on the desk and smiled. "That little girl is amusing!"

"Not from a manager's point of view," growled Montigny. "Now she's off to Spain. Good riddance! Let me never hear another word about this hysterical creature."

Why Spain? Had she any particular reason to choose that country rather than another? No. All she wanted was to get away from Paris and hide. Via Marseilles and Perpignan she reached Alicante, then Madrid. She had decided to settle there forever, to marry a bullfighter or a Spanish farmer, and, by taking his name, cause the name of Sarah Bernhardt, then very obscure, to be completely forgotten.

But she began to reconsider this matter. All her life Sarah was guilty of many extravagances, but always at the last moment she succeeded in avoiding those which would have been irreparable. Barely three weeks after she had left Marseilles she returned to Paris. This was not because she had soon become disappointed with Spain but for the very good reason that she expected a child, and she felt that she had neither the right nor the courage to bring it into the world outside of France and far from her own people.

On her return to her mother, further deception awaited her. On learning that Sarah was pregnant, Julie Van Hard, who had had three natural daughters herself by different fathers, was suddenly filled with virtuous indignation. In a blind rage she told Sarah finally that she would never allow this disgraceful child to be born under her roof!

Thus Sarah was henceforth obliged to live alone, and she rented her first apartment, a little three-room place on the mezzanine floor in the Rue Duphot, near the corner of the Rue Saint Honoré. Despite everything, she did not wish to go too far away from her mother's home. Pleased at finally having got rid of her, Julie contributed a little to the expense of the modest apartment, especially when Sarah proposed to take with her little Régina, who was ten and adored her elder sister and was delighted at going to live with her. Julie was equally pleased to have only her beloved Jeanne with her and, before the end of 1864, the family thus divided, following its avowed preferences and its obstinate dislikes.

Who was the father of the child that Sarah Bernhardt was expecting? Was it one of those vague "comrade lovers" to whom she had given herself indifferently, after she left the Théâtre Francais, during that year which was so empty and sadly gay? No. She would never have pardoned herself such a clumsy mistake; she could never have loved, as she did until her death, a son whom she had conceived under such conditions. In the best sense of the word Maurice was a love child, and his birth was the result of the most touching romance in the life of Sarah Bernhardt.

During her engagement at the Gymnase, and even before she had made her debut there, the company had been asked to give a short private performance one night in the Emperor's quarters at the Palais des Tuileries, after a private dinner given by Napoleon III in honor of a foreign prince who was passing through. As a rule, the honor of providing such gala entertainments at the Imperial Palace was reserved to the Comédie Française. Sometimes, however, the Empress Eugénie got tired of that rather solemn repertory and preferred to draw on one of the boulevard theaters.

Camille Doucet always had an indulgent affection for Sarah, in spite of the fact that she had slapped Nathalie. He had asked Montigny to include her among the actors who were to play at the well received because it was too sad, and, hoping to conclude on appier note, she began in her sweetest voice:

Lorsque l'enfant paraît . . .[2]

A poem from *Feuilles d'Automne!* More of Victor Hugo! This time he Emperor was convinced that this impudent young person was doing it on purpose and was making fun of him. The program was almost over. After Sarah Bernhardt there came only an artist of no particular importance. Even before Sarah had begun the first verse of her second piece, Napoleon III suddenly stood up; gave his arm to the Empress; and moved into the adjoining drawing room, whither all the scandalized guests followed. Meanwhile poor little Sarah, embarrassed and terrified, remained alone on the stage facing fifty empty chairs.

The director appeared from the wings, rushed toward her, and poured out a stream of insults. Sarah was not patient. Whatever mistake she may have made, she would not submit to being treated like that. She replied angrily. The angry director seized her by the wrist. She gave a cry of rage and pain. Heaven knows how the incident might have turned out had not a man's voice been heard from the far end of the room: "Kindly leave that child alone."

Petrified, the director and the young actress turned around. The young man who had just spoken was twenty-five to thirty years old, dark and fashionably dressed, with a rare distinction. As he spoke, he came toward the stage. He had been one of the last of the audience following the Emperor out of the room and, touched by Sarah's discomfiture, had stopped a moment to see what would happen to her. He had heard the gross insults hurled at her and, becoming indignant, he protested calmly but firmly.

From the stage the director replied: "Why don't you mind your own business, sir? First of all, who are you?"

The young man answered: "I am Prince Henri de Ligne. I will not allow a woman to be insulted in my presence, especially a young woman who is pretty, naïve, and defenseless, like this young lady."

On hearing the name and title of the speaker, the director mumbled some vague excuse and disappeared. And in the huge empty drawing room Sarah remained alone with her unknown defender.

Excited, in love with romance, always moved by anything noble or

[2] When the child appears . . . *Trans.*

Tuileries, thus giving her a possible opportuni
the friends of the Emperor and Empress. Althou
was the youngest and most obscure member of the c
had deferred to the wishes of the director of the Bea

On the evening of the performance, after a few "
various members of the company, and a one-act play from
of the Gymnase, played by two stars of the period, Blar
and Céline Montaland, young Sarah appeared on the impro
in a corner of the large drawing room of the Tuileries. Sl
deeply to Their Majesties and the small audience, and anne
"*Oceano Nox.* This is the title of a poem from *Les Rayons*
Ombres, by Victor Hugo." And she began:

> *Oh! Combien de marins, combien de capitaines,*
> *Qui sont partis, joyeux, pour des courses lointaines,*
> *Dans ce morne horizon se sont évanouis. . . .*[1]

Napoleon III started when he heard the title of the poem. Everyone in the audience understood the meaning and looked at one an-
other, shocked and astounded. Victor Hugo was an ardent Republican,
a deadly adversary of the Emperor, and had written *Napoléon le
Petit,* among other violent pamphlets against him. Since the latter had
come to the throne, in 1852, Victor Hugo had been in exile in
Guernsey, where he remained eighteen years. He did not return to
Paris until October, 1870, during the war, after the fall of Napoleon
III and the proclamation of the Third Republic. To recite Victor
Hugo in 1864, at the Tuileries, in the presence of Their Majesties,
was an error in taste which almost amounted to an insult.

As can readily be understood, young Sarah had no notion of this
and had acted in all innocence. At that age she read the newspapers
very little and knew nothing of politics. She adored Victor Hugo's
talent. She knew only the poet and had never heard of the politician.
She had simply learned some verses which seemed beautiful to her
and had innocently recited them as best she could. That was all. But
the effect of *Oceano Nox* on the Emperor and his guests was like a
cold shower. After the last verse the Emperor did not applaud, and
the audience followed his example. Sarah thought the poem had not

[1] Oh, how many sailors, how many captains, Who have set out joyfully on distant
journeys, Have vanished on this dreary horizon. . . . *Trans.*

rare, she was immediately deeply interested by the courtly young gentleman's vigorous defense of an unknown, insignificant little actress who had drawn attention to herself by committing—as the Prince de Ligne explained to her smilingly—one of the most colossal blunders of which an actress who had been commanded to appear at the Emperor's Palace could be guilty.

The prince, in turn, at this first meeting was visibly attracted by the peculiar beauty and the vibrant nature of the young artist. At the end of the evening he escorted her to the door of her mother's house. They met the next day and the day after . . . every day and every night until the summer. This great love soon grew into a veritable passion which was sincere on both sides, the rarest and most touching reciprocal feeling which ever united two young hearts.[3]

[3] No doubt some people will be surprised that the real name of the Prince de Ligne is given in this volume. For several centuries his family has been one of the noblest and most distinguished in Belgium and even in Europe. Hypocritical custom might perhaps have suggested that the author of this book should describe him as "a great Belgian nobleman" or "the Prince de L——."

On further consideration, it seems impossible that the undeniable details given in this work could shock or distress anybody. It could only be flattering to a man, however lofty his position, to be described as having been the object of the first and greatest love of the most illustrious artist in the world, and the father of her only son. There could be moral damage to his descendants if the Prince de Ligne had been described here in an insulting or unpleasant fashion. But the part he played in the life of Sarah Bernhardt was always particularly knightly, loyal, and generous. After sixty years her memory of him was full of tenderness and gratitude. Not to remain silent about his relations with Sarah Bernhardt would seem rather to serve and honor the memory of the Prince de Ligne.

At all times the lives of notable men and women have been retraced in all their details by those who have undertaken such a task. For example, *Verlaine tel qu'il fut*, by François Porché. If I choose this example among many others, it is for two reasons. First, Verlaine was exactly contemporary with Sarah Bernhardt, having also been born in 1844. Secondly, Porché's book is probably the most typical of contemporary biographies. I do not believe it is possible to find a more complete story of a private life. But no one has ever reproached the author with having related the love affairs of Verlaine. Like Sarah Bernhardt, he belongs to history. That being the case, no part of his life should be inaccessible to historians.

As far as this case is concerned, the question has already been settled.

Like Sarah Bernhardt, another famous French actress also lived a love story with another nobleman no less illustrious. Not only have the historians made no mystery about it, but they have given this adventure the widest possible publicity in books and plays. I refer to Adrienne Lecouvreur and the Comte Maurice de Saxe.

It may be replied that that happened a long time ago and that Adrienne Lecouvreur belongs to a distant past, whereas the centenary of Sarah Bernhardt's birth has not yet been celebrated. This argument might have some weight if the first accounts of the life of Adrienne Lecouvreur were appearing at the same time as this life of Sarah Bernhardt. But it will soon be a hundred years since Scribe,

When the summer of 1864 came around, the young prince was entrusted by the Belgian government with a long and distant mission, and had to leave Europe for several months. When the lovers had to separate it was as if they had been literally torn apart. Prince Henri did not return until the end of the year, or the beginning of 1865, first to Belgium and then to Paris. But when he reached the latter, Sarah had left the Gymnase, left her mother's home, and had forbidden anyone to give her new address in the Rue Duphot to people asking for her. It was not that she wished to break with the man she adored; far from that. But she was extremely proud, and nothing in the world would have made her appear to be taking advantage of her approaching maternity. This feeling, which was very worthy of her, was easy to understand. As she did not know whether, on his return from the long voyage, Prince Henri would still want to see her and renew their interrupted relations, to tell him that she was expecting a child, of whom he was obviously the father, would be to force his hand, to impose a duty upon him. This did not appeal to Sarah. If her lover ever returned to her, she wished it to be only his desire to see her again which brought him back to her.

Thus, unknown to the prince, Sarah, on bad terms with her mother and watched over only by Madame Guérard, gave birth to a son, who was declared to be of an unknown father and given the name of Maurice Bernhardt. He was born on December 22, 1864. Sarah was exactly twenty years and two months old.

Although Julie helped her from time to time, and so did her aunts, Sarah's life was very difficult. Instead of living comfortably and without a care in the world in her mother's house, she was responsible for her rent, the child, a nurse, and also her young sister. She would have to find work at any cost, and quickly.

She accepted a job as understudy for one of the principals in an operetta called *La Biche au Bois*, by the Brothers Cogniard, who had produced it twenty years earlier, in 1845, with great success at the Porte Saint Martin. It had been revived at the same theater early in March, 1865, with a celebrated diva of the time, Jeanne Ugalde, who

in 1849, produced his play, *Adrienne Lecouvreur*, and in 1750 Maurice de Saxe died, a Marshal of France. Thus, in the middle of the nineteenth century, nobody contested Scribe's right to show upon the stage of the Comédie Française facts which had actually happened in the middle of the eighteenth. In the middle of the twentieth century, why should it be forbidden to relate facts which actually happened in the middle of the nineteenth? *Author's note.*

played a man's part, and a charming comedienne lent by the Odéon, Mademoiselle Debay. The leading dancer was Mariquita, who, thirty years later, at the Opéra Comique, was one of the most remarkable ballet mistresses that theater had ever known.

At the beginning of April Mademoiselle Debay having fallen ill, Sarah played her part, Princess Desirée, for nearly a month. Naturally her name appeared on the playbills and in the newspapers. In this way the Prince de Ligne found Sarah Bernhardt again, having looked for her in vain for three or four months every time he came to Paris. One night at the end of the play, he came to her dressing room. The reproaches which he was beginning to make quickly ceased when she explained everything to him. Their passion was resumed as ardently as before, but more profoundly, more seriously. Now, in the room next to Sarah's own, was the cradle of tiny Maurice.

The brief appearance of Sarah at the Porte Saint Martin had not improved her position as an artist in any way. People in the theater business like artists who specialize, and those who succeed most are always those who, during their entire career, not only perform in plays of the same kind but also play the one identical part. The uninitiated might think that the art of changing one's personality, the ability to go from the humorous to the serious, from tragedy to comedy, is an indication of the rarest kind of talent and, therefore, most in demand. That is a complete mistake. A versatile actor, who appears different in every new play, always has more difficulty in achieving a reputation than an actor who can be counted upon to be eternally the same in every part.

Sardou used to say: "A complete surprise in the theater is almost always a mistake. The public does not wish to be surprised, except by what it has already vaguely guessed."

What is true of the plays is also true of the players. An actor who invariably lets his admirers see him as they expected to rarely disappoints them, and consequently he maintains his reputation more easily. If one looks over the greatest French artists of the last hundred years, one will find that, with few exceptions, those who left the most distinguished names are those who selected a type and never departed from it.

All this means that, in 1865, Sarah was far from being on the road to fame. Having appeared at the Conservatoire in tragedy and made her debut at the Théâtre Français in *Iphigénie*, she had played light comedies at the Gymnase, and now she was performing in a spectacular operetta at the Porte Saint Martin! "Soon," people said, "she will be in vaudeville [which at that time was called the café concert], or perhaps d'Ennery will want her for the next revival of *La Prière des Naufragés!*" Meanwhile nobody wanted her for anything. But this time she did not take the matter to heart. Now the existence in the Rue Duphot was marvelous. Sarah and Prince Henri passionately continued to live their wonderful love story. Every time that he could get away from Brussels, which was very often, he hastened to Paris to rejoin the young woman. In absolute understanding and complete confidence in each other, their life together was unusually and sublimely beautiful.

There was no reason why she should miss the theater. With her lover and her little boy, who was as pretty as a picture, Sarah spent her dreamlike days, with only one wish: that this blessed period should never come to an end.

Gradually, seeing that his mistress really lived only for him and that, despite a past which was not spotless, when she loved she had the tenderest heart and the noblest soul that he would ever encounter, Prince Henri, after mature reflection, decided to marry her and to recognize his son.

This was a grave decision. The last scion of the de Ligne family, this proud and noble line in which there had never been a misalliance, taking as his wife an unknown little actress, of no standing and with no money, of Jewish descent on her mother's side, who was his mistress and had a natural child by him! He foresaw that all his relatives would receive this news with horror. But his determination seemed unshakable.

He made only one condition. If she became his wife Sarah would leave the theater forever, in order to devote herself exclusively to her husband and child. She agreed to this wish, not only without regret but with enthusiasm. Leave the theater? That would be for her neither a great loss nor a great sacrifice. She had never had any success, and nothing seemed to indicate that she would someday succeed.

In the summer of 1866, during the fine weather, which is always supposed to put old people in a good humor, the young prince, in his ancestral castle on the outskirts of Brussels, courageously raised the question and, describing Sarah as an ideal wife, he announced to the entire assembled family his irrevocable intention of giving her his name.

If a squadron of bombing planes, fifty years before the achievements of these weapons were first heard of, had dropped ten tons of explosives that evening on the manor of the de Lignes, the amazement which ensued could not have been much greater. It seemed evident that Henri was the prey in Paris of a horrible and dangerous person who had captivated him by her perfidious and ambitious machinations. The matter was of the utmost importance and the peril would have to be removed with all the necessary speed and energy required. Prince Eugène de Ligne, Henri's father, could not leave Belgium on account of his health, so it was General de Ligne, his cousin, who took the train to Paris—unknown to his nephew, of course—and one day rang Sarah Bernhardt's doorbell.

He expected to see a resolute, experienced woman, sure of herself, whose feline astuteness and trickery he would have to attack with implacable vigor. And now he saw a very young woman, scarcely twenty-two years of age, blonde, sweet, and charming, who was peacefully playing on the floor in her modest living room with a baby who could not even walk, but tottered nicely. The interview still had the same object, but it was carried out in a different tone from that which the general had foreseen. Gently, almost paternally, he pointed out to her the enormous responsibility which she was undertaking. In two or three years, when all his passion had subsided, the prince would certainly hold it against Sarah that he had broken with his family—for if he married her, a break with all belonging to him was inevitable—that she had made him lose his position, his rank, and also the greater part of his fortune. The first step which his parents would take against him would be to deprive him of all of his family patrimony which did not yet belong to him personally but which would revert to him someday. Had she the right to bring such a series of catastrophes upon the man whom she loved?

Like Duval's father in *La Dame aux Camélias*—though the general did not keep his hat on—he withdrew, leaving her alone with her thoughts, face to face with this terrible question of conscience for a woman so young and so much in love to solve. However, she made up her mind quickly.

Since her customary and all-powerful savior, the Duc de Morny, had been dead for some months, she went to see kindhearted Camille

Doucet and said to him: "It doesn't matter how and the terms are unimportant, but I must get an engagement immediately in some theater. But not merely for one play. I want a long contract which will keep me very busy and give me years of hard work and with important penalties, so that in no case can I recover my freedom."

Camille Doucet was surprised and, seeing that she was violently agitated, he asked her for some explanation. In guarded terms and without mentioning any name Sarah explained.

The director of the Beaux Arts was touched and said to her quietly: "Don't worry. I understand and I have just what you are looking for. The management of the Odéon, a national theater, which is consequently under my direct control, has just been given to two new partners. One is called de Chilly, former manager of the Ambigu, a vulgar person without taste, who has contributed money, and Félix Duquesnel, a brilliant and delightful young fellow. He is not yet thirty-five. I know that he has seen you at the Théâtre Français and that he thinks you are charming. If I ask him, I'm sure that he will be delighted to take you into his company. You will hear from him within forty-eight hours."

Two days later Sarah received a visit from Duquesnel, who, instead of asking her to come to his office, had decided to go and see her. Her status as an artist being absolutely nil, it was not that the young woman deserved this mark of consideration. On the contrary, it was because her tempestuous departure from the Théâtre Français and her flight from the Gymnase, and then her almost complete inactivity, had made her undesirable almost everywhere, and the young manager was afraid, before having come to an agreement with her, to introduce her to his partner, de Chilly, who would certainly have objected to her engagement.

Camille Doucet had told the truth. Fair-haired, gay, and sympathetic, Félix Duquesnel produced the most favorable impression on Sarah and made less painful for her the tremendous sacrifice upon which she had decided.

He handed her a three-year contract already made out, signed by him "for de Chilly and Duquesnel," and said laughingly: "I am putting something over there, but it can't be helped. De Chilly will have to bow to an accomplished fact. Read this. If the terms are suitable sign it and return it, and you will make your debut at the Odéon in a fortnight."

Just as he was leaving, Prince Henri de Ligne arrived. Surprised at finding a young man there, he asked, after he had left, who he was and what he had come for. Trying, with a great effort, to appear nonchalant, Sarah replied that it was one of the managers of the Second French National Theater, who wanted to engage her. She showed the contract to the astounded Prince Henri. Had it not been agreed long ago, once and for all, that Sarah had given up the theater?

"It is true," she said, "you asked me to, and I had almost decided to. But you are away so often. Sometimes I spend weeks alone, with nothing to do, waiting for you."

"When we are married . . ." he protested.

"We are not married yet, and I have been thinking things over. Your family will never consent to receive me. I shall always be despised and ignored, whereas at the Odéon I shall be received with open arms, spoiled and cherished. You see, the manager even came here to ask me to sign a contract with him. It is a magnificent theater, and at last I shall be able to play great parts."

The young prince could hardly believe his ears. At first he thought it was a joke, that Sarah was amusing herself by trying to tease him; but a few seconds later, when he saw her resolutely dip her pen in the inkwell and sign the contract in his presence, his anger and grief broke out in reproaches whose vehemence could not be held within bounds.

"So while I, with all my heart, was trying to convince my family, to make them accept the idea of our marriage, you were secretly arranging to return to the theater! You were getting this contract, by heaven knows what intrigues and by making yourself agreeable to whom! Evidently those who wish to separate me from you were right. A cheap actress never changes! She always remains what she is and lives only for her one passion, the stage. I blush to have been so silly as to have believed in your vows and in your sincerity for so many months."

Stoically Sarah submitted to these cruel insults, which were so profoundly unfair, but apparently the prince could not guess the truth. Many times she wanted madly to cry: "It isn't true! I adore you! And it is only out of love for you that I took this step which would immediately bring about our separation." However, she said nothing. She had the incredible courage to remain silent. She knew that if she had spoken, if she had told him about the visit of General de Ligne,

Prince Henri would have gone indignantly to his uncle and, having told him what he thought of the procedure, would have been more determined than ever to marry her, thus hastening the break with his people which she had determined to avoid at any cost.

But when the young prince had gone—forever—she fell on the floor in a faint. A violent fever seized her poor frail body and, for nearly a month, Madame Guérard and her family feared for her life.

That is why, being unable to act as soon as she would have liked, Sarah did not make her debut at the Odéon until the early part of December, 1866, in the role of Silvia in *Le Jeu de l'Amour et du Hasard*, by Marivaux. She had scarcely recovered and was still upset by this horrible drama, while once again she had been given a part which did not suit her in the least. The plays of Marivaux require, particularly, qualities of preciosity, coquetry, and insincerity, which never were natural to her. Consequently her appearance at the Odéon did not attract much attention, and it was only some years later that she there acquired fame.

Nevertheless, she now belonged to a theater which she liked, where she felt protected and encouraged. For if de Chilly for a long time had no consideration for her, from the first day Duquesnel constantly displayed his good will and had complete confidence in her future. This was of the utmost importance to the hypersensitive Sarah, who always needed to feel that she could rely on people and who later could never have anyone around her whom she did not think absolutely devoted and sincere. Because of this, and not because he was an exceptional director, Duquesnel was very greatly responsible for the revelation of her talent and for its flowering, to which she henceforth devoted her nights and days.

From January, 1863, to December, 1866, for nearly four years, Sarah had done almost nothing in the theater: a few months at the Gymnase, a few weeks at the Porte Saint Martin. From the end of 1866 until the end of 1922—that is, for fifty-six consecutive years—she never ceased to act and took only rare vacations. Difficulties, obstacles, illnesses, and everything that crossed and sometimes filled her private or her sentimental life, nothing now—except the two Franco-German wars, of 1870 and 1914—was ever to turn her from the theater to which she was destined so young and where, in fact, she did not succeed very rapidly.

As a matter of fact, although she entered the Conservatoire at sixteen, it was only at twenty-two that Sarah Bernhardt really began her career, and only at twenty-five that she achieved her first success. These details may provide a useful lesson to impatient young actresses who are astonished because they are not celebrated the very next day after they have appeared upon the stage for the first time.

CHAPTER III

The Odéon, the War of 1870

SARAH BERNHARDT remained at the Odéon nearly six years,
until July, 1872, and professionally she was very happy there.
In her *Mémoires* she recalled this period with delight.

"Ah, the Odéon! The theater I loved most of all. I was very sorry
to leave it. We were all fond of one another and everyone was happy.
Duquesnel was a manager full of wit, gallantry, and youth. I remembered the few months that I had spent at the Comédie Française.
Nothing but affected, gossipy, jealous people. At the Gymnase they
talked only about gowns and hats and things far removed from art.
But the Odéon was ideal. The only thought was to put on plays. We
rehearsed morning, afternoon, all the time. I adored that. I worked
hard and was always ready to take anyone's place, as I knew every
part."

Like the Comédie Française, the Odéon was and is still a repertory
theater; that is to say, one where different plays are given alternately.
In the course of one week's nine or ten performances—every night,
and matinees Thursdays, Sundays, and sometimes Saturdays—they
often give five or six different plays, only the new ones being performed three or four times. In this way, in the course of the year, the
Odéon frequently gives fifty or sixty plays, among which about twenty
classics are billed periodically and are produced regularly every year.

Thus, until the war of 1870, Sarah Bernhardt played a considerable
number of parts. She asked nothing better because she wanted, by
dint of hard work, to forget, if possible, the man whom she had had
to leave with such heroic abnegation, and because the success which
she was experiencing at last increased tenfold her passion for the
theater—that passion which had been retarded by events and by rebuffs, but which awaited only the opportunity to express itself irre-
sistibly.

To enumerate all the parts that she played at the Odéon would be interminable and tiresome. After 1882, when her fame was enormous and decisive, each part she created was an event, and it will be the elementary duty of this book not to omit any of them. But such details are not required for the daily, routine, crowded, and often obscure work which she did at the Odéon. It was by the accumulation of different characters, important, secondary, or episodical, which she played at that theater, that Sarah Bernhardt slowly reached the top rank. Engaged for one hundred and fifty francs a month, and still quite unknown, when she left at the end of six years, if she was as yet getting only eight hundred francs a month, she had at least become the most important actress at the Odéon.

If she achieved this result it was only by making patient and constant efforts and without having had, except once during her last year, one of those sensational opening nights which in one evening reveal and launch an actress on her career.

On January 15, 1867, for the anniversary of Molière, Duquesnel had her play Armande in *Les Femmes Savantes*. It will be recalled that in 1862 she had performed the part of Henriette in the same play at her third debut at the Comédie Française, and without any success. She did not succeed much better as Armande, who, rather like Silvia in *Le Jeu de l'Amour et du Hasard*, is really only a *précieuse*. As long as they insisted on giving her parts like that, she would always be excelled by the numerous actresses who have coquetry in lieu of feeling, and who skillfully substitute virtuosity for the power and emotion which are absent but which can be completely lacking in parts of this character without doing any harm.

Among many parts in which Sarah Bernhardt went unnoticed, two characters, at the beginning of 1867, attracted the attention of the regular Odéon audiences and of certain critics: Cordelia in *King Lear*, in which she was infinitely touching and pathetic; and, especially, the youth Zacharie in *Athalie*, by Racine. It is to be noted that with two exceptions Sarah Bernhardt always succeeded in men's parts.

Duquesnel and de Chilly had had the idea of putting on Racine's tragedy with Mendelssohn's score and a large orchestra. Each of the first four acts of the play ends with a chorus, sung and spoken alternately. These choruses, which are assigned in the text to five or six "voices," were to be spoken by pupils of the Conservatoire. But, disconcerted by the music which accompanied them—and which is always suppressed at ordinary performances—these youngsters did not succeed in catching the necessary rhythm. Duquesnel then decided to entrust the entire text of the spoken choruses to Zacharie alone—assisted occasionally by his sister, Salomith. The crystalline voice of Sarah, a melody in itself, uttered the verses of Racine with exquisite sweetness and delicacy. On the night of the opening, de Chilly began to think that his partner had not been so absurd when he engaged this little Sarah Bernhardt.

That same year a play was revived once more which had been one of the greatest successes of the second half of the nineteenth century in Paris, *Le Testament de César Girodot,* by Adolphe Belot and Villetard. First produced in 1859, it was a dazzling comedy. Sarah Bernhardt played the part of Hortense, in which she showed a comic talent hitherto unsuspected. Although of little importance, the part is well written and can be played "straight." That was always for her a condition of any success.

Two other plays may be quoted among those which she performed in 1867, not because she had any great success in them, but because they show how, gradually, the important writers of the period were beginning to accept Sarah Bernhardt, if not yet as the creator of parts, as an interpreter for revivals which were more or less noteworthy. These two plays were by George Sand, *François le Champi,* first produced in 1849, in which Sarah attractively played the attractive part of Mariette, and *Le Marquis de Villemer,* a much more recent play, produced in 1864, and for that reason the object of much greater attention. In this she was given the part of the mad Baronne d'Arglade, a character with a past and much experience, for which Sarah would have needed a more authoritative and striking manner.

George Sand, who was then sixty-three years old, was at the height of her great reputation. Furthermore, since the death of Alfred de Musset ten years earlier, she was the heroine of an unforgettable romance which, in the eyes of young Sarah, excited and thrilled, made her a very considerable personality whom she was happy and proud to approach. That is why, although her personal success in them was slight, these two plays left her with her first great memories of the theater. From that time on George Sand conceived a great friendship for her and was one of those who prevailed upon her to leave the Odéon to return to the Comédie Française. At the close of 1867 Sarah Bernhardt played also in *Le Drame de la Rue de la Paix,* by Adolphe Belot, and she received friendly mention in some of the reviews.

On February 18, 1868, the Odéon was putting on an important revival of *Kean*, by Alexandre Dumas *père*, a famous play with a marvelous man's part. Since Frédérick Lemaître had created the part in 1836, all the leading actors of every country played it in turn. This night it was interpreted by Charles Berton, an actor who had a successful career during the Second Empire, though not so brilliant as that of his son, Pierre Berton, who played several parts opposite Sarah Bernhardt some years later, particularly the role of Baron Scarpia in *La Tosca*. In this revival of *Kean*, Sarah had the part of Anna Damby and made a great hit, not so much because of her interpretation of the part, but because of her courage and youthful self-possession on the stage, under very difficult circumstances.

It was at this time, faced by the more and more obstinate opposition of the Republican party, that the Emperor, having become more liberal, had to resign himself to certain concessions. Under pressure of public opinion, the Minister of Fine Arts had recently authorized the Comédie Française to revive *Hernani*, by Victor Hugo—who was still in exile. This revival, on June 20, 1867, with Maria Favart, Delaunay, Bressant, and Maubant, had been not only a literary triumph but a political event.

As a result of this tremendous success, the Left Wing press and the Odéon audiences asked the managers of that theater to revive *Ruy Blas*. Being sure of magnificent receipts, Duquesnel and de Chilly were perfectly willing; but the Ministry was opposed to it, fearing the demonstrations on the part of the students of the Left Bank would be even more noisy than at the Comédie Française. Besides, as the successful revival of *Hernani* would run until the spring of 1868, the government could not allow the two imperial theaters to be monopolized at the same time by Victor Hugo.

Born the same year, Alexandre Dumas *père* and Victor Hugo, the two great romantic writers of the century, for a long time were rivals for first place. The genius of Hugo had finally triumphed, and his long exile, which made of him a martyr, further added to the universal enthusiasm which he inspired in France.

The Odéon public, particularly the students, insisted on seeing a sort of provocation in the fact that, instead of *Ruy Blas*, which all Paris was demanding, it was precisely *Kean* that was put on, Dumas thereby usurping the position of Hugo. This was absurd, but it explains why, the night of the revival, when the curtain rose, the audience burst into a chorus of shouts: "*Ruy Blas! Ruy Blas!* Victor Hugo! Victor Hugo!"

Trying to dominate the noise, the actors raised their voices and occasionally succeeded in being heard. In the wings Dumas, who was very much upset, was walking up and down, wiping from his brow the sweat which dripped from his kinky hair and trickled down his temples. He was perfectly willing that they should have a play by Hugo or even that the great poet should return to France. But that the demonstrations of sympathy for the author of *Les Châtiments* should degenerate into hostile shouts against him was more than he could tolerate.

Before going on the stage, Sarah Bernhardt noticed his indignation and murmured to him: "Do not be uneasy, Master; if they do not stop, I will make them understand how ill-mannered they are."

Dumas looked at her, faintly incredulous.

Although he was a great favorite with the public, Charles Berton had not been able to silence the protestants when he appeared on the stage. As she promised, Sarah succeeded. She made her entrance wearing an "English costume of 1820." When the audience shortly began again to shout: "Hugo! Hugo!" she stopped playing, walked straight down to the footlights, and faced the public. In their astonishment the demonstrators ceased.

Then, with a charming smile, she said: "You wish to defend the cause of justice. Are you promoting justice this evening by holding Alexandre Dumas responsible for the decrees which have proscribed Victor Hugo?"

This simple phrase, so striking in its perfect logic, produced an immediate effect. Seeing the smiling calm of the young actress, the house burst into applause; and the show ended, not only without further incidents, but with a great success for the play, the performers, and the author, who was so delighted that he embraced his brave little player.

"I am going to write a lovely part for you, my child; I owe it to you," he said to her.

Dumas did not have time to keep his promise. A few months later he fell ill, and died in 1870.

Kean was a successful revival. The performances alternated with those of an unimportant and ephemeral play called *La Loterie du Mariage*, in which Sarah also had a small success. Quietly and imperceptibly she was making a place for herself. It was de Chilly, now completely satisfied with the young actress, who proposed to Duquesnel to raise her salary. At the beginning of the season of 1868–69, her salary was increased to three hundred and fifty francs a month.

It was a fortune or, at least, an indication that she was on her way up. Sarah had long felt cramped in her apartment in the Rue Duphot. She moved and took a larger place at 16 Rue Auber, almost at the corner of the Rue Caumartin. She was assisted in this extravagance, which would otherwise have been rather premature, by her grandmother, Lisa Van Hard.

The latter had definitely left Holland a few months before to come and live in Paris. At first Julie had given her mother a room in her own apartment in the Rue Saint Honoré. The old woman was seventy years of age, tall, bony, and hard, criticizing everyone and everything. Her humble origins were revealed every instant by her tastes, her gestures, her attitude, and especially her terrible Jewish-Dutch accent, which was infinitely more pronounced than the attractive accent of Youle. All of this soon got on the latter's nerves to an extreme degree. Since the death of the Duc de Morny, she was leading the peaceful existence of a well-to-do middle-class woman, and in spite of her forty-five years—which, in addition to giving her a taste for a quiet life, had also added to her weight—she continued to receive her little circle of men friends, who were now somewhat quieter but still very distinguished. This mother could not be "produced." Just as formerly she had refused to keep Sarah with her, because this grown daughter made her seem old, she did not want to keep Lisa, because her mere appearance only too openly betrayed her humble origins.

As goodhearted Sarah had taken in little Régina four years earlier, she now took in her grandmother. The latter made her a present of the few pieces of furniture which she had brought with her from Holland—her only possessions—and in combination with the furniture from the Rue Duphot they furnished the new apartment. While Sarah was at the theater and Régina, waiting for her, played in the Luxembourg Gardens Madame Lisa Van Hard looked after her great-grandson, Maurice, in place of the servant.

From time to time Youle paid them a visit. She stepped out of her beautiful carriage; spent ten minutes in the slightly Bohemian apartment, where, without luxury and in an almost inevitable disorder, her mother, two of her daughters, and her grandson lived. Trying to conceal her disgust, she very quickly departed, leaving on the table, when she thought of it, a few hundred franc notes, her share in the expenses of Régina's education. On going downstairs she would find her dear little beautiful Jeanne, all dressed up, waiting for her in the carriage.

The following year had scarcely opened when Sarah had her first real success. Whereas she had already played so many long parts in big plays, it was a very small play, with two characters, which was the occasion of this success. It was in verse and entitled *Le Passant*; and its author was François Coppée, a young poet of twenty-six. It opened at the Odéon on January 14, 1869, with Madame Agar, an excellent tragedienne then at the height of her talent, and Sarah Bernhardt, who that day revealed hers.

François Coppée was then unknown and in more than moderate circumstances and, despite many waits in their outer office, he had not succeeded in being received by the managers of the Odéon. So he timidly brought his little play to Madame Agar, who was well disposed toward poets. She was delighted and made Sarah read it, and the latter's enthusiasm was even greater. It was the insistence of these two actresses which prevailed upon Duquesnel to look into the slender manuscript. As a man of taste, he immediately appreciated the quality of the work and, as it would cost next to nothing—an old set from the storehouse and only two new costumes—he put it into rehearsals without even consulting de Chilly.

Le Passant was a veritable triumph. The poetic grace of the little play, its delicate lyricism, positively enchanted the public. A few days later the name of Coppée was on everybody's lips. On the night of the opening, ten curtain calls greeted the play and its perfect interpreters: Madame Agar, ideally beautiful as the courtesan Silvia, and Sarah Bernhardt, absolutely adorable as the little page Zanetto, her second part in men's clothes. In a tight-fitting, mauve doublet, which suited her perfectly, a cap ornamented with a large feather and squarely placed on her blonde wig, with her guitar slung around her shoulders, her silhouette in *Le Passant* became celebrated. In selecting her costume she very appropriately took her inspiration from the statuette well known as "The Florentine Singer," by Paul Dubois, which had been shown in an exhibition and greatly noticed three years before. On this occasion she gave the first proof of the astonishing taste with which she always knew how to "dress" a period character. She did it not only with scrupulous accuracy, but with such an intuitive feeling for what would strike the eye and the memory of the spectator that none of the characters which she created could be imagined ever afterward as having any other appearance than that which she had given them.

Until summer Coppée's little play was performed more than a hundred times. It was given at the end of the program, after most of the plays which alternated on the bills of the Odéon. If the receipts of a play fell off, it was "propped up" with *Le Passant* and they immediately rose. At the fiftieth performance of this success, Sarah Bernhardt's salary was raised to five hundred francs a month.

Toward the month of April, *Le Passant* was commanded by the Tuileries and, in the course of a great reception, was performed in the presence of the Emperor, the Empress, and the little Prince Imperial who was then thirteen.

When Their Majesties' command was transmitted by Duquesnel to Madame Agar and Sarah, the latter was at first rather perplexed. She remembered the mistake she had made at the Tuileries five years earlier. Did Napoleon III know that one of the players was none other than the little beginner from the Gymnase, who had so inappropriately chosen the poems which she had the honor of reciting in his presence?

If he did remember, he probably did not bear her any grudge; for two days after she had asked Camille Doucet the question, the latter informed her that the Emperor counted on seeing Coppée's play at the Tuileries "just as it was performed at the Odéon."

Nevertheless, Sarah Bernhardt was somewhat apprehensive when she appeared before the Emperor and Empress, and even more so when, after the performance, a chamberlain came to her and Madame Agar to tell them that his Majesty wished to present his congratulations.

When she approached Napoleon III, who was waiting for the two actresses in a corner of the drawing room, where the buffet table had been set up, she was struck by the great change in the appearance and manner of the Emperor. He seemed tired and disillusioned, and in five years he had aged fifteen. The increasingly violent attacks of which he was the object, his incessant struggle against the adversaries of his power, were positively undermining him. Whereas he was still so alert and so brilliant that other evening when she had seen him at close hand, today he looked much older than his sixty-one years.

After saying something pleasant to Madame Agar, Napoleon III turned to Sarah Bernhardt and said, with a melancholy smile: "The last time that you came here, it was you who were right, Mademoiselle. I was obliged to allow *Hernani* to be performed at the Théâtre Français. In other words, you simply foresaw before I did that I should one day have to authorize the works of Victor Hugo."

The continued success of *Le Passant* at the Odéon had brought Sarah a certain renown. The students, in particular, had taken her up. Of the entire company she was their favorite actress, and now, in every one of her parts, as soon as she came on the stage, they insured her a personal success. Not yet accustomed to this and delighted by it, spending all her days and nights at the theater, laughing, gay, and already witty, Sarah was the spoiled child of the house. From the managers to the scene shifters, everyone adored her.

An excellent person named Hortense, who was the confidante, the companion, and the stage maid of Madame Agar, conceived a genuine passion for the young woman who had created Zanetto. "Ah," she repeated, "the voice that the good Lord has given this youngster! When she speaks, you would think that gold was flowing and falling like a waterfall on the heads of the audience!" Some years later the entire world was to celebrate the "golden voice" of Sarah Bernhardt. It was during *Le Passant* that this humble lady's maid first formulated the expression which was to characterize the great artist forever.

An accident which was not serious in itself, but which came so near being serious that for a long time afterward Sarah shuddered at it in retrospective terror, gave her an opportunity of realizing that her growing popularity had become greater than she supposed. One evening in June, 1869, as the result of the stupid carelessness of her servant, a fire broke out in her absence and completely destroyed her apartment in the Rue Auber. The fire having spread with amazing rapidity to the staircase, it was only as a result of great efforts that little Maurice and Grandmother Lisa were saved. The child was asleep in bed. A ladder had to be placed against the outside wall beneath a window, whose panes the firemen broke in order to enter the room. Having wrapped the baby in a blanket, they brought him down the the same way and handed him over to his terrified young mother.

Everything was burned. Not a piece of furniture, not even a piece of jewelry, was left to Sarah. The latter had melted and become shapeless lumps of metal. And, what was even more serious, the entire apartment was badly damaged. It had to be shored up for months, and careless Sarah had always forgotten to take out fire insurance! Her landlord and the insurance companies of the other tenants claimed large sums of money—which she was all the more incapable of paying at the time, since she possessed precisely nothing.

Duquesnel and a few other friends intervened and negotiated. She did not have to face most of the suits with which she was threatened. But for the restoration of her apartment she had to pay a steep indemnity, and she anxiously wondered how she could raise the amount. The two managers of the Odéon suggested that they would give a benefit for her; that is to say, they would place the theater at her disposal free of charge for a matinee, at which she could draw up a program to suit her convenience, the receipts from which would be paid to her in their entirety. She accepted with gratitude.

It was in these circumstances that not only the sympathy of the Paris public was eloquently manifested, but that of the artists whom she asked to come to sing or act for her.

Almost all accepted willingly and lent her their assistance free, at their head Adelina Patti, the celebrated singer who, in her youth and beauty, had then reached the height of her fame. Thanks chiefly to the magical name of Patti, the house was packed, the receipts were excellent, and the victim of the fire was able to pay her debts. In the course of her benefit matinee she naturally played *Le Passant*, her one little triumph, and her entrance was greeted, not only by the students, but by the entire audience, with a touching ovation. Sarah was becoming in Paris an actress that a certain world knew and liked.

Having nowhere to go, she first asked shelter from her mother. But she never could get on with Julie. She remained with her only a few days, and soon took a furnished apartment in the Rue de l'Arcade. It was dark and gloomy and she did not feel at home in it. At the end of 1869 she moved again into a small but sunny mezzanine in the Rue de Rome, a few yards from the Gare Saint Lazare. Being too hard up to stand so many expenses, she did not take her grandmother with her this time. Doing her duty for once, Julie installed her at her own expense in a home for the aged in the suburbs of Paris.

Sarah remained seven years in the Rue de Rome, where she was happy to be alone with Régina and her little Maurice. She did not leave this apartment until the beginning of 1876, when she settled in her famous house in the Avenue de Villiers.

Prior to the war, and now much in demand by the authors whose new plays were being put on at the Odéon, Sarah created three new parts. On October 18, 1869, it was *Le Bâtard*, a drama by Alfred Touroude, a tearful story which added nothing to the slight fame of this writer but did add to the growing fame of his interpreter, who made it the occasion of a decided success.

In the early months of 1870 she played *L'Affranchi*, by Latour de Saint-Ybars, an obscure work which is lost in oblivion and probably deserves it. Then she did *L'Autre*, an interesting comedy in four acts by George Sand. This was the third play of hers in which Sarah performed, and this time it was a new one. Its success was not considerable; but by the time war was declared, these three first nights, one after the other, had decidedly placed Sarah Bernhardt among those actresses to whom first-class roles could be entrusted.

The reader will doubtless wonder what was the love life of Sarah Bernhardt during the four years at the Odéon. She was young, pretty, intelligent, and very, very amusing, gradually becoming well known in a nice way. As she lived alone, or at least without a husband or a lover, she would obviously attract the attentions of many admirers. It is certain that at this time none captured, if not her attention, at least her heart. For a very long time after she had been compelled to give up the Prince de Ligne she remained terribly hurt by this painful separation, and the slightest word of love pronounced by another hurt her physically. She could not bear to hear anyone say to her "I love you," when it was not the voice of Prince Henri murmuring those words.

It is probable that Sarah's lasting affection for Duquesnel, who remained her friend and later became her partner, grew in the course of a more intimate relationship and, a few months later, there is every reason to think that her friendship with Paul de Rémusat was not entirely platonic. The latter had a brilliant and distinguished mind and, as deputy and later senator, he played an important part in Parliament after 1871. When quite young he had been attracted to politics and was the favorite son of Monsieur Thiers, about whom he wrote a remarkable book. Rémusat was then between thirty-five and forty years of age, and Sarah was extremely drawn by his great intelligence and his perfect behavior. But no more than Duquesnel was he what might be called "beloved" by Sarah Bernhardt. Possibly at the beginning he aroused in her an interest which she thought destined to become a deeper feeling. On the contrary, their relations soon were those of affectionate comradeship. He was not the man to make her forget the father of her child.

On July 15, 1870, Napoleon III, Emperor of France, declared war on Prussia, after a fortnight during which Paris, feverishly excited by the news which constantly grew worse, expected the worst to happen every day. Overnight the theaters were deserted, and the closing of the Odéon stopped short the continued progress of Sarah Bernhardt. She did not resume the course of her youthful successes until the end of the summer following the war and the Commune—to be precise, in September, 1871.

For some weeks at first, Paris lived in a state of delirious enthusiasm. Dense and joyful crowds swarmed about the streets shouting: "To Berlin!" The early reports of military operations had been encouraging. But soon this general frenzy turned to consternation. There was the disastrous battle of Saint Privat; then, on September 2, 1870, the appalling defeat at Sedan and the capitulation of the Emperor, immediately followed by the proclamation of the Republic and the creation of the Government of National Defense.

The advance of the enemy became more threatening. In a few days it became certain that Paris would be surrounded, besieged, and possibly bombarded. Sarah Bernhardt at once decided to send away her family—especially her son, who was then barely five years old. This was in the middle of September. Scarcely had Parisians returned from the country before they were fleeing again at every railway station. It was almost impossible to find a seat on the train. After waiting for hours at the Gare Saint Lazare, Sarah finally succeeded, thanks to friendly officials who had seen her act, in obtaining, in two different trains, the six seats which she needed for her mother, Julie, her grandmother, her two sisters—Jeanne and Régina—little Maurice, and the maid. They all set out for Havre, where, in spite of the rush, Sarah was able to reserve rooms at the Frascati Hotel. But she did not leave. Why? She explains in her *Mémoires:*

"It never occurred to me for a moment that I could leave. I believed that I was useful in Paris. Useful, in what way? My belief was stupid but profound. I thought that all people who were physically able should remain in Paris, and I remained without knowing what I would do there."

She very soon knew. The war was coming nearer and nearer to the capital. Every day now long convoys brought the wounded to Paris. Sarah Bernhardt volunteered as a nurse, but the staff of every hospital was complete. So she decided to have her own hospital. With the aid of a few influential friends, particularly the Prefect of Police, Comte de Kératry, whom she knew slightly, this young woman of twenty-six received permission to open a temporary hospital on her own account at the Odéon, Duquesnel and de Chilly having agreed in advance. A few days later the Ministry of War officially recognized the Odéon as an auxiliary military hospital.

The four great months, from the end of September, 1870, to the end of January, 1871, during which Sarah Bernhardt directed the hospital at the Odéon, at first only with the help of Madame Guérard, gave her the first opportunity of showing the extraordinary energy of which she was capable when circumstances demanded it. At the same time, her ability to organize and also to give orders was revealed —which later proved to be so exceptional, when she had to manage theaters or take her companies to every quarter of the globe.

She began by turning the public foyer of the theater into a ward with fifteen beds. As the number of wounded increased every day, it soon became necessary to put beds in all the dressing rooms, the offices, the library, and finally on the stage itself—where, in order to avoid drafts, partitions were erected, covered with a low ceiling, all hastily put together with boards.

By the middle of November, the Odéon had more than one hundred and fifty wounded. Sarah did not even go home. She slept in her dressing room at the theater and, to assist her, collected some of her friends and colleagues, including an old actress, Madame Lambquin, who played duenna parts at the Odéon. The chief surgeon was a certain Dr. Duchesne, still a young man, who also never left the theater. Very often there was also Baron Larrey, now in his sixties, whose reputation as a surgeon had become very great, and who had known Sarah almost from birth. He came to the Odéon when particularly difficult or serious operations were necessary.

At the Odéon there were not only officers and men wounded in the engagements at Champigny and Buzenval. The Red Cross flag, which was raised above the theater and dominated all the neighboring buildings, indicated to the people of Paris that the Second National Theater had become a hospital. Often civilians, men and women who had been hit by the bombardment or were simply ill, knocked at the stage door to be dressed or to be admitted for a day or two.

On Christmas morning, 1870, three women came to seek refuge in Sarah Bernhardt's hospital. Three women of the people who, like so many others, stood in line every day for hours in front of the shops—which had very few things to sell—trying to get the bread, the meat or the half pint of milk which they wanted for their children. The cold was so severe that one of them had frozen feet, and two of her toes had to be amputated. The second died of fever in a few hours, and the third actually died of cold. Every care and a boiling hot bath had not succeeded in warming her.

The following day, with other men evacuated from the field of battle, Corporal Paul Parfouru, who was wounded at Avron, was taken to the Odéon. He was a young actor who had been at the Conservatoire at the same time as Sarah Bernhardt and had started a brilliant stage career under the name of Paul Porel. He was later to become the husband of Réjane and to manage first the Odéon and then the Vaudeville, with great success for many years.

Some days later, in January, 1871, a young soldier of less than twenty years of age, slightly wounded in the shoulder and with his arm in a sling, presented his hospitalization order. There was not a single bed vacant. Four had even been put in the greenroom, which is not very large at the Odéon.

As she really could not find a place for him, Sarah Bernhardt was going to send him to another hospital; but then she looked at him. He was blond, thin, and pale, and his shining eyes stared at her in respectful ecstasy. Obviously he must have seen her act, and had recognized her and felt very happy at having been directed to her hospital. When she expressed her regret at not being able to receive him, such a look of disappointment came over his face that she did not have the courage to let him return to the military wagon which had brought him. She gave him her own room, her dressing room, the only place where, from time to time, when she was dropping with fatigue, she could go and lie down for an hour or two.

Was it because she had conferred such a favor on him that Sarah conceived a friendship for this young soldier? We become attached to those for whom we have done favors. Or was it simply because he was pleasant and polite? Whenever she had time she would come and sit beside his bed, and they chatted for fifteen minutes or half an hour. He gazed timidly at the young actress—seven years his senior —who, with such smiling authority, devoted her strength, her days, and her nights to relieve as best she could the sufferings of all these men. He informed her that, having always been destined for a military career, he was a student at the Ecole Polytechnique, but that he had interrupted his studies to volunteer as soon as the war broke out.

It was not in the course of an engagement that he had been hit in the shoulder by a shell, but at the Porte d'Orléans when he was trying to reach the camp of the army of the Loire. His wound was not serious. In a fortnight he was able to leave, more resolved than ever that nothing this time would prevent him from rejoining his regiment. He did not have time to do so. The following week, on January 28, 1871, the French army surrendered. Then came the Armistice, and the first preliminaries of peace at Versailles.

Before leaving the Odéon the young soldier asked Sarah Bernhardt to give him her photograph, and she very gladly did so. Blushing, he asked her to inscribe it.

"As soon as the war is over, I will come back and see you," he swore. "Where will you be?"

"How can I tell you?" Sarah sighed. "Do any of us know today what events may do to us tomorrow or in six months?"

Just as she was writing the inscription, she asked: "By the way, I don't remember your first name. Fernand, isn't it?"

"No, Ferdinand."

"Is it really?"

On the photograph Sarah wrote: "To Ferdinand Foch, in friendly memory of Sarah Bernhardt."

In effect, the timid and blond young volunteer of nineteen and a half whom Sarah nursed in 1871 was to become the victor of the World War of 1914–1918. The great soldier always remained in friendly relations with the great artist. In February, 1915, at Bordeaux, when Sarah's right leg was amputated, one of those who visited her in the hospital was Ferdinand Foch, then a general of division.

On March 27, 1923, about ten o'clock in the morning, the writer of these lines led Marshal Foch into the room where, the night before, Sarah Bernhardt had breathed her last. The Generalissimo of the French Armies was one of the very first to come and salute the mortal remains of the woman who, fifty-two years before, had nursed him in the auxiliary military hospital at the Odéon.

The Armistice having been signed, it was thought that the Germans would occupy Paris, at least for some time. Sarah Bernhardt refused to be present at this spectacle. All her life she remained fiercely patriotic. Boiling with indignation and grief, she deeply felt the humiliation of defeat. No longer able to devote herself to the wounded, since the fighting had ceased, she decided to leave Paris and rejoin her family. She had recently learned that they had left Havre, for this region might also be threatened one day, and had taken refuge in Holland, at the Hague, with one of Julie's married sisters.

Through Paul de Rémusat she obtained from Monsieur Thiers in person a safe-conduct, permitting her to leave the capital. But a few miles farther she had to cross the German lines. She might be arrested and made prisoner. This escapade was foolishly daring, but neither advice nor entreaties could hold her back. "What on earth would they do to a woman," she replied, "now the Armistice is signed and military operations have ceased? Why should the Prussians bar my way?" On February 4, all alone, she left Paris on foot by the Porte des Ternes.

Half an hour later she came to the enemy outposts and was taken before a German general, who said to her in excellent French: "Where are you going?"

"To rejoin my family in Holland."

He looked at her safe-conduct. "Are you Sarah Bernhardt?"

"Yes."

"An actress?"

"Yes."

"You had better return to Paris. You are undertaking a very hazardous journey."

"I have already heard that."

"And yet you persist?"

"What could happen to me?"

"Everything."

"I am not afraid."

"As you will."

He signed another safe-conduct, a German one this time, because the one given her by Monsieur Thiers was invalid once she passed through the gates of Paris.

It is almost impossible to describe this journey. Going north via Pontoise, Creil, Compiègne, and Saint Quentin successively, where all regular communications were interrupted and the entire region was occupied by Prussian troops, she had to use every conceivable form of transportation: carts, carriages, garbage wagons. She did twelve miles on horseback, more than thirty on foot, and was two days in a van full of wounded who were being taken to a hospital in the country. Twenty times she was stopped by patrols or German battalions camped in the village. She slept wherever people would take her in, sometimes in a barn.

By the time she reached the Belgian frontier her brand-new safe-conduct was in tatters; it had been so often folded and unfolded, examined, viséd and stamped. Finally, at Maubeuge, she got a train which took her to Brussels and to the Hague at last. She had taken eighteen days to make a journey which is usually covered in eight hours.

About February 25 she arrived at her Aunt Mathilde's, where she found her mother, her sisters, and her darling child—her dear little Maurice, whom she had not seen for five months and for whom she had so often trembled during that terrible winter.

Some days later the entire family set out again for Paris, where they arrived in the middle of March. But when they reached Beauvais, Sarah was informed of the revolutionary movement which was rising and had already caused bloodshed in the capital. The war being over, civil war broke out—the awful Commune which, for more than two months, made so many innocent victims. To bring her family to their homes would have been sheer madness. The danger at this moment was perhaps greater than during the winter.

Turning toward the west, Sarah went to Saint Germain, in the neighborhood of Versailles, which was the provisional seat of the Republican government. With her entire household she installed herself in a little villa a few feet from the Pavillon Henri IV. From the magnificent terrace where one could see Paris so clearly she saw immense fires break out, which ravaged first one quarter and then another of the capital. Those were the exploits of the "Communards." Sometimes pieces of burnt paper were blown by the wind as far as the garden. At other times the smoke over Paris was so heavy that one could see nothing beyond Rueil or even Bougival.

It was not until May that peace was signed with the King of Prussia, William I, who in January had become Emperor of Germany, and it was not until the end of May that the abominable Commune was crushed. In the midst of the general uneasiness, in the poignant melancholy which seized the entire conquered nation, Sarah Bernhardt returned to Paris, where on every hand, from every house, even those that were intact, came the acrid smell of smoke. How many ruins, how many bereavements, and how much blood spilled in vain!

Nevertheless, life revived imperiously; and so did the theater. Taking a few weeks to restore the auditorium and the stage, Duquesnel and de Chilly announced the reopening of the Odéon and sent the members of the company a rehearsal notice. Although it was the middle of the month of August, Sarah Bernhardt had no thought of taking a vacation. People were going to work again, to try to forget those atrocious months and to endeavor to restore the country, which was momentarily crushed by the harsh conditions of peace imposed by the conquerors.

By the beginning of September she took possession of her dressing room, now restored to its original purpose; began to play the parts in her repertory; and, as early as October 11, created a new role. It was only a one-act play but of high quality—*Jean-Marie*, by André Theuriet, a little masterpiece, in which Sarah Bernhardt scored a great success in the part of a young Breton peasant. Playing opposite to her in the part of the fisherman, Jean-Marie, was Paul Porel. Like her, having stayed at the Odéon when a hospital, he was delighted to be back again now that it had become a theater.

Two other openings, one important and the other sensational, followed and finally insured to Sarah Bernhardt a preponderant position at the Odéon. One was *Mademoiselle Aïssé*, a posthumous work of Louis Bouilhet, which was perhaps not first-rate but received a warm welcome because of the recent premature death of the author, at the age of forty-seven, in 1869. It opened early in January, 1872, and Sarah

Bernhardt, in the principal part, personally achieved a large share of the success of the play.

On January 26, 1872, the celebrated revival of *Ruy Blas*, first forbidden by Napoleon III and then delayed by the war, took place. This revival, so long awaited and so often demanded, not only restored to Paris one of the major dramatic works of the century but gave the city an opportunity to acclaim Victor Hugo himself, who had finally returned to France and had personally conducted the rehearsals of his play.

It may well be imagined with what emotion and what pride Sarah Bernhardt learned, about the middle of December, 1871, that, at the instance of Duquesnel, Auguste Vacquerie, and Paul Meurice, the intimate friend and representative of Victor Hugo during his exile, the Master had named her to play the part of the Queen. He thus relied completely upon his advisers since, having been away from Paris for so many years, he had never seen Sarah Bernhardt act.

On the first day of rehearsal she was moved and also very curious to see at last the great poet of whom she had heard so much since her earliest childhood, and particularly since she entered the Conservatoire; whose immense work, political situation, literary glory, and age—he was almost seventy—commanded such respect; and who was undoubtedly the greatest figure of his time in France.

Victor Hugo made an extraordinary impression on Sarah. Extremely gentle, infinitely courteous, with the kindness and simplicity of manner which became proverbial—although he was fully conscious of his genius—he succeeded in two or three days in putting his interpreters at their ease, all of them being just as impressed as Sarah Bernhardt at working under his direction. Victor Hugo spoke the verses badly and was in no sense of the word an actor. For this reason he was not a director comparable to other dramatists who knew how to "space" their plays so exactly. However, his slightest hints, listened to with deference, were fully justified. He did not say much, but what he said was always helpful, ingenious, and clear. He was not above joking at times and always subtly. One day when he was repeating for the tenth time to a mediocre actor named Talien, who was playing the part of Don Guritan, a piece of advice that he had already given him many times before, but which the actor could not follow despite his best endeavors, Sarah Bernhardt sat down nonchalantly on a little table, swinging her legs, while waiting for the scene to continue. In the middle of the auditorium Victor Hugo stood up and declared in loud tones:

> *Une Reine d'Espagne, honnête et respectable,*
> *Ne devrait pas ainsi s'asseoir sur une table.*[1]

Embarrassed by her lack of decorum in the presence of the Master, Sarah jumped hastily to the ground. If she was always a rather difficult character and quick to reply, at this time she had not yet become obstinate when it was a question of admitting that she was wrong.

The first performance of this revival was an evening of triumph, first for the play, which was received with convulsions of enthusiasm, and then for Sarah Bernhardt, who on this occasion enjoyed the first resounding success of her career.

The cast was brilliant. The three principal parts were played by Lafontaine as Ruy Blas, Mélingue as Don César de Bazan, and Geffroy as Don Salluste. But Sarah clearly excelled them all and, during her entire part, held the public under the spell of her incomparable voice and her tragic power, which until then had only been suspected by connoisseurs and now was completely revealed. The revival ran for a long time. Until the summer, every time that *Ruy Blas* was announced, the house was packed to the ceiling. The Odéon had not seen such audiences for a long time.

Then the inevitable happened. As its title—the Second National French Theater—indicates, the Odéon is only a Comédie Française of the second order. Both theaters perform the classical repertory and also the great repertory of the nineteenth century. They alternate their productions, engage the company by the year, have subscription nights for regular patrons, and both receive a subsidy from the government. Rightly or wrongly, from an actor's point of view, the Odéon has always been regarded as a sort of anteroom to the Théâtre Français. It is understood that an artist who distinguishes himself exceptionally at the Odéon is almost always sought by the "House of Molière."

Sarah Bernhardt was no exception to this rule, and in May, 1872, she was called to the office of the general manager of the Comédie Française. It was no longer Edouard Thierry. Immediately after the

---

[1] A Queen of Spain, honest and respectable, Should not sit thus upon a table. *Trans.*

war, for reasons of health, he had asked to retire on a pension. Since July, 1871, the company had been managed by Emile Perrin, who was a remarkable official and, for fourteen years, fulfilled his delicate functions with exceptional competence and authority. The proconsulate of Perrin was an event in the history of the theater, and to this day his name is uttered there only with the greatest respect.

Nevertheless, it was only after a certain amount of hesitation that he was accepted for the post. He came with new ideas and made no secret about it: the desire to reshuffle the company, to give beginners a chance, and not to respect established reputations too blindly. This was enough to frighten the older members, who were jealous of their prerogatives and immediately predicted that, with such ideas, the new manager would soon have to hand in his resignation.

But it may be remarked that the general manager of the Comédie Française is a man whose departure is always being announced but who never leaves. It is hard to realize that for the last eighty years the theater has only had six managers: Edouard Thierry, from 1859 to 1871; Emile Perrin, from 1871 to 1885; Jules Claretie, from 1885 to 1913; Albert Carré, from 1913 to 1916; Emile Fabre, from 1916 to 1936; and Edouard Bourdet, from 1936 to 1940.

Being on the lookout for new talent, Emile Perrin was naturally greatly interested by the personality of Sarah Bernhardt, who had suddenly made such a brilliant hit in *Ruy Blas*. But he encountered a great deal of opposition to her engagement. Among the company the young actress had tenacious enemies, first, because they believed that she would quickly reach a dominating position, such as she had at the Odéon, and, secondly, because many of them—Nathalie was still there!—remembered the rude fashion in which she had left nine years earlier, and it was not without apprehension that they saw this ill-bred person coming back to them.

In order to engage an artist whose talent had attracted his attention, should the general manager consult the views of the company as a whole or, at least, those of its more important members? Morally, yes. Unlike the Odéon, where the management engages and pays the performers as it wishes, the Comédie Française is a company of actors in partnership, having an interest in the receipts and sharing the losses of the theater, if any. In a sense, therefore, they are at home.

The company at the Théâtre Français is divided into two distinct categories: the *Sociétaires* and the *Pensionnaires*. The former, as their name indicates, are those who are elected by the committee to become permanent members of the company and, in addition to their salaries, receive their share of the annual profits, according to fixed dividends known as "twelfths." The latter are the actors who are engaged on trial, among whom the *Sociétaires* are chosen after a few years' experience.

For the moment, of course, it was merely a question of engaging Sarah as a *Pensionnaire* and, consequently, Perrin might easily have done as he pleased. But it was evident that she was a future *Sociétaire*. From the point of view of courtesy and also diplomacy, the new manager thought it wiser to convince the committee that the return of the young star from the Odéon would be desirable and profitable from every standpoint. As clever as he was energetic, he succeeded without much trouble. Thus, in the course of his interview with Sarah Bernhardt, he was able to offer her a steady engagement at twelve thousand francs a year. She asked him for forty-eight hours to think the matter over because, although she was flattered, his proposal left her in a state of perplexity.

Sarah Bernhardt was now earning nine thousand six hundred francs a year at the Odéon. In view of Perrin's offer she could certainly have obtained from her managers a further increase of two hundred francs a month or more. But this kind of haggling was distasteful to her and, when she decided to tell Duquesnel and de Chilly about the offer which had been made to her, she had sworn to herself not to bring up the subject of money. Moreover, that was not what was worrying her.

Obviously she was tempted to return in glory to this theater from which she had departed, obscure and unknown, in 1863. She wanted to compete with the great actors of her day; to play in the marvelous repertory of the Comédie Française; and to achieve high rank in the company, which was then considered the leading theatrical company of the world. On the other hand, she knew only too well the jealousies, the hates, and the intrigues which she would have to encounter; the ceaseless struggle which she would have to make in order to hold her position. At the Odéon she was at peace, happy and liked by her managers and her colleagues, being already the uncontested queen of that theater. But it was on the Left Bank, which was like traveling second-class. At the Théâtre Français there was no security, and constant worries; but it was the "House of Molière."

She was still in doubt when she saw Duquesnel and de Chilly and said to them simply: "Would you be very angry with me if I left you to go to the Théâtre Français?"

Duquesnel looked at her in saddened surprise. "Would you do a thing like that?"

"I will not do it, my dear, if you absolutely want me, and if my leaving would in any way inconvenience the Odéon. It is for you to decide."

Duquesnel was about to reply, but de Chilly interrupted. He was stout and apoplectic and for some time had been suffering from heart disease, whose crises were becoming more and more frequent. He would choke, and these continual attacks, which disturbed him greatly, changed his disposition and made him easily irritable. This interview must have been on one of his bad days.

At Sarah's first word he had jumped up, and now replied sharply: "But you don't go to the Théâtre Français as if you were taking a bus, young lady. First of all, one would have to know whether they really wanted you there."

"So you don't think that they would be quite willing to receive me?"

"I'm sure of it."

"Explain yourself."

"Maubant, whom I met three days ago and who knows that you are not always easy to get on with, told me that he would prefer to resign rather than ever have you to work with."

Maubant was a rather important *Sociétaire* who played the heavy parts in tragedy. Apparently regarding his opinion as negligible, Perrin had not included him among those whom he had won over to his idea.

Piqued, Sarah smiled ironically: "Ah, Maubant told you that, did he?"

"He did."

Grumblingly de Chilly added: "Your success at *Ruy Blas* has gone to your head. I suppose you want another increase in salary? So you're trying to blackmail us with the Comédie Française. But the trick is a little stale, my dear, and is now an old chestnut. And we are not so stupid as to be caught by it."

Sarah was silent with indignation and anger. De Chilly was clumsily accusing her of exactly that which she had so carefully avoided, of a maneuver of which she was incapable because, in her pride, she thought it unworthy of her.

Faced with such injustice, she said coldly: "All right. Let us not talk about it any more."

She left the office and signed with Perrin the next day. Her engagement was to date from the beginning of the season of 1872–73.

That evening at the Odéon she showed her contract to Duquesnel and said: "Look. Read this, and you can tell de Chilly, with my compliments, that he is a fool."

Duquesnel looked at the contract and murmured sadly: "You shouldn't have signed that without talking to me about it. It's not fair. You have nothing to hold against me."

The remark was well founded. Sarah Bernhardt admitted it, and from that day she said to herself that she owed some compensation to the kindhearted Duquesnel. When she gave it to him, it was magnificent. Twelve years later, in 1884, when she was playing at the Porte Saint Martin, Derembourg, the manager, decided to retire. She intervened and persuaded him to cede his theater to Duquesnel, who had left the Odéon in 1880. From then until 1891 every time that Sarah Bernhardt played in Paris it was almost exclusively at Duquesnel's theater. He, in return, made her his partner and allowed her a share in the profits of the plays in which she acted at the Porte Saint Martin.

De Chilly was less resigned when he heard of her engagement at the Comédie Française. He flew into a violent fit of rage and, as the young actress' contract with the Odéon did not terminate for another year, he did not follow the procedure which was usual when members of that company were called to the Théâtre Français. In such cases it is customary for the contract to be canceled in a friendly fashion. On the contrary, de Chilly demanded Sarah Bernhardt's forfeit— amounting to six thousand francs. For an unforeseen and dramatic reason she did not have to pay it.

On June 10, 1872, on the occasion of the hundredth performance of the revival of *Ruy Blas*, Victor Hugo gave a large supper party for the company and the entire staff of the theater. At the dessert, in answering the toast offered by Hugo, de Chilly, as the elder of the two managers, stood up with his glass in his hand. But suddenly, before he could speak a word, he changed from purple to pale and collapsed heavily with his face on the table. He was dead! Remaining the sole manager of the Odéon, Duquesnel released Sarah from the forfeit; this attention still further increased her gratitude toward him.

Sarah Bernhardt left the Odéon during the summer, in order to have a little rest before she went to the Comédie Française. *Ruy Blas* continued without her, Emilie Broisat, who had previously played the part of Casilda, replacing her as the Queen. But, in her turn, Emilie Broisat was called to the Comédie Française, and the revival ceased in October.

Her successes at the Odéon had effectively called attention to the name of Sarah Bernhardt and her return to the Théâtre Français was awaited with very great curiosity. Now it was no longer a young beginner, fresh from the Conservatoire, whose name was advertised, but an actress of established reputation, consecrated by several successes and a recent triumph. The Comédie Française, where Sarah was to remain eight years, until April, 1880, and where she soon occupied such a considerable position, felt under the necessity of carefully choosing the part for her debut and of investing the evening with all the necessary glory.

After a great deal of hesitation Emile Perrin decided in favor of *Mademoiselle de Belle Isle*—a play in five acts, by Alexandre Dumas *père*, first produced in 1839—with Sarah Bernhardt in the principal part, supported by Bressant and Sophie Croizette. Bressant was the best leading man of the theater and Sophie Croizette was a very great actress. Although still very young, she had been with the Théâtre Français for three years and, being a great favorite of Perrin, she had already made a very nice position for herself. It was under these apparently favorable conditions that the return of Sarah Bernhardt took place, on November 6, 1872.

Nevertheless, it was not a good idea to choose this play for her debut. As a matter of fact, although the part had some strong scenes it was that of a young girl who still retained a certain naïveté; and at twenty-eight years of age, though extraordinarily slim, Sarah had acquired a maturity which made her unsuitable for ingénue parts, even though dramatic. Further, the Louis XV costume did not set her off to advantage. Very tight at the waist, her gown exaggerated her extreme thinness, which was hidden by the wide folds in which Greek and Roman heroines were draped. Also the play was in prose, and by this time it was her incomparable diction, her miraculous art

of speaking verse, which had brought her her first success. To overlook this "trump" showed unusually bad judgment. About the time
of her appearance Théodore de Banville, one of the most exquisite
poets of the nineteenth century, said of Sarah Bernhardt:

"You cannot praise her for knowing how to speak verse, for she
is the Muse of poetry herself. Neither intelligence nor art has anything to do with it. She is driven by a secret instinct. She recites poetry
as the nightingale sings, as the wind sighs, as water murmurs, just as
Lamartine used to write."

This rather summary judgment was soon to be revised by public
opinion. If Sarah had the innate gift of bringing out everything that
was poetry, it was profoundly unfair to deny that a very great art,
which was now to flower in its entirety, governed this pure voice and
this exceptional diction. It cannot be denied that the success of her
debut would have been certain in advance in any play whatsoever
in verse, whereas in *Mademoiselle de Belle Isle* the evening was not
to her advantage; it was a semifailure. The next day, in *Le Temps*,
of which he was then, and remained until his death, in 1899, the
powerful and feared dramatic critic, Francisque Sarcey wrote:

"There was a brilliant audience, and the opening attracted all
lovers of the theater. Apart from her personal merits, there have
formed about Mademoiselle Sarah Bernhardt a number of legends
which float about her and arouse the curiosity of the Parisian public.
It was a disappointment when she came on the stage. Whether her
powdered hair did not suit her face, or whether she was terribly pale
from stage fright, it was not a very agreeable impression to see emerg-
ing from a long black hood this long white face, from which the
sparkle of the eyes had disappeared and in which only the gleaming
teeth stood out. She began to speak her part trembling convulsively,
and we saw the Sarah of *Ruy Blas* only in two couplets which she
uttered in her enchanting voice, with wonderful grace. But she missed
all the strong passages. She did not really recover herself until the
fifth act. It was very late."

The article contained neither praise nor encouragement. Yet, by
its very severity, it had the most salutary effect on Sarah, who had,
in truth, insufficiently or badly studied her part, which she did not
like. Since *Ruy Blas* perhaps her confidence in herself was excessive or,
at least, premature. She told herself that in her better-chosen future
roles she would have to succeed and that the all-powerful Sarcey,

instead of attacking her, must henceforth become one of her defenders.

Thanks to her incredible tenacity, she achieved this result fairly quickly—but not so quickly as her successes at the Odéon had led her to believe. At that time, even for Sarah Bernhardt, it was not easy to establish a place for oneself at the Comédie Française.

CHAPTER IV

Sarah Bernhardt at the Comédie Française

B Y THE early months of 1873 Francisque Sarcey, who was attentively following the progress of Sarah Bernhardt, gradually
changed his point of view and, the following year, he devoted long,
enthusiastic articles to her. But it would be profoundly unjust to attribute this change of attitude to any other reasons than an increasing
esteem for her talent, to such a point that he soon foresaw that she
would be the greatest artist of her time.

I am well aware that a stupid legend was spread at this period and
lasted to our own days. It was insinuated that, by surrendering completely, Sarah Bernhardt had assured herself of the steady support and
the laudatory articles of Sarcey and that, shortly after her return to
the Comédie Française, she had had a well-known and prolonged love
affair with him. Among numerous other documents, I have before
me a book of three hundred and sixty pages, published in 1924 and
entirely devoted to the life of Sarah Bernhardt, which gives the most
precise details concerning this episode in her career. I shall quote
neither the title of the work nor the name of the author—who is a
woman and who does not hesitate to declare that Sarah herself confessed to her the interested favors she conferred on the distinguished
critic, adding that "she had left him as soon as she felt artistically
strong enough to dispense with his support."

Although this work appears to be documented, for it contains many
other correct facts, I do not hesitate to protest with all my strength
against so absurd and so venomous an accusation, which tends to
show Sarah Bernhardt as a young actress who gave herself to critics
in order to get good notices. In the first place, even granting that she
was capable of doing so, would she have admitted it with such
cynicism? That was tantamount to confessing that her success was not
due solely to her talent. Sarah Bernhardt was far too proud ever to
make such an admission.

Above everything, her dignity would have kept her from such degrading compromises; and a woman such as she could not even entertain such an idea. Her entire life was there to prove it. Although Sarah Bernhardt had a number of lovers—to deny that would be absurd and in vain—she never chose one of them for financial or professional reasons. Quite the contrary. Since her girlhood she liked to protect those who interested her, and to do more for them than they could ever do for her. Here again, was she prompted by pride or by an innate desire to dominate? Possibly both. In any case, having an invincible horror of submitting to the least restraint, she would never have consented to be under an obligation to anyone whatsoever.

Another reason, which is final for those who knew Sarah Bernhardt well, makes the fable of her calculated kindness to Sarcey perfectly ridiculous. He was an eminent man, remarkably intelligent and witty, and amazingly erudite, but physically most unattractive. He was small, with a large paunch, a short bristly beard; and he was almost bald at forty-five, which was his age in 1872. Undoubtedly Sarah would have burst into loud laughter at the mere idea of sharing the bed of this respectable paunchy bourgeois.

She always loathed ugliness and made a desperate cult of beauty. She was tremendously proud of the striking appearance of her son Maurice. Without a single exception, all the men that she loved were physically perfect. Good looks and talent, such were the two qualities which she had first to find in a man before choosing him.

Thus, as soon as she returned to the Comédie Française, she had an affair with Mounet Sully which was beyond dispute and which she could admit with pride. This adventure rather pleasantly confirmed the fact that, in order to be the recipient of Sarah Bernhardt's favors, it was not enough for a man to be good-looking; he had also to show proof of his personal qualifications. He had to be somebody.

Three years older than Sarah Bernhardt, Mounet Sully had left the Conservatoire with a prize for tragedy; and he had been engaged at the Odéon, where from 1868 to 1870 he was a colleague of Sarah's and played with her almost every day, notably in *King Lear* (where he had the small part of Cornwall), *Le Bâtard, L'Affranchi,* and twenty other plays.

She had never even looked at him!

By one of those curious phenomena which happen at the beginning of the career of certain great actors, Mounet Sully was then not exactly bad but absolutely insignificant. When the war was declared, he left the Odéon without having attracted the attention of anybody. On the restoration of peace he looked around a long time for an engagement until one day Emile Perrin, who was looking for young people, heard about him from his teacher, Bressant, but in strange terms:

"Well, yes, I did have a strange youth in my class who had been given the nickname of '*Midi à quatorze heures.*'[1] The reason was that he was possessed by some mysterious taste for the peculiar which amounted to a kind of lunacy. In that upside-down brain of his there was something; perhaps it was an artistic temperament."

On this not very reassuring recommendation Perrin sent for and engaged Mounet Sully, who made his debut at the Comédie Française in the part of Oreste, in *Andromaque,* in July, 1872. He made a success which was all the more astounding because his name was absolutely unknown until that evening. Although he still had to feel his way for the first few years, ever since then his position had been growing. When he died, in 1916, the dean of the Comédie Française, which he had never left, he had long and rightly been considered everywhere as the greatest, the most wonderful, tragic actor of his time.

It was only when she saw her obscure comrade of the Odéon at the height of his popularity at the Théâtre Français that Sarah Bernhardt looked at him carefully and said in her astonishment: "No, it can't be possible! Is it you, Mounet?"

Somewhat surprised, Mounet Sully said: "It is I."

"But what has happened to you?"

"What do you mean?"

"You are very handsome!"

"I have been told that before," Mounet replied naïvely.

"But I am not crazy. You were not as handsome as that at the Odéon, were you?"

He thought for a moment. "I think I was."

She shrugged her shoulders incredulously. "Nonsense! I should have noticed it."

"Perhaps it was because you had no time to look at me," he suggested timidly. "I was not seen very much in all the plays in which I performed."

[1] Literally "noon at two o'clock," meaning a person who vaguely expects the impossible. *Trans.*

"That may be," Sarah admitted. Then, after a silence: "Are you playing this evening?"

"Yes."

"I'll come and see you from the front of the house."

She went and was overcome, lost in reverie. Mounet Sully, in effect, was then prodigiously handsome—these words are no exaggeration. When he came on the stage, tall, admirably built, with his superb bare arms which looked as if they had been cut out of a block of ancient marble, his long hair like an aureóle about his incredibly fine face and ending in a soft, long beard, a thrill of admiration swept the house. Sarah noticed this particularly because she was seized completely by the same thrill. . . . The following week the people at the theater talked of nothing but this case of love at first sight, as sudden as it was reciprocal, between the two young actors.

The latter did not even try to dissimulate their intoxication. Why should they? Mounet Sully and Sarah Bernhardt were marvelously matched; were a unique couple, really sensational. As a good manager, Emile Perrin had them act together as often as possible: first, because people in Paris knew of their love and, seeing them on the stage in each other's arms, the public had the feeling of looking over the wall of their private lives; and, secondly, because their two talents harmonized beautifully, both being passionate to the point of violence.

It was in her second role at the Comédie Française that Sarah Bernhardt had Mounet Sully as a partner—in *Britannicus*, by Racine, in which he played Nero and she Junie—for the first time, on December 14, 1872.

It is not an important part, and she could not score any very great success. However, she definitely had her revenge for her rebuff in *Mademoiselle de Belle Isle*. Junie was a part which suited her to perfection and which she could not help playing perfectly.

A few days later they were both in *Le Cid* of Corneille, as Rodrigue and Chimène—Maubant, who had not retired, was Don Diègue—and both were warmly applauded by a house which was literally enchanted by this most harmonious and beautiful couple.

But it seemed that Emile Perrin, who generally knew so well how to use the talents confided to him, was constantly to take the wrong tack with Sarah Bernhardt. It was evident that she was a tragic actress and, above all, a lyric one. In classical repertory she could always succeed if she played Racine or Victor Hugo, whereas in comedy, whether classical or modern, her success, at this stage, was subordinate to the part.

Why, then, did Perrin risk giving her the part of Chérubin in *Le Mariage de Figaro* of Beaumarchais, on January 30, 1873? It is hard to understand why. Sarah Bernhardt, who did not like Perrin and, long after his death, had not forgotten her numerous and noisy differences with him, alleged that he tried only to give Croizette an opportunity to shine. In *Le Mariage de Figaro*, Croizette played Suzanne, an ideal part for her, and to Sarah he had purposely given Chérubin, which did not suit her at all, not only in order that she should fail in it but also that the success of Croizette should appear greater by comparison.

When informed of Sarah Bernhardt's complaints, Perrin quietly shrugged his shoulders. "She made a hit at the Odéon as Zanetto, a little Italian pageboy. I had every right to hope that she would be even a greater success as Chérubin, a little French pageboy."

Quite true, but *Le Passant* was a lyric poem.

Two months later, on March 28, 1873, the same situation recurred on the occasion of the revival of *Dalila*, a dramatic comedy, by Octave Feuillet, first produced at the Vaudeville in 1857 and placed in the repertory of the Théâtre Français in March, 1870.

There are two almost equally important women's parts in the play, which had been performed by Maria Favart and Sophie Croizette three years earlier. The latter, in the part of Marthe, had had a great personal success. She was certain to repeat it, as she had already played the part and had mastered it, whereas, coming after Maria Favart, Sarah was attempting for the first time the difficult role of the Princess Léonora (Dalila). This time again, Croizette alone received all the applause and Sarah Bernhardt's anger against Perrin increased. She was more and more convinced that he was only interested in putting forward his pretty favorite.

However, that same year he gave her two little parts to create—very small parts! Alternating between successes and semifailures, Sarah Bernhardt had not yet achieved sufficient standing at the Comédie Française for the important writers of that theater to be safe in asking for her in an important new play.

She created the leading role in *L'Absent*—a nice little one-act play in verse, by Eugène Manuel—and, on July 23, in *Chez l'Avocat*—

a one-act, by Paul Ferrier, also in verse but very amusing—which she played with Coquelin *aîné*, the great Coquelin of the future, who was then also at the dawn of his fame. The play was a sort of rhymed light comedy, a comic discussion between a husband and wife who want to be divorced and are reconciled at their lawyer's. The wife's part seems to have been written for Cassive or for Jeanne Granier, at least, and on reading it one is quite surprised to discover, in the list of the cast, the name of Sarah Bernhardt. Nevertheless, she proved to be dazzling—the worthy partner of that marvelous comedian who played the man's part.

But all this merely produced pleasant results, more or less noteworthy attempts, which disappointed Sarah Bernhardt's admirers. She had to wait until summer to win her first big success at the Comédie Française. It was in the part of *Andromaque* in Racine's tragedy, which she played for the first time on August 22, 1873, with Mounet Sully as Oreste.

Four weeks later, on September 17, she played Aricie in Racine's *Phèdre*, Mounet Sully playing Hippolyte. One after the other, these were two splendid successes for Sarah Bernhardt. This time she had really arrived. As Andromaque, with dignity and poignant grace, she had equaled her most distinguished predecessors on the first night, and as Aricie, a minor role, she had eclipsed all the other actors and really made a success of the evening.

It was the year 1874, when she was thirty, which definitely established her position at the Théâtre Français, where in a few months she had aroused fervent enthusiasms and solid hates, not only among the actors and friends of the house, but also among the public.

"But you must take into account," her defenders cried, "that here is an exceptional, a unique personality. No such tragic actress has been seen since Rachel. What a voice! What grace! What majestic serenity in her deportment and her gestures!"

"Agreed," her enemies replied, "she is very good as a tragic princess, but she should confine herself to such parts. She is bound to them in perpetuity and will be incapable of ever playing anything else!"

Often during the intermissions, in the lobbies of the Comédie Française, these arguments echoed loudly and people almost came to blows: "She'll succeed!" "She'll not succeed!" The bets were open. This hullabaloo was the best proof of the undoubted talent of the young actress. So many people, most of whom had never spoken to her, would not have become so excited over a doubtful personality which would not have deserved so much interest.

Yet it is a strange and incontrovertible fact that Sarah Bernhardt's renown had preceded her success, instead of being the logical result of it. At the end of 1873 the noise made about her greatly exceeded the proofs which she had given of her real quality. She owed it to herself to justify as soon as possible this premature popularity, if I may so describe it.

It was in a perfectly minor role, almost an unimportant one, that Sarah Bernhardt achieved the success which her faithful admirers expected of her. And it was in a play which, as dangerous competition, included another part of a young woman which was much more important, full of effective lines, and in which the character died in the last act in a powerfully pathetic scene. It was called *Le Sphinx*, by Octave Feuillet. It opened at the Comédie Française on March 23, 1874.

When the author brought the work to the general manager, they both agreed at once to cast Sophie Croizette for the principal part— Blanche de Chelles, a magnificent character, both virtuous and passionate, frank and impenetrable.

In the first act, one of the characters, Lord Astley, says of her: "Every woman is an enigma, and she, more than any other, has the right to take the sphinx as a symbol."

A fine part and, in addition, one wrapped in mystery—what a windfall for an actress!

For the part of the other woman, Berthe de Savigny, Perrin immediately suggested Sarah Bernhardt, arguing quite intelligently as follows: "Her noisy partisans accuse me of confining her to classical plays and demand that she be given an original part to create. Well, here is one. If her critics are right, if she really cannot succeed in a modern play, her part is so unimportant that it cannot compromise the success of the latter."

Sarah Bernhardt listened attentively when the comedy was read to the company and she immediately realized to what extent her part was eclipsed by Croizette's. At first she was inclined to refuse it, but she changed her mind. After all, she had been the success of the evening as Aricie—who is to the character of Phèdre approximately what Berthe, in *Le Sphinx*, was to Blanche. Moreover, her part did call for two or three scenes which gave her an opportunity to "put herself over," as they say backstage. Giving proof of unusual foresight, she judged that the part of Blanche was obviously superb but actually did not suit the talents of Croizette so very well.

The latter was essentially destined for the part of the "young coquette." She had succeeded, or was soon to succeed, as Antoinette in *Le Gendre de M. Poirier*, as Camille in *On ne badine pas avec l'Amour*, as Suzanne in *Le Demi-Monde*, as Célimène in *Le Misanthrope*; and her greatest success was then Adrienne in *L'Eté de la Saint Martin*, a one-act by Meilhac and Halévy, which she had created in July, 1873. It is a delightful play, but light and smiling, in which her part was solely one of charm and seductiveness. Would she have the dramatic power required for the important leading young woman in *Le Sphinx*; and if she had it, would she be able to get the exact tone and maintain the reserve necessary?

From the time of her beginnings at the Odéon, Sarah Bernhardt had taken as her motto *"Quand même!"*—which magnificently expresses her unconquerable energy, her bravery, and her determination to conquer enemies and obstacles. Croizette's note paper bore the heading *"A outrance"*—which characterized most exactly the beautiful and brilliant Sophie, whose talent, like her life, proved that she was not one of those who understand moderation. Sarah was counting simultaneously on the advantages which she felt she could derive from her own part and on the manner in which she guessed that Croizette would play hers.

The performance proved that she was right. Perfect in the scenes of charm at the beginning, Croizette completely missed her last act— or, more correctly, she played it with an amount of exaggeration and vulgar realism which delighted a certain section of the public but deeply shocked the regular patrons of the Théâtre Français. In his *Comédiens et Comédiennes*, published in 1877, Sarcey wrote:

"What was our surprise when the denouement occurred! Mademoiselle Croizette drank a bottle of poison and fell dying in a chair. Then we witnessed a really hideous spectacle. With the aid of certain tricks, whose secret was subsequently revealed in the newspapers, the actress' face suddenly became greenish, horribly decomposed, wrinkling in fearful contractions; her glazed and haggard eyes rolled in their sockets, her hands and legs trembled convulsively, and her head was shaken in the convulsions of lockjaw. These terrible spasms

lasted only a few seconds, but they seemed very long. The whole
house was seized with a shudder of revolt, and some women cried out
in horror. Somebody in the orchestra stalls hissed.

"In the part of Berthe de Savigny, which ceased to be a minor one,
Mademoiselle Sarah Bernhardt won the applause of the connoisseurs.
She played with noble and discreet grace, which was all the more noticeable because her rival had allowed herself to be carried away by
her temperament. She had very little to say in the early acts, but she
knew how to evoke prolonged applause with a few words or a gesture
of her outstretched hand. In the last act, where she is the outraged
wife who forgives, she displayed an intensity of passion, both dignified and vehement, which aroused real shouts of admiration. Each
one of these words: 'You want to know if I have your letters?' came
from her trembling lips, as sharp and cutting as darts whistling
through the air."

That was what might be called a personal success! The partisans
of Sarah were triumphant, while Croizette's admirers, coming ener-
getically to her defense, declared that her suicide in the last act was
not only an artistic masterpiece but a marvel of accuracy. Distinguished doctors were invited to the theater and asked to give their
opinions. Some concluded that Sophie Croizette reproduced scrupulously every phase of death by poisoning, while others insisted that
it was not plausible—that it was, as we say today, "phony." There
were two camps in Paris, the Croizettists and the Bernhardtists. In
her *Mémoires*, Sarah correctly defined these two opposing parties by
saying: "All the bankers and all the old gentlemen with high blood
pressure were in favor of Croizette; on my side I had all the artists,
the students, the dying, and the failures." Needless to say, the play
was helped by all this agitation and had a long run.

Six years later, when Sarah Bernhardt left for her first tour in
America, among the eight plays of which her repertory consisted, *Le
Sphinx* was included. Then, of course, she played the principal part
and, demonstrating what Croizette should have done, she rendered
the death of Blanche de Chelles with perfect art. The scene was just
as impressive; but this time the effect was produced without any
trickery, either easy or vulgar.

In the course of her career Sarah Bernhardt almost began to specialize in death scenes, in which she was always incomparable and
showed the greatest diversity. Possibly her usual authors took advan-

tage of this by making Sarah die inevitably in the last act. I believe that after 1882, when her great career in Paris began, Sarah died in at least three plays out of four.

It may be objected that I am hardly in a position to make such a comment, since *Daniel* and *Régine Armand,* the two plays of mine which she created in 1920 and 1922, also ended in the death of the character she was playing. I admit it. Like my more famous predecessors, I allowed myself to be tempted by an ending which was always certain of its effect when played by her.

Shortly after *Le Sphinx,* Sarah Bernhardt opened in a nice one-act play by a then unknown young author, Louis Denayrousse, entitled *La Belle Paule.* On August 6, 1874, she had another immense success in a brilliant revival of Voltaire's tragedy, *Zaïre,* which, it will be remembered, had been her part in the competition at the Conservatoire in 1861, in which she had obtained a second prize for tragedy. She was supported by Mounet Sully, a splendid Orosmane, and by Laroche, a fine actor, who was excellent as Nérestan. The Bernhardtists rejoiced. After Junie, Chimène, Andromaque, and Aricie, it was the fifth tragedy in which the success of their idol was striking and undeniable. She showed herself to be almost without a rival in the noblest and highest art.

Compelled to admit this fact, Perrin decided upon a daring stroke. Without waiting any longer, he gave her the most formidable part in the repertory of tragic plays—the most beautiful, but the most difficult, one, which generally requires of its interpreter greater experience on the stage than Sarah Bernhardt could have at that time. This was the part of Phèdre in the tragedy of Racine. In order to attract attention to her first attempt at this part, instead of having her play it on any ordinary evening, he advertised it for the anniversary of Racine, which is a little celebration every year at the Comédie Française.

It was therefore on December 21, 1874, that Sarah Bernhardt appeared for the first time as Phèdre, which she was to play for forty years in every part of the world and which was, of all her roles, without exception, the one upon which she most strongly stamped her personality and in which she most completely unfolded her genius.

All the great French actors of that period had their own special part, in which they surpassed themselves; with which their names were identified; and in which their admirers wanted to see them repeatedly, rather than as any other characters. With Mounet Sully it was *Oedipe roi,* by Sophocles; with Coquelin *aîné, Cyrano de Bergerac,* by Rostand; with de Féraudy, *Les Affaires sont les Affaires,* by Octave Mirbeau; with Le Bargy, *Le Marquis de Priola,* by Lavedan; with Lucien Guitry, *Samson,* by Henry Bernstein; with Bartet, *Bérénice,* by Racine; with Réjane, *Madame Sans-Gêne,* by Sardou; with Silvain, *Le Père Lebonnard,* by Jean Aicard. In Sarah Bernhardt's considerable repertory two parts stood out from all the others. The crowd demanded *La Dame aux Camélias,* but the connoisseurs preferred her in *Phèdre.*

It was only gradually, in two or three years, that she achieved the amazing mastery which she ultimately displayed in this part, which no actress in the world has ever been able to play perfectly at the first attempt. However, the evening of December 21, 1874, remained the most sensational in Sarah Bernhardt's career. She was not only undertaking a part bristling with difficulties but also following in the footsteps of Rachel, the celebrated tragedienne of the early nineteenth century. She died at the age of thirty-seven, in 1858, and many in the regular audiences of the Théâtre Français could have seen her in this same part sixteen years previously, when it had also been for her the occasion of a resounding triumph.

One solitary critic, Paul de Saint-Victor, who was very intimate with Dinah Félix, Rachel's younger sister, who played the soubrettes of Molière and Marivaux at the Comédie Française, tried, by invoking the name of the great deceased artist, to "chastise the impertinent presumption of Mademoiselle Bernhardt," who dared to pit herself against a memory so great and so recent. All the others, headed by Sarcey, recognized that she was already as good as Rachel, at least in the second act, and that in future performances she would certainly surpass her from the beginning to the end of the play.

Phèdre sealed the reputation of Sarah Bernhardt, who, from then on, enjoyed her first taste of real glory. The Bernhardtists now became innumerable. All Paris had gradually joined their little group.

It must be added that, particularly during the last two years, the personality of Sarah Bernhardt had impressed itself completely on the public; that is to say, also outside the theater. During her stay at the Odéon she had constantly played the most numerous and most varied parts, rehearsing almost every day. At the Théâtre Français everything was very different. The company was large, comprising about twenty *Sociétaires* and thirty-five *Pensionnaires*; and at least fifteen of these fifty-five actors played leading parts and shared them. In this way Sarah found herself condemned overnight to a life of semi-inactivity which far from suited her temperament.

From November, 1872, to December, 1874, these pages have enumerated only a dozen parts played by Sarah Bernhardt at the Comédie Française. For an actress in an ordinary boulevard theater that would be a lot. Six plays a year would almost constitute a record. At the Théâtre Français it is very different. It is not unusual for an actor to play twenty or even thirty parts in a year. But, because they alternated, how often did he appear in each play? While a new play, if a great success, can reach a hundred performances a year, the works in the repertory, such as *Andromaque, Le Cid,* or *Britannicus,* are rarely given more than five or six times a year, if that. Consequently, apart from *Le Sphinx,* a new play which was billed three times a week for months, Sarah Bernhardt had probably not given, in all, more than sixty to eighty performances in two years. This means that in the course of a week she was at leisure on an average of five nights out of seven.

Exasperated by this idleness, she sometimes went to see Perrin and asked for other parts. But this role was reserved for Madeleine Brohan, that one to Maria Favart, another was promised to Suzanne Reichemberg, and, of course, a couple of others to Sophie Croizette!

One fine day, just to keep herself busy, Sarah began to sculpture. She took some fifteen lessons, and at the end of a few weeks she even astonished her teacher. An excellent pianist, a painter in her odd moments, the young woman was evidently endowed with all the talents! Feeling encouraged, she devoted herself to this new art with that passion which she put into everything. Her apartment in the Rue de Rome being too small for her to work there comfortably, she rented a large studio, at 11 Boulevard de Clichy, and from 1873, every morning about ten o'clock, she went there and remained all day when she was not rehearsing. Until the middle of the afternoon, trowel in hand, she modeled in clay. And at teatime her friends came to see her.

Her studio soon became one of the meeting places of the rising celebrities of the period. They talked of the theater, politics, and literature. Among those around Sarah Bernhardt were François Coppée; Pierre Berton; Alfred Stevens, the painter; Marie Lloyd, a young actress from the Comédie Française; Louise Abbéma, who later became a celebrated painter and remained Sarah Bernhardt's best friend for fifty years; the two sisters Rose and Blanche Baretta, the latter an adorable comédienne who soon married Worms, the eminent artist of the Théâtre Français; Arthur Meyer, the future editor in chief of the *Gaulois*, who was then beginning in journalism; Sophie Croizette, for the two rivals were very good friends; Félix Escalier, the architect; and the painter Georges Clairin, most faithful of all, who, having first been received as a lover, afterward became the portraitist in ordinary and in extraordinary, as well as the devoted daily friend, of Sarah, in whose shadow he happily passed his entire life, almost without leaving her, for forty-five years.

At this time Sarah sculptured the busts of several of her friends— notably that of her younger sister Régina, who was seriously ill and died of tuberculosis in the autumn of 1874. Her funeral gave rise to a tragicomic incident which the press took up and which helped to increase Sarah Bernhardt's reputation for originality.

I have mentioned that, when she began at the Odéon, her health seemed very precarious and was a source of constant uneasiness to her own circle for many years. Often, at the end of a performance in which she had made a particularly strenuous effort, she would fall breathless into a chair and be seized with terrible spells of vomiting blood. Without daring to say so, people not unreasonably concluded that, like Régina, her lungs were affected and she would die young. Sarah had quietly become accustomed to this idea, and from one week to another she expected to be carried away by a more violent attack. In advance she had had the coffin built in which she wished to be buried, a pretty rosewood coffin, lined inside with white satin, which stood in a corner of her apartment.

During her last days, when Régina was too ill to get up, Sarah did not leave her in her room, which overlooked the courtyard. In order to distract her a little she gave her her own bedroom, which looked out on the street, and her own bed, from which—the apartment being on the mezzanine floor—she could follow the movement of carriages and pedestrians. In order to watch over Régina, whose end might come any moment, Sarah slept in her coffin for about a week, having brought it into her room and placed it beside the bed.

On the morning of Régina's funeral, when the undertaker's men arrived at the apartment to remove the body, they went into the bedroom and were confronted by two coffins. Losing his head, the master of ceremonies sent in hot haste for a second hearse, which arrived shortly afterward to the rapid trot of its two horses. Naturally, it had to be sent back; but from that day everyone in Paris knew that Sarah Bernhardt slept in her coffin!

Already suffering from the heart trouble which was to carry her off, in her turn, two years later, Julie Van Hard felt the loss of her third daughter more profoundly than might have been believed. After so many brilliant years, as she approached fifty, her life had become very melancholy. Extremely busy with her theater, her sculpture, and her friends, Sarah saw little of her. Since she had left her mother's house, their relations had always been affectionate but distant. As she often did not feel very well, Julie had almost ceased to receive people; and gradually the circle of her admirers of yesteryear had deserted the beautiful apartment in the Rue Saint Honoré. What had really reduced her to despair was that, shortly after the war, her darling Jeanne had also left her. She was twenty in 1871 and, being crazy about the theater, where her eldest sister, Sarah, was making such a place for herself, she had also decided to become an actress.

She made her debut in 1872, playing small parts here and there in little theaters. In order to be known more quickly, she had obtained Sarah's permission to call herself Bernhardt—a name to which she had no right but which was already popular, especially since *Ruy Blas.*

Never having been recognized by her father—whose identity, in any case, was doubtful—and having hitherto called herself Mademoiselle Van Hard, Jeanne became henceforward Jeanne Bernhardt, giving up her mother's name and house, in order to try to earn her living. She did not succeed very well. A more than mediocre actress, she was given only sketchy parts and did not have a real role until Sarah took her with her on tour after 1880. Frivolous and scatterbrained, she never could inspire any lasting feeling and went from one adventure to another until she died in 1884, aged thirty-three, still pretty, although an alcoholic, a morphine addict, and quite depraved.

The bust of Régina by Sarah Bernhardt was exhibited at the Salon of 1875, some months after her death. It attracted a great deal of attention. But it was the following year, at the Salon of 1876, that Sarah achieved a considerable success—and "honorable mention"—with a group entitled "After the Storm," which remains celebrated.

It represented a Breton peasant woman holding on her knees the body of her son, which has just been thrown upon the shore by the sea. This group is really a very fine thing, and a distinguished professional would not disown it.

Later on, having no longer so much leisure as when she was at the Théâtre Français, she gave herself up less regularly to sculpture. However, she never completely abandoned it and finished several works of undoubted merit, notably a proud and magnificent "Medea" and a bust of Victorien Sardou which was astonishingly like him.

Although the distance was not very great from the Rue de Rome to the Boulevard de Clichy, Sarah soon was irritated by having to divide her time between two homes. Her friends never knew where to find her. When they came to see her at the studio, she had just gone to her apartment. If they went to the latter, she had just gone to the studio. Moreover, she felt cramped in this little apartment; and the noise of the traffic, which was considerable, near the Gare Saint Lazare, often prevented her from sleeping. So she decided to move, but this time she wanted to settle definitely in a quiet part of the city, on the west side of Paris, and in her own home; that is to say, in a private house large enough for her to have a studio and which she would have built according to her own ideas and to plans drawn up by herself.

This meant a great deal of expense and, at the Comédie Française, her salary was only fifteen thousand francs a year, as a *Pensionnaire*. Fortunately, as a result of her triumphant success in *Phèdre*, her colleagues and the manager a few days later made the obvious move and, on January 30, 1875, promoted her to be a *Sociétaire*, at the same time as her fellow player Laroche.

Now, seeing a more certain financial future and having inherited about a hundred thousand francs from one of her aunts in Holland, she bought an attractive triangular plot situated at the corner of the Avenue de Villiers and the Rue Fortuny, and the construction work began immediately. She moved in the following year, and this was her penultimate home in Paris. It was only twenty-two years later that she moved to a much larger house at 56 Boulevard Péreire, where she spent the last twenty-five years of her life and where she died.

Although the interior decoration had been carried out entirely by Clairin and some of his friends, the house in the Avenue de Villiers, including the ground and the building, cost her more than five hundred thousand francs. At the time, in gold francs, it was a very large amount of money, although the Crédit Foncier had granted her a loan and all the contractors gave her long periods in which to pay. But they were insufficient, and it took Sarah years to pay off completely this first rash venture—to be followed by so many others which caught her forever in the circle of living on credit, from which she was almost never again to escape.

Up to that time, as she lived a reasonable life in a small apartment, her income more or less met her expenses. As soon as she was settled in this new house, and especially after 1881, on her return from America, she lived on a royal scale, keeping up an incredible household, with eight or ten servants, two carriages, several horses, and constantly giving luxurious receptions. For this reason, during the space of forty years, Sarah could never keep her profits from a play or a tour. Always, and no matter what was the amount, the profits from any business which she undertook were earmarked in advance to meet some bill, to pay one or more urgent debts.

Often, when one or two plays in succession did not succeed, she found herself in complicated situations, and her friends wondered how, burdened with financial worries, she was able to maintain complete mastery of herself and to act most calmly every night. It makes one's head turn when one thinks of the fabulous sums which Sarah Bernhardt earned in the course of her life, and remembers, at the same time, that never at any period did she succeed in putting aside fifty thousand francs.

From 1875 to 1880 Sarah's popularity grew constantly and rapidly. More and more her way of living, her varied talents, her strange way of dressing, her contempt for fashion, her rather conspicuous extravagances, and her peculiarly individual appearance were the subject of every conversation. Sarah Bernhardt was then extraordinarily thin. It was not until about 1884, at the age of forty, when she had become a little stouter, that her always slender figure became normal. During her years at the Théâtre Français her slenderness was legendary. It was Aurélien Scholl who once wrote: "An empty carriage stopped, and Sarah Bernhardt got out."

But her originality alone would not have been sufficient to feed the legend and, above all, to fill the Théâtre Français when her name was advertised. What definitely consolidated her reputation was that, after

Phèdre, Sarah experienced at that theater only successes, which grew greater from year to year.

On February 15, 1875, she created, supported by Mounet Sully, the only feminine part, Berthe, in *La Fille de Roland,* a drama in verse by Henri de Bornier. The play, more avenging than literary, was well constructed, however, and was inspired by a great breath of patriotism. As the title indicates, the action took place in the reign of Charlemagne, who appeared in the guise of Maubant. However, the public was very chauvinistic and saw constant references to contemporary events and to the impending revenge for the defeat of 1871, which everyone desired. This certainly greatly helped the success of this work, which was very considerable.

Sarah Bernhardt's part included a very difficult scene to play. In the third act, standing at the window of a room in the Castle of Aix-la-Chapelle, she follows from a distance, with anguish, a duel taking place in a neighboring field, in which the opponents are her fiancé, Gerald, and the Saracen, Noethold. The public cannot see anything of a combat whose course it learns only by a narrative in some twenty lines—necessarily broken by long pauses—which Berthe tells the Emperor, who is near her.

Describing what she sees, alternately she trembles, is moved, regains hope, despairs, and finally proclaims joyfully the victory of Gerald. This monologue, explaining to the audience a struggle which they must imagine solely by means of what the actress tells them, ran the risk of arousing the impatience of the audience or of even making them smile. But Sarah Bernhardt succeeded in giving it such intensity that the scene was applauded. The play has often been revived since; but no matter who plays the part of Berthe, the scene at the window generally passes unnoticed.

On April 27 Perrin made his last mistake, so far as Sarah Bernhardt was concerned, by having her play, with Coquelin *aîné, Gabrielle,* a play in verse, by Emile Augier, first performed in 1849. Augier was then one of the great authors of the Comédie Française, to which he had brought some tremendous successes, many of which were lasting. To this day two of his plays, *L'Aventurière,* dating from 1848, and *Le Gendre de M. Poirier,* created in 1854, always fill the house whenever they are announced.

But the dramatic works of Emile Augier consist of two kinds of plays: those in prose, which are almost all well done; and those

in verse, which are all most inferior with the single exception of
L'Aventurière. The reason is that Augier was anything but a poet
and that his verses are the flattest in literature, also that he han-
dled in Alexandrines subjects of middle-class comedy—introducing
ordinary, everyday types, well drawn and sometimes involved in an
interesting plot but as little designed to express themselves in verse
as would be today the characters in *Topaze* or *Le Sexe Faible*.

Consequently, in Augier's plays in verse, there is such a discrep-
ancy between the familiar things his heroes talk about and the noble
rhymes in which they express themselves that nowadays his plays appear to us slightly ridiculous. I believe it is Tristan Bernard who
said: "I have a great admiration for Emile Augier, but I do not know
if it would survive a first reading."

In 1875 Augier's vogue was enormous; people did not notice so
much his lack of poetic inspiration, and every revival of *Gabrielle*
brought in handsome receipts. Perrin was therefore right in reviving
the play again; but it was madness to give Sarah Bernhardt such a
part, she being essentially a lyrical creature designed to play prin-
cesses of tragedy or heroines of legend. She was detestable in *Gabrielle*; the contrary would have been surprising. She had her revenge
by establishing herself in the title role of *Phèdre*, which she played
about ten times in the course of the year.

On September 19, after the second act, she fainted and could not
continue the play. The stage manager then made an announcement
to the public, stating that, in place of the three last acts of *Phèdre*,
they would play *Le Dépit Amoureux*, in two acts, by Molière, with
Got, the dean of the Comédie Française, and the distinguished
"junior lead" of the company, Delaunay.

The majority of the audience did not want this substitute. They
had come to see Sarah Bernhardt. In spite of the popularity of the
two great artists who saved the evening on the spur of the moment,
half the audience got up and left.

On October 22, 1875, Marshal de MacMahon, President of the
French Republic, accompanied by his wife, was present at the seventy-
fifth performance of *La Fille de Roland*. More than ever the flam-
boyant tirades of Bornier were drowned in applause. When Charlemagne said "France has need of a strong arm!" the entire house
turned toward the presidential box and acclaimed the Chief of State.
At the end of the performance, when he got up, another ovation

saluted the great soldier, who threw a sheaf of flowers onto the stage for Sarah Bernhardt. Shouts arose from the orchestra seats: "Long live Sarah!" Bowing to MacMahon, with her flowers in her arms, Sarah replied: "Long live France!"

Fifteen minutes later, at the stage door, three hundred spectators waited to applaud her again. The Marshal, who was adored by the Parisians, had come that night officially to recognize the growing genius of the great artist.

On February 14, 1876, with a dazzling cast, which included Got, Coquelin, Thiron, Mounet Sully, Febvre, and Madeleine Brohan, the two young stars of the Comédie Française, Sarah Bernhardt and Sophie Croizette, created the two principal parts in *L'Etrangère*—a new and anxiously awaited play by Alexandre Dumas *fils*, which was destined to be a triumph.

Two years after *Le Sphinx*, Perrin cleverly brought together the two rivals again and, as in the play of Feuillet, it was Croizette who had the most important part, the Duchesse de Septmonts. But, although not so long, the part of Mrs. Clarkson, which was played by Sarah, was worthy of her and, with Coquelin and Febvre, it was she who scored the big success of the evening. When she performed the play in America, she kept the part which she had created.

On April 1 the bill announced the "retirement performance" of Madame Nathalie—the plump *Sociétaire* whom Sarah had slapped thirteen years previously, under circumstances which may be remembered and which had led to her departure from the Théâtre Français. When a *Sociétaire* gives this farewell performance, the house is handed over to her, the entire receipts are hers, and she can arrange the program exactly as she pleases. Not only can members of her own company appear, but also singers and actors from the boulevards, the music halls, or even the circus. Obviously the recipient of the benefit always tries to get the most famous stars on the program, in order to augment the receipts as much as possible. The first of her colleagues at the Théâtre Français whom Nathalie asked was Sarah Bernhardt! She had forgiven her long ago, and she knew how valuable her name already was at the box office. On this occasion Sarah played *La Nuit de Mai*, by Alfred de Musset, with Mounet Sully.

Early in May, 1876, Julie Van Hard died at her home in the Rue Saint Honoré, after ten days of terrible suffering. Sarah watched over her every night. On May 24 her strength gave out; she had to take to her bed and hand over for some weeks her part in *L'Etrangère* to her comrade and friend, Marie Lloyd. Unimportant in itself, this incident showed at the time how great the vogue of Sarah Bernhardt already was. For a whole week a regular procession of notables filed through the house in the Avenue de Villiers, into which she had moved a few days earlier. In the anteroom a visitors' book was filled with hundreds of well-known signatures, words of sympathy for the death of her mother, and, above all, wishes for her recovery. Every day the newspapers published a "Bulletin on the Health of Sarah Bernhardt"—long articles on her plans, her future parts—and deplored the long convalescent holiday which she was obliged to take.

Reporting the Salon of 1876, the art critics tarried, longer than over all the other pictures, over the two large portraits of Sarah Bernhardt, one by Louise Abbéma and the other by Georges Clairin. Having briefly described and appreciated the pictures, they spoke chiefly of the model because they knew that their readers would devour everything concerning her. This was real popularity, and Sarah Bernhardt was not yet thirty-two!

On September 27, with Mounet Sully, she gave the first performance of *Rome Vaincue*, a play in verse by Alexandre Parodi. Perrin had first cast her as Opimia, the young vestal virgin, but now she had acquired sufficient authority in the theater to express her opinion. She refused the part and asked for that of Posthumia, a blind old Roman woman of seventy, which seemed to offer her more opportunity. Although astounded, Perrin gave in to her. Prudently he did not argue any more! And Sarah created an absolutely sensational character with this part.

Twenty years later, in 1896, at the Renaissance, when the grandiose manifestation called "Sarah Bernhardt's Day" was staged in her honor, from her immense repertory she chose for her appearance on this occasion only the second act of *Phèdre* and the fourth of *Rome Vaincue*.

The year 1877, during which she, of course, played her usual parts, was marked for Sarah by only one great opening, but one whose glory surpassed that of all its predecessors. It took place on November 19. That evening, for the first time, she played *Hernani*, by Victor Hugo.

The word "opening" is incorrect, because it was really the fourth revival since the first performance in 1830. It had been played again in 1838, with Firmin and Marie Dorval; in 1841, with Beauvallet and Emilie Guyon. Then, after the long ban placed upon the works of Victor Hugo by Napoleon III, the revival of 1867 took place. That of 1877 brought together an entirely new cast, with Mounet Sully as Hernani, Worms as Don Carlos, Maubant as Ruy Gomez, and Sarah Bernhardt as Doña Sol. All things considered, it is possible to say that, with such a cast, this revival was a real opening.

In 1872 *Ruy Blas* had been a success at the Odéon. Sarah Bernhardt declared that it was modest compared with that of *Hernani* at the Théâtre Français in 1877.

Having definitely abandoned those eccentricities with which he had been reproached for so long, Mounet Sully, then thirty-six, was at the height of his powers; already at certain moments his genius revealed itself. The old subscribers were delighted, declaring that he was the best of all the interpreters of the part—which he played, by the way, at the Comédie Française for thirty-five years. I saw him in 1910 and I shall never forget him.

The following day Sarah Bernhardt received this letter:

> Madame:
> You were great and you were charming. You moved even me, an old warrior, and at a certain moment, while the touched and delighted public was applauding you, I wept. That tear which you caused to flow is yours. Allow me to present it to you.
>
> Victor Hugo.

With the letter was a jewel case containing a small gold chain from which a diamond hung in the shape of a drop. Sarah kept this piece of jewelry until her death. Forty-five years later, in 1922, in the third act of *Régine Armand*, she still wore around her neck the tear of Victor Hugo!

The revival of *Hernani* had a hundred and sixteen performances between November 19, 1877, and December 31, 1878—which was immense for that period.

On February 27, 1878, Bressant gave his farewell performance on retirement. As Nathalie had done, he asked for the co-operation of Mounet Sully and Sarah Bernhardt, who were then drawing everyone in Paris. They performed one act of Shakespeare's *Othello* in a new adaptation by Jean Aicard, which the latter had brought to the Comédie Française for "the couple" and which was to be staged in its entirety the following season.

It was not performed, in effect, until 1899. Sarah Bernhardt having left the Comédie Française, for twenty years Mounet Sully could find no actress there worthy to succeed her as Desdemona and refused to perform the play. Finally, giving up the struggle, he accepted Lara, who was mediocre, and Aicard's *Othello* did not have a great success.

While Emile Perrin, with remarkable regularity, always tried to advertise the couple as often as possible, looking out for plays which would bring the two artists together, their liaison had long ago ended in a very friendly way. This was not surprising, for then Sarah was particularly absorbed in sculpture and painting. During the run of *Hernani* she painted, among others, a large picture, about six feet high—"The Young Girl and Death," which she exhibited at the Salon in 1879. It was natural that an actor should interest her less and that she should choose a painter from the many aspirants who were eager to please her. And it had been Georges Clairin. His hour came in 1877, and for a year or two he succeeded Mounet Sully in the affections of Sarah Bernhardt.

Barely more than a year older than she, tall, robust, energetic in appearance, his pointed beard neatly trimmed, a successful portrait painter, and a medal prize winner at the Salon, Clairin had touched her by his complete devotion, his boundless admiration, his docility with all her caprices, and also his intelligent advice in painting. But all these qualities were those of a friend rather than of a lover, and their relationship was neither passionate nor lasting. Even before her departure for America, Sarah had gradually changed "Georges darling" to "dear old Geogeotte," the name which remained with him until his death and by which he was always called by the entire Sarah Bernhardt family, when he became an intimate of the household.

On April 2, 1878, for the first time, Sarah played Alcmène in Molière's *Amphytrion*, and Perrin, being a man of traditions, did not fail to give the part of Jupiter to Mounet Sully. This time, however, the part was not at all his type of thing; for Mounet had never any lightness of touch, irony, or sense of comedy, and he was not good. But that was of no importance, as Sarah and Mounet on the bill were sufficient to bring in receipts. She was adorable as Alcmène, displaying wit and grace which were noble, languid, and smiling, in which a new aspect of her talent was revealed.

Three months later an incident which made a great deal of noise at the time gave unexpected publicity to her liaison with Georges Clairin. This was Sarah Bernhardt's flight in a balloon.

Among other attractions the Universal Exhibition of 1878 relied chiefly on Pierre Giffard's captive balloon, which was installed in the garden of the Tuileries facing the Louvre. For a modest sum visitors to the international fair, to the number of four or five persons per journey, could go up in the air for half an hour and were then brought back to earth by the rope which attached the airship to the ground. At that period this was an astonishing innovation and a sensational attraction.

Attracted by all that was new and original, Sarah Bernhardt had made many ascents of this kind; but her dream was to go up in a free balloon. On reasonable terms, owing to her celebrity she persuaded Pierre Giffard to equip a balloon for her and to place a pilot at her disposal. On a fine Saturday in July, without a trace of wind, about six in the evening, she launched herself upon this daring adventure alone with Clairin. They counted on making a "little tour" of two or three hours and coming down about nightfall, after looking at the lights of the city from a height of six thousand feet.

Today, in this century of airplanes, all this looks like a childish amusement; but it must be remembered that it took place in 1878, after the invention of the first dirigibles but long before they were in regular use, when the spherical balloon was by no means a form of transportation but an experimental apparatus jealously reserved for professionals alone.

About eight o'clock the wind suddenly rose, and the balloon was carried away at a great speed toward the southwest. How far were the passengers going to be carried? It was impossible to foretell. Meanwhile clouds were coming up, and the thermometer in the basket, which had gradually fallen, now indicated ten degrees below zero. Sarah Bernhardt was shivering and, unaccustomed to such an altitude, her ears were drumming and her nose was bleeding. In short, feeling most uncomfortable, she asked to be taken down. The pilot opened the valve, but because of the wind the descent had become more difficult and had to be made very slowly. It was nearly mid-

night when they landed—in the middle of a field, near a village called
Emerainville, Seine-et-Oise, about thirty miles from Paris. There was
nothing to do but spend the night there, in the waiting room at the
station—the only place where Sarah and Clairin could take refuge,
as the entire village had long since gone to sleep.

At the matinée the following day, at half past one, Sarah was to
play Zaïre, which had been revived for the hundredth anniversary of
Voltaire's death at the Comédie Française. She did not reach the
theater until one o'clock, dead tired and not feeling very well. She had
to ask them to hold the curtain for a while, but explanations were
unnecessary. All the morning papers had already related her adventure, and that she had spent the night up in the air with Clairin!

The disciplinarian Emile Perrin was shocked, and that evening he
fined Sarah Bernhardt a thousand francs for having traveled without
the authorization of the Théâtre Français. In the contracts which the
actors at the Comédie signed, there was a clause forbidding them to
leave Paris without special permission. An argument arose. "Leave
Paris?" If there had been no wind, Sarah would have descended at
the exact spot from which she had left. Could she be held responsible
for changes in the elements? Naturally, the press took up the matter
and discussed it for a long time. At the intervention of the Minister
of Fine Arts, Edmond Turquet, the fine was rescinded; but once again
the newspapers were full only of Sarah Bernhardt.

I have found a long article by Albert Millaud which appeared in
the Figaro at the beginning of August, 1878. I believe I should quote
some parts of it, because it is a fairly typical example of what used
to be written and what was the attitude of the press toward Sarah
Bernhardt.

"In Paris and in all fashionable circles, there is talk only of the
actions and gestures of Mademoiselle Sarah Bernhardt. Even the question of Bosnia has receded into the background. The chief editors
of the Paris papers forget everything, in order to concentrate on
Mademoiselle Sarah Bernhardt and her recent ascent in the balloon
of M. Giffard. The reason is that Mademoiselle Sarah Bernhardt is
not an ordinary woman. There is something of the goddess, something
aerial and ideal, about her. Her slenderness is merely the result of
the dissolution of matter. She is as uncorporeal as possible, all dreams,
all vapor, all spirit. On this account she aspires to the clouds, to the
blue, to the azure. Not having wings with which to fly, she applied to

M. Giffard; and they say that she does not begin to breathe until she is above the towers of Notre Dame.

"For my part, I believe that Mademoiselle Sarah Bernhardt is surrounded by clumsy people who, with their insistent advertising and the stories they peddle, end by injuring their favorite artist. Nobody more than I appreciates the grace, the charm, of the young actress. Everywhere people praise her wit, her education, and her noble artistic aspirations. Why do some of her courtiers succeed in spoiling all that by giving her a reputation for strangeness and eccentricity which, I like to hope, she does not care for in the least? They say she sleeps in a coffin, that she dissects dogs and cats, that she dresses like an undertaker, that she produces both pictures and statues, that she dyes her hair blonde because her cheeks are too fresh for her to remain brunette. Such stupidities can only hurt Mademoiselle Sarah Bernhardt. They encourage her to continue her system of childish extravagance. A day will come when, in order to fill the gossip columns of the papers, she will become her own chimney sweep or her own cook. Then her friends will cry out in admiration: 'Seeing her in *Phèdre* is nothing. You should see her when she's peeling onions. That's what brings tears to your eyes! And how sublime she is when she comes down from the chimney covered with soot and declaims in her silvery voice: "And there too, I can pass!" '

"The end of it will be that Mademoiselle Sarah Bernhardt will look like Harlequin in the classical Italian comedy, about whom so many plays have been written. We shall have 'Sarah Bernhardt in a Balloon'; 'Sarah Bernhardt, the Farmer'; 'Sarah Bernhardt, Sculptress'; 'Sarah Bernhardt and Her Eleven Fathers'; 'Sarah Bernhardt, the Hoaxer'; etc. All these Sarah Bernhardts are not worth the one whom I applauded in *La Fille de Roland* and cheered in *Hernani*. For my own part, I prefer to think only of the latter."

Sarah Bernhardt did not like this article very much. She dismissed hundreds of them with a shrug of the shoulders. Albert Millaud being an important personality, she replied in a letter, which the *Figaro* published, from which I quote the following lines:

"Your good will toward the artist prompts me to defend the woman. It is not my clumsy friends who thus throw me in the face of the public, but clever enemies. It exasperates me to be unable to do anything without being accused of eccentricity. I had great fun going up in a balloon, but now I dare not do so. I assure you that

I have never skinned dogs nor burned cats. And I regret that I cannot prove that I am a natural blonde. My thinness is eccentric, people say. Well, what can I do? I should very much prefer to be deliciously 'ripe.' So my illnesses create a disturbance? They attack me without warning and leave me insensible wherever I may be. I cannot be expected, before feeling ill, to ask people who happen to be there to leave the room. I am accused of trying to do everything except act: sculpture, painting, piano playing. Whom does that disturb, if my work at the Théâtre Français has never suffered?"

After a revival of *Le Sphinx* on October 28, 1878, Sarah for the first time, on February 7, 1879, played the part of Monime in Racine's *Mithridate* with Maubant as Mithridates and Mounet Sully as Xipharès.

On April 4 of that year, having been first performed at the Renaissance in 1838 and revived at the Porte Saint Martin and the Odéon, *Ruy Blas* was admitted to the repertory of the Comédie Française. Naturally, Sarah resumed the part of Queen Maria of Neubourg, with Mounet Sully as Ruy Blas, Coquelin *aîné* as Don César de Bazan, and Frédéric Febvre as Don Salluste.

The play had the same brilliant success as at the Odéon—perhaps even greater, because the male cast was very much better. While Febvre was far from being as good as Geffroy, the admirable Don Salluste of 1872, Coquelin *aîné* was astounding as Don César, far superior to Mélingue, who was an assured actor but whose sense of comedy dated somewhat; and Mounet Sully, extraordinarily romantic, greatly surpased his predecessor, Lafontaine. Moreover, Coquelin *cadet*, who had left the Théâtre Français early in 1875 in a sudden fit of anger and who had returned repentant in December, 1876, after a regrettable flight to the Théâtre des Variétés, showed astonishing spirit in the small part of the lackey in the fourth act and, in five minutes on the stage, achieved an extraordinary personal success.

This revival, whose performances continued for a year, consecrated Sarah Bernhardt as the greatest favorite of the Comédie Française public. Although the company at that era was then exceptionally brilliant, including at least twenty first-class artists, Sarah undeniably surpassed them all, by her personality, her reputation, and, above all, her talent. What was more miraculous was the fact that, although greatly criticized and at times mediocre, when she joined the Comédie

Française she had conquered this absolutely dominating position through hard struggles and almost solely because of the repertory, that is to say, by her interpretation of parts already played before her by many other actresses, some of whom were often very remarkable.

As a matter of fact, during eight years at the Théâtre Français, apart from three plays in one act, Sarah Bernhardt did not create, altogether, more than four parts in new plays: *Le Sphinx, La Fille de Roland, L'Etrangère,* and *Rome Vaincue.* From October, 1876, to April, 1880, she did not create *any new part.* During those three years and a half her reputation was maintained only by her performances in *Hernani* (revival); *Ruy Blas* (revival); and in classic roles, particularly *Phèdre* and *Andromaque.*

As important alterations had to be made in the auditorium and on the stage, the exceptional announcement was made that the Théâtre Français would be closed during the months of June and July, 1879. The words "annual closing" are unknown at the Comédie Française, which is open three hundred and sixty-five days a year. Immediately an offer had been made to the general manager by Hollingshead and Mayer, managers of the Gaiety Theatre, London, and a contract had been signed by the terms of which the entire Théâtre Français company was to go to London, from June 2 to July 12, and give a series of forty-two performances of the principal plays in its repertory.

It was then that a very significant incident occurred. Emile Perrin spent days carefully drawing up the program for the London season, endeavoring to give each artist his due, according to rank and merit, to have all the principal *Sociétaires* appear, each as frequently as the other, in their best parts. Having done this, he sent the London managers the list of plays chosen, with their casts. The opening night included *Le Misanthrope* and *Les Précieuses Ridicules.* Sarah Bernhardt was not playing in either of them. By return of post Perrin received a letter from Hollingshead and Mayer asking him to change this program for the opening. More than half the reservations had been made on the mere name of Sarah Bernhardt. It was absolutely necessary that she should appear on the first night.

Perrin was greatly embarrassed. During the interval the London program had been announced to the members of the company. To change the opening program would be to eliminate one or more of

them, who had already been told that they would be part of it. There
would be certain protests, shouts, arguments, and perhaps some refusals to go to England at the last minute. With the London opening
only a few days away, the slightest disturbance was to be avoided at
any cost. After prolonged reflection and a voluminous exchange of
telegrams with the English managers, it was decided to keep the program of the opening night as arranged but to include the second act
of *Phèdre* for Sarah, between the two plays of Molière. This was done.

It constituted a veritable revolution in the customs of the Théâtre
Français. To put on a single act from a five-act tragedy, solely in order
that one artist should appear, was to draw attention to her to the disadvantage of all the others; to make her a star, whereas there had
been no stars for three hundred years at the Comédie Française. On
the playbills the names of the performers are invariably printed in
one column underneath each other, in small type, and in the order
of their seniority at the theater. This means that it may easily happen
that the actor whose name appears first plays an unimportant part,
and the one who has the leading part may be last. In order of
seniority in 1879, Sarah Bernhardt was the tenth woman *Sociétaire*.
Here an exception was being made for her of which there is probably
not another example in the entire history of the "House of Molière."
But, while insisting on their prerogatives, her colleagues also were
anxious that their expedition to London should succeed. So, realizing
the paramount importance which the English public attached to the
presence of Sarah, nobody protested. On June 2, 1879, at the inaugu-
ration of the official performances of the Comédie Française at the
Gaiety Theatre, London, Sarah, who was a member of the company,
actually played as a "featured" star!

The performances as a whole were very successful. After the final
performance the *Times* held a referendum, asking those of its readers
who had followed the performances to send in a kind of roll of honor;
that is, a list of the principal artists in the order of their preferences.
Adding the votes obtained by each player, and giving him one point
in twenty according to the totals, the results were the following:
Sarah Bernhardt, 19; Got, 14; Coquelin *aîné*, 14; Sophie Croizette, 12;
Emilie Broisat, 10; Febvre, 10; Delaunay, 10; Worms, 10; Coquelin
cadet, 9; Jeanne Samary, 8; Thiron, 8; Mounet Sully, 8; Maria Favart,
7; Madeleine Brohan, 6; Blanche Baretta, 6. This was the first time
that Sarah Bernhardt performed outside of France. From the follow-

ing year on, during her entire life, she was to divide her artistic activities between Paris and abroad.

During the six weeks which she spent in London she made the acquaintance of a man who was later to have a decisive influence on the direction of her career, and who then visited her for the first time. This was the American impresario Edward Jarrett. Having often seen Sarah act in Paris, he happened to be staying in England while the Comédie Française was giving its performances. There he quickly realized that Sarah alone, as an "attraction," was worth all the other members of the company put together.

So he went to see the actress who had triumphed in *Hernani* and *Phèdre*, and said to her: "Would you like to make a fortune?"

"Certainly," Sarah replied. "In what way?"

"By going to America."

At first she did not know what to say. "What would I do?"

"Well, obviously, you would give performances. I make you an offer to do a grand tour of the United States and Canada. Your own dates will suit me."

"But I do not speak a word of English."

"I'll act as your interpreter."

"That is not what I mean," said Sarah smilingly. "I suppose one would have to act in English over there?"

"Not you. You have so much personality and, then, I have so much material to advertise you. You will act in your own language. Almost nobody will understand you, but I guarantee you a triumph all the same."

Sarah remained thoughtful. Her success in London had certainly given her a taste for performing abroad.

"How long would this tour last?" she asked.

"Six months, at least."

"The Théâtre Français will never grant me the necessary leave."

"You never can tell. Moreover, in your position, Mademoiselle, one does not ask; one demands. Here are my three addresses, in New York, London, and Paris, where I come from time to time. The day that you decide, call me."

Having saluted her, Jarrett—who was a great gentleman with a white beard, cold and infinitely polite, and who never smiled—withdrew, leaving Sarah in a state of perplexity. She had often heard that, in 1855, Rachel had made a tour of the United States which was still famous: enormous receipts, fabulous profits, but no real success. The Americans had not yet understood the noble but austere art of the famous tragedienne. And this rebuff, which had hurt her very much, certainly helped to shorten her life.

On the other hand, Sarah noted that with the English public she had at least as much success as in Paris. But would it be the same in America? In any case, the proposal was worth studying. She thought of it often in the months that followed.

When leaving for England, Sarah, always in need of money, thought that perhaps she might take advantage of her popularity in London to sell some of her works there. In her luggage she had brought about ten of her own pictures and the same number of busts or statues. She exhibited them at a gallery in Piccadilly and sent out five hundred invitations to the *vernissage*. London society crowded the place. Among the visitors were the Prince of Wales—the future King Edward VII—and the Prime Minister, Gladstone, both of whom often came to the performances at the Gaiety. Sarah sold almost all her works, chief of which was a bronze reproduction of her group "After the Storm"—which was bought for ten thousand francs.

After her return to Paris the Comédie Française reopened on August 2.

A few days before she left England, Sarah had been told about a famous menagerie in Liverpool, kept by a man named Cross, where one could buy every animal in creation. She went there one day when she was not playing at night—and embarked at Dover with a leopard, a monkey, and seven chameleons. Several of her colleagues cried out in terror at the appearance of the leopard on the deck of the boat. Her return to France with this menagerie and her settling in the house in the Avenue de Villiers, where there were already three dogs, two tortoises, and a parrot, did not help to diminish the owner's reputation for eccentricity.

The immense success of *Ruy Blas* continued during the last months of 1879 and the first weeks of 1880. On February 25, 1880, the fiftieth anniversary of *Hernani* was celebrated successfully, it having been first produced at the Comédie Française on February 25, 1830. Still robust, in spite of his seventy-eight years, Victor Hugo came to the anniversary performance, which consecrated the lasting triumph of his work. After the performance, on the stage and in the presence of the entire company, which had assembled to pay its respects to the Master, he affectionately embraced his marvelous Doña Sol. This was the last big night of Sarah Bernhardt at the Théâtre Français.

In March, Perrin suggested to her a revival of *L'Aventurière*, by Emile Augier, to which she consented, Coquelin *aîné* playing Annibal; Frédéric Febvre, Fabrice; and Martel, Monte-Prade. The first performance was announced for April 17. Having been indisposed for a few days, Sarah Bernhardt had not been able to take part in all the rehearsals; and the night before, not feeling ready, she asked Perrin to postpone the play. But the booking was considerable and the revival anxiously awaited. He refused.

On the appointed date Sarah appeared as Doña Clorinde, in *L'Aventurière*, and, as she often admitted, she was bad. In more or less polite language, the entire press the next day commented on her failure; and Auguste Vitu, the critic of the *Figaro*, concluded his article with these words:

"Finally, the new Clorinde, especially in the last two acts, moved her arms and body in a cheap, vulgar way which astounded us. We did not have the feeling of seeing *L'Aventurière* of Augier, but big Virginie in *L'Assommoir*, by M. Zola, who had somehow managed to find her way onto the noble boards of the Comédie Française."

This article made Sarah violently angry. In all conscience, vulgarity is the one fault with which no one could ever reproach her. She saw in this challenge a trick of her enemies, a concerted offensive by all those who were jealous of her and were taking advantage of an isolated failure to overwhelm her with articles which were, in truth, much too severe. She was too susceptible to accept such criticism. On April 18, at six o'clock in the evening, she broke with the Comédie Française, sending by messenger to Emile Perrin a letter which closed with these lines:

"You forced me to play when I was not ready. What I anticipated has happened. *L'Aventurière* is my first failure at the Comédie Française; it will be my last. By the time you receive this letter, I shall have left Paris. Kindly accept my resignation. Yours truly."

In order that nobody should intervene, which would inevitably happen, in order to make her break irreparable, she sent a copy of her letter to the newspapers, with a request for publication, and left for Havre. At the Hotel Frascati, where she arrived veiled and registered under a false name, she did not want anyone to join her, for a few days at least, or even to know where she was.

Her decision was clearly irrevocable and, because of a few bad notices, it was perhaps carrying things too far to break overnight with a company of which she was a *Sociétaire*, with a theater where she was certain of a dazzling career all her life and where, as a spoiled child of the public, she held a position which was not only privileged but absolutely exceptional. Further, when she was elected a *Sociétaire*, in 1875, she had signed a twenty-year contract, and she could not break it without leaving herself open to a suit which the Théâtre Français would certainly bring against her, and which she had lost in advance.

But it is permissible to surmise that, during the winter of 1879–80, Sarah Bernhardt must have heard frequently from Jarrett, and perhaps seen him; that the proposals which he had made to her in London had been clarified by definite figures; and that she had the assurance, therefore, that the money which she would bring back from her American tour would enable her to pay the Comédie Française, without noticing it, the fine to which she would certainly be condemned.

Another consideration gradually led her to take this decisive action. At the Théâtre Français, whatever her success, she would always remain one of the *Sociétaires*, subject to the decisions of the general manager. While she was in London she had really been treated as a star, by both the press and the public. She had realized that, on her own, she could attract receipts and, by placing her name at the top of the bill, become henceforth the only star in the plays in which she acted. When necessary, she could put them on herself, and thus become her own producer. This view of her future in the theater certainly suited much better her forthright, masterful, and essentially enterprising character. A fairly definite indication that, if not premeditated, her resignation from the Théâtre Français had at least been considered for a long time is furnished by the fact that, less than four days after it was announced in the papers, Sarah signed a contract with Jarrett who, by a curious coincidence, just happened to be in Paris. On the basis of ten per cent of all the money she earned, he guaranteed her a contract with Henry Abbey—one of the most important managers in New York.

The latter, on receipt of a cable from Jarrett, immediately took a steamer and arrived in Paris two weeks later. The contract which

Sarah Bernhardt signed for her first great tour of the United States and Canada was drawn up in the following terms:

One thousand dollars (equal, at the time, to five thousand French francs) for each performance, plus fifty per cent of all receipts above four thousand dollars; that is to say, in the case of receipts amounting to five thousand dollars, for example, her share would be fifteen hundred dollars, or seven thousand five hundred francs. In addition, she received two hundred dollars a week for hotel expenses. Whenever she traveled on the American continent, she was to have a private car, containing a drawing room, a dining room, a bedroom for herself, a neighboring room for Madame Guérard, two compartments with two beds each for her staff, and a kitchen. The contract guaranteed a hundred performances in four months, to be extended by mutual agreement. Abbey also made himself responsible for the expenses of the company, the members of which would be chosen by her. Her repertory was to consist of eight plays.

This contract between Sarah Bernhardt and Henry Abbey was signed at the beginning of May. However, the season being then too far advanced, it was agreed that the tour would not begin until the following October. These miraculous terms, absolutely extraordinary for that time, now enabled Sarah Bernhardt to contemplate with complete calm the loss of her suit with the Comédie Française. On June 9, 1880, she was condemned to pay a hundred thousand francs' damages, losing, in addition, forty-three thousand francs from her pension fund; that is, fifty per cent of her share in the profits from 1875 to 1879.

Every year a *Sociétaire* receives only half his profits, leaving the other half on deposit in the theater. The amount thus accumulated is paid in a lump sum when he leaves, on condition, of course, that his departure is agreed to by the management and is not contrary to their wishes.

By May 1 Julia Bartet, a newcomer at the Comédie Française, had assumed the part of the Queen in *Ruy Blas*, and on May 8 Croizette that of Doña Clorinde in *L'Aventurière*.

It was in London that Sarah Bernhardt learned that she had lost her case and the terms of the verdict. As soon as they heard of her resignation from the Théâtre Français, the managers of the Gaiety Theatre, Hollingshead and Mayer, who had brought the Comédie Française to

London the year before, had rushed over to Paris and engaged Sarah for a month, to begin at once, she being the only star this time. She had accepted and signed an agreement for a hundred and fifty pounds for each performance, plus one half of the profits. The London performances took place from May 24 to June 27, 1880. She played six of the eight plays selected for her future American tour, which enabled her to become settled, in advance, in those parts which she had not previously performed. These six plays were *Hernani, Phèdre, Le Sphinx*, and *L'Etrangère*, with which she was familiar, and two which she performed for the first time: *Froufrou*, the excellent dramatic comedy by Meilhac and Halévy, first performed by Aimée Desclée at the Gymnase in 1859, and *Adrienne Lecouvreur*, by Scribe, a part created by Rachel at the Théâtre Français in 1849. These two plays, the only ones which she had not already performed in London with the Comédie Française in 1879, had the greatest success. But the whole series of performances was a triumph. Every day her English public received her with prolonged ovations.

This season in London was the beginning of the long series of tours by Sarah Bernhardt which did not cease until her death; and it was the first time that she was starred alone, supported by a company which she had formed herself. In order to appear again before English audiences, which had seen her the previous year with all her distinguished colleagues from the Théâtre Français, she was careful about those whom she chose. Her company consisted principally of Pierre Berton, Dieudonné, Talbot, Train, Mary Jullien, Marie Kalb, and her sister Jeanne Bernhardt—who, among other roles, played that of Berthe in *Le Sphinx*, which Sarah had created, the latter taking the part of Blanche.

Encouraged by this success, which was really considerable, Sarah remained only a few days on her return to Paris. Almost at once she left for Brussels and then Copenhagen, where she played *Adrienne Lecouvreur* and *Froufrou* during the months of July and August. As she was not leaving for America until sometime in October, during the entire month of September she undertook a series of performances in the principal towns of France, with the same two plays. Félix Duquesnel, who had given up the management of the Odéon six months earlier, organized this tour. This was the first business deal that he had with Sarah Bernhardt, with whom he subsequently collaborated again for so many years.

Although she was on the point of leaving France for months and of undertaking a distant and tiring journey, Sarah did not take one day's holiday. No sooner had she left the Comédie Française than the intensive and uninterrupted exploitation of her talent and her fame began.

At the end of June, when she had gone through Paris, Perrin and the Minister of Fine Arts had semiofficially delegated several of her colleagues to attempt to persuade her to return to the Théâtre Français. The press, headed by Francisque Sarcey, demanded her return to the fold. They knew of the reception she had had in London, and deplored the fact that the general manager of the "House of Molière" should have allowed anyone so valuable, artistically and commercially, to get away. It was Got, the dean; then Delaunay; then Coquelin *aîné*; then Mounet Sully, who, employing the various arguments suggested by their different natures, went in succession to the Avenue de Villiers. She opposed with the same obstinacy the affectionate requests of the one; the wise counsels of the other; and the warning of the third, against the risks of this new and adventurous life compared with the quiet security of the Théâtre Français. She was resolute. Nothing in the world could now persuade her to return to the Comédie Française. For one thing, on her own in London she had brought in larger receipts than that theater had earned in its entirety the previous year. It was only too evident that the Comédie Française needed her, but she had no need whatever of the Comédie Française.

During the first two weeks of October, 1880, Sarah Bernhardt rehearsed her repertory with the company which she was taking to America, and worked up the two parts which, with those already performed in London, completed the total of eight plays stipulated in her contract with Abbey. One of these was *Antony*, a very early drama by Alexandre Dumas *père*, first performed in 1831, in which, however, she did not act. The play was announced; but in the course of her journey to the United States she decided it was too old-fashioned and substituted, at the last moment, *La Princesse Georges,* by Alexandre Dumas *fils*, which dated only from 1871 and had been one of the greatest successes of Aimée Desclée at the Gymnase. The other was *La Dame aux Camélias,* which, from that day, was to be included in all her tours and was revived in Paris almost every year until 1914. In all, she performed it more than three thousand times.

Sarah did not know the play. Obviously she had heard about it, because since it was first performed with Madame Doche and Fechter at the Vaudeville, on February 2, 1852, it had been revived several times.

But it had never met with such success as might have brought it to her attention. At the Gymnase, in 1872, Blanche Pierson, who was an excellent actress, had been just adequate, nothing more.

It was the actor Pierre Berton who suggested *La Dame aux Camélias* to Sarah Bernhardt, when she was looking for an eighth play for her repertory and had been wondering for weeks which one finally to choose.

At first Sarah made a face. "Isn't that the part of a courtesan?"

"It is a magnificent part."

"Yet of all the people who have played it, up to now, none has succeeded very well."

"But you will have a magnificent triumph in it."

Sarah was incredulous, but to please Berton she concluded: "I'll have to read it. Be a dear and send me a copy."

That evening Berton, who was not going with her to America and whose advice was consequently completely disinterested, sent her the script of *La Dame aux Camélias*. She read the play the same night, and liked Marguerite Gautier. She felt that, as played by her, the last act would create a profound impression. The sacrifice in the third act seemed touching. This woman, who adores a man but leaves him through the intervention of his family, without being able to tell him her real reasons for doing so, evoked in her personal memories—memories which were not yet completely effaced.

She included the play in the program of her American tour—but without any particular enthusiasm, strange to say. How would this play be received, which dated back twenty-eight years and had never been more than a moderate success? Evidently she was quite sure that she could produce an effect, but she would never have supposed that the success of *La Dame aux Camélias*, during her entire life, would far eclipse that of all her other plays.

Following a remark which I have already made, I will point out that among the eight plays of which Sarah Bernhardt's repertory consisted there were at first seven in which she died at the end. Only Mrs. Clarkson in *L'Etrangère* was alive in the last act. When she substituted *La Princesse Georges* for *Antony*, there still remained six plays which ended with the death of the character which she portrayed.

On October 15, 1880, on the French steamship *Amérique*, Sarah Bernhardt, then exactly thirty-six years of age, with her entire company and her impresario, Jarrett, embarked at Havre for New York, where she began her first conquest of the New World.

CHAPTER V

America, Return, Jacques Damala

DURING the few days preceding Sarah Bernhardt's departure, the Paris papers had commented widely on the event. But all were not entirely favorable. While some of the dailies predicted—and often wished—her success, in view of what had happened in England, Belgium, Denmark, and the French provinces, many others, recalling Rachel's unfortunate tour in the United States, were reserved and puzzled and did not augur from this distant journey anything of any advantage to the fame, the prestige, and the quality of her talent. Arsène Houssaye, who was general manager of the Comédie Française at the beginning of the Second Empire and who had since achieved great authority as a journalist, wrote:

"Having spent five hundred thousand francs for her house in the Avenue de Villiers, Mademoiselle Sarah Bernhardt needs money; so she is leaving for America. Be careful, Mademoiselle; to great art these distant peregrinations are not congenial and it suffers from the deplorable habits which are derived from this traveling-circus existence, lived slapdash between the hotel which one has left and the new theater to which one is going. What sort of haphazard public is this, which understands nothing of either your language or your genius? An elephant walking on bottles in a circus would be more to its taste. For a French actress, real wealth is the applause of French hands. Like the conquerors of old, this restless genius imagines that she has but to appear in order to conquer, to set up the flag of French Art at the other end of the world. I greatly fear that she will soon have to give up her illusions. In vain she will cast the fire and flame of her talent before a public which, not being familiar with our masterpieces, will come to see her only in order to be able to say: 'I was there.'"

Most humorous were those who did not pardon her for having left the Comédie Française. At first they believed that it was a whim, a momentary caprice, a desire to go alone as a star and give a few performances in London. When, at the instance of Sarcey and some of his colleagues, so many steps—almost official and known to everyone—were taken to beg Sarah to resume her position at the Théâtre Français, no one doubted that she would quickly succumb to these flattering requests. Then they had observed that, far from considering them, she quietly shrugged her shoulders and continued her expeditions in Europe and America.

Finally a section of the press and of her admirers was seized with a kind of spite. They were annoyed by the carelessness with which Sarah was leaving the foremost theater in the world and a devoted public, which acclaimed her loudly every time she appeared. When she had definitely left France and broken with the Comédie Française, the injured tone of the newspapers gradually turned to bitterness, to irony, and soon to hostility. Early in 1881, in Paris, when she was too far away to reply, to defend herself as she so well knew how, her enemies were unleashed and, succeeding to their hearts' content, mobilized public opinion almost completely against her.

This was not yet the case when she took the train for Havre at the Saint Lazare station. A large number of friends and hundreds of curiosity seekers accompanied her, and she was greeted by an ovation when she appeared at the window of her compartment. At Havre, the next day, there were further manifestations of affection as the steamer left. Her intimate friends had come from Paris to be with her until the moment when the *Amérique* raised anchor. These were Clairin Louise Abbéma, Duquesnel, William Busnach—the author of the plays based on Zola's novels—and, of course, Maurice Bernhardt, who was now a little more than fifteen years old and was entrusted by Sarah, during her absence, to the care of his Aunt Henriette and his Uncle Faure—henceforth her only family. Her grandmother, Lisa, had just died, following to the grave her granddaughter, Régina, and her daughter, Julie. Rosine, Julie's frivolous sister, had left France, probably with some lover. No one ever heard what became of her.

Jeanne Bernhardt was a member of the company and was to have embarked with Sarah. But, some days before the departure, she fell sick and suffered from a violent crisis induced by narcotics, those horrible poisons the abuse of which caused her death four years later. Now she had to remain at a sanitarium in Paris in order to undergo treatments, it being understood that she would join the tour in the United States as soon as she had recovered.

At the last minute Sarah Bernhardt engaged an actress then fairly

popular along the boulevards, Marie Colombier, to replace her sister.
If her name is still remembered today, it is not because of her success
as an actress, which was always modest, but solely because, on returning from the tour, she had a quarrel with Sarah and published a
venomous book about her, full of perfidious and sometimes obscene
anecdotes, entitled *Sarah Barnum*. The mere title of the volume re-
veals its intentions. By the change of name of Bernhardt to that of the
owner of the famous circus, the reader is informed in advance that
he will find an exposure of the secrets and devices for noisy publicity
with which her enemies reproached Sarah Bernhardt so very much.
Nasty, but quite amusing, the book had a certain success. It was well
documented, because Marie Colombier not only had almost never left
Sarah during the long tour but had also been a friend of hers for
years and knew her well.

The rest of the company which went with Sarah Bernhardt to
America was quite mediocre. It included only one really good actor,
Angelo, who played all the male leading parts: Hernani; Maurice de
Saxe, in *Adrienne Lecouvreur*; Armand Duval, in *La Dame aux
Camélias*; etc.

The crossing was bad. The *Amérique* was not a very large ship. The
pitching and tossing kept Sarah lying down in her cabin during almost
the entire journey. On October 23, when she came to wish her a
happy birthday, Madame Guérard found her sick "as she could not
have imagined it was possible for anyone to be!" When would they
arrive? When would this torture end? It ended on October 27. At that
time it took twelve days to cross from Havre to New York.

For three months there had been formidable publicity in New
York and all over the United States—about Sarah Bernhardt "the
greatest French actress." In addition to innumerable newspaper articles, enormous advertisements, and huge posters on the walls, a
pamphlet of a hundred pages, illustrated with many portraits and
giving the details of her life and career, had been printed in tens of
thousands of copies and generously distributed among all sections of
the American people. This colossal and unusual effort had produced
results. For weeks seats for the performances, which were to begin in
ten days at the Booth Theater, had been sold for twenty, thirty, and
forty dollars, and then offered at auction, such was the demand!

It was not yet eight o'clock in the morning when the *Amérique* came into port. Yet an immense crowd had been waiting quite a long time for the arrival of the ship, which some hundred privileged persons had been allowed to board, in order to welcome the great artist. Henry Abbey, the manager of Sarah's tour, led the way. There were compliments, flowers, and speeches in English, a reply from Sarah in French. A fanfare of music: the *Marseillaise, The Star-Spangled Banner.* A queen could not have been received with greater pomp and circumstance. Crossing on the same steamer was an elderly lady, dressed in black, who was returning to the United States after spending the summer in Europe. She waited patiently in the dining room until the crowd had dispersed; then disembarked quietly, unrecognized and unknown. This was the widow of Abraham Lincoln, whose husband had been assassinated fifteen years previously by the brother of the famous actor Booth—the very man whose name was given to the theater where Sarah was going to perform.

The carriage with two horses which awaited Sarah at the pier passed between two unbroken lines of curiosity seekers—who stood on one another's shoulders in order to see her—and took her to the Albemarle Hotel, where she stayed for a month. Fifty reporters were already waiting for her. But, being very tired after the journey and the noisy reception at such an early hour, she begged to be allowed to sleep for a while. Jarrett was amazed. It was long before the era of skyscrapers. Her apartment was on the mezzanine floor. By standing on his toes, a man on the sidewalk could almost touch with his fingers the floor of the balcony upon which the windows opened. The noise in the street, where small groups of people were discussing her arrival, together with the noise of the conversation of the journalists in the next room, would certainly prevent her from closing her eyes. However, lying down on her bed, Sarah demonstrated the opposite then and there.

Like Napoleon I, she had all her life the marvelous ability to sleep when she wanted to, wherever she might be, whatever the noise about her, and for the length of time which she had fixed in advance. It was certainly extraordinary. How often have I heard her say, in her dressing room at the Théâtre Sarah Bernhardt or on tour: "It is six. We'll dine at seven. I'm going to sleep for three quarters of an hour." Immediately, forgetting everything that was happening around her, she would fall soundly asleep and would open her eyes punctually, without having to be awakened, three quarters of an hour later, just as she had said. It was undoubtedly this astonishing faculty which enabled her, up to her old age, to make such constant efforts and to withstand superhuman fatigue which nobody else could have resisted.

The questions of the American reporters amazed Sarah. She had long been accustomed to the fantastic stories of the press concerning her; but she thought it must be a joke when she was asked seriously, by ten people at once: "What do you eat on getting up? What do you drink during intermissions? Are you Protestant, Catholic, Jewish, Mohammedan, atheist, Orthodox Greek, or Buddhist? What are your superstitions? What is the exact value of your jewelry? What size shoes do you wear? What is your weight, dressed and undressed? Is it true that you cannot learn a part unless taking a foot bath in boiling water? When can you receive our artist, who wants to make a sketch of you lying in your coffin?" And so forth and so on.

She was impatient and taken aback, and would have liked to tell all these intruders to go to the devil; but Jarrett looked on impassively, murmuring quietly in his white beard: "Don't discourage publicity!"—the phrase which, during her entire tour and whenever she felt nervous, he had so often to repeat to her.

The next day Henry Abbey, who was a greater expert at publicity than Jarrett, discovered an ingenious way of bringing Sarah into contact with the American public before her performances. Abbey was the manager of another theater in New York, the Park, where a very celebrated American actress, called Clara Morris, was then playing. She happened to be performing in a French play, *La Comtesse de Sommerive*, by Théodore Barrière, adapted into English under the title of *Alix*.

Abbey announced in the press that, before appearing herself on the New York stage, Sarah Bernhardt had insisted on applauding first of all her great American colleague, and would go to pay homage to the talents of the interpreter of *Alix*. Very naturally, that evening, the Park Theater was packed. Clara Morris on the stage and Sarah Bernhardt in the audience! A unique spectacle!

Accompanying Sarah, Abbey and Jarrett were careful not to arrive until the middle of the first act. When she entered her stage box, the actors, instructed by the management, stopped playing and the orchestra began the *Marseillaise*. There was a sensation. The performance having been resumed, two minutes later Clara Morris made her entrance amid loud applause. Instead of saying the first lines of her part, she walked down to the footlights, threw a bouquet into the box, and with both her hands threw Sarah a kiss. Sarah took the flowers and pressed them to her heart—and, in her turn, threw onto the stage a sheaf of flowers, which Jarrett handed to her, wrapped in ribbons of the American colors. There was prolonged excitement, the entire house applauding the two artists. More than ever the opening of the "Sarah Bernhardt season" promised to be an event.

As a matter of fact, it was. Her first performance in New York took place on Monday, November 8, 1880. After the success which she had already had in Europe with this play, she had chosen *Adrienne Lecouvreur* for her debut. Her character did not appear in the first act. Certain members of the audience were dissatisfied and were already talking of getting their money back. But in the second act her entrance, carefully studied and greeted with interminable applause— which Abbey paid for that night—produced a profound impression. In the third act the big scene between Adrienne and the Princesse de Bouillon was applauded. In the fourth, the famous tirade of despairing hate, which Sarah emphasized with admirable intensity, left the public palpitating. And the death of Adrienne in the fifth act brought the enthusiasm to its height. There were twenty-seven curtain calls; and the receipts were five thousand, six hundred and thirty-four dollars, or twenty-eight thousand, one hundred and seventy francs.

On her return to the hotel, during her supper, Sarah was still the object of the ovations of the crowd, which had collected beneath her windows shouting her name and trying to sing some lines of the *Marseillaise*. Draped in a cloak, she was obliged to reply several times to the shouts of applause. It was not an accident that Jarrett had chosen for her this suite with a balcony, whose usefulness was suddenly revealed in spite of its being winter.

The next day some papers thought it more dignified to be reticent, but the bulk of the press was enthusiastic. Summing up the general opinion, the *Commercial Advertiser* wrote:

"Sarah Bernhardt's reception was grandiose. Certain critics, looking down from the heights of their grandeur at the artist who dazzled Europe, judged her to be a mediocre artist. But all true connoisseurs will find her a dramatic genius of the highest order."

While the actress was accepted, the play provoked almost unanimous reservations. Not that its dramatic interest was denied, but it was considered unacceptable from a moral point of view. Adrienne

Lecouvreur, in effect, is the mistress of Maurice de Saxe, who is also the lover of the Princesse de Bouillon—a married woman whose husband, the Prince, appears in the play. The drama ends with the assassination of the actress—poisoned by the great lady, her rival. This was quite sufficient to outrage the puritanism of certain circles, whose prudery was incredible sixty years ago and makes their own descendants smile today.

When it was learned that almost all the other plays in Sarah's repertory contained situations equally risqué, there was a veritable explosion of indignation in the press—which was increased by the sermons of the preachers of New York from their pulpits. The latter denounced the "perverted Parisienne" to the faithful and exhorted them, in the name of religion, to stay away from her performances. Moreover, the same sermons were preached in almost every town in the United States and also in Canada. Among the most violent was the Bishop of Montreal.

Uproar of any kind always helps a theatrical enterprise. This one, particularly, had the result which its instigators might have expected. The crowd rushed to the performances of Sarah Bernhardt more than ever. The newspapers not only proclaimed her immense talent but now were pointing out the fearful immorality of the works which she interpreted! Who could have resisted this twofold attraction? Only certain families in society, who were particularly rigid, ostentatiously refused to appear at the Booth Theater. A women's club became indignant and, through the pen of a certain Dr. Crosby, launched a public protest against "the European courtesan, who has come to ruin the morals of the American people."

Once a current of public opinion gets started, not only is it difficult to stop it but almost always it brings exaggerations in its train. So many people pretend to be better informed than their neighbors. Because a certain section of the press now presented Sarah as a woman "without shame or morals," other papers went one better, rivaling one another in their inventions, and published the most astounding and most fantastic "information" about her. Very soon carts were going around the streets of New York on which enormous panels of painted canvas announced in large letters: "The Loves of Sarah Bernhardt. One Volume. Twenty-five Cents."

This pamphlet, which was sold in all the bookshops and even offered along the sidewalks to pedestrians by hawkers, contained an inconceivable jumble of stories, each one more farfetched than the other. The author gave unheard-of details concerning the beginnings of Sarah, her family, her habits, and her whims. He particularly noted that, although never having been married, "La Bernhardt" had four children, whose names and ages were indicated with the utmost precision. As for her father—whom her mother had known only during a single furtive encounter—it could not be stated whether it was the Emperor Napoleon III or Pope Pius IX, but it was certainly either one or the other!

Sarah was outraged and talked of bringing an action for libel, of leaving immediately for Europe, but placidly Jarrett calmed her with the same eternal phrase: "Never discourage publicity!"

When a reporter came to ask Sarah what she thought of these stories which were being peddled about her, Jarrett prompted her to reply: "I am accused of having four children and no husband. That is not true; but it would be better than to have four husbands and no children, like certain women in this country!"

Some days later, when she was asked what she thought of the sermon about her preached by the Reverend Pastor X, she replied: "Everybody knows that, having no religious convictions, this man is a comedian. Therefore I consider that he is acting toward me like a disloyal colleague!"

These witticisms, published the next day and reproduced in all the newspapers of the United States, were greatly appreciated and brought to Sarah Bernhardt the sympathy of many people who were hesitating. The hubbub concerning the French actress did not stop there. There was so much talk about Sarah Bernhardt that very soon her name was also used for commercial advertising. A liquor dealer covered New York with posters representing two Sarah Bernhardts beside each other, one outrageously thin, sickly, and with glazed eyes, the other plump and glowing with health. Underneath appeared the legend: "After using our bitters for six months."

Sarah Bernhardt cigars were on sale everywhere, and a perfumer brought out Sarah Bernhardt soap and face powder. There were Sarah Bernhardt gloves, handkerchiefs, stockings, and even eyeglasses, although she was then far from needing the latter! Such intense and furious publicity could not but bear fruit, the more so as, from a strictly artistic point of view, Sarah was having an increasing success in her other parts. *Froufrou* had aroused ovations, being even better received than *Adrienne Lecouvreur*. *Phèdre* and *Hernani* had perhaps not succeeded quite so well, not because she was less appreciated in them, but because these two works, being more austere, rather puzzled the general American public.

Le Sphinx was also greatly applauded, but not *L'Etrangère*. Unable to understand why Sarah did not play the principal part, one paper confidently asserted that, feeling tired, the great actress had relinquished her part—the Duchesse de Septmonts—to another actress in the company, and played Mrs. Clarkson "in order to rest herself." This warning had a salutary effect on Abbey and Jarrett. From that day *L'Etrangère*, in which the star was not sufficiently prominent, was almost completely banished from the repertory.

But Sarah's triumph was in *La Dame aux Camélias*, which she played, for the first time in her life, in New York, on November 16, 1880. The play produced such an effect, was called for again and again with such insistence, that the program of the entire tour in the other towns of the United States was changed by telegram. It had been arranged that in the places where Sarah would play only one day she would give *Froufrou*, and where there were two performances they would be *Froufrou* and *Adrienne Lecouvreur*. Because of the reception which each of the plays, respectively, had enjoyed in New York, she played *La Dame aux Camélias* wherever she gave only one performance; and in the towns where two shows were needed they were *La Dame aux Camélias* and *Froufrou*.

Sarah Bernhardt's New York season ended on Saturday, December 4, with a seventh performance of *La Dame aux Camélias*. She had given twenty-seven performances, the average receipts being four thousand, three hundred and twenty-seven dollars, or twenty-one thousand, six hundred and five francs, a performance. She had performed in seven plays. *La Princesse Georges* was held in reserve as a novelty for the three or four towns—including New York—where she was to stop a second time before returning to France, after having covered the entire United States.

On Sunday, December 5, before going to Boston, where she was opening the next day, Sarah paid a visit to Thomas Edison at Menlo Park, with two or three members of her company. Thinking of the accounts which would appear in the press, it was Abbey who had organized this meeting between the great artist and the distinguished scientist, who was then, with General Grant, the most outstanding personality in the United States. Thomas Edison had accepted with great pleasure the visit of the celebrated French actress, about whom the whole country was talking, and he politely regretted that his work, which kept him night and day at Menlo Park, had prevented him from going to applaud her in New York.

After many other miraculous discoveries, Edison, who was then only thirty-three years old, had just invented the phonograph, and had quite recently perfected the current and universal use of electric light. In 1880, even in America, apartments and theaters were still lighted by gas. He showed off his latest inventions to Sarah Bernhardt, and then recorded her voice on his phonograph. She recited some verses from *Phèdre* into the apparatus. A few seconds later the wax cylinder —for cylinders were used then and not disks—repeated them in a somewhat nasal voice to the astounded little company, which was overcome with admiration. Who is the happy collector who possesses today the first phonograph record made in 1880 at Edison's by Sarah Bernhardt?

The fortnight during which she played in Boston witnessed a repetition of the triumph which she had won in New York. She opened in *Hernani* at the Globe Theater on December 6. Trying to outdo one another in their enthusiasm, the local critics were even more dithyrambic than their New York colleagues. After her performance of *La Dame aux Camélias*, the *Boston Herald* wrote:

"In the presence of such perfection, analysis is impossible."

Restored to health, and having left Havre a fortnight earlier, Jeanne Bernhardt rejoined her sister's company toward the end of the latter's stay in Boston, and henceforward shared with Marie Colombier the parts assigned to her. The day of her arrival in Boston she was accosted by a strange individual who stopped her in the hall of the Vendôme Hotel, where Sarah Bernhardt was staying. He was a thickset little man, square-shouldered and very polite, with a fur cap in his hand. For three days he had been trying in vain to approach the great artist. Abbey, Jarrett, and their secretaries, while indulgent to anything in the shape of a reporter or a journalist, jealously spared her the useless fatigue of receiving intruders. Having given up hope of seeing Sarah Bernhardt herself, and having heard at the hotel desk that her sister was expected, the little man had planted himself there to wait for her and to present his request.

Although he could scarcely speak any French, Jeanne was able to understand him. His name was Henry Smith. He was the owner of boats which fished for cod along the coast of the Atlantic; and one of them, the week before, had harpooned a whale, which it had succeeded in bringing back to land alive and which was now in Boston harbor. Since then his one dream was to show his capture proudly to the great French artist. One visit, one simple visit, to the whale by Sarah. The capture of one of these gigantic beasts was such a rare event. He wanted to offer this sensational spectacle to the woman whom the entire United States admired, and whom he alone admired more than all the other citizens of the United States put together.

Young, full of laughter, scatterbrained, and delighted with her journey, which enabled her to discover so many new things, Jeanne promised him her help and, after her first effusions with Sarah, transmitted the request of her unknown protégé. For her own part, she was greatly amused at the idea of going to see this whale. She had never seen one, and she had made up her mind to accompany Sarah on this expedition. Delighted at seeing her sister arrive in good health, bringing news and letters from Maurice and her friends, Sarah accepted without difficulty. The next day, with Jeanne and Jarrett, who never allowed Sarah to take a step alone, she went to the harbor in the port of Boston where the whale was installed, its complete immobility raising a doubt as to whether it was as alive as Henry Smith asserted.

The latter, who was delighted and had been feverishly awaiting Sarah since morning, went with her down a little stairway leading to the whale and asked her to stand on its back. "That will bring it luck," he declared. For the sake of peace, Sarah consented; and, clinging to Jarrett's arm, almost falling at every step, she took a few steps on the slippery back of the poor cetacean, without noticing that two or three artists, stationed a short distance away, were busily sketching the scene.

Having satisfied her sister's caprice and finished this visit, which had not amused her particularly, she returned to her hotel. After a magnificent farewell evening in Boston, in *La Dame aux Camélias*, she set out for New Haven, then Hartford, before crossing the frontier to Canada. On arriving at the hotel in New Haven, Sarah again encountered Henry Smith in the hall, with his fur cap in his hand. She was surprised. The man with the whale! What more could he want of her?

She found out very soon. An infernal noise of drums and trumpets drew everyone to the windows. She also looked out and was astounded to see an enormous carriage on which some ten Negroes, dressed as minstrels, were dancing and singing. The carriage was framed by large panels, crudely painted, showing Sarah Bernhardt standing on the whale, which was resisting, and pulling out one of its fins. Sandwichmen followed, bearing the following announcement:

"COME AND SEE the enormous cetacean, killed by SARAH BERNHARDT, who herself pulled out its fins, to be used as whalebones for her corsets, which are made exclusively by Madame Lily Noé, the famous corset maker of X Street, New York. Address all orders to Mr. Henry Smith, sole representative of Madame Lily Noé for the entire United States."

Other placards described the whale, its weight, its length, and the enormous quantity of salt with which it had been filled to preserve it during the journey, etc.

Sarah Bernhardt flew into an indescribable rage. As Henry Smith was there, blissfully delighted and possibly expecting congratulations, she gave him two terrific slaps with all her strength. Without flinching, the little man bowed low and left. A little later, on entering her room, Sarah Bernhardt found a superb basket of flowers, with Henry Smith's card and his "grateful homage."

She was furious and had the flowers taken away. But she was doomed to have many others taken away because, during her entire itinerary, in every hotel room she found a bouquet from Henry Smith —and in every town the whale, which covered almost the whole tour at the same time as Sarah! Seeing the immense celebrity of the French actress, the little man had immediately thought of using her name to "pep up" the exhibition through the entire country of the animal he had captured. And such was his invention! As a matter of fact, his idea turned out to be an excellent one. Everywhere, thanks to Sarah Bernhardt's packed houses, the whale also did very good business.

After Hartford, Sarah gave four performances at Montreal which ended on Christmas day. She played *Adrienne Lecouvreur, Froufrou, La Dame aux Camélias,* and *Hernani,* in that order. Having a public almost exclusively French, she had an unbelievable success. As a protest against the order of the Bishop who, after her first performance, had pronounced anathema against her and threatened to excommunicate her—likewise Scribe, the author of the play, who had been dead for nineteen years—the crowd gave Sarah an endless ovation. On the last night the horses of her sleigh were unharnessed and important citizens fought for the honor of dragging it themselves and taking her back in triumph to her hotel.

After one performance of *La Dame aux Camélias* at Springfield, Massachusetts, she gave five in Baltimore, where she and the company celebrated the New Year of 1881. Then she had a week in Philadelphia and two weeks in Chicago. In the latter place the Bishop, through the violence of his sermons, had given the French actress such a great advertisement that Sarah's manager wrote him this letter:

> Monseigneur:
>
> It is my custom when I come to your city to spend five hundred dollars on publicity. But, as you have done it for me, allow me to send you two hundred and fifty dollars for your poor.
>
> Henry Abbey.

The letter was published in some of the papers and further contributed to draw the crowd. After New York the tour in all the other towns of the United States definitely promised very well. Sarah would have been completely satisfied if only the abominable Smith, his whale, and his deafening publicity had not pursued her eternally, like a nightmare from which she thought she would never awake.

At St. Louis, where she played one week, from January 24 to 31, Sarah was surprised to discover there a sort of southern Montreal. Everybody spoke French. This town had been the capital of Louisiana, which, like Canada, was formerly a French possession. In short, here was a public which understood what was being performed and did not merely applaud on trust. She would have liked to remain at St. Louis during the last three months of her tour. But she had to go on: Cincinnati for three days; then New Orleans, where she had to give eight performances. At the end of the long journey between these two cities—two days and two nights—a dramatic incident occurred, a real movie episode. The story can be found in the American papers of February 7, 1881.

Continuous rain for several days had flooded the rivers and lakes in the entire region to such an extent that the bridge crossing the Bay of St. Louis, to the east of Lake Pontchartrain, over which Sarah Bernhardt's special train was to pass, reaching New Orleans two hours later, had been announced as likely to collapse at any moment under the furious pressure of water. The driver of the locomotive hesitated to cross. He had stopped the train in a little station some miles before arriving at the Bay of St. Louis, and he proposed to turn back. By a long detour the dangerous bridge could be avoided, but they would not be in New Orleans until the next day. This meant losing the night's receipts—which, according to the telegrams, promised to be considerable—and upsetting the program of all the plays arranged for this city. Abbey had returned to New York, leaving the management of the performances to Jarrett. The latter consulted Sarah, who, with her customary impetuosity, was immediately in favor of crossing "even so." Jarrett, for his part, had no opinion of his own. He was content to agree with his star. Negotiations then began between the impresario and the engineer, who agreed to attempt to cross—but on one condition. He had just been married and, before taking the risk, he demand the sum of twenty-five hundred dollars, which he would send at once by telegraph to his wife, who lived in Oklahoma. If he arrived safe and sound in New Orleans, he would return the money. Otherwise it would remain the property of his widow.

Delighted with his courage, Sarah gave him the amount at once. A quarter of an hour later, slowly at first, her train resumed the journey. It consisted of only three cars and the locomotive. The company was left in ignorance of what had happened. Only Madame Guérard and Jeanne Bernhardt, who was traveling in the same car as her sister, were aware of the facts. Gradually the train gathered momentum and, at a dizzying speed, rolled across the bridge, which shook under its weight.

It was only at that moment that Sarah realized how, on her own authority, she was risking the lives of thirty-two persons—all her actors, her staff, and the employees of Abbey. But it was too late to retreat. In two more minutes—which seemed to her like a century— literally bouncing along the tracks, the train reached the opposite shore. Almost instantaneously there was a tremendous crash, and an immense column of water gushed up and fell like a fountain. The bridge had collapsed!

More dead than alive, Sarah at last breathed freely and allowed the brave engineer to keep the twelve thousand five hundred francs which he had well deserved. For a long time, however, she was terribly remorseful for having dared to do such a thing. When an actor in the company spoke to her about his child, his wife, or his mother, whom he would be so happy to see again on his return to France, she felt herself turning pale and was seized with a dreadful retrospective terror. Suppose the train had not got across?

The week which she played in New Orleans was less successful because, at the same time as Sarah, the famous singer Emilie Ambre was also giving a series of performances. On the very evening when Sarah was playing *La Dame aux Camélias* she was singing *La Traviata*, the libretto of which is based on that play. The competition which they gave each other interfered with the financial success of the performances of both stars.

In Mobile, the next day, a single performance of *La Dame aux Camélias* began with a well-filled house, but it did not finish. The stage of the theater in this town was so small that once the supper table in the first act was placed within the set there was no room for the actors to sit at it. There were four more acts to be played under these conditions, including the fourth, at the club, which had a number of characters. At the slightest gesture they would collide and push one another about. The performance threatened to collapse in ridicule. Sarah felt this and, being already nervous, she had not the courage to show herself for a whole evening on these tiny boards. Therefore she decided to simulate a scene, to faint. The curtain had to be lowered and the ticket money returned. Jarrett was not pleased, but Sarah was able to go to bed early just for once.

This existence was becoming more and more tiring for her. Up to this time the tour had not noticeably deviated from the main line of the large cities; but now came the series of towns of second- or even third-rate importance, where the company remained only one day or, to be more correct, only a few hours. Leaving at night, after the performance, having spent ten or twelve hours on the train, sometimes more, Sarah would arrive in the next town between noon and six in the evening. She acted from eight o'clock until half past eleven and then set off again that night.

From time to time they did not leave until the following morning, but that was rare. They had to be on the safe side and take into account the delays unavoidable for a special train, which must often wait on a siding until the regular trains have passed. This daily timetable was hard on the company, which was less comfortably installed than the star; but, apart from Angelo, each actor actually played only minor parts and did not appear in all the plays. Sarah, however, had always to carry the weight and the responsibility for the performance. Besides, she was obliged to begin to study on the train *La Princesse Georges*, which she rehearsed from time to time, in one theater or another, before the evening performance, when they chanced not to arrive too late in the afternoon.

She performed in succession in Atlanta, Nashville, Memphis (where she was on February 18), Louisville, Columbus, Dayton, Indianapolis, St. Joseph (Missouri), Leavenworth, Quincy, Springfield (Illinois), Milwaukee, Detroit, Cleveland, Pittsburgh, Bradford (where she played on March 17), Toledo, Erie (where she took the time to visit Niagara Falls), Toronto, Buffalo, Rochester, Utica, Syracuse, Albany, Troy, and finally Boston—to which she returned, thus interrupting for a moment her frenzied race, four months after her first visit, giving a new series of six performances beginning on March 28. The last of these was *La Princesse Georges*, which was played for the first time and was received with the enthusiasm which henceforward was the rule for everything that Sarah Bernhardt performed.

Next came Worcester, Providence, Newark, and Washington—where she gave one performance of *Froufrou* and one of *La Dame aux Camélias*, on April 9 and 10. Finally, after a second visit to Baltimore and Philadelphia, Sarah returned to New York, where a short series of farewell performances took place. Beginning, of course, with *La Princesse Georges*, which was a "novelty," she closed on her last night with *La Dame aux Camélias*, which took place on May 3, 1881, and at the end of which, receiving ovations, covered with flowers, Sarah said good-by to her American public, which kept on shouting: "Come back again! Make it soon!"

The next day the newspapers recorded these unanimous wishes and joined in them. She was to grant them with pleasure and to return very often, for she made eight more tours in America. The next was in 1886–87 and the last during the World War, in 1916–17–18.

During her first journey to the United States and Canada, Sarah Bernhardt had given a hundred and fifty-six performances in a total of fifty-one towns during her stay of six months and a half on American soil. She had played *La Dame aux Camélias* sixty-five times, *Froufrou* forty-one times, *Adrienne Lecouvreur* seventeen times, *Hernani* thirteen times, *Le Sphinx* seven times, *Phèdre* six times, *La Princesse Georges* four times, and *L'Etrangère* three times. The average receipts for the whole tour had been thirty-eight hundred and seventy-six dollars a performance, or nineteen thousand, three hundred and eighty francs. Personally she had made one hundred and ninety-four thousand dollars net, or nine hundred and seventy thousand francs.

On May 5, accompanied to the pier by hundreds of people shouting "Long live Sarah! Bon Voyage!", she sailed for France on the steamer which had brought her in October, the *Amérique*, and reached Havre on May 17. The following day she was in Paris, where she thought she would reappear in some theater at the beginning of the following season; but she did not act again until nineteen months later, in December, 1882. The fact was that, during her absence, many things had happened which she was to learn with stupefaction, and many more were to happen which had most unexpected repercussions on her life and her career.

In Havre, with Maurice—who had grown much taller and whom she embraced most warmly—she found her intimate circle, under the care, as usual, of Georges Clairin and Louise Abbéma. In Paris, however, although the papers had announced her arrival—very quietly, it is true—the platform of the Saint Lazare station seemed deserted when her train arrived. Where was the enthusiastic crowd which, seven months previously, at the same station, had taken her to the train? Had the constant excitement ceased which her mere name aroused in theatrical circles? Had Paris forgotten those arguments, sometimes so passionate, which used to take place concerning her, and in which the violence of her adversaries was exceeded only by the burning ardor of her devotees?

In effect, that all seemed very distant. Officially, at least, Sarah no longer had even enemies. The latter had gradually transformed their hatred into pity and, affecting to be sorry for Sarah because of the acrobatic profession to which she was condemned by her perpetual money troubles, they had given accounts of her American tour which were not only uncomplimentary but pitiful. Her journey was described as a long disaster, both artistically and financially. In this way they had succeeded in turning public opinion away from her. She was no longer criticized; she no longer exasperated people. She had become a matter of indifference. In February, 1881, J. J. Weiss, a bitter polemicist but widely read, had written in *Le Figaro*:

"Poor Sarah Bernhardt! Poor passionate lover of fame! If she sinned by loving uproar too much, she has been well punished over there.

When she acts in *Phèdre*, in order to make the play tolerable for Americans, the orchestra plays the quadrilles from *La Belle Hélène* during the intermissions. Mademoiselle Sarah Bernhardt went to the United States to capture everything—hearts, applause, bouquets, and, especially, plenty of money. She imagined that the drawing rooms of New York and Washington would compete for the honor of receiving her. But in America they have not yet reached that lack of social discrimination which we have in Paris. Mademoiselle Sarah Bernhardt, humiliated and angry, has had to renounce her success in the drawing rooms as well as in the theater, where her noisily announced performances take place in half-filled auditoriums of people who do not understand them. It was for this pitiable result that she threw her contract as a *Sociétaire* of the Comédie Française in M. Perrin's face! Poor Sarah Bernhardt!"

Such was the perfidious cleverness of these articles. It was as much as to say to the people of Paris: "The Americans, whom Sarah preferred to you, are not as naïve as you are. They quickly recognized the mediocrity of this actress. Now that she returns to you, driven back to France by the disdain of the Yankees, I hope you will receive her with the coldness which her eagerness for money and her ingratitude deserve. The Parisian public is surely not going to prove less intelligent than that of the United States."

To remind the French of how intelligent they are is the surest way of making them do what one wants. Preached at cleverly, her once idolatrous public had easily succumbed to the idea of no longer caring about Sarah Bernhardt. Moreover, she had not acted in Paris for more than a year. Out of sight, out of mind—how true that is! Her successes in *Phèdre, Hernani,* and *Ruy Blas* were already fading from memory. When people spoke of her it was the right thing to reply, with an air of superiority: "Oh, no! She's through! She can't fool us again!"

It took Sarah only a few days to realize the profound change which had taken place in public opinion concerning her, and she immediately perceived its gravity. The more celebrated an actress is, the less she can afford to neglect the approval of the crowd. As soon as possible she would have to find an opportunity to conquer it again.

Before she left for the United States she had received a visit from Raymond Deslandes, one of the authors of *Un Mari qui lance sa Femme*—the play in which she had acted at the Gymnase in 1864 and which she had recklessly abandoned at the second performance. Des-

landes had since become manager of the Théâtre du Vaudeville. Needless to say, he had pardoned in the great actress the escapade of the
beginner and had offered her, on her return from America, a chance
to appear at the Vaudeville in a new play by Victorien Sardou, for
which the latter had an idea and which he proposed to write specially
for her during her absence.

At this time Sarah Bernhardt knew Sardou very slightly. He was
thirteen years older and, having had his first successes while quite
young, was already a well-established author before she even entered
the Odéon. All her life, even after their successes together, Sarah regarded Sardou with complete deference. She never addressed him
otherwise than as "dearest Master." She had unbounded admiration
both for his talent as a dramatist and for his knowledge as a director.

Shortly before she resigned, in February, 1880, Sardou had given
a new play to the Théâtre Français, *Daniel Rochat,* in which Delaunay
performed and in which Julia Bartet had created her first important
part at that theater. Just then Sarah had had several talks with him
when she met him in the theater, and they had met again, the night
before her departure, after her conversation with Raymond Deslandes.

While deploring, like many others, her break with the Comédie,
Sardou had confirmed the fact that he would be happy if she would
"come back" in the play which he had in mind for her, and for which
the Vaudeville seemed to him the ideal setting. Moreover, it was a
setting which he knew well; for since *Les Femmes Fortes,* in 1860, he
had had nine or ten plays produced there, including such successes as
La Famille Benoîton, L'Oncle Sam, Dora, and the famous *Rabagas.*

On her arrival in Paris, Sarah Bernhardt expected to hear from
Sardou and to receive a line or a visit from Deslandes. There was not
a move by either of them. This was getting serious. Resolutely she
then asked for an appointment with Sardou, who received her at once
and was very cordial but slightly embarrassed. Since their last meeting,
he said, he had been very busy, especially with the rehearsals of
Divorçons at the Palais Royal, which had been difficult. The play which
he wanted to write for Sarah was not "working out" as well as he had
hoped. . . . He had scarcely begun it. . . . He could not say exactly
when it would be ready. In short, without saying so frankly, he gave
her to understand that the realization of the project formed so
enthusiastically in October, 1880, seemed to have become rather prob-
lematical in May, 1881.

As for the reasons for this change of attitude, Sarah was too intelligent not to grasp them on the spot. The venomous campaign against her during her absence, the changed attitude of the public toward her, rendered her reappearance in a theater henceforth not only less desirable for the first author whom she interpreted but almost dangerous. Heaven knows what her reception would be! Sardou, who knew her very slightly, had never had her in any of his plays and did not care to involve himself in such a risky adventure, as he had as yet felt no particular friendship for her. Their conversation had lasted barely a quarter of an hour, by which time Sarah realized the effort she would have to make in order to re-establish a position which was not only compromised but almost ruined, at least in Paris.

Obviously it would have been easy for her to hire a theater and, on her own account, put on an immediate revival of some sort: *La Dame aux Camélias* or *Froufrou*. But this appeared too simple. Something better was needed; and she would have to force the great dramatist and Deslandes to keep their promises, both being so strangely pusillanimous. During her American tour she had become accustomed to the idea of playing this new piece of Sardou's at the Vaudeville. It was a project which appealed to her. Now that difficulties had arisen, she felt more strongly about it than ever! It was in this play and in no other, in this theater and in no other, that she would stage her "comeback" in Paris. It was merely a question of employing the necessary tactics.

In London, of course, the press had no reason to adopt toward her the same attitude as that of Paris, and it asked nothing better than to receive Sarah any time she wanted to act there. She had two plays, both ready and unperformed in England: *La Princesse Georges* and *La Dame aux Camélias*, above all. Without announcing it in the Paris papers, she left Calais with the company from America. She had made a contract with the Shaftesbury Theatre for a season of three weeks, beginning June 2, in the course of which she would give only those two plays. Her success was such that she extended her stay for eight more days. Having given *La Princesse Georges* for one week, she played *La Dame aux Camélias* twenty-four times in succession! This was her third season in London in three years, and each year her reception there was more enthusiastic.

Professional circles in Paris had been informed of this success, which seemed improbable in advance, and there was a certain skepticism. How could Sarah, who was considered "finished," be feted to such an extent by the English public? Clearly there must be a great deal of exaggeration on the part of those who related this success. The Paris press had remained silent concerning the performances in London. Decidedly this hostility persisted and would not be easy to overcome.

Not in the least upset, Sarah returned to Paris on June 30. There she learned that for the national holiday on July 14, in the evening after the free matinee, a great gala performance had been organized at the Opéra. Jules Grévy, the President of the Republic, would be present with Jules Ferry, the head of the government. That year not only the national holiday was being celebrated, but the tenth anniversary of July 14, 1871—the day which marked the liberation, immediately after the war, of the French territory which had been invaded for months by the German Armies. For that reason the celebration of July 14, 1881, assumed a particular importance.

The program included three acts of *Robert le Diable*—the opera of Meyerbeer, first performed in 1831, which had been successfully revived on its fiftieth anniversary—also interludes by several important artists of the Comédie Française and the boulevard theaters, and the *Marseillaise*, of course, which was to be recited by Agar—the statuesque tragedienne who, twelve years earlier, had acted in the first performance of *Le Passant*, at the Odéon with Sarah Bernhardt.

Agar was then almost fifty. Engaged by the Comédie Française at the beginning of 1870, she had left it in 1872 in order to go on several tours in Europe, had returned for a few months in 1877, had left again in 1878, and was to return, for the third time, in 1885. The reasons for these somewhat unusual comings and goings were not exclusively artistic. Still magnificently beautiful, Agar was, to express it in the style of Racine, "one of the preys to which Venus entire seemed most often attached." Her life consisted of one adventure after another, all ardent and passionate. At the time of *Le Passant* it was whispered that she had a very strong weakness for young François Coppée. If she left, not only the Théâtre Français, but also Paris, so frequently, it was generally to shelter her love of the moment in some corner of the world. In 1881 Agar felt an imperious emotion for a captain of dragoons, an officer garrisoned at Tours. Gossip of this had reached Sarah's ears, and immediately she decided on a plan.

The reader may perhaps not have forgotten Hortense, the kindly old companion of Agar, who, during the years when her employer and Sarah were colleagues at the Odéon, had conceived such a deep affection for the young actress of Zanetto and even then praised her golden voice. Sarah arranged one day to meet this excellent person without her mistress' knowledge, and had no difficulty in getting her to promise her necessary help.

Toward the end of the afternoon of July 14 Agar was resting at home, lying down in a little drawing room whose closed curtains protected her from the sun and the heat, when suddenly Hortense entered and, looking greatly disturbed, told her about someone she had just met. The orderly of the captain, of the man who was the tragedienne's only reason for existence, had arrived that morning posthaste in Paris to find a surgeon and bring him back on an urgent mission to his master in Tours, who had fallen from his horse. A fracture of the thigh was feared. In order not to frighten Agar, the officer had purposely forbidden anyone to tell her; and his orderly had warned Hortense to say nothing. But she did not feel that she had a right to be silent. She knew how much her mistress adored the captain. If his condition was more serious than they thought, if complications, which are always possible, should arise, she would never forgive herself for not having spoken.

Agar did not even give her time to finish. Half an hour later, having packed her bag in a hurry, she was in the train for Tours, after telling Hortense to go to the Opéra and immediately warn the organizers of the performance that night. Her sudden failure to appear, which might have been serious if she had been acting in a play, was not very important for the *Marseillaise*. Although the summer season had already caused many artists to leave for the country, there remained in Paris at least ten sufficiently important to recite the national anthem on this solemn occasion. Among these the managers of the Opéra could easily select a woman of talent who would be kind enough to replace Agar, so suddenly prevented from coming.

The reader will have guessed that Hortense did not notify anybody.

That evening, about a quarter past eleven, a few minutes before the end of the performance, while the managers were looking at their watches and becoming uneasy at Agar's unusual delay, Sarah Bernhardt suddenly appeared, wrapped in a large cape with a hood, in the wings of the Opéra.

The organizers of the evening, both the employees of the Opéra and those sent officially by the Ministry of Fine Arts, were astounded. Nobody had seen Sarah since her return; and she had not appeared on any stage in Paris for fifteen months, since the unfortunate revival of *L'Aventurière* at the Théâtre Français. Where had she come from and what was she doing there? As one of the artists who had undertaken to act in the interludes, Mounet Sully walked off the stage in evening dress—having just recited *L'Aigle du Casque*, by Victor Hugo.

"Good evening, Jean," Sarah said quietly, "would you mind holding my cloak?"

Having taken it off, she appeared in the classical costume which tragediennes wear when they recite the *Marseillaise* at an official ceremony: a long white gown; a sash in the three national colors, with loose ends; and on her head a black moiré cap, with wide wings like those of the Alsatian peasant women.

People looked at her in frightened astonishment. "What? . . . Is it you who . . ."

"Who what?" Sarah asked calmly.

"What about Madame Agar?" one of the managers asked.

"Oh, that's true; I was forgetting. She had to leave Paris an hour ago, having been called urgently to the bedside of a sick friend. She sends her apologies and has asked me to take her place. I need hardly say that I am very glad to do so."

Then she added, with a friendly smile: "I hope that nobody here will have any objection to my taking her place."

The entire administrative general staff of the evening looked at one another in perplexity. It was impossible not to close the performance with the *Marseillaise*. On the other hand, as everybody knew, Sarah Bernhardt had practically the whole of Paris against her. Was it not dangerous to allow her to go on the stage, especially in such circumstances? Suppose her presence, as was very possible, should arouse protest? A disturbance must be avoided that night at any price: the chief of State was in the stage box. In the neighboring boxes were members of the government, of the diplomatic corps; and from floor to ceiling of the immense auditorium, filled to overflowing, so many notable people had rarely been seen.

This was precisely what Sarah had anticipated, and was the reason why she had carefully chosen that night to face the public of Paris once more. She looked at Mounet Sully, who was disconcerted, and at the others, who were greatly disturbed, and burst into a rather nervous laugh.

"Don't put on such glum faces," she said to them. "I am risking much more than you, and you can see how calm I am!"

A few moments later, the orchestra having brilliantly begun the opening measures of the national anthem, the President of the Republic stood up, immediately followed by the entire house. Then, perfectly at ease, Sarah Bernhardt appeared with a flag in her hand, and slowly advanced to the middle of the stage.

The public, which was expecting to see Agar, had recognized her immediately, of course. At first there was a moment of stupefaction. Greatly excited, the entire audience whispered: "Sarah Bernhardt! Sarah Bernhardt!" The leader of the orchestra was taken aback and stared at her, forgetting to beat time. Then, out of respect for the President, the murmuring died down. Having voluntarily waited a few moments, during which a glacial silence reigned, Sarah Bernhardt, in a half whisper and an almost toneless voice, but with prodigious intenseness, slowly began to enunciate the simple and sublime verses:

> *Allons, enfants de la Patrie,*
> *Le jour de gloire est arrivé. . . .*

In an instant the three thousand members of the audience were seized with an indescribable emotion. Never had Sarah, merely by reciting a few lines which everybody knew by heart, burned with such a flame and conveyed such superhuman strength. When, for the last time, she repeated the refrain:

> *Aux armes, citoyens! . . .*

all the women wept and many men also wiped their eyes, while the entire audience was positively overcome. Finally, at the last words:

> *Qu'un sang impur abreuve nos sillons! . . .*

Sarah raised as high as possible the flag which she held in her right hand. It unfolded widely behind her and, with her two hands raised to heaven, she stood motionless, all in white, in front of the three French colors.

The enthusiasm was beyond description. The audience shouted: "Bravo! Sarah! Sarah!" Grévy himself, extremely moved, did not stop applauding and recalling her. In the front row of the theater Gambetta, wiping his brow, actually yelled his admiration. As the shouts did not cease, she had to repeat the *Marseillaise* from beginning to end a second time and, as she put even more emotion into it, there was such bedlam that she was compelled to recite it a third time. Then the curtain fell.

After that there was really a kind of delirium. All over the house people who did not know each other spoke to one another, their eyes red with tears, exchanging congratulations and embraces as if some great and happy event had just taken place. People were heard saying: "It's incredible! She is prodigious! I've never seen anything like it! She is the greatest of them all! I was sobbing! The most beautiful night of my life!" In a quarter of an hour Sarah Bernhardt had turned Paris around and had regained all her old popularity. On going into the wings she found the managers and officials, who were also weeping and blowing their noses violently.

She smiled: "Didn't I tell you that there was nothing to be alarmed about?"

A moment later hundreds of spectators, friends, and strangers left the auditorium, came through the iron door, and rolled like a sea of humanity toward the corner of the stage where she was seated. Some shook her hands; others embraced her; while still others stared at her, petrified, as if she were a supernatural being, some women kissing the hem of her gown!

In her life Sarah Bernhardt knew many triumphs, but she rarely had any of the same quality as this.

When she was told how her substitute in the *Marseillaise* had been received, Agar, who was very fond of Sarah, far from holding the trick against her, congratulated her, and also forgave Hortense without difficulty. First of all, she was too happy at having found her lover in perfect health at Tours; and she was almost equally pleased that her friend had been able, by such wit and with such self-confidence, to reconquer her position, the first place, which a handful of envious people had almost succeeded in making her lose so unjustly.

The next day and during the days following, the Paris newspapers could not avoid noting the extraordinary triumph which Sarah had won at the Opéra, in such an original and unexpected fashion. But she had resolved to take no more notice of the expressions of admiration aroused by her audacity than she had of the hateful prejudice displayed in the accounts of her journey to America and her performances of *La Dame aux Camélias* in London. Now she knew that, whenever she wanted to act again in Paris, so far from risking anything, she would be received with enthusiasm. Nothing else mattered. A few days later she went away to Sainte-Adresse, near Havre, where she had bought a chalet on the heights which had been fitted up during her stay in the United States. It was only five years later that she acquired at Belle Isle the fort mentioned in the first chapter, which became her first villa in that region.

In the quiet of the country, alone with her son and Madame Guérard, Sarah began to reflect and was suddenly seized with one of those fits of cold anger to which she was occasionally subject. So that was the Paris public, to which she had exclusively consecrated the first eighteen years of her career! Slowly and patiently she had mounted the steps which led her to the first place, having never had a failure in seven years except *L'Adventurière*—which was the mistake of an evening. On the contrary, having accumulated successes such as no other actress in that city had achieved, she had seen herself denied, forgotten, and almost despised, solely because a perfidious press had cleverly exploited her absence. After that, this same ungrateful Paris public, merely because she had known how to recite the *Marseillaise*, was making an idol of her again and loudly demanding her immediate return!

Well, no! These people did not deserve her! Paris did not want her when she returned from America. She would go away again for a long time, and would not return until she saw fit. Not when people begged her to, but at her own convenience! This sudden decision revealed again the stubborn nature, easily irritated and violently masterful, of Sarah Bernhardt, who, during the following weeks, prepared the itinerary of a grand tour of Europe.

It must be added that she had been warmly encouraged in this project by an actor of a certain talent, endowed—needless to say—with a superb face, the veritable head of a Roman emperor. His name was Philippe Garnier, and he had at the time, and particularly three years later, such an influence on Sarah that it is doubtful whether she never felt more for him than a cordial friendship. Cleverly using her resentment against Paris, it was he who persuaded her to exploit more widely the repertory, now well developed, which she had built up for herself and to make use of all these plays which, without almost any rehearsing, she could take and play everywhere, with the company she had in America—strengthening it, when necessary, with one or two good actors, including, of course, Garnier himself!

The day after the night of July 14 the extraordinary details were relayed to Raymond Deslandes, who immediately realized the mistake he had made by not seeing Sarah Bernhardt on her return to Paris. Sardou also was only too willing to repair what he recognized as a great mistake on his part. But it would have been a greater mistake to take the train to Havre and descend upon Sarah, three days after her triumph at the Opéra. The famous dramatist and the manager of the Vaudeville, therefore, decided to wait until she was back in Paris, which would be about the end of August. If another management made any offers to Sarah Bernhardt meanwhile, they would be notified in time as news travels quickly in theatrical circles in Paris. The idea of a tour had not occurred to them. After an absence of more than a year, they did not imagine that Sarah would dare to leave again and would not profit immediately by the excitement— which was really enormous—aroused by her ingenious return in the *Marseillaise*.

It was, therefore, with complete confidence that Raymond Deslandes rang the bell at the house in the Avenue de Villiers on the morning of September 1. Sarah received him immediately, and he ingenuously announced that, during recent weeks, Victorien Sardou had been able to work more and better than he had expected, that his new play was finished, that he was delighted with it, and that its title was *Fédora*.

"It is a dramatic comedy, without elaborate scenery," added Deslandes, "with only fifteen characters and four very simple sets. Will you see Sardou tomorrow? He will read you the play. If you like it, and I have no doubt you will be enchanted by it, we can rehearse next week and open on October 10."

Suppressing her laughter, Sarah had allowed him to talk without interrupting, apparently taking the deepest interest in his story. When he had finished, she assumed an air of great sadness.

"What a pity you did not tell me all that six weeks earlier—say, sometime before July 14!" she added, with a faint smile.

"But why?"

"Because that is the time when I made all my arrangements for the coming season, and at present I am no longer free."

Deslandes started. "Have you signed a contract elsewhere?"

"Why, yes."

"With what theater?"

"Oh, about thirty! Particularly the Célestins, in Lyons, where we are opening on the twenty-second of this month."

"Are you going on tour again?"

"Until May of next year."

Deslandes turned pale. "A whole year?"

"Not exactly, but it might be more! You never can tell. This being understood, I shall be delighted to hear Sardou's play. Tomorrow; whatever time suits him will suit me."

A dramatist and a director of genius, Sardou also read extraordinarily well—playing all the parts, living his play rather than reading it. When he had finished, Sarah was greatly tempted by the admirable role of Fédora in a play which could not fail to be a hit; and she had a good mind to send her tour to the devil. But her pride was stronger. She was quite willing to pardon Sardou and Deslandes for having doubted her, but on condition that they awaited her pleasure. They really deserved this little lesson.

When the reading was over, Deslandes rejoined them and insisted on beginning rehearsals at once. Sarah did not yield.

Then, thinking he had a master stroke, he said to her: "Well, I will convince you. Postpone your tour. Let us do Fédora at once, and I offer you one thousand francs for each performance. There is a guarantee of a hundred performances; and half the money will be paid in advance, if you so desire."

This was a considerable offer, for then no boulevard star was paid more than three hundred or, at most, four hundred francs a day. Sarah smiled sweetly.

"I am very sorry on your account, my dear Deslandes, and especially on yours, my dear Master," she added, looking at Sardou, "but, in spite of all my desire to play in this admirable piece, I could not be at your disposal before October, 1882. As for the terms, I suppose that my dear Deslandes was joking?"

"How do you mean?" said Deslandes in astonishment.

"When the house is full, the Théâtre du Vaudeville can take in eight thousand francs. I will never act there for less than fifteen hundred francs a performance, plus one quarter of the profits."

"Fifty thousand francs a month!" Deslandes and Sardou looked at each other.

She continued, still smiling: "I hasten to add that if this amount seems to you too much, and if it is impossible for you to wait for me, I shall not hold it against you in any way if you put somebody else into the play. I should be heartbroken on my own account, but I should find it perfectly legitimate."

Sardou grumbled: "Someone else? As if you did not know that only you can play Fédora."

"You are far too kind, my dear Master," said Sarah modestly, having the time of her life. "I shall be happy and proud to rehearse under your direction . . . next year."

What else could they do? Wait for Sarah and postpone *Fédora*. That was what they did. Having always two or three plays ready, or almost ready, Sardou quickly finished a comedy called *Odette*, which was put on at the Vaudeville in November, 1881, with Réjane, Blanche Pierson, Maria Legault, Adolphe Dupuis, and Pierre Berton, and was, moreover, a brilliant success.

Meanwhile Sarah was preparing her tour of Europe, which, after Lyons and the south of France, included Italy, Greece, Hungary, Austria, Sweden, Norway, Denmark, England, Spain, Portugal, Switzerland, Belgium, and Holland. It was during the final rehearsals for this tour, about the middle of September, 1881, that Sarah Bernhardt, to her great misfortune, made the acquaintance of a man who, for many years, was to occupy such an important place in her life: Jacques Damala. And it was her sister Jeanne, most unhappily inspired that day, who introduced him to her.

It will be recalled that for some years Jeanne Bernhardt had been a terrible morphine addict. She had already taken five or six cures but always returned to her vice, which aroused a morbid horror in Sarah. One day while *La Dame aux Camélias* was running in London, seeing Jeanne more livid than usual, with glassy eyes and thick speech, Sarah was suddenly filled with furious anger. She locked the door; seized a whip and flogged her sister, who vainly begged for mercy. But neither reprimands nor prayers nor arguments could cure her. Nine out of ten addicts are incurable. Without exception they all seek one another out, recognize one another, attract one another, and get together. Through her sister and especially through her husband, Sarah Bernhardt suffered so much from morphine addicts that she knew them well and often spoke of them with disgust.

She used to say: "It is the same with addicts as with homosexuals, Lesbians, smokers of opium, and all other human beings tainted with any vice. Conscious of their degradation, they find a sort of excuse in the fact that they are not alone in being affected. That is why they not only always look for people like themselves but also try to make converts. A Lesbian always surrounds herself with other Lesbians, even if she has no intimate relations with them. The number and the constant society of her own sort finally give her a feeling that she is not so very abnormal, since so many others suffer from the same perversion. Drug addicts act in exactly the same way. They can almost recognize one another at the first glance. There exists among them a kind of freemasonry, of tacit complicity, of instantaneous loyalty, even toward someone unknown, the very moment that he proves to be one of themselves."

In effect, all over the world, there are mysterious little circles where morphine and cocaine addicts meet; help one another; get false prescriptions; suggest complaisant doctors who sign them for a low fee, and pharmacists who deliver forbidden doses without difficulty. It was under these conditions that Jeanne Bernhardt had made the acquaintance of Jacques Damala, like herself an inveterate morphine addict and—a frequent result of this vice—a completely amoral man, whose cynicism was unequaled and who was capable of the lowest forms of depravity.

A Greek by birth, but speaking almost impeccable French, Damala was connected with the Greek Legation in Paris. He was then thirty-four years old, three years younger than Sarah, and even his name must have been unknown to her, because he frequented principally diplomatic circles and lived as far as possible from the theater and life backstage. But his scandalous adventures were known and discussed everywhere. Two women of the best society had got divorces on his account, and another had committed suicide because Damala had broken with her. Gradually he had become a kind of hero in a perverted novel. When his name arose, Casanova, Lovelace, the Duc de Richelieu, and the Marquis de Sade invariably occurred to the journalists writing about him.

That year his scandalous exploits had finally moved official circles. The Ministry of Foreign Affairs had discreetly asked the Greek Legation to transfer, if possible, this too-famous attaché, who was decidedly a threat to domestic security. The government of the Hellenes had deferred to the wishes of the French government, and Damala had just been appointed to Saint Petersburg. He was to join his new post on October 1 and was perfectly willing to accept this change of residence. Why should the Russian women be more insensible to his charms than the Parisians?

His repeated successes were understandable. Almost as handsome as Mounet Sully, Damala was tall and perfectly built. He had regular features; a pointed, light brown beard; and very long and very thick eyelashes which gave a sort of disturbing softness to his somber glances, which bowled women over. But, while their features were alike, how these two men differed in their expressions! Mounet had a frank look, a noble air, and was loyal above all things, with a loyalty which was almost naïve it was so strict; he at once gave an impression of absolute honesty. Oriental, feline, his eyes always hidden beneath his eyelashes, Damala was inevitably bound to inspire mistrust in those women whom he did not immediately conquer.

One day, at the end of a rehearsal in the studio of Sarah Bernhardt's house, this handsome Greek had come to fetch Jeanne and was waiting for her outside in the Avenue de Villiers. As she was kissing her sister before she went downstairs, Sarah asked her whom she was going to meet in such a hurry. Jeanne mentioned Damala.

Sarah smiled. "Ah, the famous lady's man! It would be amusing to see him. Ask him up for ten minutes."

Damala entered, perfectly at his ease, in no way impressed by the famous artist whom he was meeting for the first time. He treated her politely, like any other woman, but with complete detachment, in which there was almost a note of condescension. However, her approaching tour interested him. He told her that in his youth he also had wanted to be an actor, but his family was against it and had compelled him to enter the diplomatic service. Since then he occasionally played in amateur performances, and that rather amused him.

"So you're not sorry that you gave up the theater?" Sarah asked.

"I never regret anything," replied Damala indifferently. "It is all the same to me what I do."

"Nothing interests you?"

"Nothing particularly."

"You're not in love with anybody?"

"Oh, Heavens, no!"

"Wouldn't you like to fall in love someday, just to see what it's like?"

"To see what?"

"Whether it is pleasant."

After reflecting, he said: "That does not tempt me very much."

The type is obvious. Extremely bored, condescendingly polite, he would certainly have irritated Sarah extremely if he had not been so handsome. But he was handsome, that could not be denied. He looked like Apollo in person, this Greek with the long eyelashes. And he made a profound impression on Sarah Bernhardt. For fifteen years no man had ever disturbed her to such an extent. Did she see him again before she went on tour?

That is probable, for it certainly was not at this first meeting that he said: "I see that your itinerary will take you to Scandinavia. Why not come on as far as Saint Petersburg? In the first place, you would probably make a great hit. And, secondly," he added nonchalantly, "such a move would touch me. It would show that you wanted to see me again."

Sarah was dumfounded. No man had ever spoken to her in such tones. Men begged for the favor of coming to tea or having dinner with her. All those who loved her immediately became her slaves. Every day her letters contained frantic declarations, which she ran over with indifference or even threw into the waste-paper basket without reading them. Only Damala dared to assume such an attitude! He was suggesting to *her* that she should behave in such a way that he might eventually be touched by it! This was outrageous! Alas, this very impudence intensified the interest which Sarah already felt in Damala. She was extremely nervous, excessively irritable, complaining of everything and finding fault with everyone, when she left Paris to begin her long tour, with a week at Lyons, at the Théâtre des Célestins, and another week in Marseilles, at the Gymnase.

Early in October she was in Italy, beginning with Genoa. There she opened in *La Dame aux Camélias*, which was henceforward the play in which she performed first in every city. On the second day she had a real nervous attack which shook her with convulsive tremors for hours, so that she could not play and the money had to be returned to the public. Doctors were called who prescribed a few days' rest, but that was not the remedy. It was only when, in reply to long telegrams sent to Russia, she received the assurance that a theater in Saint Petersburg would be at her disposal on the dates she wished that suddenly, after three days in bed, her health revived and the tour could continue.

The last part of her itinerary was instantly changed by telegram. London, Lisbon, Madrid, Barcelona, Geneva, Lausanne, Brussels, Amsterdam, and the Hague, where she was to play in succession from March until the end of May, were postponed from April to the end of June. She was to be in Copenhagen from February 20 to 24, and she kept to this. For the twenty-eighth she made an agreement for a performance at Reval in Estonia, a normal stage on the way to Saint Petersburg—where she had an engagement to play during the entire month of March, 1882. Ten contracts with different theaters had to be canceled, solely in order to enable her to meet Jacques Damala again. Philippe Garnier, who did not know, of course, the reasons for this upheaval, could not make head or tail of it.

"Why this insistence on playing in Saint Petersburg?" he naïvely repeated. "The journey is so long and so expensive for twenty people. Admittedly, the receipts will be good. But will they even cover the enormous cost of traveling?"

Sarah, who was now satisfied, smiled. "Don't worry. I am certain that I shall be very happy in Saint Petersburg."

As a matter of fact, she was; but not for very long. What tears, what deceptions, what rages and humiliations, were to follow a few months of illusory happiness!

CHAPTER VI

Marriage, Rupture, Apotheosis

TO FOLLOW, city by city, this first tour of Sarah Bernhardt's across Europe would be interminable, perhaps monotonous, and would consist of little more than a repetition of the successes which she had already achieved in England and the United States. If, since 1876 and, especially, 1879, her fame had spread to the New World, with all the more reason it had reached every part of the European Continent. Consequently, almost everywhere she met with the same triumphant reception; the same packed houses, where the seats had brought exorbitant prices. In every country magnificent receptions were given in her honor; all the literary and political celebrities made it a point of being present at her opening nights; and usually she was asked to give a private performance at the palace of the reigning sovereign, who proved his gratitude and admiration by giving her a magnificent present.

The souvenirs which she brought back from her various tours all over the world were innumerable. In the Boulevard Péreire I have often seen lying in disorder in the drawers of some piece of furniture in her office the diamond brooch from King Alfonso XII of Spain; the necklace of cameos which the Emperor Franz Josef himself placed around her neck, after a performance of *Phèdre*; the fan from King Umberto of Italy, a magnificent water color on parchment representing an evening dance on the terrace of a palace in Venice at the time of the Doges; and how many other marvels! Toward the end of her life, unfortunately, many of these presents were no longer in her possession. After one play, whose sets and costumes had been expensive and whose receipts proved insufficient, Sarah had to sell, at any price, treasures priceless not only because of their value but also because of the triumphant occasions which they represented to her.

In January, 1882, when she arrived in Vienna, the Archduke Friedrich placed at her disposal, for the length of her stay, one of his palaces, "not wishing to see a queen living in a hotel." While she was playing in Copenhagen, King Christian IX invited her on his yacht in order himself to show her over Elsinore, Hamlet's grave, and the castle of Marienlyst. Then, at the end of her farewell performance, he summoned her to his box and, in the presence of the entire audience, decorated her with the Danish Order of Merit.

When she was about forty, Sarah Bernhardt was already a Commander or a Grand Cross of all the National Orders of every country in the world. Incredible as it may seem, France alone waited until January, 1914, to make her a Knight of the Legion of Honor, when she was sixty-nine. At her death she was only an Officer, the second rank of the French National Order. In our time certain women considerably less famous received greater honors when they were very much younger. One could mention an eminent novelist, whose prestige is not comparable to that of Sarah Bernhardt, who was made a Knight at forty-eight and Commander at sixty.

It was at Saint Petersburg that the success of Sarah Bernhardt assumed the most considerable proportions. At that time and until 1914, the entire aristocracy and high society of Russia spoke faultless French. It may also be noted—all artists have experienced it—that the Northern peoples are much more enthusiastic and demonstrative than those of the South. England and Scandinavia, for example, produce theater audiences which are incomparably more receptive and whose demonstrations of feeling are ten times more clamorous than those of an Italian, Spanish, or Algerian audience. There is no explaining this fact, but it is incontestable.

Russia gave Sarah a grandiose reception. For hours every day the crowd waited for her to come out of her hotel in order to acclaim her. Every evening on her arrival at the theater a large red carpet was quickly unrolled on the sidewalk, so that she would not have to step in the snow when she got out of her sleigh. Special trains from Moscow had been arranged to enable the inhabitants of that city to come and see her performances. The grand dukes and all the members of the imperial family came daily to the theater, where all the nobility and the most illustrious people in Saint Petersburg crowded.

Twice she was commanded to appear at the Winter Palace, the residence of the Czar—in whose presence she played, first, *Le Passant* and the death scene in *Adrienne Lecouvreur*, then two acts of *Phèdre*. The night she was presented to Alexander III, whom she had deeply moved, he stopped her hastily as she bowed and, in the presence of the court, said to her: "No, Madame. It is for me to bow to you!"

How and in what circumstances exactly, six months after their few meetings in Paris, did the first encounter of Sarah Bernhardt and Jacques Damala take place in Saint Petersburg? The details are of little importance. What is certain is that three days after her arrival the handsome Greek and Sarah were inseparable. She was radiant, and accepted no invitation unless he was also invited. Without him she would go only to purely official affairs, where the procedure and etiquette of the occasion did not decently permit her to make such a request.

Their liaison was soon the talk of Saint Petersburg, and already in every circle people judged more or less severely the rather shocking lack of restraint of the great artist. Suddenly a sensational piece of news circulated in the city. Jacques Damala had resigned from the Greek Legation and had been engaged as an actor by Sarah Bernhardt. Being now a member of her company, he would play the part of Sartorys with her in *Froufrou*, the following Tuesday! This startling news was followed by something which went unnoticed by the public but which constituted quite an event in Sarah's company: Philippe Garnier, giving bronchitis as his excuse, was leaving the tour and returning in dignity to Paris. Sarah had freed him from the end of his engagement on friendly terms.

This romantic adventure at once increased the curiosity of the crowd tenfold. During his five months' stay in Saint Petersburg, Damala had had time to be introduced into the best Russian society and to break absent-mindedly a few hearts. There was enough to arouse endless commentary in the fact that this handsome diplomat had suddenly become an actor, abandoning his post to follow the great actress and to be her partner for the rest of her tour.

In the absence of exact reports on the subject, it is easy to imagine what the debuts of Damala in Saint Petersburg were like. Although he had often played in comedy as an amateur, he obviously lacked professional skill and, in spite of the efforts of Sarah, who taught him his parts with tireless patience and care, he was certainly not equal to his task. More than madly in love with the handsome Greek, she soon wanted to have him as her partner in all her plays. Not satisfied with giving him, one by one, all the roles of Philippe Garnier, she gradually took away from poor Angelo some of the parts which he filled more than adequately. She even made Damala play Armand Duval in *La Dame aux Camélias*—and Hernani! In this latter part, which is difficult and very long and which demands style, first of all, as well as an actor who knows how to speak verse, Damala proved particularly inadequate. But, far from admitting this, Sarah Bernhardt thought him admirable and predicted for him a wonderful career as an actor. Love rendered her more blind than any other woman. However, she did not dare to have him play Hippolyte in *Phèdre*, but that was probably only because Damala's memory was not capable of the effort of learning so many plays in so short a time.

As far as Sarah Bernhardt is concerned, the reasons for this rash move are evident. During the beginning of her tour, she had feverishly waited for the day when she would finally see Damala again. Over and over again she wondered how he would receive her, whether he would even come to see her, whether she would not find him in love with another woman or, at least, yielding to the unfamiliar charms of some Russian princess. After this long period of anxiety, when she had seen him and he had finally consented to crown her passion, she was filled with such a feeling of joy and triumph that her only idea was to attach this man to herself, first, professionally and soon, alas, legally.

But what prompted him, who had never felt the slightest sentiment for Sarah any more than for any other woman? Was he dazzled by her success and tempted by the satisfaction of appearing in everybody's eyes as the happy conqueror of the woman about whom all Saint Petersburg was talking? Or, more prosaically, did the enormous receipts which she earned everywhere she acted open up to him the perspective of living henceforth a luxurious existence, of which she alone would bear the expense? In spite of appearances, this latter hypothesis can be dismissed. Not that Damala was disinterested; but even in Saint Petersburg he could have chosen any mistress he liked, richer than Sarah Bernhardt and equally generous. What is more probable is that this sudden turn of the steering wheel of his existence appealed to the Oriental adventurer in him. It was something different, something new, something unforseen, something picturesque. Perhaps he also liked the thought that, in this way, he could soon return to Paris, which he had been discreetly asked to leave as an attaché and from which he could no longer be sent away if he reappeared as an actor protected by Sarah Bernhardt.

After a month of triumph, culminating in an apotheosis, Sarah left Saint Petersburg on March 30. Taking her train by assault, some fifty enthusiasts accompanied her as far as the frontier. She had to promise to return very soon and very often; and then she set off directly for London, where she opened on April 2. On April 4, 1882, at the church of Saint Andrews in Wells Street, she committed the gravest mistake of her life: Sarah Bernhardt married Jacques Damala.

When the news reached Paris there was general consternation; and also in London among her company, all of whom adored Sarah. People knew the frightful reputation of the young Greek diplomat, whose conduct with women was ignobly notorious. Above all, many knew what Sarah was still ignorant of because, during their stay in Saint Petersburg and despite their intimacy, he had succeeded in concealing it from her: that he was a formidable morphine addict, so far advanced that he was practically incurable.

But what could her actors and her friends do? Sarah was transfigured, and gave such an impression of desperate happiness and radiant pride! Nobody would have dared to risk the slightest observation—not even Jeanne Bernhardt, who knew the defects of Damala better than anybody. Out of affection for her sister she had, indeed, thought of warning her, of telling her to be careful; but she was restrained by that complicity which exists between morphine addicts. They always stand by each other. Possibly she also feared the vengeance of the Greek, who was said to be brutal and hot-tempered. In short, she said nothing and made the best of it, like the others, congratulating the young couple.

This was Sarah Bernhardt's fourth season in London in four years and, to vary her repertory, she played *L'Aventurière*, by Emile Augier. Now she had had the time to build up the part of Doña Clorinde, which she had mastered so imperfectly when she played it at the Théâtre Français. The English press thought her so magnificent that Francisque Sarcey made the journey especially to see it. He took advantage of the opportunity also to see a performance of *Adrienne Lecouvreur*, which she had not yet played in Paris. On his return he devoted an entire article to her in *Le Temps*, concluding with these words:

"She is unique and no one will ever take her place. What an irreparable loss for the Comédie Française!"

This was the theme which he repeated every time he spoke of
Sarah Bernhardt.

After Portugal, Spain, and Switzerland, Sarah passed through Paris,
stopping a few days, before finishing her tour in Holland and Belgium. She was asked if she would be willing to assist at a gala performance, organized at the Théâtre de la Gaîté, for the benefit of the
widow of the well-known painter-decorator Chéret. She accepted and,
as a play, proposed *La Dame aux Camélias*, with Damala in the part
of Armand Duval. This would be the first time in Paris that she played
in this work of Dumas *fils*, which she had been performing everywhere
else for nearly two years. And she was going to appear in it with the
man who had been her husband for six weeks! This was something
to arouse the curiosity of the public! At the first announcement of
this performance the box office of the Gaîté was absolutely invaded.
This unique performance took place on May 25, 1882.

Supporting Sarah Bernhardt, who was at last giving Paris an opportunity of applauding her as Marguerite Gautier, the cast included
Jeanne Bernhardt as Nichette; Mesdames Laurence Grivot, Angèle,
de Cléry, Depoix, Sydney; Messieurs Jacques Damala as Armand,
Dumaine as Duval *père*, Dieudonné, Cooper, Romain, Joumard. To
make the program more exciting, Saint-Germain, the famous comedian, had agreed to resume for one evening the part of Saint-Gaudens,
which he had already played quite often in Paris.

On her appearance Sarah Bernhardt was greeted with prolonged
applause. From one act to another her incarnation of the famous
character of Marguerite filled the house with admiration. After
Madame Doche, who created the role in 1852, it had been played in
Paris in succession by Blanche Pierson and Aimée Tessandier. Personally all three of them had achieved only a moderate success. In
their day it was the play which "carried" the actor. With Sarah
Bernhardt it was quite different. In the third act, particularly, she rose
very far above the work, which that evening the public had the impression of really discovering. In the fifth act, where her slow agony
and death were realized with sovereign art, she almost reached the
sublime moments of the death of Phèdre. It was a triumph for her,
and she was repeatedly recalled.

Unfortunately, the "juvenile lead" was very far indeed from sharing this success. About him the press was cruel. As a typical example, this is what the critic of Le Rappel, Edmond Stoullig, said:

"Monsieur Jacques Damala was cast for the part of Armand. As may be imagined, the sight of Madame Sarah Bernhardt's husband was one of the great attractions of the evening. His entrance in the first act created a sensation. 'Damala! There he is!' Then the opera glasses were turned on the handsome fellow with the dark eyes, who had had the honor of being lovingly elected by the great artist to the high office of her husband in the eyes of the law. While Armand Duval conquered all hearts, from a physical point of view, the same could not be said from an artistic standpoint. His lack of experience was colossal; his voice so deep that it was indistinct, his speech was thick and handicapped by a very pronounced foreign accent, while his bearing was uniformly sad and frightened. In truth, this passionate lover appeared very cold and very awkward to us. In short, this 'exhibition' was not very fortunate. However, in the fourth act, which is almost entirely Armand's, Monsieur Damala had his little revenge. He struck a few moving and sincere notes. If he works very hard, he may possibly become an actor. He certainly has with him a teacher whose lessons should be helpful to him."

On reading these articles, which were all about the same, Sarah Bernhardt shrugged her shoulders.

"They were just as severe on me when I began," she said to her husband. "That made no difference, as you can see. Consequently, don't let it discourage you."

By a curious aberration she had and always retained a complete admiration for Damala the actor. At the end of her life, while sadly admitting all his defects and vices, she persisted in believing that "he might have been an actor of genius," in which belief she was alone.

At the time, in Madrid, when she agreed to give this performance at the Gaîté, Sarah wrote to Victorien Sardou and Raymond Deslandes to be sure to come and see her. She did not conceal the reason. The leading man's part, Loris Ipanoff, in Fédora, the play in which she was to open at the Vaudeville on her return, was a great lover, for whom she thought Damala was the ideal interpreter. She did not doubt that, having seen him in La Dame aux Camélias, both Sardou and Deslandes would be of the same opinion. She set out for Amsterdam on the twenty-seventh.

The night before she had seen Sardou, who said evasively: "Very good . . . a handsome fellow . . . interesting. . . . Let us talk about that when you get back."

These few words were sufficient to make her believe that Damala had been accepted, and she announced to him triumphantly that he would open with her in *Fédora*.

At the beginning of July, when she definitely returned, explanations became necessary. As skillfully and considerately as possible, Sardou gave her to understand that it would be doing a poor service to Damala to have him open in Paris in the principal part of a new play. The professional actors over whose heads he would thus be promoted would not pardon him for this sudden piece of luck. Incited by them, the press would be merciless; and the play would suffer. For her own sake did Sarah not think she should be more circumspect? After fourteen years at the Odéon and the Théâtre Français, *Fédora* was the first play in which she was going to perform on the boulevards; and it would mark her return to Paris after a long absence. She would be eagerly expected and should be careful to have all the trumps in her hand, particularly by making sure of a partner who was a well-known actor and popular with the Parisian public.

She insisted, entreated, and threatened not to play herself if her husband was not given the part of Loris. Sardou would not be swayed; she had to give in. At the bottom her heart, while thinking Damala remarkable, she had to admit that the author of *Fédora* was right. But how could she announce this to Jacques without annoying him? After only three months of marriage she had already observed that he was excitable, easily irritated, and perhaps capable of violence.

She then secretly began a feverish search for a play for him—one with a very fine man's part, whose author would be willing to entrust it to Damala. After having approached in vain several different writers, she turned to Catulle Mendès, a poet, dramatist, and critic, who was almost a contemporary of Sarah's and had been her friend for years. Among his manuscripts he had a dramatic comedy entitled *Les Mères Ennemies*, with a powerful central situation and a superb leading male character. As a favor to Sarah he consented to give her this play for Damala, on condition, of course, that she found a manager who would accept the play and the interpreter.

That evening, on her return home, Sarah Bernhardt waved a manuscript and said to her husband: "Jacques, darling, I have something marvelous for you, the finest present I could possibly make you."

"What could that be?" Damala asked quietly.

"A play by Mendès, a masterpiece, with the most marvelous part for you ever written for an actor."

"Really?"

"It is quite simple. Since I read *Les Mères Ennemies*, I have been wondering whether you should not play that rather than *Fédora*. Sardou will be heartbroken; he wants you so much. But you can imagine your success means more to me than his. Please read it, and tell me what you think of it."

Damala read the manuscript and agreed that it was a fine play and the part was magnificent. But he could not make up his mind. To act at the Vaudeville, a very important theater, in a new play by such a master as Sardou, with Sarah Bernhardt in all the splendor of her glory, seemed to him such a certain success in advance.

"No doubt," Sarah agreed. "But, in a play with me, you will always come second." Then she added, as if to excuse herself: "I have been in the theater for so many years, whereas in the play of Mendès you will come first—you alone. You cannot help having the success of the evening."

Being vain, in addition to everything else, Damala allowed himself to be convinced by this argument. Now it remained to have the play accepted. This might involve long and perhaps disappointing negotiations. Therefore—to such follies could she be driven by love!—Sarah leased a theater on her own, solely in order that Damala should perform. Having heard that the Ambigu, which was then in the hands of a man named Chabrillat, was not doing very well, and that the manager might lease it on favorable conditions, she got in touch with him and acquired a lease on the theater at the end of July.

Nowadays this would seem to be an undertaking of slight dimensions. For some years theaters have been hired by the season, for six months, or even for the run of the play. In 1882 that was not the case. Theaters could be had only on a very long lease—ten or fifteen years, at least—and often there was a clause forbidding the tenant to sublease. It was in such circumstances that Sarah Bernhardt became manager of the Théâtre de l'Ambigu, where she never played herself and where she was to lose a small fortune in a few months.

She did not take the theater under her own name, but under that of her son. The news astonished the professionals. As Maurice Bernhardt was then seventeen and a half years old, how could Sarah entrust the destinies of a theater to him so early and, above all, why?

Because Maurice had accepted his mother's marriage with chagrin and almost with sorrow. Up to that time she had lived with him alone, lavishing her tenderness and all kinds of attention on him. As we know, she had a feeling of real adoration for her son which she preserved, intact and passionate, till her death. Since their marriage Damala had installed himself in the house in the Avenue de Villiers, where he reigned as master. Maurice suffered from both his presence and the obvious love which his mother had for Damala. In a word, it was more or less to soothe Maurice, to make him forgive her marriage, and also in order to try and render his relations with his stepfather more cordial, as he was now to be the latter's manager, that Sarah set up this youth in the manager's office of the Ambigu.

In reality, she handed over the practical administration to a shrewd and competent business manager, Auguste Simon, whose name appeared with her son's on the playbills and programs. Of course, it was she alone, in the background, who remained the real mistress of the undertaking. Having paid one hundred thousand francs to Chabrillat for the business and good will, Sarah Bernhardt began by redecorating the theater, which cost her another hundred thousand francs. By the end of August rehearsals might have begun, but the opening of *Fédora* at the Vaudeville would not take place until some time in December. It was, therefore, necessary that the play of Mendès should not be presented before November at the earliest. The sole purpose of this arrangement, planned only to protect the *amour-propre* of Damala, was to keep him at the Ambigu during Sardou's play, and not before it, in order to be able to say: "It is not Sardou who did not want him in *Fédora*. It is Damala who was not free."

To gain time a revival of *Cartouche*, a melodrama by d'Ennery, first performed in 1858, opened the doors of the brand-new Ambigu, on September 9, 1882, "under the management of Maurice Bernhardt and Auguste Simon." Not thinking that there was any use in going to much expense for this stopgap performance, Sarah had got together only a very mediocre company which did not include more than two good actors—Paul Deshayes and Cooper. As might have been expected, the receipts were no better than the actors. For sixty-five performances the revival of *Cartouche* cost Sarah Bernhardt something more than fifty thousand francs.

At last, on November 17, the first performance of *Les Mères Ennemies* took place. Supporting Damala, the principal parts were played by Agar, who had become completely Sarah's friend since the *Marseillaise;* Antonine, who played the other mother; and Paul Deshayes. It was a success; nothing extraordinary, but a success. The play, which was well constructed and full of pathos, was perfectly at home at the Ambigu, and Damala, whom Sarah compelled to work desperately, was applauded and considered superior to what he had been in *La Dame aux Camélias.* The handsome Greek was delighted and Sarah was full of hope. Would those scenes which were already making her married life so difficult possibly become less frequent?

As a matter of fact, she had now discovered why Damala was sometimes so touchy, so strange, or so silent, remaining depressed for hours. Having often seen Jeanne in a similar condition, Sarah realized that her husband was a victim of the same vice as her sister; and he had confessed as much. She then courageously undertook to cure him, locking up his poison and giving him only small doses, which she gradually decreased every day. But to cure a drug addict is a superhuman task, demanding the constant attention and presence of whoever undertakes it. As soon as his nurse goes away, a morphine addict always finds a way of getting the drug. Obviously Sarah's kind of life did not permit her to watch over Damala day and night. There was nothing for her to do but resign herself, to hope against hope, to pray that his success in the theater would gradually turn him away from his vice. After the opening of *Les Mères Ennemies,* she thought that perhaps this happy experience would arouse his ambition to recover his health.

On December 11, at the Vaudeville, *Fédora* opened. It was not only a success but a triumph, almost an event. Not only did the return of Sarah Bernhardt, who had not played in Paris—at least in regular performances—for two years and eight months, arouse wild curiosity, but also, after so many previous masterpieces, Sardou had produced in *Fédora* one of the most gripping and most admirable dramas he ever wrote. From beginning to end of the four acts, the rapid and exciting action concerning a Nihilist plot, which takes the participants from Saint Petersburg to Paris, held the public absolutely breathless. The dialogue, nervous, vivid, without long speeches or tirades, consisting entirely of short and sharp exchanges of dialogue, gave the situations an extraordinary intensity. At the end, the death of Fédora

Sarah Bernhardt in *Le Passant*
(*Odéon—1869*)

The Parisian Theatrical World in 1875

A Picture by Alfred Stevens

(By courtesy of the John and Mable Ringling Museum of Art, Sarasota, Florida)

From Left to Right: Edouard Lockroy, Ernest Reyer, Adrien Proust, Léon Cladel,
Georges Ohnet, Paul Hervieu, Henry Becque, Sully-Prudhomme, Jules Massenet,
Madame Adam, Henri Meilhac, Ludovic Halévy, Emile Augier, Francisque Sarcey,
Julia Bartet, Jules Lemaitre, Victorien Sardou, Sarah Bernhardt, Edouard Pailleron,
Jules Claretie, Suzanne Reichemberg, Georges Bizet, François Coppée, Edmond Got.

Sarah Bernhardt at the Comédie Française

A Picture by Jules Bastien-Lepage (1879)

Two Incidents of Sarah Bernhardt's First American Tour
Sarah Bernhardt on the back of the whale in Boston harbor (*December 1880*)

The collapse of the bridge over the bay of Saint-Louis, just after the crossing of the
"Bernhardt Special" (*February 1881*)

Sarah Bernhardt as *Théodora*
(*1884*)

Sarah Bernhardt in *La Dame aux Camélias*
(Around 1885)

Sarah Bernhardt and De Max in *Gismonda* (First Act)
(*1894*)

Sarah Bernhardt as *Phèdre*
(*1896*)

Sarah Bernhardt as *Hamlet*
(*1899*)

Sarah Bernhardt in *L'Aiglon* (First Act)
(*1900*)

Sarah Bernhardt and Coquelin Ainé in *Cyrano de Bergerac* (Third Act) (*New York, December 1900*)

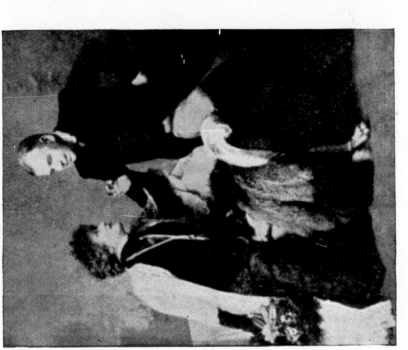

Sarah Bernhardt and Coquelin Ainé during the rehearsals of *L'Aiglon* for their American Tour (*November 1900*)

Sarah Bernhardt and Victorien Sardou during the rehearsals of *La Sorcière*
(*1903*)

Sarah Bernhardt in her own play *Adrienne Lecouvreur*
(*1905*)

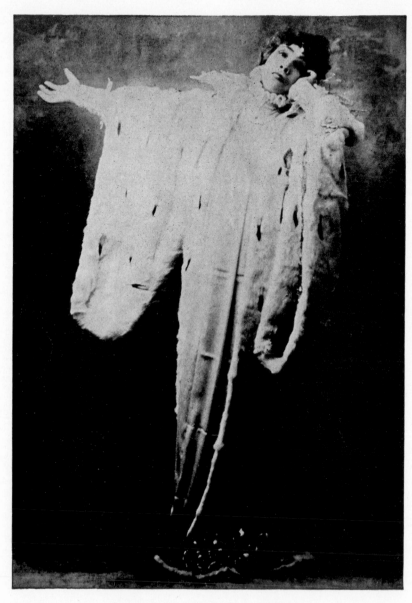

Sarah Bernhardt in *La Reine Elisabeth*
(*1912*)

Sarah Bernhardt at Sixty-nine in *L'Aiglon*
(*American Tour, 1913*)

Sarah Bernhardt in *Daniel*
(*1920*)

(still another!) gave Sarah Bernhardt an opportunity of surpassing herself. Moreover, all the other parts were performed remarkably—especially that of Loris Ipanoff, which was a great personal success for Pierre Berton.

Psychologically, it was a very curious evening for Sarah. From one act to another she felt the success growing and spreading, and she was both delighted and upset by it. For herself, obviously, she was enchanted by this triumph. But what would her husband say? Would he not begrudge her and Sardou a success infinitely greater than that which he himself had had with Mendès?

On leaving the Ambigu, after the performance, Damala rejoined Sarah at the Vaudeville. He arrived just as the curtain was being lowered. A few minutes later there was the same rush of people into her dressing room as on her great occasions.

To those who congratulated her, Sarah, touching almost to the point of naïveté, pointed to Damala and repeated: "You know he's the man who was to have played Loris. Sardou insisted on him absolutely. But he is having such a success in the play of Mendès! He could not leave Les Mères Ennemies. Have you been to see him at the Ambigu? You must go. He is wonderful!"

All this went on while her friends, overpowered by the performance which they had just witnessed, tried in vain to talk to her about herself, about Fédora, and did not care in the least about Damala. The next day, delirious with enthusiasm, the press greeted the dazzling triumph of Sarah Bernhardt and Victorien Sardou. The box office of the Vaudeville was besieged, and the whole house was sold out for six weeks in advance.

For three or four days the atmosphere was heavy in the house in the Avenue de Villiers. Damala scarcely spoke, but it was easy to guess the feelings which agitated him. On December 16, about midnight, the storm broke.[1]

[1] The reader may be astonished that, sixty years after the event, I can give so exactly the date when this scene took place, that I have given it within a day. Nothing could be easier. It was after this discussion that Damala suddenly threw up his part in the play of Catulle Mendès at the Ambigu. And it was on December 18, 1882, that the Paris papers announced that he had been replaced the evening before in Les Mères Ennemies.

It is by means of such verifications that I have been able to give exactly all the dates mentioned in this work. Generally speaking, my researches were easy. The slightest actions and gestures of actors are always related in detail by the press. *Author's note.*

Thinking to please him, on returning from the Vaudeville, Sarah said to her husband: "I have just come to an agreement with Sardou. No matter what the receipts are, I'll stop playing in *Fédora* at the end of April."

Slumped in his armchair, Damala was smoking a cigar and did not reply.

Then she continued: "I gave him to understand that if I went on tour with the play in May, June, and July I should make much more money in Brussels and London than in Paris, where we shall already have given more than a hundred performances. He agrees and, of course, you will play Loris everywhere."

Damala looked up and said sharply: "Are you trying to fool me?"

"What do you mean?"

"So I am just good enough to replace Monsieur Berton, no doubt because he cannot get away from Paris! And you have the impudence to make this proposal to me?"

"On the contrary, it seems to me that . . ."

"Because you have neither tact, nor intelligence, nor decency! For three months I have put up with this insult in silence. I can't stand it any more!"

"This insult?"

"You relegated me to the Ambigu, while you spread yourself at the Vaudeville. You made me give up an admirable part in *Fédora*, in order to play in an asinine piece by Monsieur Mendès! You are trying to squelch me, to stop my career. You do everything to prevent me from succeeding."

"Jacques! How can you?"

"Moreover, I know very well why. You're dying of jealousy. You're afraid that some other woman will get me. So you are very careful that I shall not be anywhere where I can shine. You poor idiot!"

Sarah turned pale at this insult. "Jacques! You are going too far!"

In his exasperation he continued: "I repeat. You poor idiot, you have no conscience! When I think that I have sacrificed my career for you, that I lived in the most agreeable and most aristocratic circles in Saint Petersburg! I gave all that up to follow a cheap actress, and this is all the thanks I get for it! She buries me at the far end of the Boulevard Saint Denis, and then she has the nerve to ask me to take up, in the provinces, a part which I was not considered good enough to create in Paris!"

Losing her patience, Sarah replied: "Is that my fault?"

Then Damala lost his temper completely. "What use is it to me, then, to be your husband? Why should I live with a mad woman, whose bad taste and eccentricities make me blush, if not in order to play whatever parts I like? You should have told me in advance that, in spite of your so-called position, you are incapable of making authors accept the partners whom you choose. In that case, you may be certain, I would never have married you!"

"You'd better be careful!"

"Of what? You are no more capable of hurting than of helping me. What's more, I defy you to do so—because you'll never see me again!"

Slamming the door violently, he left the room. Panic-stricken, Sarah ran after him, imploring him. Madame Guérard was awakened and intervened; Maurice was also called and, seeing his mother in tears, was most reluctantly obliged to ask his stepfather to remain. Nothing helped. Hastily throwing a few clothes into a bag, Damala noisily left the house in the Avenue de Villiers, about two o'clock in the morning, and went to finish the night in heaven knows what dive or with which of his former mistresses.

The next day he did not appear at the Ambigu, where his understudy replaced him. Two days later all the Paris papers published this brief announcement:

"Théâtre de l'Ambigu. Since yesterday evening, the part of André Boleski in *Les Mères Ennemies*, created by M. Jacques Damala, has been played by M. Montigny."

The departure of Damala was a terrible blow to Sarah Bernhardt. She suffered atrociously, and it was through a miracle of energy that she was able to continue in *Fédora* without losing one evening. Furthermore, this was not to be the end of her relations with her husband, from whom she was not really freed until his death, seven years later, in December, 1889.

While the triumph of *Fédora* continued regularly at the Vaudeville she had to provide shows for the Ambigu, of which she was now in charge. Following *Les Mères Ennemies*, on January 27, 1883, the first performance took place of a magnificent play, entitled *La Glu*, by a young poet who, some years later, made a considerable name for himself in Paris: Jean Richepin. Although it was admirably performed by Réjane and Agar, Decori and Lacressonnière, the play was not a success and ran for only fifty performances. It did not succeed until it was revived, and its production again cost Sarah Bernhardt some fifty thousand francs.

To surmount this failure, on March 15, she put on a play by Pierre Decourcelle, entitled *L'As de Trèfle*. This also closed after thirty-five performances. Then they revived *La Bouquetière des Innocents*, a play by Anicet Bourgeois and Fernand Dugué, first produced twenty years earlier, which was no more successful. Bad luck continued and they had to give up the struggle.

At the end of May, 1883, after an almost uninterrupted series of failures, "Monsieur Maurice Bernhardt" retired, giving up the management of the Ambigu, which the business manager, Auguste Simon, continued on his own account. In ten months of management, Sarah Bernhardt had produced five plays and lost a total of four hundred and seventy thousand francs. Almost half a million was swallowed up by the Ambigu, the theater which she had taken solely for Damala and where he had played four weeks!

However, she did not unduly regret this costly undertaking because during the rehearsals of *La Glu* she had come to know the author better, and he appealed to her greatly. In addition to his undoubted talent Jean Richepin was a fine specimen of a man, thirty-four years of age. With his broad shoulders, square beard, sonorous voice, and tousled curly hair, he was the exact incarnation of the celebrated play *Le Chemineau*, which he wrote fourteen years later. Like everybody else in Paris, Richepin knew about the rupture between Sarah and Damala and, like everybody else, he was full of sympathy for the great artist so vilely treated by her unworthy husband. For her part, once the first days of depression were over, she recovered herself and, being proud and disliking to be pitied, felt the necessity of concealing her grief from the public by flaunting a new happiness, even if it was only for show. So she encouraged Richepin to come and see her often, both at home and at the Vaudeville, even asking him to write a new play for her.

On the evening when an announcement of this forthcoming work appeared in the press, Damala returned to the house in the Avenue de Villiers, while Sarah was at the theater, and quietly resumed possession of his room as if he had never left it! When Sarah returned after the performance she found waiting for her in the hall Madame Guérard, who whispered to her that Damala had come back. This was the month of February, and about two months had elapsed since that

stormy night when he disappeared. Highly indignant, Sarah went
upstairs to the Greek's bedroom and found him lying down, calmly
reading the papers.

"What are you doing here?"

"As you can see, I am reading for a while before going to sleep."

"How can you dare to come back here?"

"Why not? I am your husband and this house is our conjugal residence. This is where I belong."

"But you deserted it weeks ago. You have no right to . . ."

"You're completely mistaken. Did you have my absence legally
certified? Did you catch me in *flagrante delicto?*"

"No. So you are cynically taking advantage of my kindness?"

"Don't talk to me about your kindness. You didn't think of taking
the necessary legal steps, doubtless because you were too deeply
absorbed in Monsieur Jean Richepin."

"It seems to me you're hardly the person to put on a jealous act."

Nevertheless, by pretending to have learned of the constant presence
of the author of *La Glu* with his wife, and to have suffered by it,
Damala obtained her forgiveness. The very next day Sarah and he
resumed their life together. Richepin was told of this and shrugged
his shoulders.

As he then had no right to interfere with Sarah's private life, he
merely said to her: "Suit yourself! The next time, when you've had
enough of this creature, kindly inform me!"

She was destined to follow this advice without delay. During the
weeks after he had left the Avenue de Villiers, Damala had doubtless
become more than ever addicted to morphine. When he returned to
his wife, his condition was frightful. Alternately overstimulated in the
extreme or completely prostrate, being unable to sleep in either case,
he could not stand being alone for one hour. In the middle of the
night he would go into Sarah's room, sit at the foot of her bed, and,
having decided to take up acting again, expound the most unrea-
sonable projects. Or again, lucid but in despair, he would sob for
hours over his physical downfall, crawling on the ground and begging her to cure him.

At this time Damala was giving himself as much as eight and ten
injections of morphine daily. He had ceased even to take the trouble
to uncover and rub with alcohol the part of his body which was to
receive the platinum needle. He pricked himself in the thigh, through

his trousers, while continuing the conversation which he had begun. It was a lamentable spectacle, this magnificent man whose condition got worse from day to day and who was gradually becoming a mere rag before the eyes of the powerless Sarah. But she loved him and still had infinite indulgence for him. A more violent scene than usual, almost a scandal, was necessary before she decided, not to ask for a divorce, which was never granted to her and Damala, but to regain her liberty at least.

One day in April, exasperated by the more and more frequent crises of her husband, she had entered his room, searched the drawers, and angrily thrown away all the bottles and containers of morphine which she could find. On returning in the evening Damala discovered the disappearance of the drug, which was now as necessary to him as the air he breathed. He broke into a bestial rage, shouting, yelling, breaking everything within reach, until he could no longer stand it. Then he rushed out bareheaded into the avenue, running like a mad-man to whatever friend or pharmacist could give him his indispensable poison immediately. He did not reappear for two days.

This time Sarah took advantage of his absence to escape from this calvary. She asked the courts to grant a separation between her and her husband. She received it in a few weeks. In order to obviate the further return of Damala, she called in Richepin on the pretext of asking him for news of the play which he was writing for her. A few days later their relationship was known all over Paris. Richepin did not have to defend Sarah against another intrusion by her husband. Seriously ill, Damala went to a sanitarium where he remained six months. He came out cured, at least momentarily.

On April 25, 1883, the one hundred and thirtieth—and last—performance of *Fédora* took place at the Vaudeville. It was a short run for such a hit. But almost always, being pressed for money, Sarah Bernhardt interrupted in the midst of their success the plays which she was performing in Paris—in order to go on tour, where the profits were naturally greater. As soon as she could, she revived the plays whose career was prematurely interrupted in this way. During the months of April and May she played *Fédora* in all the large towns of France and Belgium and in June in London, where she had her fifth season. Always fêted by the English public, she was henceforth to appear in London almost every year.

For the beginning of the season of 1883–84, encouraged by the success of *Fédora*, Sardou had written for her another play, *Théodora*, which he urged her to play at the Porte Saint Martin, whose large stage was required by this work with its elaborate settings. But Richepin had almost finished his play, and he had Sarah Bernhardt's promise. She wanted, in turn, to insure, as soon as possible, a success for the man to whom she now devoted all her attention. Once again Sardou had to wait. With Sarah he had to get accustomed to that!

On September 17, 1883, Sarah Bernhardt reappeared, in all her glory, at the Porte Saint Martin, where, eighteen years earlier, she had modestly understudied Mademoiselle Debay in *La Biche au Bois*. For eight years it was in this theater that she gave almost all her performances in Paris.

As she did not wish to launch Richepin's play until midseason, she first suggested a revival of *Froufrou* to Derembourg, then manager of the Porte Saint Martin. Sarah Bernhardt's name was one to conjure with, especially since *Fédora*; so Derembourg did not raise the slightest objection. He was "playing" the actress, not the play. If Sarah had proposed a Palais-Royal farce, or a tragedy from the Chinese, he would have agreed, provided she appeared in it. On the other hand, it was with a certain astonishment that the press received the announcement of this play. Not that there was any question about this magnificent comedy, which is probably the masterpiece of Meilhac and Halévy. But it was feared that it might be rather slight for the enormous dimensions of the Porte Saint Martin, whereas it would have been perfectly suitable for a theater on the same scale as the Gymnase, where its first performance had been a triumphant success.

These fears were unfounded. Sarah Bernhardt performed the miracle, not only of perfectly filling the setting she had chosen for *Froufrou*, but also of surpassing the great Aimée Desclée, who had been dazzling in the part twenty-four years previously. Supported by the excellent actor Marais as Sartorys, Angelo, Colombey, Marie Kalb, and Antonine, Sarah was acclaimed in this very varied and difficult part, which demands simultaneously so much lightness and dramatic power. Everyone who saw her in *Froufrou* was convinced that in the domain of comedy this was probably Sarah Bernhardt's most perfect achievement. Planned for a month or six weeks, this revival brought such receipts that it could not be decently withdrawn until its hundredth performance.

It was not until December 20, 1883, that the first performance took place of *Nana Sahib*, the long-awaited play of Jean Richepin, upon which both Sarah and Derembourg counted with such great hopes. The action took place in India, in 1857, at the time of the Sepoy Rebellion against British domination. Nana Sahib was a Hindu chief, played by Marais, and Sarah Bernhardt was his mistress, the voluptuous and sanguinary Djamma. It was a complete flop! The story seemed puerile, melodramatic, and confused. "It is a play for children, which should rightly be at the Châtelet," said the press. The name and the talent of Sarah Bernhardt were not sufficient to ward off disaster.

An accident aggravated the situation on the seventh performance. Marais fell ill and was forbidden to act for several weeks. Thereupon, on Sarah's insistence, the author himself, Jean Richepin, played the part of Nana Sahib from December 26 onward. This greatly pleased Sarah, who was happy to appear on the stage with the man she loved —as she had been the year before with Damala as partner. But it probably was less pleasing to the public, which would have preferred to see a good actor as the leading character, rather than a poet, undoubtedly splendidly handsome but quite ignorant of the profession of acting, who was then not sufficiently well known for his mere presence on the stage to constitute an attraction. By playing the part, Jean Richepin very likely hastened the end of his play—which did not run to even forty performances.

This failure was triply cruel for Sarah Bernhardt: first, because it made her realize that she was powerless to save a play which did not please the public; secondly, because the disappointment of Richepin hurt her; finally, and above all, because, by a strange turn of fortune, at the very moment when she suffered this failure, Jacques Damala, who was cured and had returned to the stage, scored a considerable personal success, contrary to all expectations, by performing, two hundred yards from the Porte Saint Martin, in a play which was hit. This was *Le Maître de Forges*, by Georges Ohnet, which opened at the Théâtre du Gymnase, on December 15, 1883, with Jane Hading, Lina Munte, Jacques Damala, and Saint-Germain in the principal parts.

By what series of extraordinary circumstances had Georges Ohnet, an already established author who could choose his interpreters from the best actors in Paris, been persuaded to entrust to Damala a part so important as that of Philippe Derblay, the ironmaster? How and by whom had Damala been introduced to him, and recommended to such an extent as to be preferred above all others? This, in truth, is almost inexplicable. An amateur actor turned professional at thirty-five, having barely played one month in *Les Mères Ennemies* at the Ambigu, whose only claim to fame was to have been Sarah Bernhardt's husband and to have made her as unhappy as all his other mistresses— his claims to create this big part were open to question. The fact remains he played it, and the play was so successful that Damala seemed excellent.

"In order to succeed in the profession of acting," Maurice de Féraudy said, "there is no harm in having ability, but one must have, first of all, good plays."

Nothing could be truer. A public that is bored will have difficulty in finding an actor of genius acceptable. A public that is amused is ready to regard as admirable the most ordinary actors. After the prodigious success which *Le Maître de Forges* had as a novel, the play based on it aroused equal enthusiasm and continues to do so to this day. For the last sixty years it is certainly one of the plays most frequently revived in France.

The exasperation of Sarah Bernhardt and Jean Richepin may be imagined when, every evening on their way to the Porte Saint Martin, where they faced an empty house, they passed in front of the Gymnase —the approaches to which were protected by a special detail of police, so huge was the crowd. The Porte Saint Martin gave extra matinees on Thursday. The Gymnase had none. On the first Thursday of January, 1884, as Sarah came onto the stage, she perceived Damala all alone in the front row of the orchestra. Behind him there were, at most, two hundred scattered spectators. During the entire performance, every time that he felt Sarah or Richepin was looking at him while acting, Damala ostentatiously turned around toward the auditorium, which he looked at, from floor to ceiling, shaking his head with an air of commiseration. He seemed to be saying: "This is lamentable! Poor Sarah! You're playing to an empty house, my child!"

Such insolence was intolerable. At the end of the performance Richepin did not take his curtain calls, but hastily threw a cloak over his Hindu costume, waited for Damala at the entrance, and gave him a masterly trouncing. That night, on the stage of the Gymnase, the handsome ironmaster had some difficulty in sitting down and getting up. To Jane Hading's inquiries, he replied: "I think I must have twisted my back!"

Le Maître de Forges ran for more than three hundred consecutive performances. It seemed as if Damala were made. But that was far from the case. The story of his successes is restricted to the single part of Philippe Derblay. Not that he ceased to act. After *Le Maître de Forges* he again had the luck to open in *Le Prince Zilah*, by Jules Claretie, at the Gymnase, in February, 1885, and on December 18, 1885, in *Sapho*, the admirable play by Alphonse Daudet. Yes, Damala was the first to play the part of Jean Gaussin, with Jane Hading as Fanny Legrand.

He appeared again in three other plays, three revivals. In October, 1885, in *Les Mères Repenties*, an old comedy by Félicien Mallefille; in March, 1886, in *Serge Panine*, the play by Georges Ohnet, in which he played the part created by Marais; and finally, in October, 1886, in *Froufrou*, the first play in which he had acted with Sarah Bernhardt in Saint Petersburg and which he had revived this time with Jane Hading. In each of these five plays he was as colorless and as insignificant as in the beginning. Nobody could understand it. After all, he was perfect in *Le Maître de Forges*, as people said. What had happened to him? How could this incredible decline be explained? But it was not a decline. Damala had never been an actor. One part, by pure accident, had "carried" him, doubtless because he found in it exact scope for his qualities and, especially, his defects. As any other character he was bound to fail, normally speaking. People should have been surprised, not by his repeated failures, but by his success in *Le Maître de Forges*. He did another short revival of this play at the Gymnase in December, 1886. At the end of January, 1887, after a career of three years, he again abandoned the theater or, more correctly, the theater abandoned him.

Meanwhile, at the Porte Saint Martin, it had become necessary to stop the performances of *Nana Sahib*, which threatened to ruin poor Derembourg forever. In order to enable him to recuperate his losses safely, on January 26, 1884, Sarah Bernhardt revived *La Dame aux Camélias* or, rather, she at last gave in Paris her first series of performances in the play of Dumas *fils*. From that day there became evident the great success which she always had with this play, revived in Paris twenty-two times in all, between 1884 and 1914. In this first revival Marais played Armand Duval. Jeanne Bernhardt, who was very ill, was not able to resume the part of Nichette, which she had been playing everywhere with Sarah for the last four years. She died a few weeks later, drugs having got the better of her.

The receipts were so considerable that Sarah might easily have continued to play *La Dame aux Camélias* until summer. But, to make the public forget his recent failure, Jean Richepin had hastily written for her another play or, to be exact, had finished an adaptation of Shakespeare's *Macbeth*. In *Nana Sahib* he had been accused of having written a play for children. This time he could not be criticized for doing the same thing. Moreover, he would no longer venture to act himself! But it was written, no doubt, that the association of Jean Richepin with Sarah Bernhardt would never meet with any success. Remembering the triumphs which this great poet later achieved in the theater, his long and brilliant career, one is tempted to believe that, on the day of his birth, a wicked fairy leaned over his cradle and said to him: "You will succeed always and everywhere, except with a woman named Sarah Bernhardt!"

His version of *Macbeth* was an even greater failure than *Nana Sahib*. Yet Sarah played Lady Macbeth in a masterly fashion. In the sleep-walking scene she positively aroused cries of admiration in the audience. But Richepin's very free adaptation had failed to please. Once again de Féraudy's remark was verified: "Act in good plays!"

Macbeth opened on May 21, 1884. By June 18 it had to close, and in great haste Derembourg revived for the summer an old drama by d'Ennery, first performed in 1845—*Marie-Jeanne*, or *La Femme du Peuple*—while Sarah Bernhardt went to play *Macbeth* in London. She gave the play at the Gaiety, opening on June 22, 1884. "In Paris we played it too late in the season," she had said to Richepin. "The early heat was against us, but it will be quite different in London. Also, a play by Shakespeare will always be better received by the English public. You'll see!"

He did not see. In London, as in Paris, *Macbeth* was a failure. After a week at the Gaiety she had to revive *La Dame aux Camélias*.

On the whole, the season at the Porte Saint Martin had not been a good one. The profits on *Froufrou* and *La Dame aux Camélias* had not compensated for the enormous losses on *Nana Sahib* and *Macbeth*.

To follow *Marie-Jeanne*, which drew nobody, Derembourg had tried a revival of *La Tour de Nesle*, by Dumas *père*, which also failed. At the end of his tether, he had to put his theater up for sale. Supported by Sarah and by Victorien Sardou, from whom now, to be sure, she demanded *Théodora*, Félix Duquesnel entered the running, negotiated with Derembourg, and, on September 15, 1884, took over the management of the Théâtre de la Porte Saint Martin. It was with joy that Sarah Bernhardt met again the first manager who, as far back as 1866, had had confidence in her—at the old Odéon, where she had been so happy.

As a favor to Sarah, Duquesnel began his management by reviving, without enthusiasm, *Macbeth*. But the play did not succeed any better in autumn than in spring. Obviously it was not the fine weather which had prevented it from making money. After a fortnight it had to close again. On October 3, in despair, Sarah left for Sainte-Adresse—where she shut herself up in her chalet, refusing to see anybody and weeping over the thrice-repeated failure of this play, which she liked, and also her rupture with the author.

La Glu, Nana Sahib, and *Macbeth* had disappointed them in turn. Their love had not survived so many rebuffs. Liaisons in the theater are strengthened by hits, but failures destroy them quickly. What exactly had happened? Had Sarah become tired of holding up with a great effort an author who seemed absolutely doomed to failure, at least with her? Or did he leave her, holding her responsible for all these failures? This is actually of little importance. The fact remains that, in order to arrange the casting of *Théodora* in agreement with her, Sardou and Duquesnel had twice to take the train to Havre, because up to the time of rehearsal, seeking forgetfulness in solitude, Sarah refused to put her foot in Paris.

Théodora has some thirty characters, but there were two men's parts in particular, the most important, for which the actors had to be carefully chosen: Andreas, Théodora's lover, and her husband, the Emperor Justinian. For the former, Sardou wanted Pierre Berton, who had done so well as Loris Ipanoff in *Fédora*; but Sarah preferred Marais, who had just played with her in *Froufrou, Nana Sahib, La Dame aux Camélais,* and *Macbeth*, successively, and was perfect in these four parts.

"Let us give Justinian to Berton, then," said Sardou.

"That is impossible," said Sarah. "Berton is too much the 'juvenile lead.' He is not broad-shouldered enough; he lacks presence and weight. An actor should represent his character physically, in the first place. Let us find an actor who has the face of an emperor; there must be such a thing."

"Have you anybody in mind?" asked Duquesnel.

She reflected for a while, lost in thought, and then said suddenly: "Why not Philippe Garnier?"

Duquesnel and Sardou were struck by the idea. In effect, there was nobody more suitable physically. Besides, he could fit the part, his speech was impressive, and he had a certain majestic appearance. So Garnier was accepted, but he did not accept immediately.

When Sardou sent for him, he expressed his astonishment. "Did Madame Bernhardt really suggest me for this part?"

"Why, of course," said Sardou, who could not understand his surprise.

"For an actress, she has a very bad memory!" said Garnier in acid tones.

"But what ever happened between you and her?"

"Oh, nothing very much. I had the bad taste to be with her in Saint Petersburg when she became engaged to Monsieur Damala. I realized that I was in the way, so I left."

Sardou shrugged his shoulders. "Is that all?"

"It is something," said Garnier, standing on his dignity.

"My friend," said Sardou, "if we remembered all these little stories, it would be impossible to cast a play. Do me the pleasure of signing the contract which our friend Duquesnel has drawn up, and don't attach importance to things that don't deserve it."

With great dignity and a beautiful flourish, Garnier signed, and he was never to regret it.

Théodora was produced for the first time at the Porte Saint Martin on December 26, 1884. It was assuredly Victorien Sardou's greatest success with Sarah Bernhardt, and also one of the greatest successes she ever had.

Quite unlike *Fédora*, which was a modern play, a "drawing-room piece," the action of Sardou's new work took place in Byzantium in 532, at the time of the Emperors. With seven different sets, picturesque, marvelously directed by the author, with a numerous cast and well-staged crowd scenes, it showed Théodora, the ex-dancer of the circus, who had been singled out by the Emperor Justinian, married to him, and made the Empress Augusta. Under an assumed name she continued her gallant adventures and learned one day that her lover of the moment, Andréas—who believed that his mistress was a young widow of no particular importance—was at the head of a conspiracy to assassinate the Emperor and Empress; that is to say, herself! Justinian discovered the plot and also his wife's infidelity, condemning her to torture. She died, strangled by the hangman's rope.

For exactly one year there was a veritable rush for the Porte Saint Martin. The play was performed more than three hundred times, until December 25, 1885, with a single interruption of two months, beginning on June 18, during which time Sarah played *Théodora* in London and then had to take a few days' rest.

Théodora marked the real apotheosis of Sarah Bernhardt, who was then forty. *Théodora* was her Austerlitz. As an actress and as a woman she had now reached her full development. Her celebrated slenderness, which had persisted until after her tour in America, had disappeared. As she herself had so long desired, her figure was now "ripe." Her strange beauty no longer awakened reservations. Her genius, of which she had furnished so many proofs, had become universally recognized. In addition to her salary she was largely interested in the profits of the Porte Saint Martin, and earned considerable sums of money. Her son was twenty and as handsome as a picture. Her dressing room in the theater and her house in the Avenue de Villiers were the meeting places of all the celebrities in Paris. It was impossible for an actress to have simultaneously more glory and more happiness.

Why had the obscure name of Philippe Garnier to be connected with this brilliant period? He was a fair actor and played the part of Justinian very well; but he was a pale and pretentious personality who, at the very first rehearsals of *Théodora*, had taken his revenge for the rather abrupt release which he had been given two and a half years earlier in Saint Petersburg. Finding Sarah separated from Damala and from Richepin, morally at a loose end, he maneuvered so cleverly that he gradually acquired a complete influence over her, to such an extent that, in everything concerning the theater, it was henceforth he who decided and not she. Whereas such a success should never have been interrupted, it was he who, contrary to the advice of Sardou and Duquesnel, persuaded her to go and give *Théodora* in London, which she might have done just as well the following year. Very soon he was to make her commit another mistake which was much more unfortunate.

On May 22, 1885, Victor Hugo had died at the age of eighty-three. His funeral, which took place on June 1, is still remembered. According to the wishes of the great poet, his coffin had been placed in a pauper's hearse; and it was behind this modest vehicle that the entire population of Paris escorted the author of *Les Misérables* to his last resting place. Sarah had always preserved a tender memory of Victor Hugo, and she followed him on foot, like everybody else, unnoticed among the thousands of people.

Then something moving happened. Having recognized her, and remembering how much the deceased had loved her, all the people about her gradually stepped back, so that, by degrees, she reached the front ranks of the procession. Long before they arrived at the cemetery, immediately after the poet's family, among whom his grandchildren, Georges and Jeanne Hugo, were most noticeable, Sarah Bernhardt walked alone, the crowd following her only at a respectful distance.

That same year, in honor of Victor Hugo's memory, each of the leading theaters of Paris revived with success one of his plays. Sarah Bernhardt was the first, and she asked Duquesnel to get permission from the Théâtre Français, which had the most important Hugo works in its repertory, to put on *Marion Delorme* at the Porte Saint Martin. It is a magnificent play, almost as good as *Ruy Blas* and *Hernani*, and Sarah had never played the part. This revival promised to be sensational. They counted on a very great success, which everything seemed to promise.

Fifty-four years after its first production, at the same theater in 1831, Sarah Bernhardt revived *Marion Delorme*, which she performed, for the first time, on December 30, 1885. With her, Marais played Didier; Philippe Garnier, Louis XIII; Pierre Berton, Saverny; and Dumaine, the Marquis de Nangis. But, to the general amazement, it was nothing more than a moderate success. Sarah spoke the lines magnificently, and particularly the fifth act was a triumph for her. She was acclaimed at the famous last verse: [*]

Regardez tous: Voilà l'homme rouge qui passe! [2]

However, by the beginning of January, it was evident that this revival would not last. Another play had to be found in a hurry.

[2] Look, all of you: It is the red man who goes by! *Trans.*

Every day Sarah received manuscripts, and Duquesnel submitted others. Berton suggested reviving *Fédora*, which had been stopped at the height of its success three years before at the Vaudeville. Although excellent, this suggestion had been received without enthusiasm. We shall see the reason why. I have before me a letter in the handwriting of Victorien Sardou, addressed to Pierre Berton, which shows how much Sarah's real friends deplored her incomprehensible weakness for her favorite of the moment, who took advantage of his influence with "the star" to forward his own little personal ambitions. This letter is dated January 1, 1886:

> My compliments, my dear friend, on your Saverny, and all my best wishes to you and yours.
> You are right about *Fédora*. That would be better than a new play, which would undoubtedly be a failure. But why do you want Sarah to play *Fédora*, in which Garnier has no part? Now it is Sarah—that is to say, Garnier—who runs everything today in this madhouse of which Duquesnel imagines he is the manager and in which he is a "pensioner" much more than he believes.
> Greetings,
> V. Sardou.

As Sardou had foreseen, it was, indeed, Garnier who chose the play to follow *Marion Delorme*, and the result was tragic. For years Philippe Garnier had cherished a dream: to play *Hamlet*. He thought this was a good opportunity and persuaded Sarah to have Duquesnel put on an adaptation in prose of Shakespeare's play, by Lucien Cressonnois and Charles Samson. But, what was more serious, in order to have her name on the program, he further persuaded her to play the part of Ophelia. This not only was in bad taste but was extremely stupid, as he was soon to realize.

This incredible performance of *Hamlet* appeared for the first time at the Porte Saint Martin on February 27, 1886, with a very ordinary actor in the monumental part of the Prince of Denmark, while, for love of him, the greatest French actress retired into the background in the insignificant character of Ophelia. The newspapers discreetly emphasized the "touching abnegation" of Sarah Bernhardt, but the general public did not take such a lenient view of the situation. When confronted by certain facts that are really scandalous, political, artistic, or otherwise, Paris sometimes has these astonishing movements of revolt, which are so sudden and violent that nothing can stop them.

Paris would not allow a mediocre actor, whom Sarah Bernhardt had highly honored by choosing him, to parade like a peacock in *Hamlet* while thrusting the idol of Paris into a part of third-rate importance, in which she humbly did little more than give him his cues. By the second or third performance, every evening Garnier was hissed, howled down, and booed by audiences which were daily enraged. Not that they thought him bad; for, in truth, he was adequate, as usual. The people were not against the actor, but against the man. Hundreds of letters informed Duquesnel and warned the actor himself that, as long as this revolting spectacle was performed at the Porte Saint Martin, he would not be allowed to make himself heard. There was nothing to do but close the play. They finally resigned themselves to this, after some ten stormy performances. Garnier retired in dignity to his property at Bois Colombes, and on March 16, with Pierre Berton, Sarah revived *Fédora*. This revival was limited to a few weeks because, as a result of the semifailure of *Marion Delorme* and the disaster of *Hamlet*, Sarah had decided to go off again on a long tour.

During her entire life her journeys were usually decided in this way. While everything was going well in Paris and she was making plenty of money, she remained. The moment one or two failures reduced her monthly income and, when she was a manager, caused her often to spend large sums, she quickly organized a tour, hastening to regain abroad what she had just lost in Paris. This time she undertook a long journey: South America, Central America, North America, then all the British Isles. She was to remain absent for fifteen months, from April, 1886, to July, 1887.

Shortly before her departure she experienced another great emotion. It was during the revival of *Fédora* at the Porte Saint Martin. One evening, as she came off stage, Sarah found a visitor waiting for her in her dressing room. When she recognized him, she was overwhelmed and silent. . . . It was Prince Henri de Ligne! She had not seen him for twenty years. He was now nearly fifty, with graying hair, and he seemed sad, distant, and prematurely aged. She asked him how and why, after so many years, he had thought of coming to see her again.

He replied gently: "Why should I be the only person not to come and applaud Sarah Bernhardt? Since you have been playing here this has become the foremost theater in Paris, and you have become the foremost French actress. Decidedly, it is you who were right. And you made the decision, at that time, which was necessary. The life which I offered you could not give you the happiness which you have found in the life you have made for yourself."

Sarah looked at him. So he did not know? He had never learned of her sacrifice? She was tempted to tell him, but she thought better of it. What was the use now? So she said nothing. With some hesitation the Prince asked about his son—their son.

"Come and have lunch with me tomorrow," said Sarah simply, "and you will see him. He is twenty-one; he is magnificent. He is very like you."

That was the truth. Maurice bore a bewildering resemblance to his father. The latter could never have denied him. Moreover, he did not think of such a thing; quite the contrary. On seeing him the next day, the Prince was greatly struck by this resemblance and also by the distinction, the breeding, and the bearing of the young man.

After lunch, when Sarah left them alone, he looked at Maurice for a long time and then said: "Do you know who I am?"

"When she introduced me to you a while ago, my mother mentioned your name."

After a silence the Prince made his thought clearer: "I mean do you know who I am—for you?"

Silently Maurice gave him a look of acquiescence.

Then the Prince continued: "I did not expect to find you as you are, charming and sympathetic. Since I have seen you, an idea has occurred to me."

"I am listening."

"You see," said the Prince with a slight effort, "I am a widower and am therefore free to do something which, in a different situation, would be impossible. In a word, I am prepared to recognize you."

"I don't understand."

"Yet, it is quite easy. You were born of an unknown father. I offer you my name, my title, and, after me, the share of my fortune which would legally be yours."

Maurice reflected, but only for an instant, then shook his head. "I thank you, but I cannot accept."

"Why not?"

"Since my birth, my mother alone has brought me up, sometimes with great difficulty, and has made every sacrifice for me. Whatever

I am, I owe it only to her. The only way in which I can prove my gratitude is by remaining her son, and hers alone. Your offer is very flattering, but I prefer to continue to call myself Bernhardt."

The Prince bowed. "I will not insist. I understand your feelings. They do you honor and are worthy of respect."

Next day Prince Henri returned to Brussels, and out of politeness Maurice accompanied him to the Gare du Nord. In the entrance hall an enormous crowd blocked the way to the platforms. As he was a little late, the Prince was afraid that he might miss the train at any moment. He stopped an employee.

"Could you get me through ahead of all these people?" he said to him. "I am Prince Henri de Ligne."

"Never heard of him," said the man sharply. "Do like everybody else. Stand in line and wait."

Then Maurice intervened and spoke to the same employee. "Could you help us to get through at once? I am the son of Madame Sarah Bernhardt."

On hearing this famous name, at the moment the most famous in France, the man gave a smile of sympathy and admiration.

"Is Sarah Bernhardt your mother? In that case, follow me. I will take you to the platform by a way I know. What train are you taking?"

"The four-fifty to Brussels."

"Come this way."

Two minutes later Prince Henri, accompanied by Maurice, was at the door of his car.

He said good-by to the young man, who concluded with a smile: "So, you see, it is also a very good thing to be called Bernhardt."

CHAPTER VII

Tours, the Renaissance

SARAH BERNHARDT embarked at Bordeaux during the last days of April, 1886, going directly to Rio de Janeiro, the first city on her itinerary. From June 1 she gave a full month's performances. Her son, Maurice, went with her on this long voyage. At the head of her company was Philippe Garnier, who resumed all his parts of the European tour of 1881, playing, in addition, Loris Ipanoff in *Fédora* and Philippe Derblay, Damala's part, in *Le Maître de Forges*. Because of its enormous success in Paris, Sarah had included Georges Ohnet's play in the repertory of her tour—herself playing the part of Claire de Beaulieu, which Jane Hading had created.

This was the first time that she performed in South America. The reception given her on her arrival at once assured her that her reputation there was already greater perhaps than in North America. Her entire stay in Rio was one prolonged triumph. The Brazilian public received her with transports of enthusiasm. At the end of each performance there was a veritable rain of bouquets and flowers on the stage. The Emperor of Brazil, Dom Pedro II, came to every play in which she acted. The great singers of the period, Nilsson and Adelina Patti, the idols of the South American public, never had any greater success.

During the journey from Rio to Buenos Aires, a painful event greatly saddened Sarah Bernhardt. Old Jarrett, her American impresario, who had managed her tour in 1880–81 and was still her agent for the present one, suddenly died. She had both affection and gratitude for this excellent man, who had revealed the New World to her, and she was deeply affected by his sudden disappearance. The management of the undertaking was then taken over by Sarah's secretary, Maurice Grau, who, as Jarrett's successor, was henceforth to be the impresario of all her tours for twenty years.

It was in the part of Fédora that Sarah Bernhardt made her debut at Buenos Aires, on July 17, 1886. She stayed there six weeks, during which she took in the biggest receipts which were ever recorded in that city. Then came Rosario and Santa Fé; then Uruguay—she played eight days at Montevideo. She continued her journey to Chile, one week at Valparaiso and four days at Santiago, and to Peru, where she gave a short series of performances in Lima. From there she went to Havana, where she was in September; then to Mexico, where she made two hundred and sixty thousand francs in ten performances. After this she arrived in the United States via Texas. She resumed the long tour of small and large American towns which she had made five years earlier. She wound up in New York, where she played during the month of April, 1887.

In May she was in London, and for the first time she made a tour of the cities of England, Scotland, and Ireland. Everywhere she met with the same triumphal reception. Wherever she arrived, the mere announcement of her name inevitably meant enormous crowds waiting for hours at the station or the pier, grandiose demonstrations, maximum receipts, enthusiastic acclamations, stages strewn with flowers, entire cities talking only of her.

In his remarkable work *Les Contemporains*, Jules Lemaître wrote: "More than any other, she will have known immense glory, concrete, intoxicating, maddening, the glory of the conquerors and the Caesars. In every country in the world she has been accorded receptions which are not given to kings. She has had what the princes of the mind will never have."

What is really extraordinary is that Sarah was never intoxicated by this unheard-of and prodigious success, such as no other actress had ever known and no other will probably ever know. She was perfectly aware of her genius, of both her artistic and her commercial worth, yet she remained as simple as in the beginning, perhaps more so. How many others, in her place, dazzled by such a fate, would have quickly become unapproachable!

In his brief biography of Sarah Bernhardt, Maurice Baring observes: "She took for granted that she was the greatest actress in the world, just as Queen Victoria took it for granted that she was Queen of England. Sarah Bernhardt estimated her position correctly, but never spoke of it, nor gave to it another thought."

Nothing could be more true. If some insolent or half-witted person had said to her: "Such and such an actress played such and such a part better than you did," she would certainly have considered him, without anger, as a man devoid of reason. But this was in no way a form of vanity. The vain person is one who notices his own superiority at every turn, delights in it, acts and speaks with condescension, and treats everyone who comes near him as an inferior. Sarah never had this odious fault. It is true she had whims, a difficult character, and sometimes made insufferable demands. But these were by no means manifestations of pride. She was by nature intractable, and she had always shown the same fits of temper. It will be remembered that she was only eighteen and had a very obscure name when she slapped Nathalie, and had to leave the Théâtre Français. At the height of her glory Sarah always maintained complete control of herself, and that is also why she was a great woman. She well knew that those who are really great are modest.

Shortly after her return from this long tour, in September, 1887, while she was resting at Belle Isle, where she lived for the first time in the fort which she had recently bought, her return to the Comédie Française was semiofficially announced. Why? Because in Paris the most fantastic statements are launched and spread without the faintest reason. This time the news was not entirely inaccurate. Emile Perrin had been dead for two years, and Jules Claretie was now general manager of the Théâtre Français. As a critic, he had often devoted dithyrambic articles to Sarah. His wholehearted admiration for her was known, and it had been rumored that, as soon as she returned from her tour, he would make her an urgent offer.

He did so, as a matter of fact; but Sarah had a thousand plans. Her successes in all the foreign countries where she had played made it possible for her, and almost made it an obligation, to return. These perpetual absences were hardly compatible with the regular and exacting service which an actress at the Comédie Française must give. On the other hand, by making a special effort in her case, perhaps the "House of Molière" could guarantee her a maximum of a hundred and fifty thousand francs a year. At the time Sarah was easily living on a scale of sixty to eighty thousand francs a month. In short, her return to the Théâtre Français was practically out of the question, and the negotiations, which were brief, were doomed to failure in advance.

But the press revealed them in sufficient detail for her partisans and adversaries to have another opportunity to taking sides. In *Le Gaulois*, at the beginning of October, 1887, Albert Delpit, the author of *Le Fils de Coralie*, wrote:

"What tradition does Madame Sarah Bernhardt represent, may I ask? Greedy for money, it is now seven years since she left the Théâtre Français in search of adventures. In the declining years of her career, does the Comédie want to take her back? How ridiculous! Monsieur Jules Claretie, among his *Sociétaires*, has artists of very great talent, such as Mademoiselle Bartet and Mesdames Baretta, Reichenberg, and Dudlay. He has just engaged Mademoiselle Brandès, who will soon occupy an important position. My eminent colleague and friend has no need of Madame Sarah Bernhardt. She is forty-three and, with her changed voice and her diminished talent, she cannot be of any further use to the Comédie. Further, what kind of parts could she play? I can only see her in maternal roles, and she would never accept that. If the former fugitive really did return to the Comédie, is she not afraid that some nasty person might throw a wreath of immortelles at her, as happened long ago to Mademoiselle Mars?"

As this book is written in the hope of contributing to the glory of Sarah Bernhardt, in my modest fashion but with all the strength of my tenderness for her, the reader may perhaps wonder why I thought it necessary to quote these treacherous lines. Well, precisely in order to show what was the extraordinary power of Sarah Bernhardt's personality. We see that, already in 1887, certain people thought her old and said so brutally, advising her to play maternal roles. *Thirteen years* after such articles, what other artist, at fifty-six, could have created *L'Aiglon* and had a triumph in it, and seven years later, at sixty-three, create the part of Prince Charming in *La Belle au Bois Dormant* and be acclaimed, not only for her talent, but also for her astounding youthfulness?

The article of Albert Delpit, backed by others even nastier, by Emile Bergerat in *Gil Blas*, was not only cruel but profoundly unfair. A few days after it appeared, Sarah Bernhardt gave the first performance of *La Tosca*; and once more Paris was stunned by this radiant apparition. Who has not looked with delight at the numerous portraits of Sarah in the part of Tosca, whose costume is still celebrated? In her long Empire gown, with her large black velvet hat and tall cane, she is both sumptuous and adorable.

La Tosca was the third play which Victorien Sardou had written for Sarah Bernhardt. It was first produced at the Porte Saint Martin on November 24, 1887, and was again a tremendous success, equal to that of *Fédora* and *Théodora*. Three times in five years Sardou and Sarah triumphed together. Perhaps *La Tosca* was an even more solid and more enduring triumph. The opera of Puccini, based on Sardou's play, was performed in 1903, with the great success which we all know. Logically, its career should have interfered with that of the play. However, Sarah revived *La Tosca* in Paris up to 1909, and in New York up to 1913, and it was always one of the plays in her repertory which people wanted to see over and over again.

At the opening Pierre Berton played Baron Scarpia; Dumény, Mario Cavaradossi. They were both excellent, particularly Berton. The other parts are not very important. Consequently none was worthy of Philippe Garnier, who, since "the tragic story" of *Hamlet*, had lost much of his prestige, which was not restored by the long tour which followed. Soon he was to play again on two occasions with Sarah Bernhardt, but now everything had finally resumed its proper place. He was merely an actor, like the others, playing respectfully opposite the star.

At the end of March, 1888, Sarah Bernhardt was ill and had to interrupt the performances of *La Tosca*, in which she had played only one hundred and twenty-two times. The considerable amount of work which she had done since her departure from the Théâtre Français, the exhausting journeys, the perpetual strain, relieved by always too brief vacations, had finally overcome her resistance temporarily. She rested for several weeks before going on tour in *La Tosca*, which she played during May and June in the larger cities of France and in July at the Lyceum in London. Eagerly awaited, Sardou's play had the same great success in England as it had in Paris.

Before leaving London, for one week, Sarah played *Francillon*, a new play by Alexander Dumas *fils*, which Julia Bartet had created at the Théâtre Français the previous year, in January, 1887. It was a very modern and gay comedy, with a few dramatic scenes—a play in the manner of *Froufrou*, in which Sarah Bernhardt had found an opportunity for such a great success. London thought her admirable in *Francillon*. Paris, unfortunately, was never to see her in this part.

On her return an important event occurred in the life of Sarah Bernhardt: the wedding of her son, Maurice, who was not yet twenty-four. He married a young Pole, named Terka Jablonovska, and left his mother's house, where he had hitherto always lived. Although she warmly approved of the marriage, which gave her the most charming daughter-in-law in the world, it was a great loss to Sarah no longer to have under her roof this son whom she adored. All of a sudden the house in the Avenue de Villiers seemed to her very empty!

That same year, 1888, witnessed Sarah Bernhardt's beginnings as a dramatist. They were not very brilliant. Among the various strings to her bow, the literary talent of Sarah Bernhardt was certainly not the greatest. She was a sculptor of undoubted merit, but she was never a writer. How was it that this woman, whose conversation was so brilliant and witty, lost all her wit and simplicity as soon as she took it into her head to write? She is herself only in those short replies to critics, some of which have been quoted in the preceding pages. She was lively only when she contradicted!

Her dramatic and literary work is, incidentally, of slight importance. Apart from her *Mémoires,* which stopped at the year 1881 but were written as late as 1906, she was the author of a novel entitled *Petite Idole,* a rather childish story in the manner of Zénaïde Fleuriot, and three plays. In addition, she wrote a certain number of articles and stories for the newspapers; but none is worthy of mention. Chronologically Sarah Bernhardt's first play was a drama in one act, *L'Aveu,* which was first performed at the Odéon on March 27, 1888. It was a play which she had written for herself, for her tours, two or three years earlier, in which she had already performed here and there abroad. It generally shared the program with *Le Passant,* the second act of *Phèdre,* and, sometimes, *Chez l'Avocat*—the merry little play by Paul Ferrier, which she had first performed at the Comédie Française in 1873 and which she revived from time to time. Thus she had added to her repertory a program in which, during the same evening, she appeared as three or four totally different persons.

Played by Sarah Bernhardt, *L'Aveu* produced a great impression and, on her return from the tour, she proposed it to her friend Porel, who was made manager of the Odéon on January 1, 1885. It was impossible to refuse Sarah Bernhardt anything. So Porel accepted the little play, more as a favor to her than in the hope of a success, and cast it with Paul Mounet, the brother of Mounet Sully; Marcel Marquet, the father of Mary Marquet; Marie Samary, Jeanne Kerly, and Raphaèle Sisos in the part played on tour by Sarah Bernhardt. *L'Aveu* is a short melodrama which takes place at the bedside of a dying child. At the instant when the mother feels that he is lost, she confesses to her husband that the child is not his. The real father is waiting anxiously for news of his son in the adjoining room. A violent scene takes place between the two men. The death of the baby, which affects the three of them equally deeply, peacefully ends a quarrel whose object has ceased to exist. Without the genius of Sarah Bernhardt in the part, this little work did not have an enthusiastic reception in Paris. Only twelve performances were given at the Odéon in the course of the year 1888.

After spending the month of August with her family at Belle Isle, with her son, her daughter-in-law, Madame Guérard, Louise Abbéma, and Georges Clairin, Sarah Bernhardt set out again, in September, 1888, on a tour of Europe for six months, which took her for the first time as far as Turkey and Egypt. After Belgium, Holland, and Switzerland she reached Austria on November 1, opening in Vienna with *La Tosca*. After four nights in Budapest she was in Cairo and Alexandria in December, at Constantinople in January; left for Saint Petersburg, where she gave twenty triumphant performances, and returned through Sweden and Norway. She was back in Paris on March 1, 1889.

News awaited her which upset her more than one might have thought. Jacques Damala was very ill and begged her to come and see him. She did not hesitate for a moment. First of all, she still legally bore his name and, secondly, in spite of everything that had happened between them, she kept her affection unchanged for the Greek with whom she had known ephemeral but immense happiness seven years earlier. She hastened to him and was overcome when she saw him. Worn out and undermined by morphine, Damala was almost unrecognizable. Enveloped in a long dressing gown, horribly thin, with hollow cheeks, a ghastly pale complexion, his dark eyes glassy and lifeless, he himself came to open the door of his modest apartment where he lived alone, abandoned by all—men and women. His good looks had always been his only attraction and, these having disappeared, nothing remained to arouse admiration, but only sympathy. That is the fate of these great ladies' men who spend their youth driving to despair all women who approach them. When age overtakes them, or they are laid low by sickness, not a friendly hand is stretched out to them and they end their days in solitude and sadness, if not in poverty.

Thanks to Sarah, whose generosity was touching, Damala escaped this sad fate. He was visibly doomed. Perhaps he had a few months or weeks to live. She did not want her husband to have a lamentable end. The next day she had him taken to a sanitarium, where she went to see him every day and where he was looked after with such attention, with such determination to cure him once more if that was humanly possible, that the miracle soon appeared to be happening. Six weeks later, hidden in a box with a grating, Damala was able to be present at the first performance of the new play in which Sarah Bernhardt was opening.

This was a dramatic comedy in four acts, entitled *Léna*, which Pierre Berton had taken from an English novel by F. C. Philips, *As in a Looking Glass*. The opening was at the Théâtre des Variétés, on April 16, 1889, Pierre Berton playing the principal male part in what was his first attempt as a dramatic author. The result ought not to have encouraged him in this new career, for *Léna* was a complete failure. Nevertheless, Berton was undoubtedly a dramatist. He was later to prove it often, having several quite remarkable plays produced. The best known is *Zaza*, which was first performed, with Réjane and Huguenet, at the Vaudeville in 1898, was revived for years, and remains one of the great successes of the beginning of the century.

Léna was a melodrama of inferior quality, in which we see a married woman made the victim of blackmail by a former lover. Believing that she has lost the love and esteem of her husband, she commits suicide. The sole interest of the play was to provide Sarah Bernhardt with an opportunity to die in a manner hitherto unknown. The last act ended with a silent scene of at least five minutes—which is enormous in the theater—in which Léna, alone on the stage, prepared with the utmost detail for her death.

First she took a dagger, hesitated, then threw it away. Then she poured the contents of a bottle of chloral into a glass, placed her husband's portrait in front of her, and, staring at the picture, slowly drank the poison. She let the empty glass fall; then remained seated, facing the public, with a fixed stare, waiting . . . for the moment when she toppled over and fell forward with her face on the ground. Her husband, who had always adored her, burst open the door and rushed on the scene. She had ceased to breathe. This Grand Guignol scene, which Sarah played with her usual mastery, was as displeasing as the play itself.

It was about this period that she began to have a less regularly enthusiastic press in Paris, and that success, instead of being assured in advance, could be achieved only if the entire play really deserved it. Hitherto, several of the plays in which she had performed had obviously not succeeded, but even in these failures she personally had always had her success as an actress. After *Léna* things changed a little. In the first place, people would have liked her to be more strict in the choice of her plays. Many felt that the gifted interpreter of Racine and Victor Hugo should appear only in works of distinction, signed by established names. In the second place, and perhaps rightly, people accused her talent of having lost some of its quality in the course of her long and frequent tours, during which the fatigue of daily journeys did not allow her physically to play each evening with the same conscientiousness and intensity. It was regretted that she had brought back from these expeditions a kind of carelessness which she did not correct when she played again in Paris. Jules Lemaître wrote: "The newspapers have told you that Madame Bernhardt is wonderful in the death scene of *Léna*. It is true. But in the rest of the play she gets on one's nerves. She recites her lines like a schoolgirl intoning her prayers the night before her first communion. Is this because she has got used to performing before audiences which do not understand French? I am rather inclined to believe that she has become so accustomed to scenes of violence and torture, which are so generously dispensed in the sanguinary dramas of Victorien Sardou, that she has gradually lost the faculty of expressing the ordinary sentiments of everyday life. Madame Sarah Bernhardt does not become herself again until she is killing someone or dying."

Although he was then only thirty-six years of age, the authority of Jules Lemaître was already very great. This reproach deeply impressed Sarah, who despised nasty remarks and calumnies but was never indifferent to intelligent and fair criticism. But the actual time was lacking in which to correct her interpretation of *Léna*, for the play lasted only four weeks. Another play was urgently needed, because she had leased the Théâtre des Variétés for three months.

It was then that Sarah made a very nice and infinitely touching

gesture. Although still very ill, Damala was going out again and clinging to life with all the strength that remained to him. She wanted
to give him one last joy in this world, for she well knew that he would
never recover. She suggested to him that they revive *La Dame aux
Camélias* for a series of performances—the play in which he had performed only once in Paris, seven years previously, soon after their
marriage. This was an enormous favor to the poor dying man, who
suddenly had the feeling that he was living again. The revival took
place at the Théâtre des Variétés on May 18, 1889, and lasted until
June 30. Sarah enjoyed her usual triumph. To her husband the press
showed indulgence and pity. Edmond Stoullig wrote in *Le Rappel*:

"What are we to say of Monsieur Damala? The handsome 'ironmaster,' obviously ill and painfully emaciated, is today only the
shadow of his former self. The uncertainty of his acting and the
weakness of his diction would lead one to suppose that, lacking force
and vigor, he was imprudent in returning to the theater before he
had completely recovered. Where, alas, is the handsome Armand
Duval, whom we saw for the first time a few years ago at the Gaîté?"

This revival brought in handsome receipts, for Sarah Bernhardt
never played *La Dame aux Camélias* to other than packed houses;
but these performances were very sad. Every night she wondered
whether Damala would last out his part, or whether he would collapse on the stage exhausted. In the fourth act, which demands so
much warmth and violence from the actor, the poor man was often
not able even to stand up, and he was obliged to play the famous last
scene while seated: "You are all witnesses that I have paid this woman
and no longer owe her anything!"

But he was so happy to be with his wife again, the only woman
who held out a helping hand to him in his distress, so proud to reappear with her before the Paris public, that Sarah was touched and
helped him with all her heart, acting the play alone, so to speak, and
making up for what her partner lacked by redoubling the intensity
of her effort.

The day after the last performance of *La Dame aux Camélias* at the
Variétés, she went off to London, where, beginning on July 2, she
played *Léna* at the Lyceum, while Damala tried desperately to get
better in a country retreat.

On September 4, 1889, Sarah Bernhardt reappeared in Paris at
the Porte Saint Martin in a revival of *La Tosca*, with Pierre Berton.

On October 7 she revived *Théodora*, with Garnier. The play ran for another sixty magnificent performances, terminating at the end of November.

The very night of the last performance of *Théodora*, Damala died, the victim, like Jeanne Bernhardt, of the merciless drugs. He was forty-two years old. Although separated from him officially for six years, Sarah mourned him for a long time and was genuinely grieved. During the brief and moving revival of *La Dame aux Camélias*, her tenderness for her husband had revived. Moreover, it was a memory of the past, a part of her distant youth, which was disappearing!

Sarah Bernhardt was now forty-five, but she made no effort to conceal it. On the contrary, she took a certain delight in publicly revealing certain facts of her private life which tended, rather, to add to her years and which another person would probably have kept secret. During the month of November, 1889, the new play in which she was going to act was announced by *Le Gaulois* in these picturesque terms. The theatrical columnist of the paper wrote:

"We have recently received the following letter, signed by some fifty well-known names in Paris:

" 'Sir:—You who know Madame Sarah Bernhardt, could you not tell her that many women and young girls would like to applaud her; but the kind of plays in which she acts prevents them from going to the theater where she has her triumphs. Sometimes she plays the part of a vicious queen, sometimes a strumpet, sometimes a great lady but of doubtful morality. How many of us would go to applaud her with enthusiasm, if she would at last play a pure heroine in a moral work.'

"We sent this letter at once to Madame Sarah Bernhardt, whose reply was as follows:

" 'For years I have been considering the project of playing Jeanne d'Arc, but I have not found a play on the subject which pleases me. Finally, that delightful poet Jules Barbier has just brought me one which is magnificent. I believe I am satisfying your wishes by asking my friend Duquesnel to produce it immediately. Moreover, I could not wait any longer. Soon I shall be too old to play Jeanne d'Arc. After all, I am a grandmother! Yours, Sarah Bernhardt.' "

It so happened that the wife of Maurice, Terka Bernhardt, had given birth a few mouths earlier to their elder daughter, Simone. The theatrical world of Paris knew nothing of it and, just as she was going

to incarnate the Maid of Orleans, Sarah Bernhardt might have refrained from announcing it in the press. But she knew very well
how young she always looked, and doubtless she took a certain pleasure in making people say that, also physically, she was extraordinary.

The *Jeanne d'Arc* of Jules Barbier, with a splendid score by Charles
Gounod, was first performed by Sarah Bernhardt at the Porte Saint
Martin on January 3, 1890. Contrary to what she had announced, it
was by no means a magnificent play. It was far from it, being old-
fashioned in construction, with a redundant style and a facile kind
of patriotism. Yet it had a rather good run: sixteen weeks, ending
April 30, 1890. But Sarah Bernhardt herself did not achieve one of
those great successes of which she had had so many and which she
was to have again so often. She intoned her part a little. Perhaps it
was difficult to show any genius in a play so totally without it. What
insured its success was the spectacular performance, superbly staged
by Duquesnel or, more correctly, by Sarah Bernhardt—who, except
when playing Sardou, now directed her plays herself, another art in
which she was to prove incomparable.

After her annual season of one month in London, in May, Sarah
Bernhardt finally took a real holiday during the summer of 1890.
She spent three whole months at Belle Isle, where the first of the
villas surrounding the fort had just been built, following the marriage of Maurice and the birth of Simone. The family life, of which
she was so fond during the second part of her career, began at this
time for Sarah Bernhardt, collecting about her her son, her daughter-
in-law, and her granddaughter, who were henceforth to be the sole
objects of her love. She had sworn this on the day after Damala's
death. This year she was anxious to prolong her stay at Belle Isle,
for she was not going to be able to return there for two years. It was
at the beginning of the following year that she undertook the longest
tour of her entire career.

Before that she performed in Paris the fourth play written for her
by Sardou. This was *Cléopâtre*, a play in five acts and six scenes,
which was performed for the first time at the Porte Saint Martin on
October 23, 1890. Playing for the last time with Sarah Bernhardt,
Philippe Garnier took the part of Anthony. The rest of the cast was
just adequate. The play had much less success than the three others
by Sardou which Sarah had previously created. It was performed only
ninety-eight times, until January 15, 1891, and was never revived after-

ward. For Sardou it almost amounted to a failure. The truth is, *Cléopâtre* is not a very good play. It is a long love duet between the two leading figures, in which that wonderful dramatist did not display his usual mastery. The dramatic devices are feeble and, in the fourth act, it required all the authority of Sarah Bernhardt to make acceptable a situation which might easily have seemed ridiculous if played by anybody else.

The scene is laid in Actium. Having learned that Anthony has married the sister of Octavius, mad with jealousy, Cleopatra wishes to see her rival in her own house. With the complicity of Anthony's attendant she gets in, wrapped in a carpet which is carried onto the stage by slaves who are not aware that the Queen of Egypt is hidden in it. Then she hides again behind a curtain where for more than a quarter of an hour—one half of the act!—she listens to everything that is being said. After this she appears and says to Anthony: "I wanted to see. I have seen!" These are exactly the same words which Athalie says as she makes her exit in the second act of Racine's tragedy, a reminder which was a little too exact. The "carpet" in *Cléopâtre* aroused smiles in the press. The death of the Queen on the body of her murdered lover saved the evening. Sarah Bernhardt reproduced wonderfully her slow agony, after the asp had stung her arm.

This was the last play which Sarah Bernhardt performed at the Porte Saint Martin, and it was also the swan song of Duquesnel. After the departure of his most important star he produced a few plays of the most varied type, not one of which succeeded. In July, 1891, he retired, after a revival of *Le Petit Faust*, the operetta by Hervé, which was played by Jeanne Granier, Cassive, Cooper, and Sulbac. He was fifty-nine years old, and devoted himself henceforth to literature. He had a fine career as a dramatist, which lasted until his death in 1915.

The great world tour of Sarah Bernhardt began on February 5, 1891, in New York, where she made her debut in *La Tosca*. As before, her third stay lasted four weeks. Then she covered Canada and the entire United States, playing out West for the first time—in California. From there she embarked for Australia, arriving at the end of October. She made a long stay in Sydney, then in Melbourne; and embarked for Turkey, where she arrived via Madagascar, the Red Sea, and the Suez Canal. After Constantinople, Athens, and Russia she went all over Europe during the year 1892; then reached North Africa, performing in Egypt, Tunis, and Algeria. She next sailed again from Dakar to Central America; then to South America, where she again visited each country during the spring and summer of 1893. At last she returned to Lisbon, where she ended, in September, 1893, this colossal expedition, which had lasted thirty-two months, in the course of which she had gone around the world.

As usual, her company consisted of about thirty actors, at the head of which was Duquesne—who, on his return, played the part of Napoleon in *Madame Sans-Gêne*—her faithful Angelo, Fleury, Jeanne Méa, and Suzanne Seylor. Her repertory consisted of twenty plays. It was in the course of this tour that she played, for the first time, *Gringoire,* the immortal one-act play of Théodore de Banville, in which she had the part of the vagabond poet, created by Coquelin *aîné* at the Comédie Française in 1866, said to have been one of the most original creations of Sarah Bernhardt.

When she returned, Coquelin said to her: "I swore to you that if you ever played *Gringoire,* wherever it might be, I would take the train to see you, because you must be marvelous—and then you go and play it in Australia! That's not a nice trick to play on an old friend."

This tour was the handsomest money-making undertaking which Sarah Bernhardt ever had. In two years and eight months, all expenses for the company and for traveling deducted, her net profit was three million and a half gold francs. It must be admitted that such an effort deserved this brilliant result. Moreover, it was solely to her genius that she owed it now, and not, as formerly, partly to publicity. Her tour of 1880–81 had been chiefly a success of curiosity. That could not be said of her tour in 1891–92–93. With the exception of Australia all the countries where she went had already applauded her on two or three occasions, and it was because she had left an unforgettable memory that everywhere people rushed to see her again.

On her return Sarah Bernhardt at last became her own manager. For a long time, at the Porte Saint Martin, she did more or less what she wanted; but, in spite of the infinite good nature of Duquesnel—which was quite natural—she was still not complete mistress of the situation. For example, when she left Paris he had to see that the house was not idle during her absence, and often, when she got back, she found a success running at the Porte Saint Martin which could not be interrupted. Then she had to wait or go to another theater. For this reason she had to put on *Léna* at the Variétés, which for eighty years had been classified as a theater for operettas and light comedies. Apart from its lack of standing, it was not the right setting for this somber lady.

On April 1, 1893, the Théâtre de la Renaissance was open to contract. It is situated exactly beside the Porte Saint Martin, in what was then the theatrical district. Within a radius of five hundred yards were grouped the Eldorado, the Scala, the Menus Plaisirs (which was to become the Théâtre Antoine), the Renaissance, the Porte Saint Martin, the Ambigu, the Folies Dramatiques, the Déjazet; in the neighborhood were also the Gymnase and the Gaîté. The stage of the Renaissance is not large and is completely lacking in outlets. But the building was then admirably situated, at the corner of the main boulevards and the Rue de Bondy. In short, Sarah was tempted and telegraphed an offer. It was not accepted immediately, for there were many competitors. She then sent to Paris her impresario, Maurice Grau, who got into direct communication with the company that owned it. In June, 1893, the newspapers announced that Sarah Bernhardt had become the manager of the Renaissance.

The news was gladly received by the press, which declared unanimously: "Perhaps, now that she has her own theater in Paris, Madame Sarah Bernhardt will not absent herself in the future so often."

This hope had only an appearance of logic. When she was a manager, Sarah Bernhardt traveled as much as she had in the past. She had acquired the habit and retained it until her death. And she had become the greatest international star, with as much of an obligation to the rest of the world as to France. Besides, the need of money often compelled her to go away again. Despite the attraction of her name and the casts which she assembled, always perfect and often brilliant, her management of the Renaissance did not turn out well financially. Far from it. She managed this theater for five years, until December, 1898. During that period and among numerous revivals, she produced twelve new plays for the first time. Only one of these, *Gismonda*, reached its hundredth performance. Two others, *Izéil* and *Lorenzaccio*, had barely more than seventy performances, which was far from being brilliant. The nine others were all catastrophes, not to mention several other plays in which she did not act herself, but produced on her own account, which also failed.

By a strange turn of fate the only very great success at the Renaissance, during Sarah Bernhardt's management, was a play in which she did not have a part: *Amants*, by Maurice Donnay.

Yet it was always with great care that she chose her plays, endeavoring to extend her repertory, to put on the works of new writers, and also to surround herself with young people. Renouncing those actors who had been her partners till then, and whose technique perhaps now dated a little—Marais, Philippe Garnier, and even Pierre Berton —she began by placing at the head of her company three actors of the new school, all three at the dawn of their career. Two were remarkable and the third excellent: Lucien Guitry, De Max, and Abel Deval.

Lucien Guitry, who was to become the great and admirable actor whom we subsequently knew, was then thirty-three years of age. But he had spent nine years in Russia, engaged by the year at the Théâtre Michel in Saint Petersburg and, not having returned until 1891, he had not yet had time to make a brilliant name for himself in Paris. It was in the roles which he performed at the Renaissance, under the management of Sarah Bernhardt, that he achieved an important position, which became preponderant when, in his turn, he became manager of the same theater in 1902.

Edouard De Max was still younger, being only twenty-four when Sarah Bernhardt took the Renaissance. He also was launched by Sarah, under whose management he played, with few interruptions, until 1910. De Max was one of the most admirable actors of his time. For thirty years he astounded Paris in fifty successive creations, all masterly and prodigiously varied. At the Renaissance, at the Théâtre Sarah Bernhardt, at the Odéon, and then at the Comédie Française, which he joined in 1915, he had a dazzling career. Much more than Guitry, a superior actor but moderate and unlyrical, De Max was ideally constituted to act with Sarah Bernhardt. His talent was in complete harmony with that of his great manager. After Mounet Sully, De Max was certainly Sarah's best partner. Imposing, regal, splendidly handsome, he incarnated particularly well the great heroes of tragedy and of costume plays—kings, legendary princes, great lords of times past. As Nero in *Britannicus*, Petronius in *Quo Vadis*, Marc Antony in

Julius Caesar, particularly, all who had seen him considered him irreplaceable.

In 1893 Abel Deval was thirty. He was far from being an actor in the same class as Guitry and De Max, but he had superb presence, a magnificent voice, self-assurance, and a cutting manner. He played a number of parts perfectly, notably, after Pierre Berton, Baron Scarpia in *La Tosca.* In 1900 he became manager of the Théâtre de l'Athénée, and was the father of Jacques Deval, the author of *Tovaritch.*

Having done some important remodeling and redecorating in the theater, it was with these three actors that Sarah Bernhardt inaugurated her management of the Renaissance, on November 5, 1893, with a first performance of *Les Rois,* in five acts, by Jules Lemaître.

This was by no means a costume play. The action took place in 1900; that is, in the future. Noble, austere, magnificently written, but more literary than dramatic, the play had no success. By the way, it is remarkable that never, or almost never, has a dramatic work succeeded which showed a period in the future. In more recent times, how many plays whose action takes place in the year 2000, or even 1950, have failed similarly? Here is a peculiar psychological phenomenon which has been verified a hundred times. The public does not like to see "tomorrow" on the stage. I think this can be explained by the fact that the future is the only hope of man, and whatever the form in which it is shown to him it disappoints him because he wants this future to be more beautiful. "Well, if that's all we can expect . . ." he thinks, and accuses the author of not being more optimistic. It is also possible that a play situated in the future, and consequently a hypothesis, thereby takes on an even greater unreality than those numerous dramatic works in which the scene is laid "in an imaginary country," which also very rarely succeed. *Les Rois* had exactly thirty performances, with very small receipts, and the result was largely a deficit.

Sarah did not hold this against the author who, on the contrary, became a very affectionate friend for whom Sarah had a very great liking until his death in 1914. A few years younger than Sarah Bernhardt, Jules Lemaître distinctly marked the turning point in the sentimental life of the great artist. Until then her numerous adventures, like her marriage, had been stormy and passionate. I have mentioned the more important ones, those that all Paris knew, which it is positively impossible to ignore. In retracing the life of Sarah Bernhardt I could not pass them over in silence, when all the newspapers of the period spoke of them openly. But I do not forget that during her last two years Sarah Bernhardt was my "step-grandmother," and out of respect for her memory I have strictly refrained from revealing anything in her life that was secret or, in any case, less official. I have tried to combine my duties as a historian with those of a grandson. Moreover, everybody knows, more or less exactly, that the first thirty years of her life as a woman were exceptionally adventurous. It is useless to dwell on the fact. It was at the time when she took the Renaissance and met Lemaître that everything changed. She was then forty-nine and, as we have seen, she was far from forgetting both her age and the dignity which it imposed upon her.

Jules Lemaître was calm, peaceful, almost cold, decorous even in his youth, with a pointed beard, not very handsome, and a bit of a pedagogue, but highly intelligent. He was exactly the kind of man to interest a sensible woman approaching fifty.

For his own part, while he had criticized her severely at times, Lemaître had a boundless admiration for Sarah, and often said: "She is not only an actress of genius, but a woman of genius. Nothing escapes her. A few moments of attention are enough to make her acquainted with subjects most foreign to her. Astonishingly witty and clear-sighted, she could just as well have succeeded in any other art, in science, or in politics. She had only to wish it."

During the performances of *Les Rois*, Sarah had revived at classical matinees *Phèdre*, which she had not played in Paris for thirteen years —since her departure from the Théâtre Français. Then she gave the play daily, every evening for two weeks, from December 2 to December 15. A tragedy of Racine as a regular performance! Only Sarah Bernhardt would have dared to do such a thing. She had asked De Max to play Hippolyte, but he would never consent.

"Mounet Sully was and still is too marvelous in this part," said he. "As long as he is alive it would be an impertinence on my part to play it. And, then, I do not wish to risk a comparison which would crush me."

De Max, therefore, took the part of Thésée, and played it nobly. But who could achieve a personal success as this pompous and credulous character? On the other hand, as Phèdre, Sarah had as great a triumph as in her finest days at the Comédie Française. In connection with this revival, Francisque Sarcey wrote in his *Quarante Ans de Théâtre*:

"It is strange, astounding, inexplicable, but nevertheless true that Madame Sarah Bernhardt is younger and more beautiful than she has ever been. Her beauty has become, if I may say so, more artistic. The admiration which she inspires is that which one experiences at the sight of an ancient statue. Her Phèdre is a masterpiece of artistry. Such an interpretation almost borders on the miraculous."

On December 16, in order to be sure of handsome receipts during the Christmas holidays and on New Year's day, Sarah revived *La Dame aux Camélias*. This was the third series of performances of this play which she gave in Paris. After Marais and Damala, it was Lucien Guitry who played Armand Duval. Of course, the play of Alexandre Dumas *fils* packed the house, but it must not be overdone. On other occasions, Sarah might be compelled in a hurry to revive this blessed play, which was a certain source of revenue.

She stopped it prudently, in order to create a new part in a play by Eugene Morand and Armand Silvestre, *Izéil*, which she played with Guitry and De Max, on January 24, 1894. To their three names she added that of Marie Laurent, a great dramatic actress who was then nearly seventy, whose name Sarah courteously placed ahead of her own on the program. Having India as its setting, six centuries before Jesus Christ, *Izéil* was a picturesque work but rather colorless, and it lasted only two months. Then Sarah Bernhardt finished her season in Paris by reviving *Fédora* on April 3, with Lucien Guitry as Loris Ipanoff, and closed the Renaissance on May 29. The combined result of these first efforts was rather unsatisfactory.

In June she went to London and gave *Les Rois, Izéil,* and *Phèdre*. On her return she engaged as manager of her theater Victor Ullmann, whose name appeared for the first time on the programs of the Renaissance in 1894. During the last thirty years of his life he remained the business manager of all Sarah Bernhardt's undertakings in Paris, while Maurice Grau devoted himself exclusively to her tours.

Sarah Bernhardt's second season at the Renaissance began on September 17, 1894, with a revival of *La Femme de Claude*, by Alexandre Dumas *fils*, first performed by Aimée Desclée at the Gymnase in January, 1873. Supported by Guitry, De Max, and Abel Deval, Sarah Bernhardt was admirable. I saw her in another revival of the play in

January, 1905, and I shall never forget her regal cynicism as the spy, Césarine. But the play was never a financial success, and the revival in 1894 ran only six weeks. It was followed by *Gismonda*, a new play by Victorien Sardou, which was produced for the first time on October 31, 1894, with Sarah Bernhardt supported by her three usual partners.

Better than *Cléopâtre* but much less powerful than the preceding plays written for her by Sardou, this new work had a satisfactory run: a hundred and three performances. Luxuriously staged, the play was set in Athens in 1450. As the curtain rose, the first set, representing the Acropolis dominating the sea in the distance, received prolonged applause. But Sarah Bernhardt's part was no more touching than dramatic. Instead of dying in the end, she married Lucien Guitry—which was a disappointment. Sarah and Sardou had accustomed the public to being "shaken" more deeply.

On January 5, 1895, after the performance, Sarah invited her company to her dressing room for an intimate celebration of the seventy-fifth performance of *Gismonda*. She seemed thoughtful and preoccupied and Sardou questioned her. At eight o'clock in the morning she had got up to go to the Ecole Militaire, where, among a few privileged persons, she had been present at the degradation of Captain Dreyfus, condemned by the court-martial three weeks earlier. Maurice Barrès, Léon Daudet, Henri Rochefort—all convinced of his guilt—were there. But she had found herself on the side of the manager of *Le Figaro*, Fernand de Rodays, who was then one of the few who doubted his treason. The impassiveness of Dreyfus during his degradation and his protestations of innocence had profoundly impressed Sarah. "But suppose he were not guilty?" she kept repeating.

That night everybody laughed when she formulated this hypothesis. Ten high-ranking French officers had judged him "in their souls and consciences." How could they be wrong? Nevertheless, Sarah remained thoughtful. Two years later she was to recall that evening and that discussion. She alone had had a presentiment of the truth.

At the same time, the Renaissance suddenly became the object of general attention in theatrical circles.

In 1888, after twenty years' service, Coquelin *aîné* had asked for his pension from the Comédie Française. He had made many tours, particularly in the United States, and had then returned to the Théâtre Français as a *Pensionnaire* in 1891, in order to play in

Thermidor by Victorien Sardou. The following year he had again left that theater but had not yet performed in Paris. In principle, he actually had no right to. Every actor who signs the deed of the associated players of the Comédie Française undertakes never to appear *during his life* in any other theater in the capital, even after he has drawn his pension. A *Sociétaire* who is dismissed is free to play in Paris, but one who decides to retire can perform only in the provinces and abroad.

In December, 1894, it was announced that the famous actor had been engaged by Sarah Bernhardt and would make his debut at the Renaissance the following month. There was great excitement, and the newspapers discussed the news at great length. As was its duty, the Comédie sued the actor and his manager, who for the second time in her life received the process servers of the Théâtre Français. It was she who had persuaded Coquelin to ignore the prohibition stipulated in his old agreement with the Comédie Française. He was then fifty-four, and he could not be expected to renounce playing on the boulevards until the end of his life. It was better to risk a lawsuit and lose it. He knew the costs: a hundred thousand francs and some additional expenses. It was worth the money to recover the right to act in Paris, and Coquelin allowed himself to be convinced.

Beginning in January, 1895, while *Gismonda* was still running in the evening, Coquelin *aîné* gave about twenty performances at the Renaissance, but only at matinees. The first play in which he appeared was Molière's *Amphytrion*, with the following magnificent cast: Sarah Bernhardt as Alcmène, Coquelin *aîné* as Sosie, Lucien Guitry as Jupiter, Abel Deval as Amphytrion, Jean Coquelin as Mercure. (Jean Coquelin, then a youth, was the son of Coquelin *aîné* and the nephew of Coquelin *cadet*.) As a curtain raiser the Renaissance company gave *L'Infidèle*, the delightful one-act in verse by Georges de Porto-Riche.

The second "Sarah Bernhardt–Coquelin Program" consisted of *Le Médecin malgré Lui*, by Molière, in which he played Sganarelle, and *Jean-Marie*, the one-act play by André Theuriet, which Sarah Bernhardt had first performed at the Odéon in 1871 and was now reviving for the first time in Paris. With her Lucien Guitry took the part of Jean-Marie, created by Porel. Naturally these few performances were a triumphant success. What playgoer would have missed such a windfall as these two great artists, back once more on the boulevards fifteen years after their last successes together at the Comédie Française?

Unfortunately, the evening performances were not so brilliant. Following *Gismonda*, on February 13, 1895, Sarah Bernhardt first played in *Magda*, a play by Hermann Sudermann, translated from the German by Maurice Rémon. It was a drama of the middle class, interesting but showing her in too familiar and too commonplace a guise. With rare exceptions—*Froufrou* is the most striking—Sarah was less successful in modern dramatic plays. The public wanted to see her in costume plays. As Sarcey said at the time, she was "condemned to parts of great heroines." *Magda* had twenty-seven performances.

We shall never know why she then attempted to revive *Izéil*, which she had to close at the end of one week. On April 5 she opened in *La Princesse Lointaine* by Edmond Rostand. This was not that great poet's first attempt at the theater. During the previous season he had given *Les Romanesques* to the Comédie Française. This was, therefore, his second play. In her interviews, before the opening, Sarah Bernhardt had said: "The play may not make a cent, but I don't care. I think it is superb. An artist could not fail to put on *La Princesse Lointaine*."

She produced it with unbelievable care, love, luxury, and ingeniousness, achieving real miracles of stage management on the small stage of the Renaissance. As presented by Sarah Bernhardt, *La Princesse Lointaine* was not only an admirable play, a lofty poem, but also a spectacle of the utmost beauty. The cast was absolutely first-rate, with Sarah Bernhardt as a marvelous Mélissinde; Guitry as a splendid Bertrand; and, particularly, De Max, who was incomparable as the dying poet, Geoffroy Rudel. The play ran for thirty-one performances, costing Sarah Bernhardt more than two hundred thousand francs!

Heartbroken, on May 2 she revived *La Dame aux Camélias*, with Guitry, and made forty times the maximum! But these successive rebuffs, these two burdensome seasons, had disgusted her with the Renaissance for a time. She handed over the direction to Guitry and prepared to return again to America for ten months. She had to make money. "What?" people exclaimed. "Already?" Two years earlier she had brought back three and a half millions. True, but the Renaissance had already cost her seven hundred thousand francs, Belle Isle almost as much. Above all, there was her mode of life—growing ever more luxurious and extravagant. This "household" employed innumerable overseers, secretaries, valets, and female servants; three or four carriages, six horses, two coachmen. Since she kept practically open house, at almost every meal Sarah Bernhardt had from ten to twenty guests around her table.

By the beginning of October, 1895, she was touring in Belgium and the large towns of France. During her absence Guitry produced at the Renaissance *Amants*, the magnificent play by Maurice Donnay, in which he himself played, with Jeanne Granier. It opened on November 5 and was a triumph, at last. On her way through Paris, Sarah went to a performance of the play, saw the packed house, and said sadly: "All I have to do is go away, and they make money here!"

As a farewell to Paris, at the end of December, she performed at the Renaissance, once in *Phèdre* and once in *La Dame aux Camélias*. On January 3, 1896, she left Havre for the United States.

Her repertory consisted of the plays which were always asked for again in the New World: *Phèdre, Adrienne Lecouvreur, La Dame aux Camélias, Froufrou, Fédora, La Tosca,* etc. To these she added four new plays not yet seen in America: *Gismonda, Izéil, Magda,* and *La Femme de Claude*. This time she began her tour in Chicago, and did not reach New York until May, 1896, after having played in the West. Her biggest success was still *Fédora*, which she had to keep on the program for two weeks in succession.

During her absence the success of *Amants* continued at the Renaissance. Then, for the second half of the season, Guitry produced and appeared in two more plays, *La Figurante,* by François de Curel, and *La Meute,* by Abel Hermant, neither of which was a success.

Returning to France at the end of July, Sarah skipped Paris and went directly from Havre to Belle Isle, where all her family had already settled for the summer. It had now increased, for Lysiane, the second daughter of Maurice Bernhardt, had been born the year before. Simone, the eldest, was now seven. Other close friends were impatiently awaiting her return. These few weeks' rest at Belle Isle were Sarah's reward every year. Belle Isle recompensed her for all her fatigue, all her worries, and her losses at the Renaissance. Belle Isle, which brought Maurice and his two little girls under her roof for a time, was the joy of her life.

She returned to the Renaissance on September 30, 1896, in a revival of *La Dame aux Camélias*. This time she played it longer and with more magnificent results than usual; for more than two months the box office was sold out. The reason was that, for this revival, Sarah Bernhardt had the idea of putting on the play in the settings and costumes of the period. Played in the atmosphere of 1896, it was beginning to date a little, forty-four years having passed since its first performance. Revived in the fashion of 1852, the play was "rejuvenated" in an extraordinary way and its success mounted higher than ever. This new setting of *La Dame aux Camélias* was destined to insure the eternal success of this play, which is as dazzling in France today as it was ninety years ago when it first opened.

On October 8, for one evening, there was no performance at the Renaissance in order to allow Sarah Bernhardt to appear at an entertainment given at Versailles in honor of Czar Nicholas II, on his official visit to Paris. In the name of the Minister of Fine Arts, the French Ambassador had asked the Czar, before he left Saint Petersburg, whether he had any particular wish concerning this program. The Emperor of Russia replied with the simple words: "Sarah Bernhardt."

December 3, 1896, was a great date for Sarah. It was that of the first performance of *Lorenzaccio*, the play by Alfred de Musset, written in 1834, which had never been performed on the stage. At Sarah's request Armand d'Artois adapted it for the stage, making only a few respectful changes destined to reduce to only five acts and an epilogue the work of Musset which, in its original form, consisted of thirty-nine scenes. It was one of the greatest personal triumphs of Sarah Bernhardt, one of the five or six successes of the highest rank which surpass all others in her wonderful career. This victory appeared all the more brilliant as, for sixty years, it was generally believed absolutely impossible to play Musset's drama, and especially the very singular and very complex character of Lorenzo de Médicis. He is a sort of Hamlet, less courageous, more disturbing, and still more difficult to play. Having very often astonished Paris in the space of twenty-five years, Sarah succeeded in astounding those who thought they knew best what she was capable of doing. This is what Jules de Tillet wrote in *La Revue Bleue* of December, 1896:

"This time her triumph was unbounded and unreserved. She went beyond the summit of her art. She gave life to the character of Lorenzo, whom nobody had dared to approach before her. Admirable from beginning to end, without tricks and without garbling, neither going to extremes nor shouting, she led us into the very depths of the soul by the simplicity and accuracy of her diction, by the sovereign art of her attitudes and gestures. She reached the sublime. I have never seen anything in the theater to equal what she gave in *Lorenzaccio*."

The supporting cast was just average. There were no well-known names. She alone was the entire performance. Obviously, it was not a play for the general public. She knew this before she produced it. She was, therefore, neither surprised nor disappointed when she closed it after seventy-one performances. It is certain, however, that *Lorenzaccio* did as much for the fame of Sarah Bernhardt as the plays of Sardou in which she had performed three hundred times.

A week after the opening of *Lorenzaccio*, on December 9, 1896, the first official glorification of Sarah took place in Paris. An eminent journalist of the period, Henry Bauer, organized "Sarah Bernhardt Day," a sort of apotheosis of the great artist, the public crowning of her career. First there was a banquet of five hundred covers at noon, in the Grand Hotel, Rue Scribe. All the celebrities of the world of art and letters in Paris were present. Around the tables every seat was occupied by some personality. Sarah Bernhardt presided, having on her right the Minister of Fine Arts and on her left the personal representative of the President of the Republic. At the end of the banquet only one speech was made, by Victorien Sardou. He outlined the career of Sarah Bernhardt, her triumphs; and, in striking homage to her genius, he expressed in affectionate terms the admiration of Paris and of all France for her. Sarah replied briefly, and prolonged applause greeted her as she sat down.

At half past two o'clock, at the Renaissance, in the presence of a packed house, where the seats had been bought up for a fortune, she played the second act of *Phèdre* and the fourth act of *Rome Vaincue*, by Alexandre Parodi, which she had first performed at the Comédie Française twenty years earlier. Between the two plays she mounted a sort of throne on the stage, and in succession François Coppée, Catulle Mendès, André Theuriet, Edmond Rostand, and Edmond Haraucourt came in person and each recited a sonnet which he had written to her fame. Then the orchestra of the Concerts Colonne played a "Hymn to Sarah Bernhardt," specially composed for the occasion, with words by Armand Silvestre and music by Gabriel Pierné.

The mere story of this demonstration gives one an idea of what

Sarah Bernhardt's position was at the time. A queen, a leader of vic-
torious armies, Pasteur or Victor Hugo themselves, could not have
been the object of greater honors. She was then only fifty-two, but
already her name was gradually becoming a legend. She was one of
the national glories of France. She was a unique and exceptional
personality, a sort of being apart, above humanity, and very naturally
Paris treated her as such. For twenty-seven more years, more than a
quarter of a century, she retained this unheard-of prestige which was
improbable and without a parallel in the world. In every country she
was to be the heroine periodically of a "Sarah Bernhardt Day" or a
"Sarah Bernhardt Night" of this kind, comparable, within certain
limits, to the triumphs of the Roman Emperors of old. Nevertheless,
by the incredible irony of fate, the two last years of her management
at the Renaissance were nothing but an uninterrupted series of
failures.

On February 28, 1897, she acted in a new play by Sardou, called
Spiritisme. The greatest men have their little weaknesses. Sardou
blindly believed in communications between this world and the beyond. He believed in turning tables, in mediums, in the occult in-
fluences of the subconscious, and in the constant intervention of the
dead in all our actions. In all seriousness he had written a modern
drama in which the principal scene aroused "sensation in the house."
It took place between his two principals: Simone, played by Sarah
Bernhardt, and her husband, d'Aubenas. The latter, owing to an
erroneous report, believed that his wife had been killed in a railway
accident the day before. On seeing her reappear he was not in the
least astonished, but instead of concluding logically that she had
escaped from the accident he chatted calmly with what he believed
was the ghost of his wife! People refused to accept the situation, and
Spiritisme had twenty performances. This was Sardou's only failure
with Sarah Bernhardt, but it was colossal. For years in Paris, whenever one wanted to quote an example of a complete flop, *Spiritisme*
was mentioned.

On March 3 Sarah Bernhardt revived *La Tosca*, with Abel Deval
in the part of Scarpia for the first time. On April 13, for the Easter
holiday, she gave the first performance of Edmond Rostand's *La
Samaritaine*, which she put on for a few matinees only as she did
not believe it was possible to give a "gospel" regularly every evening
in succession. The author himself had thus entitled his work, but

the future happily proved that Sarah Bernhardt was wrong. While the creation of *La Samaritaine* was only a brilliant literary success, its frequent revivals were to become more and more fruitful. It must be added that, after *Cyrano de Bergerac* and *L'Aiglon*, the fame of Edmond Rostand was such that every play signed by him attracted the public.

Toward the end of April it was announced that Eleonora Duse, the great Italian actress, would come to give a series of performances in Paris at the end of the season. She had already performed all over Europe and also in the United States, but France had never yet seen her. Her impresario, Joseph Schurmann, was negotiating with different boulevard theaters. Hearing of this, Sarah Bernhardt sent for him and told him that she would be happy to place her theater at his disposal free of charge. This meant that the receipts, instead of being divided according to agreed proportions between the Renaissance and the foreign company, would be handed over entirely to her young and famous colleague.

Duse was then thirty-eight, fifteen years younger than Sarah. The latter did not know her personally, but, because of her already considerable fame, she made it her duty and pleasure to receive her under these exceptional circumstances. On being consulted by telegram Duse accepted Sarah's offer, and a contract was signed under which Duse was to give at the Renaissance, between June 1 and June 30, 1897, ten performances, in the course of which she was to appear herself in four different plays of which a list was to be sent a few days later to the manager of the Renaissance. These performances of Duse's were to take place alternately with those of Sarah Bernhardt herself, who was to continue the current revival of *La Tosca* on the evenings when Duse was not playing, until the end of June.

About May 15, as had been agreed, the list was published of the plays which Eleonora Duse was to play at Sarah Bernhardt's theater, and there was general stupefaction in theatrical circles. The list included *La Dame aux Camélias* and *La Femme de Claude*, by Dumas *fils*, on the same bill with *Cavalleria Rusticana*, by Verga; *Magda*, by Sudermann, and *La Locandiera*, by Goldoni, on the same bill with *Il Sogno d'un Mattino di Primavera*, by Gabriele d'Annunzio.

When the program was first shown to Sarah Bernhardt, she thought it must be a mistake. She knew that Duse's repertory was composed essentially of the works of Ibsen, *A Doll's House, Hedda Gabler, Rosmersholm,* and *The Lady from the Sea.* Among her other regular dramatists Schurmann had mentioned chiefly Goldoni, Gherardi di Testa, and Marco Praga, whose *La Moglie Ideale* was one of her greatest successes. If she wanted to appear in French plays when performing in Paris, which was perfectly admissible, she had in her repertory *L'Abbesse de Jouarre,* by Ernest Renan; in which she alone had scored a success; *Divorçons, Fernande,* and *Odette,* by Sardou; *Denise* and *Le Demi-Monde,* by Dumas *fils*; and a great many other plays in which Sarah Bernhardt had never acted. When Duse was about to be the guest of the Renaissance, that she should have chosen to appear there precisely in *La Dame aux Camélias,* which had morally been the exclusive property of Sarah for sixteen years, and also in *Magda* and *La Femme de Claude,* two plays in which the latter had been performing for less than three years in her theater—this really looked like a challenge, a kind of provocation. The least one can say of it is that it was a lack of tact.

However, Sarah did not raise the slightest objection, not even when she learned that Duse had decided to give her first performance in Paris in *La Dame aux Camélias.* But the press was not so generous, and commented very severely on the contents of the Italian actress' repertory. Merely by the announcement of the titles of her plays, and before her arrival, she had predisposed the critics against her. This was a serious mistake and a very surprising one. What could have happened, and why this change in her program at the last moment?

At this time the liaison, which made such a sensation, between Eleonora Duse and Gabriele d'Annunzio had just begun. In 1897 she had performed in only one play of his, the very brief *Il Sogno d'un Mattino di Primavera,* which was included in her performances in Paris. It was not until the following year that the series of important works began which he wrote for her: *La Gioconda, La Gloria, La Figlia di Jorio, Più che l'Amore, La Fiaccola sotto il Moggio,* etc. But she had already devoted to the poet of *Le Laudi* the desperate love which was the misfortune of her life, and the slightest wish that he expressed, a word said in passing, became to her orders which she executed slavishly.

When d'Annunzio learned that Duse was going to play in Paris at Sarah Bernhardt's theater, his imagination, which was constantly in a state of effervescence, immediately saw an opportunity for a tournament between the two great actresses, for a sort of competition in which Duse would be the victor, he did not doubt, because of her youth. If it is possible to find an excuse for him, it may be added that, at this time, he had not yet been in Paris and had never seen Sarah Bernhardt act. In advance he could imagine all the French critics dazzled by the genius of his mistress, handing her the palm in long, ecstatic articles, and declaring Sarah conquered, crushed, and finished—whereupon Sarah would immediately cease to be the idol of Paris. It was in order to render more striking the victory of his interpreter and friend that he had persuaded her to produce in Paris the same plays in which Sarah performed. In a state of perpetual admiration before her lover, Duse allowed herself to be convinced. She soon realized how ill-judged her docility had been.

Beyond any doubt, Duse had a considerable success due to curiosity in Paris; and there were packed houses for all her performances. As she was wisely playing only ten nights, and not in succession, which was very little for Paris, her name alone guaranteed receipts for such a short stay. But the press did not even begin to compare her and Sarah Bernhardt. From the choice of her plays it was evident that she had sought and demanded such a comparison. It was not only to evade this rather imperative suggestion that the critics refrained from measuring the two artists. It was because, in fact, no parallel between them was possible. I will not quote the articles of Jules Lemaître. His intimacy with Sarah might make him suspected of partiality. What is worth recording is that, with infinite good sense, he remarked that, if there was a French actress with whom Duse could be compared, it was not Sarah Bernhardt but Réjane.

Nothing could be more true. The comparative studies which were later made in different countries of the respective talents of Duse and Sarah Bernhardt never made any sense and had no reason for existence. The two actresses were both very celebrated. One was the greatest French artist, the other the greatest Italian. But there precisely all points in common between them stopped. The idea of opposing one against the other was as absurd as if a journalist had taken it into his head to establish a competition between Mounet Sully and Coquelin aîné, for example. The former was a tragedian whose art was very elevated, reaching the heights of *Oedipe* and *Polyeucte*. The latter was an admirable comedian whose repertory extended from *Scapin* to *Cyrano* but who, obviously, would never have dared to play Corneille or Sophocles. Similarly, Sarah was primarily a tragedienne and, because her talent was infinitely diverse, she also succeeded in romantic and modern plays. Duse was a magnificent dramatic actress; but she could never rise to the great classical heroines, and never, moreover, interpreted them.

In *La Dame aux Camélias* the Paris critics thought Duse interesting and pathetic, especially in the third act, but physically too middleclass, too remote from the demimondaine who was Marguerite Gautier. She was more pleasing in *Magda*, but the play remained as dull in Italian as in French. Greatly applauded in *La Femme de Claude*, she did not outshine either Sarah or even Desclée. She had her greatest success in the joyful *Locandiera*. This eloquently proves how impossible any parallel was between Duse and Sarah Bernhardt, who could never have played Goldoni's Mirandolina. Gay, malicious, and witty, Duse was delightful in the spontaneity and intense life with which she invested the playful innkeeper. As the ardent Santuzza in *Cavalleria Rusticana* and in *Il Sogno d'un Mattino di Primavera*, in which she played a gentle madwoman, a sort of modern Ophelia, she was intensely interesting. Without further or particular enthusiasm, it was finally concluded that "she was equal to her reputation."

One can get a fairly exact idea of the tone of the French papers toward Duse from the following concluding lines of an article by Emile Faguet, whose authority was then considerable:

"Madame Duse is nothing more than an actress of melodrama, but above the first rank, let us admit. Let her beware of trying to play *Andromaque* in particular. As her acting is lacking in style, she ought to know that grandeur and poetry are closed to her. She must realize this, however, for she does not even try *Bérénice* and contents herself with *Magda*. But in the latter type of work she is marvelous. She is devoted exclusively to melodrama, I repeat; but she gets out of it everything it contains, adding to it and ennobling it, for her power of conveying a sense of reality, on the one hand, and of moving the public, on the other, is unequaled."

On June 14 an extraordinary performance took place at the Renaissance on behalf of the subscription for a statue to Alexandre Dumas *fils* (who had died two years before) which was to be erected in the Place Malesherbes. On the same night, Eleonora Duse played the second act of *La Femme de Claude* and Sarah Bernhardt the fourth and fifth acts of *La Dame aux Camélias*. The receipts were thirty-one thousand francs, which was colossal at that time. This was the only occasion when Sarah Bernhardt and Duse appeared on the same program.

On the morning of this performance d'Annunzio arrived in Paris. He was then thirty-four years old, four years younger than Duse, and spoke absolutely perfect French. After his final break with his famous interpreter, it was in French that he wrote his last three plays: *Le Chèvrefeuille* for Le Bargy, *La Pisanelle* and *Le Martyre de Saint Sébastien* for Ida Rubenstein. It did not take him many hours to realize what was happening in Paris and that, far from having "crushed her rival," Duse, by acting in the repertory of Sarah, and especially in *La Dame aux Camélias*, had merely succeeded in having proclaimed once more the immense superiority of the French interpreter of Marguerite Gautier.

D'Annunzio was greatly struck by this and wanted to be present that very evening at the gala performance where Sarah was playing the two last acts of the play of Dumas *fils*. He wanted as soon as possible to discover the reasons for the undoubted preference of the French public, to see why and how this woman of fifty-three still retained this inexplicable power after her young Italian rival had shown herself to Paris. For the first time he saw Sarah Bernhardt act and quickly understood. Dumfounded and overcome with admiration he returned to the hotel at midnight and said to Duse:

"You were completely mad, my dear, to have attempted to pit your-self against this creature of genius! She is the greatest artist I have ever seen, and no other could be compared to her. For my own part, from this night on I shall have only one ambition in the world: to have her as an interpreter, and it is for her that I shall write my next play."

This simple anecdote enables one to understand how Duse nearly died of the continual sorrows and deceptions which her liaison with d'Annunzio brought her. It lasted eleven years, after which, in 1909, at the age of fifty, she retired from the world and believed that she had left the stage forever. Compelled to gain a livelihood, she re-turned to the theater in 1921, after a retirement of twelve years, and she died at Pittsburgh in 1924, at the age of sixty-five.

D'Annunzio saw the realization of his dream. It was Sarah Bern-hardt who first acted in the play which he wrote during the summer and autumn of 1897, which was *La Città Morta*. Translated by

G. Hérelle, it was first performed in French in Paris at the Renaissance; and it was only a few months later that Eleonora Duse played it in Italian. But this purely gratuitous insult offered to his mistress by the great Italian poet did not bring him luck. In Paris *La Ville Morte* was a complete failure. The subject of the play—the incestuous love of a brother for his sister—shocked the public profoundly, and d'Annunzio took a long time to recover in France the prestige which this play alone had seriously compromised.

Early in October, 1897, Sarah gave a series of performances for two months in Brussels and the large towns of Belgium, while Lucien Guitry gave a first performance at the Renaissance, on October 2, of an American play by William Gillette, called *Secret Service,* adapted by Pierre Decourcelle. This was another total failure. After thirty performances Sarah had to return hastily and revive the inevitable *La Dame aux Camélias* at the beginning of November. The play had fifty superb performances, which permitted her to rehearse at leisure her next new play, *Les Mauvais Bergers,* by Octave Mirbeau. It was to open during the month of December and to be performed by Sarah Bernhardt, Lucien Guitry, and Abel Deval.

On her return Sarah was surprised by the stormy atmosphere which reigned in every circle. Paris seemed in the throes of some kind of fever. The reason was that, while she was away, the Dreyfus Case had come up again and was now entering its acute phase.

In September of the year before, the newspaper *L'Eclair* had revealed that the court-martial of 1894 had pronounced judgment after studying a secret dossier of which neither the accused nor his lawyer, Maître Demange, had any knowledge. In view of this unjustifiable irregularity, Mathieu Dreyfus, the brother of the Captain, had been multiplying his efforts for months to secure a review of the case. In November, 1896, Bernard Lazare had published his first pamphlet: *A Judicial Error: the Truth about the Dreyfus Case.* His second and much more detailed pamphlet appeared at the end of October, 1897, and profoundly disturbed public opinion. Gradually France was dividing into two camps, the Dreyfusards and the Anti-Dreyfusards. During the two or three following years the entire country was shaken by this tremendous affair. Five Ministers of War and three Prime Ministers in succession were obliged to resign. From the top to the bottom of the social ladder everyone took sides, according to his personal, political, or religious convictions. Families were divided, brothers quarreled, and couples were divorced solely because of the Dreyfus Case. Never in the history of France had a judicial scandal reached such proportions.

Sarah Bernhardt's circle and her family provided an exact picture of the dissensions which then arose. Jules Lemaître, her wise and gentle counselor, had taken the part of the army against Dreyfus from the beginning. He was soon to found the *Ligue de la Patrie Française*, which was constituted solely to rally the Anti-Dreyfusards. The other leader of this movement was François Coppée, the author of *Le Passant* and Sarah Bernhardt's friend for twenty-eight years. And one of the first members was her own son, Maurice Bernhardt.

On the other hand, her master and friend, Victorien Sardou, had been greatly upset by the revelations of Bernard Lazare, and he was to play an active part in favor of Dreyfus by being the first to sign the public protest against the arrest of Lieutenant Colonel Picquart, the courageous defender of the prisoner. Moreover, every day Sarah saw, at the rehearsals of his play, the fiercest Drefusard in the world of letters: Octave Mirbeau.

A writer and pamphleteer whose violence nothing could restrain, Octave Mirbeau was a sort of wild animal. He did not discuss, but literally fell upon his interlocutor. With the exception of *Les Affaires sont les Affaires*, his plays are pretty well forgotten today, but his novels are well known: *L'Abbé Jules, Le Journal d'une Femme de Chambre, Le Calvaire, Sébastien Roch,* and many others. All are furious attacks against the individuals or groups which he indicts. They are executions as much as literary works. Mirbeau can be imagined as he wrestled with the most enormous iniquity of the century. With his eyes starting out of his head, with foam on his lips, thundering and vociferating, he spent the rehearsals of *Les Mauvais Bergers* insulting the judges of the court-martial, shouting his hatred of du Paty de Clam, Colonel Henry, Gonse, Mercier, or de Bois-deffre. The play was slow in getting ready, and the peaceful Renaissance had never echoed to such imprecations. But there was lofty intelligence and complete lucidity behind these jackal yells. Little by little, by dint of listening to him and having always doubted the guilt of Dreyfus, Sarah acquired the conviction that his innocence was beyond discussion.

On November 15, acting on the advice of Scheurer-Kestner, Vice

President of the Senate, Mathieu Dreyfus, in an open letter to General Billot, Minister of War, denounced Esterházy as the author of the *bordereau* attributed to Captain Dreyfus, the only basis of the accusation against him and the only official reason for his condemnation. This came like a clap of thunder in Paris. The Dreyfusards could not remain inactive, but they were not organized in groups like their adversaries. The *Ligue pour la Défense des Droits de l'Homme et du Citoyen*, to which all the partisans of Dreyfus rallied and of which Yves Guyot was the president, was not formed until later. Until then, in order that their efforts might be effective, it was necessary for the movement to be led by an eminent man, admired, respected, known for his wisdom and also for his judicial habit of mind. The fulminating Mirbeau had already drawn up a manifesto, which he wished to publish in the press and post on all the walls of Paris. But it was a tissue of insults and violent statements, which thereby invalidated it. Moreover, the personality of the signer was not important enough to give his proclamation sufficient force.

Then Sarah Bernhardt had an idea. Through William Busnach, a friend of her youth, she had met Emile Zola, of whom Busnach was a disciple and admirer, having adapted with both skill and devotion all the plays based on his novels: *Nana, Pot-Bouille, L'Assommoir, Germinal,* etc. She said to herself that Zola was the only man in France who had sufficient prestige to lead the revisionist movement and bring out the innocence of Dreyfus. But would he want to do this, and what, in the first place, was his opinion of the Dreyfus Case? On November 15, after the rehearsal of *Les Mauvais Bergers*, Sarah went to see Zola at his home in the Rue de Bruxelles and explained to him in detail her point of view—which is to say she repeated exactly the arguments of Mirbeau, merely suppressing the invectives.

An indefatigable worker, who went out very little and devoted himself exclusively to his writing, Zola had never paid any attention to the Dreyfus Case. The clear, lucid, and irrefutable manner in which Sarah expounded the facts was a revelation to him. The very next day he saw Scheurer-Kestner, and three days later his mind was made up. Interrupting all other activities, he would now have only one object— to free the innocent man. On November 25 his first article on the subject appeared in *Le Figaro*, ending with the celebrated phrase: "Truth is on the march, and nothing will stop it." On December 14, after three other articles in *Le Figaro*, Zola published as a pamphlet his *Lettre à la Jeunesse*, exhorting all young men to take their stand on the side of justice. It excited passionate comment.

The next day, on December 15, 1897, the first performance of *Les Mauvais Bergers* took place at the Renaissance. It was a play of social significance, the title referring to selfish employers who were hard on the workers. Abel Deval was the manager of the factory, and Guitry the leader of the workers on strike. Although mediocre on the whole, the play had some good scenes; but people's minds were so over-excited by the Dreyfus Case that a mere anecdote left the public indifferent. Only such dialogue was underlined as could be interpreted as referring to current events. This simple phrase "It is not within the reach of everybody to be just" aroused thunders of applause, to which hisses and shouts replied. Twenty similar harmless phrases provoked incidents of the same kind.

Walking up and down the stage behind the scenes, Octave Mirbeau watched the demonstrations, his blood pressure rising. He had completely forgotten that it was a play of his own whose fate was being decided at that moment. Only one thing concerned him: Were the demonstrations against the court-martial definitely the stronger? In other words, was there a majority of Dreyfusards in the house? As for *Les Mauvais Bergers*, he was as little concerned about it as the public! Performed in such an atmosphere, it was difficult for a play to run a normal course. During the following evenings the Renaissance looked more like the hall of a public meeting than the auditorium of a theater.

On January 10, 1898, Esterházy was tried and acquitted; on January 11 Picquart was arrested and taken to the fortress of Mont-Valérien. Two days later Emile Zola published in *L'Aurore* his famous letter *J'accuse*, in which he mentioned by name all the high-ranking officers whose machinations had led to the condemnation of Dreyfus. It was an event.

Next day the Anti-Dreyfusards were unleashed and asked for the immediate arrest of Zola, demanding his head. Violent demonstrations took place in the principal cities of France, particularly at Marseilles, Lyons, and Nantes. But nowhere were they so bad as in Paris, where, about six in the evening, a furious column marched up to the Rue de Bruxelles shouting "Death to Zola!" and besieging the novelist's little house. The police had to be called in great haste. Suddenly a window opened on the second floor, and Sarah Bernhardt appeared. She had come to congratulate Zola on his courageous campaign, which she had initiated two months earlier. She was revolted by the shouts of these madmen and her mere presence in his house at that moment showed which side she was on. When they recognized her the disconcerted disturbers were silent, and soon the police hastened along and dispersed them. But the following morning the Anti-Dreyfusard papers announced in large letters:

"Sarah Bernhardt at Zola's. The great artist is with the Jews against the army!"

Soon further demonstrations, this time against her, took place around her theater. In order to avoid conflicts the Prefect of Police begged Sarah Bernhardt to close the Renaissance, which was obliged to suspend performances for eight days. Thus the run of *Les Mauvais Bergers* was abruptly interrupted, after thirty performances. But her visit to Zola had another consequence more painful for her. Being a member of the *Ligue des Patriotes*, Maurice Bernhardt had applauded the acquittal of Esterházy; and he considered Zola's articles as so many insults to the honor of France. His consternation was great when he learned from the papers the attitude adopted by his mother. That same evening he left for Monte Carlo with his young wife, without having informed Sarah or even seen her again. For months they did not speak to each other. It was not until the suicide of Colonel Henry, which revealed to all men of good faith the innocence of Dreyfus and of Picquart and the certain guilt of Esterházy, that Maurice returned repentant and convinced at last. Never again from that day was the Dreyfus Case mentioned in Sarah's presence. It alone had succeeded in momentarily disuniting this mother and her son whose love for each other nothing up to then and nothing ever afterward affected.

On January 21, 1898, Sarah Bernhardt reopened the Renaissance with a first performance of *La Ville Morte*, the play which Gabriele d'Annunzio had asked her to play in French before it was performed in Italian. In the supporting cast were Abel Deval, Brémont, and Blanche Dufrène. Sarah was applauded and considered sublime in the perilous role of Anne, the blind woman; but the play was unanimously slaughtered by the press and barely reached thirteen performances. This was another costly failure, following that of *La Princesse Lointaine, Spiritisme, Secret Service,* and *Les Mauvais Bergers.* Sarah was discouraged and tried what had already succeeded with *Amants* two years previously: to produce a new play by Maurice Donnay without acting in it herself. The Renaissance gave the first performance of

L'Affranchie, with Guitry, but the play was mediocre and closed after two weeks.

Making a further effort, Sarah Bernhardt herself created the leading part, on April 20, 1898, with Lucien Guitry and Abel Deval, in a new play by Romain Coolus. As a special tribute to his manager and interpreter he had called it *Lysiane*, after the name of Sarah's second granddaughter. It was a dramatic comedy devoid of interest and was also a complete failure, reaching only twenty-four performances. What was there to do? Nothing but to revive the inexhaustible *Dame aux Camélias* for one month. To this Sarah Bernhardt resigned herself on May 12, and by the middle of June she left for Belle Isle.

Prior to her departure she attended the opening performance of the great Italian actor Ermete Novelli, who came with his company to the Renaissance for two weeks—during which they performed *La Morte Civile, Ghosts, Le Père Lebonnard, Michel Perrin, Don Pietro Caruso*. Then, in July, the two admirable Spanish actors, Maria Guerrero and Diaz de Mendoza, took possession of the Renaissance, where they gave some twenty performances.

When she returned, Sarah Bernhardt made another attempt; but she had vowed that it would be the last. If it failed, she would give up. On October 28, 1898, she appeared in the first performance of *Médée*, by Catulle Mendès. She gave it a luxurious production, a powerful performance by herself of the legendary wizard; but the play had only twenty-three performances!

By this time she had had enough of it. Convinced that there was an evil spell on the theater, that nothing could ever succeed at the Renaissance, she put her lease up for sale and asked the City of Paris to let to her the Théâtre des Nations. It had a very large auditorium and it was situated on the quays of the Seine, opposite the Théâtre du Châtelet. The Municipal Council eagerly accepted her offer and she signed a lease for twenty-five years, beginning January 1, 1899.

In order to say good-by to the Renaissance "nicely," on November 18, 1898, she gave a last revival of *La Dame aux Camélias*, with a new Armand Duval, Pierre Magnier, whom she engaged for several years. And on December 11, 1898, Marguerite Gautier died for the last time on the stage of the Renaissance, which Sarah Bernhardt definitely abandoned. There, in five years, she had lost two million gold francs. A few weeks later she opened the Théâtre des Nations, which was renamed the Théâtre Sarah Bernhardt.

CHAPTER VIII

The Théâtre Sarah Bernhardt

SARAH had four essential reasons for leaving the Renaissance and taking the Théâtre Sarah Bernhardt. First, as we have seen, she was convinced that the Renaissance brought her bad luck. Secondly, she wished to have a larger house which, in case of a hit, would make it possible to take in large receipts. The Renaissance had nine hundred seats; the Théâtre Sarah Bernhardt had seventeen hundred. The box-office capacity of the Renaissance was six thousand francs, or forty-eight thousand francs a week; that of the Théâtre Sarah Bernhardt was eleven thousand five hundred francs, or ninety-two thousand a week.

A show like *Gismonda*, for example, carried expenses of thirty-two thousand francs a week at the Renaissance. Therefore, even if the house was full every night, the weekly profit could not exceed sixteen thousand francs. The same show, produced with the same artists at the Théâtre Sarah Bernhardt, would cost perhaps forty thousand francs a week. But, if it took in maximum receipts daily, the net profit could reach fifty-five thousand francs a week. The difference was enormous.

Moreover, large theaters are always better to run, because their expenses do not rise in proportion to the possible increase in receipts. The cost of the actors, for example, does not vary according to the theater in which they play. At that time an artist like Guitry received a thousand francs a performance. But he would have asked that amount just as well if he were playing at the Bouffes Parisiens, where there are seven hundred seats, as at the Châtelet, where there are twenty-two hundred. What is more expensive in a large theater are light, heat, and stagehands, because they are more numerous, and sets, because they are larger. But that is infinitesimal compared with the other expenses, which are fixed, whereas the receipts can be much more important.

Thirdly, Sarah Bernhardt's new theater had an immense stage with a considerable number of outlets. The sets for four or five plays could be kept there at the same time and thus used alternately, a method which Sarah particularly liked and whose advantages she had learned to appreciate at the Odéon and the Théâtre Français.

Fourthly—and perhaps this was the principal reason—she felt that she was growing older and, on the stage of the Renaissance, she was too close to the public. The dimensions of the Théâtre Sarah Bernhardt would enable her to withdraw from them by seating the nearest spectators at a more prudent distance. As a matter of fact, she was fifty-five when she took the Théâtre Sarah Bernhardt. Thirty-seven years had elapsed since her debut in Paris at the Théâtre Français. She knew that she could still create an illusion, but on condition that she was not looked at too closely.

She was happily inspired when she gave up one theater for the other, for her tenancy of the Renaissance was, on the whole, disastrous. At the Théâtre Sarah Bernhardt, it is true, her success was not constant; but she did produce several big successes and one triumph, *L'Aiglon*. In the long run the results of her enterprise were incomparably better.

Her management of the Théâtre Sarah Bernhardt, the only theater in Paris where she performed during the last twenty-three years of her life, falls into two distinct periods. The first lasted fifteen years, from 1899 up to the war of 1914, during which time she controlled the theater herself, performing there constantly; and both as an actress and as a manager her activity was tireless. During those fifteen years she appeared at the Théâtre Sarah Bernhardt in some forty different roles, of which only about fifteen had been played by her before—at the Comédie Française, the Porte Saint Martin, or the Renaissance. Up to 1914 alone, she acted at the Théâtre Sarah Bernhardt in about twenty-five new plays, or works which she interpreted for the first time.

After 1915 she handed over the management of the enterprise entirely to her son, in association with Victor Ullmann, and it was under their management that she reappeared at the Théâtre Sarah Bernhardt in the four plays which she performed there at the end of her life. By way of salary she then received fifteen per cent of the gross receipts; but she was in no way concerned with the profits and losses of the undertaking, which were assumed by Maurice Bernhardt and Ullmann on their own account.

When she took the Théâtre des Nations, it was very old, very ugly, and very dirty, and it was imperatively necessary to redecorate it; but she was in a hurry to open. She therefore decided to postpone this work until the following summer, and inaugurated her management of the Théâtre Sarah Bernhardt, on January 21, 1899, with a revival of *La Tosca*, in which she played with André Calmettes, as Scarpia, and Pierre Magnier, as Mario. Presented in a setting more vast than that of the Renaissance and even that of the Porte Saint Martin, where it had been first produced, Sardou's play seemed to take on a new life, and this revival was far better than that of 1897. Sarah was delighted and felt very much at home in this large theater. "At last, there is breathing space here," she used to say, and, recalling the Renaissance which she now execrated in retrospect, "How did I ever keep so long that bird cage where you could not open your arms without banging against the walls!"

Every night, after the act of the reception at the Marquis Attavanti's, Ullmann brought her the statement of the receipts, which were very satisfactory indeed. Decidedly, everything in her new theater seemed to be as favorable as possible. At the end of this brilliant revival, *La Tosca* reached its three hundredth performance in Paris.

Why, then, was she seized by the extraordinary notion of reviving *Dalila*, which she had played without any success at the Théâtre Français twenty-six years earlier? Sarah Bernhardt had a strange nature, willful and, above all, incredibly obstinate. She would not admit failure. It will be remembered that, in spite of the lack of success of *Macbeth*, she had insisted three months later on reviving the play, whose revival was even more disastrous than its first performance. Doubtless a similar feeling prompted her to produce *Dalila* again. She had failed in it in her youth—all the more reason to revive the part and now achieve the success in it which her mature talent should insure her.

In 1899, however, the play of Octave Feuillet was more than forty years old and fully looked its age. It is an intimate drama with eight characters and would inevitably be lost in the great spaces of the Théâtre Sarah Bernhardt. That is exactly what happened. Over night empty houses took the place of the well-filled seats at *La Tosca*. Revived on March 8, *Dalila* was removed from the playbill on March 20.

For the Easter holidays, on March 25, she revived *La Samaritaine*. And, on April 9, *La Dame aux Camélias* occupied the Théâtre Sarah Bernhardt, where it was to be revived henceforth every year without exception. At this first revival the play of Dumas *fils* proved to be as solid and as "sure" at the Théâtre Sarah Bernhardt as everywhere else. Thanks to it, and very soon to *L'Aiglon* also, Sarah was able to indulge in the luxury of putting on everything she liked, the plays with only the slightest public appeal but in which there was a tempting role for her. After two rehearsals *La Dame aux Camélias* could be made ready and rushed to the rescue of all catastrophes.

At the same time, during the first months of her management, in order to demonstrate the trend of her new theater to young people and to students, she had revived *Phèdre*, at classical matinees, beginning in February. But *Phèdre* could no longer be considered a revival. For several years she had been playing Racine's tragedy regularly in Paris, on an average of ten times a year.

As a result of her triumph in *Lorenzaccio*, Sarah Bernhardt for two years had decided to play *Hamlet*. She rightly thought that, having succeeded strikingly as Lorenzo de Médicis, who was only an imitation of Hamlet, she must succeed equally as the original. But the official French adaptation of Shakespeare's play did not please her. This is the one which was, and still is, in the repertory of the Comédie Française. It is a version in five acts in verse, by Alexandre Dumas *père* and Paul Meurice, which departs very noticeably from the English text and whose lines are very mediocre. In the very first scene, on the terrace at Elsinore, Bernardo says:

> *La bise est âpre et coupe en sifflant, le visage.*[1]

And this is not the most peculiar verse in the adaptation!

Why, Sarah Bernhardt wondered, should one modify or "arrange" Shakespeare? He does not need a collaborator. A well-written translation of his play is better than any adaptation. Therefore, she asked Marcel Schwob, a very fine man of letters, and Eugène Morand, one of the authors of *Izéil*, to write for her a prose version of *Hamlet*, following exactly the original English work. They had brought her their manuscript during the summer of 1898; but already at that time Sarah Bernhardt was thinking of leaving the Renaissance, and

[1] The wind is sharp, and cuts in whistling the face. *Trans.*

she preferred to keep this *Hamlet* until she was settled in a better and more spacious theater.

She gave the first performance at the Théâtre Sarah Bernhardt on May 20, 1899, and, like *Lorenzaccio*, it was an immense success. Her *Hamlet* will always remain one of her most astonishing characterizations. Maurice Baring is of the opinion that, on seeing Sarah Bernhardt in the part, the French public finally got, for the first time, an exact idea of what Shakespeare's play is. Her characterization was absolutely her own and aroused heated commentaries. Catulle Mendès fought a duel with one of his colleagues solely on account of their respective and contradictory opinions concerning Sarah in *Hamlet*. In certain scenes she aroused cries of admiration: the famous monologue, "To be or not to be," which she murmured sitting down, almost in a whisper, instead of reciting it to the public; the scene with Ophelia, "Get thee to a nunnery"; and, above all, the scene with the players, in which she thought of a new and extraordinary piece of stage direction.

Usually Hamlet stands in the middle of the stage staring at the King, who is on the right looking at the performance of *The Murder of Gonzago*, which takes place on the left. On the contrary while the players were performing, Sarah almost disappeared from view behind the courtiers. Then she gradually approached the King, and, suddenly standing behind him and pointing toward the players, shouted almost in his ear: "Look!" The public was startled, at the same time as the King, by her sudden reappearance; the effect was striking.

Mounet Sully was told of her enormous success in the part of the Prince of Denmark, which he had been playing himself for years at the Comédie Française. He had gone to see her and was so much impressed that he returned the next day. Ten times in the course of the year 1899 he was present at the performance from beginning to end, attentively studying the acting of Sarah Bernhardt.

During the intermission or after the performance, he would go to see her in her dressing room and ask her: "At a certain word, tell me why do you do that?"

She would laugh and give him the explanations which he wanted. He often said that he did not agree with her.

"That nervous fear which you show in the scene with Rosencrantz and Guildenstern has no justification. At that moment Hamlet does not yet know that the King has decided to kill him."

"Excuse me," Sarah replied, "he is sure of it, ever since the scene with the players, ever since he decides to kill the King, having become convinced that the Ghost told the truth and that the King is, indeed, the murderer of his father. From that moment he has the certainty that the King fears him and, consequently, will put him out of the way at the first opportunity."

"That is very subtle," said Mounet.

"Well, don't you think that *Hamlet* is subtlety itself?"

Often at two o'clock in the morning they were still arguing in Sarah's dressing room.

In order to allow the contractors to take possession of her theater, Sarah Bernhardt closed on June 15 and went to play *Hamlet* in London, where her characterization aroused the same debates as in Paris.

At the end of the summer she did not tarry at Belle Isle, but returned in September to supervise the work herself. Needless to say, it was longer and more considerable than she had foreseen. She could not reopen in *Hamlet* until December 16, 1899, with a brilliant first night. All Paris first-nighters were present, and the stage box was occupied by the new President of the Republic, Emile Loubet, who had succeeded Félix Faure a few months previously.

Sarah Bernhardt had promised that her new theater would be the most beautiful in Paris, and she kept her word. There were cries of admiration when people saw the enormous auditorium of the old Théâtre des Nations entirely redecorated, brilliantly lighted, and—a remarkable innovation—draped from floor to ceiling in yellow velvet. All theaters in Paris had always been red. Nobody then could have imagined an auditorium any other color. This break with tradition was quite a little event. In the large public foyer, whose windows looked out on the Place du Châtelet, ten tall murals by Georges Clairin, Louise Abbéma, and Mucha depicted Sarah Bernhardt, life-size, in some of her most striking roles: *Lorenzaccio, Gismonda, Phèdre, Théodora, La Princesse Lointaine,* and *La Tosca.*

Because she knew that, more than ever, she would spend the greater part of her time in the theater, Sarah had given particular care to the arrangement of her dressing room, which was a veritable apartment consisting of no less than five rooms on two floors. Communicating directly with the stage, from which she was separated only by a double door and three steps, there was, first of all, an anteroom eighteen to twenty-one feet long and twelve wide. Then there was a large Empire drawing room, hung with yellow satin, with a huge divan in one corner, numerous bookcases, and magnificent period furniture. Finally came Sarah's dressing room, properly speaking, with a tall dressing table, closets capable of holding fifty costumes, a monumental washstand, a bathtub, and a gigantic mirror with three panels. These three communicating rooms were on the second floor of the theater, their windows overlooking the Avenue Victoria. In addition, from the anteroom a narrow stairway led to the ground floor, to a dining room large enough to seat a dozen guests comfortably around the table. To one side there were a pantry and a little kitchen.

For twenty-three years the entire theatrical world of Paris, on opening nights, passed through Sarah Bernhardt's dressing room, whose luxury and vast proportions were famous. Every Sunday, in the dining room on the ground floor, between the matinee and evening performance, she invited to dinner her friends, her authors, and her most important actors. After 1915, when she could no longer walk, in order to avoid going down the narrow staircase, she abandoned the dining room on the ground floor and ate her meals in the Empire drawing room on the first floor. It was there that I dined almost every Sunday from 1920 to 1922, when Sarah Bernhardt was in Paris.

In its new and embellished setting, *Hamlet* had a better reception than in the spring. Alternating with *La Dame aux Camélias*, Sarah played in Shakespeare's tragedy for nearly three months, until March 10, 1900.

The day after it reopened, on December 17, 1899, at half past one, on the stage of the Théâtre Sarah Bernhardt, Edmond Rostand read *L'Aiglon* to the company. Two years earlier, on December 28, 1897, at the Porte Saint Martin, the resounding, incredible, and fabulous opening had taken place of *Cyrano de Bergerac*, the most extraordinary triumph ever witnessed by Paris. In one night Edmond Rostand, who had achieved only three pleasant *succès d'estime*—with *Les Romanesques, La Princesse Lointaine,* and *La Samaritaine*—awoke next day to find himself the foremost dramatic author of his period, as well as "the" French national poet.

In any event, and even if *L'Aiglon* had not been the masterpiece which it is, the prodigious popularity of *Cyrano* insured an immense success to the new play to be given by Edmond Rostand. Before the reading, the flies above the stage were carefully searched to make certain that no indiscreet journalist had hidden there in order to take down as they were spoken, and publish the following day, any verses from *L'Aiglon,* which had barely been announced and was already feverishly awaited.

Rostand read admirably—as well as Sardou, but in a very different style. He also might have been an extraordinary actor, and Sarah Bernhardt begged him, for twenty years, to play at least once the part of Cyrano. But Rostand never consented to that. To make up, to wear a costume, to work at this still somewhat despised profession, even on an exceptional occasion, seemed inconceivable to him. He was seen on the stage reciting his own verses only on very rare occasions, in the course of absolutely sensational gala performances.

Of all the distinguished men whom I have known, Edmond Rostand was certainly the most marvelously French, in the complete and brilliant sense of the word. He was of medium height, very slim, perfectly but quietly dressed; and his famous baldness rendered perhaps even more interesting his delicate face, with its stamp of high breeding and fine features, to which so much character was also lent by his light brown mustache curled up at the ends. Distant without being haughty, with no insolence in his bearing, obliging and generous when he wanted to be, he was really the direct descendant of those great gentlemen of old as they are shown to us in their most flattering pictures. Rostand was not of noble birth, but it was impossible to imagine a more perfect aristocrat, in his demeanor, his gestures, and his language. Around 1900 to resemble Edmond Rostand was the dream of all young men between twenty and thirty, provided they had the slightest taste for distinction and "class."

Already at this time Rostand was in delicate health and had ceased living in Paris. At Cambo, some thirty miles from Biarritz, he bought a magnificent piece of property called Arnaga, where he spent ten months of the year. He did not suffer from this forced retreat, because he had gradually taken an aversion to society and honestly despised the hectic life of cities, which he had had to renounce. Strictly speaking, he was not a misanthrope; but he kept more and more to himself, and it was not easy to reach him. When his arrival in Paris was announced, he immediately received hundreds of invitations but refused almost all of them. His innumerable female admirers, particularly, exasperated him.

"Light women are very tiresome," he used to say, "but respectable women are a deadly bore."

Sometimes he added, with his slight disillusioned and ironical smile: "But for its pleasures, life would be tolerable." He had not much respect for theatrical people, actors, and dramatists. Speaking one day of his friend Léon Bourgeois, an old politician who, in the course of twenty-five years, had occupied all the Ministries in succession, he said: "It was not until the day when he took over Public Instruction and Fine Arts that he fully realized the depths to which meanness, hatred, jealousy, and moral ugliness can descend."

In the theater the two great friends of Rostand were Charles Le Bargy—the admirable actor who, after the death of Coquelin *aîné*, left the Comédie Française in order to revive *Cyrano* at the Porte Saint Martin—and Sarah Bernhardt, for whom he had a real veneration. Certain people, who imagine that they are in the know, have insinuated that a tender idyl had momentarily united the poet of *L'Aiglon* and his divine interpreter. People are very much inclined to associate great authors and their distinguished performers in this way. But these collectors of piquant or sensational stories would do well to open an encyclopedia. There they will see that Edmond Rostand was twenty-four years younger than Sarah Bernhardt. He might easily have been her son; in fact, Maurice Bernhardt was four years older than Rostand. Neither of them—she, particularly—could have forgotten this fact.

Similarly, as I was recently running through one of the numerous books devoted to the life of Sarah Bernhardt I discovered that its author states with the utmost seriousness that, when *Ruy Blas* was revived at the Odéon in 1872, Sarah Bernhardt addressed Victor Hugo in terms of intimate familiarity. In this work the great poet and his interpreter are represented as two comrades of about the same age. Now, Victor Hugo was actually forty-two years older than Sarah Bernhardt, who never spoke to him except in terrified respect. Why do these manufacturers of anecdotes, before peddling them around, never think of verifying dates of the facts to which they refer? This elementary precaution would limit their discoveries to adventures which are at least probable, and would spare us the reading of disconcerting puerilities.

The complete admiration and the unshakable tenderness which Edmond Rostand felt for Sarah Bernhardt were always combined with the profoundest respect. For that reason his devotion to her was probably more complete and more attentive. He would never miss a reception, or a gala of any kind, organized in her honor. As soon as he was notified he took the train and hastened to Paris, even if it was only for twenty-four or forty-eight hours. And she also never appealed to him in vain, being able at all times to ask him for a poem, for his advice, or for his presence. The triumph of *L'Aiglon* had bound them definitely to each other. Shortly before the war of 1914, Rostand was dreaming of a *Faust* for Sarah Bernhardt. But in 1915 her right leg was amputated, and in 1918 Rostand died of Spanish influenza. He was fifty years old. That day Sarah lost her most devoted, most faithful, and most fastidious friend. And the whole of France was in mourning, a greater and more irreparable mourning than was at first realized. For twenty-four years nobody has replaced him. Edmond Rostand was the last great French dramatic poet.

Because he read both very well and very rarely, it was doubly a treat to hear him. His reading of *L'Aiglon* to the company was unforgettable. Delighted and touched, the actors were wiping their eyes and embracing one another, utterly delighted to have a part in the performance of such a work. From that day its triumph was certain. Yet Sarah was not completely satisfied. Edmond Rostand had conceived *L'Aiglon* for her and for Coquelin *aîné*, for whom the part of Flambeau was written. At the beginning and on the basis of a scenario of the play, Coquelin had agreed to, and Sarah had already settled with him, the terms of his engagement: fifteen hundred francs a performance.

However, when the play was finished, Coquelin discovered not only that his character appeared in neither the first nor the last act but also that the part was much less important than Sarah's. He became evasive and embarrassed, alleging that tours, revivals of *Cyrano* every year in Paris, which *L'Aiglon* would prevent him from undertaking . . . in short, he refused the part. Because of Coquelin's refusal, it was Lucien Guitry who was to create the part of Flambeau. But this did not please Sarah at all. She was tremendously fond of Guitry both as an actor and as a man; but more than anyone else she knew his talent, which she had been using at the Renaissance for five years.

Guitry had been admirable in *Amants*, perfect in *Les Mauvais Bergers*, and excellent in *Fédora*, *La Femme de Claude*, and *La Dame aux Camélias*; but he had been mediocre in *Amphytrion*, *Izéil*, *Gismonda*, and very inferior to De Max in *La Princesse Lointaine*.

Guitry was essentially a modern actor, and Emmanuel Arène held that he was not at his ease in what he called "disguise"; that is, period characters. But this was not true, for he was not at all hampered by wearing a costume. He was wonderful in *Le Juif Polonais*, and prodigious in *Le Misanthrope*. What he lacked was poetry. He played badly in *Chantecler* and, very wisely, never tried *Cyrano*, and Sarah guessed that he would not be good as Flambeau. She was uneasy about Guitry in that part and, at the same time, she was unconsolable for the absence of Coquelin, against whom she felt a grievance because of his decision. Coquelin was her old comrade, her partner at the Théâtre Français, twenty-eight years earlier, in so many plays. In 1895 she had opened the doors of the Renaissance to him, thereby deciding him to begin an independent career which turned out to be so brilliant. Coquelin should not have refused to play *L'Aiglon* with her. Obstinate as we know her to have been, she was later to have her way. Employing an ingenious means for achieving her end, she persuaded Coquelin to play Flambeau, not in the original performance of the piece, but in its first revival in Paris.

The first night of *L'Aiglon* took place on March 15, 1900, and was a triumph equal to that of *Cyrano*. From one act to another its success built up to the scene of Wagram, which was the culminating point of the evening and in which Sarah was sublime. In the sixth act, in the death of the Duc de Reichstadt she reached the topmost summit of her art. Prolonged ovations greeted the author when he appeared on the stage beside his inspired interpreter. After thirty curtain calls, the house was still demanding Edmond Rostand and Sarah Bernhardt. It would be in vain to analyze in detail Sarah Bernhardt's interpretation of *L'Aiglon*. Her creation of this character was such an event that all the most eminent critics of every city in the world, where she played the drama for fourteen years, devoted innumerable articles to it. In the long list of roles which she created or revived, *L'Aiglon* is one of the three most celebrated, the other two being *Phèdre* and *La Dame aux Camélias*.

André Calmettes was excellent as Metternich. On the other hand, as she had foreseen, Sarah Bernhardt told me that Guitry was much inferior to his task as Flambeau. Moreover, he never revived the part —in which he played only for the first series of performances. These had a long and perfectly triumphal run. Interrupted only during the month of August, so that Sarah could rest, the play ran until October 30, two hundred and thirty-seven performances, the receipts totaling two million six hundred and seventy-seven thousand francs, or an average of eleven thousand three hundred francs a performance, approximately the maximum. In its day it was one of the greatest financial successes ever achieved in Paris.

The play closed to houses which were as full at the last as at the first performance. Sarah might easily have continued to play it as long again and have brought it to its five hundredth performance. But after this triumph she had been called again to America and had made an engagement for a new tour of six months in the United States, from November, 1900, to April, 1901. It was understood that she would revive L'Aiglon in Paris on her return. As she had the fixed idea of having Coquelin as Flambeau in this revival, she had recourse to a stratagem.

By prearrangement with her, Maurice Grau, her impresario, came to an understanding with the Paris representative of Sarah Bernhardt's American managers, and told him what to do.

One evening this agent went to see the creator of Cyrano in his dressing room, at the Porte Saint Martin, and said to him: "We are in negotiations with Madame Sarah Bernhardt to have her come again to America, but her popularity over there is beginning to fall off. This will be the fifth time in twenty years that she will appear in the United States. We are afraid that henceforth she herself will not be sufficient to guarantee the receipts. Ah, if you would only act with her! Your name is so famous that it would support hers, which is weakening. Backed by Coquelin, Sarah Bernhardt can still hold out; but without him the affair is doubtful. Could we count on you?"

Coquelin was very vain, and the question as to his intelligence has never been solved. In 1888, with Jane Hading, he had made a tour of the United States which was brilliant but whose success could not be compared with the indescribable triumphs which Sarah Bernhardt had achieved there. His name linked with that of Sarah Bernhardt could in no case increase the receipts by five cents. But what actor in his place would have been clearheaded enough to realize it? Stated in these terms, which had been dictated by Sarah, the proposal was to flatter him in the extreme.

"The thing is not impossible," he replied.

"How fortunate! Ah, Monsieur Coquelin, you have saved us!"

"But," he immediately added, "I will consent to come only on condition that I play *Cyrano*. On the nights when this play is given, Sarah can take a rest; that's all."

The impresario pretended to think. "But why should she rest?"

"Because she would never be willing to play Roxane," said Coquelin. "Compared to mine, the part is of too slight importance."

"And if I persuaded her to play Roxane," said the American quickly, "would you play Flambeau in *L'Aiglon*?"

"I could not loyally do otherwise," Coquelin conceded.

"In that case, leave it to me. I will undertake to convince her."

He was all the more certain of succeeding because Sarah had guessed the scene in advance. Coquelin would insist on playing *Cyrano*; and she would "have" him as Flambeau provided she played Roxane, to which she had no objection. And that is how Sarah Bernhardt persuaded Coquelin to play not only Flambeau in *L'Aiglon* but also Scarpia in *La Tosca*, which he learned specially for this tour. He even played, unbelievable as it may seem, the father of Duval in *La Dame aux Camélias*, a part which has only one scene, and the First Grave-digger in *Hamlet*, who has twenty lines in the last act!

Coquelin was so happy, so proud of expanding as Cyrano while the great Sarah modestly effaced herself as Roxane, that he would have accepted many other "bits." He would even have gone so far as to play Panope in *Phèdre* if that had been in the repertory of this tour. According to the actors at one's disposal, the very short part of Panope can be played as readily by a man as by a woman.

The Sarah Bernhardt–Coquelin tour was made with only five plays. They opened in New York at the Garden Theater on November 26, 1900, in *L'Aiglon*, which they played for two weeks. Beginning on December 10, they played *Cyrano* for one week; on the seventeenth, *La Tosca*; on the eighteenth, *La Dame aux Camélias*; and *Hamlet* on the twenty-fourth, closing their performances in New York on January 2, 1901. Beginning the next day, they covered all the large cities of the United States, reappearing at the Metropolitan Opera House in New York on April 8, 1901, in *L'Aiglon*, in which they again played for two weeks. After a few performances in Washington and Philadelphia, Sarah Bernhardt and Coquelin said farewell to the American public by giving one performance on April 29, 1901, in the course of a gala program at the Metropolitan Opera House, of a play in one act by Léon Gozlan, *La Pluie et le Beau Temps,* from the repertory of the Comédie Française. On the following day they left for England, and from May 15 to the end of June, 1901, they gave *Cyrano* and *L'Aiglon* in London. At the beginning of July they were back in Paris.

The Théâtre Sarah Bernhardt had not remained closed during the absence of its manager. On the contrary, the beautiful new house had been brilliantly occupied. On March 8, 1900, a fire broke out at the Comédie Française. During the rebuilding, the players were obliged to seek refuge in other theaters in Paris. After having acted on different stages from March to October, they had settled in the Théâtre Sarah Bernhardt, which, during the months of November and December, 1900, became the temporary stronghold of the "House of Molière." The great artist and her former comrades had forgotten their quarrels, which now dated back twenty years.

On July 14, 1901, the day of the National Holiday, Sarah Bernhardt opened her theater for one evening, giving a single performance of *L'Aiglon* with Coquelin. Edmond Rostand, who had not yet seen the creator of Cyrano in the part of Flambeau, was present at the performance, and at midnight he said to Sarah: "Obviously, there is no comparison!"

He was speaking of Coquelin, who was dazzling as Flambeau, with such a mastery of the part that Guitry could not even be compared with him.

Beginning September 7, Sarah revived *La Dame aux Camélias* with Pierre Magnier for six weeks; and on October 17 she revived *L'Aiglon* for a series of performances, with Coquelin *aîné.* "Now that you know the part," she said to him, "and have had a triumph in it, you cannot refuse to play it for me in Paris also."

He had agreed and had accepted. At last! . . . The newspapers all said the same thing: "Why did he not create this part?" And the revival, which was as brilliant as the opening, brought in maximum receipts for a hundred performances. Sarah Bernhardt was beside herself with joy. Living constantly in a state of excitement, her feelings in regard to the same people, according to circumstances, would go from fierce hatred to overflowing tenderness. A few months earlier,

when Rostand had announced decidedly that they must not count
on Coquelin, that he had refused Flambeau, she had conceived a
deadly hate for the great actor and would willingly have strangled him
with her own hands. Since he was playing the part at last—and with
what success!—she was filled with a sort of adoration for him—strictly
artistic, I need hardly say—and she did not know what to do to please
him and demonstrate how happy she was.

One of Coquelin's best roles at the Théâtre Français had been
Mascarille in *Les Précieuses Ridicules* of Molière. One evening Sarah
Bernhardt offered to put on the play for him at the Théâtre Sarah
Bernhardt and to play Madelon, one of the *Précieuses*. At first Coquelin thought that she was joking. Madelon is a charming character
but quite unworthy of Sarah Bernhardt. With Cathos it is half a part
as the two characters are always on the stage together, alternately
furnishing the dialogue with Mascarille. Why did Sarah Bernhardt
want to take the trouble of learning and playing such a part?

"Why, just to give you pleasure, my 'Cock,' " she said to him. "You
are admirable in the play, and I want you to have your usual success
in my theater."

At classical matinees Sarah Bernhardt played Madelon in *Les
Précieuses Ridicules* with Coquelin *aîné*, as Mascarille, opening on
December 12, 1901. The show began with *L'Aveu*, the play in one act
by Sarah Bernhardt, first performed at the Odéon in 1888. I shall not
pretend that Madelon was the triumph of her career, but she amused
herself enormously, in any case.

After the Christmas holidays and New Year's day, Coquelin had to
return to the Porte Saint Martin, of which he was now co-manager. In
order to go to America with Sarah, and then to her theater, he had
abandoned his own theater for more than a year, and his people
there were asking for him. Heartbroken at his departure, and not
wishing to play *L'Aiglon* without him—at least, for some time—Sarah
Bernhardt closed Rostand's play. During the first three months of
1902 she inaugurated alternating programs at her theater, playing
in *Théodora*, with Desjardins as Justinian and Pierre Magnier as
Andréas; in *Phèdre* and *La Femme de Claude*, on the same bill as
Jean-Marie and *La Samaritaine*. This continued until her next opening in a new part, which took place on April 22, 1902.

It was a play by an American dramatist, Marion Crawford, entitled *Francesca da Rimini*, in a French translation by Marcel Schwob,

the scene of which was laid in Italy during the Renaissance. It was not a success and had only twenty-five performances. The part of Francesca did not bring any great personal success to Sarah Bernhardt. The few who were privileged to see the play remember De Max in particular, who made his return in it. Seven years earlier he had stopped acting with Sarah, after *La Princesse Lointaine*. In *Francesca da Rimini* he gave an extraordinary performance as the lame Giovanni Malatesta, hopelessly in love with Francesca. He brilliantly resumed his position with Sarah Bernhardt, on whose payroll he was to remain for eight years.

At the end of May, Sarah gave *Francesca da Rimini*, with De Max, in London and for the first time played Alphonse Daudet's famous *Sapho*—first performed by Jane Hading and Damala at the Gymnase in 1885 and since revived by Réjane, who had made a great hit in it. For years *Sapho* was to be one of the plays most frequently performed by Sarah, who placed it in the repertory of all her tours. On every hand she was asked to revive it in Paris, but she never had an opportunity to do so.

The following season the Théâtre Sarah Bernhardt opened on October 5, 1902, with *L'Aiglon*. But Sarah Bernhardt did not play the Duc de Reichstadt; it was De Max. In agreement with Edmond Rostand she had entrusted her own part to this magnificent member of her company, rehearsing him herself and showing him in detail all the effects and all the "tricks." If I am not mistaken, this was the only time that the part of the Duc de Reichstadt was played by a man. What actor can have both the talent and the youth demanded by this twenty-year-old character? A woman of fifty can play it convincingly, and Sarah Bernhardt did so until she was sixty-nine. But a man shows his years much more quickly than a woman. As soon as an actor is more than twenty-eight or thirty—that is, when he is beginning to have enough experience to play it well—the part is forbidden to him by his age.

De Max was then thirty-three, but he was astonishingly thin and slender. He had dyed his magnificent black hair blond, and was physically the Duc de Reichstadt in person. After Sarah Bernhardt he was certainly the best *Aiglon* that Paris ever applauded. For forty years the part has been played by many often remarkable artists. Until her death Sarah Bernhardt saw them all. She adored *L'Aiglon* and, being no longer able to perform it herself, since her operation, she liked to see it come to life again in the persons of those who succeeded her. She always said to me: "I have seen only one perfect *Aiglon*: De Max."

However, it was not solely in order to hand over her part to him that Sarah had not revived it at this time. It was because, for the first time in her life, she had agreed to go on tour in Germany. It will be remembered how painful to her was the defeat of 1871. Against the conquerors she had preserved a tenacious hatred, and had never been willing to act in Germany. Her first European tour had taken place in 1881, and since then no six months ever passed without her receiving offers from Berlin. Politely and without giving any explanations, she declined them regularly. While performing constantly in all the neighboring countries—Switzerland, Italy, Austria, Russia, and Denmark—she always excluded Germany from her itinerary.

After refusing for more than twenty years, why did she accept this time? For one simple reason. Because she now had *L'Aiglon* in her repertory. Not only was this a triumph, but it also contained so many avenging verses, so many lines exalting the victories of Napoleon by recalling the defeats of the European allies, particularly the Austro-Germans. Thanks to this play, her performances in Germany could assume the appearance of a semiofficial propaganda tour. When signing her contract she had insisted that *L'Aiglon* should be played at least once in each city, and this condition had been accepted. However, not wishing to give this clause the appearance of a provocation, she had not asked to open in every town with Edmond Rostand's play. It was in *Fédora* that she appeared before the Berlin public for the first time, on October 16, 1902.

It must be admitted that her success was relative, for Sarah Bernhardt was then fifty-eight years old. After she had triumphed all over the entire world, it was felt that she had waited a little too long to allow the Germans to applaud her finally. The press was polite, but no more. If she did not receive in Germany the ovations to which she was accustomed, at least her receipts were considerable. She played for seventeen days in Berlin, and every evening to full houses. Kaiser Wilhelm II came twice to applaud her and invited her to Potsdam, where he gave a large luncheon in her honor. Before and after Berlin she also appeared in Munich, Nuremberg, Dresden, Leipzig, Hamburg, Bremen, and Frankfort, performing for a total of six weeks in Germany. On November 15 she returned to Paris; and on the nineteenth, at the Théâtre Sarah Bernhardt, she revived *Fédora*, with Pierre Magnier as Loris.

On December 23 she gave the first performance of *Théroigne de Méricourt*, a spectacular play in six acts, by Paul Hervieu, about the French Revolution of 1789. Sarah Bernhardt had a great belief in this play, which she mounted with unheard-of prodigality. It consisted of a great number of characters, numerous walk-on parts, and a succession of splendid tableaux. The sustaining company was perfect, with De Max, Desjardins, and Pierre Magnier. But the work required more ample treatment. As treated by Sardou, the same subject would probably have resulted in an important work, a second *Thermidor*. Hervieu was not the man to create these great historical frescoes. His successes have been in cold, incisive, moderate, modern plays—*L'Enigme, La Course du Flambeau, Les Tenailles*—in which the action is concentrated among three or four characters and is not burdened with any episodic or spectacular afterthought. In *Théroigne de Méricourt* he had forced his talent. Willy said: "It's a drama by Victor Hugo, written by Jules Renard."

Nothing could be truer. The long speeches were stilted; the characters lacked inspiration; the big scenes of passion were written with reserve. Plays of this kind must soar, but this one did not.

The production of *Théroigne* confirmed the hopes which Sarah had founded on the size of her theater. As the houses were full at first, the expenses were paid in a month; and the play could close after seventy-one performances with a deficit that was not serious.

Meanwhile the classical matinees were becoming more and more frequented. Often, on certain Thursday afternoons, without doing so on purpose, Sarah advertised *Phèdre*, when Racine's tragedy was being performed at the Théâtre Français on the same day and at the same hour. In such cases, no matter who played the part at the Comédie Française, it was not there that the fullest houses were to be found. Sarah Bernhardt in *Phèdre* had become a sort of national institution, one of the wonders of Paris, something that one had to see.

On February 7, 1903, Sarah Bernhardt performed a professional feat which she alone could have dared. She revived Racine's *Andromaque*, which may be recalled as having been one of her first big successes at the Comédie Française, thirty years earlier. For a few weeks she advertised it every Thursday, appearing herself alternately in the two roles of the play. One Thursday she was Andromaque; and the next, Hermione. De Max was a magnificent Oreste, equaling Mounet Sully. Perhaps he was even better in the last act, in the scene of the Furies. Blanche Dufrène played every Thursday whichever of the two roles was not chosen by Sarah Bernhardt.

These performances attracted all Paris. The two characters are as dissimilar as possible: Andromaque, worthy, chaste, sad, and solemn; Hermione, ardent, vindictive, and passionate. It was a miracle to see Sarah Bernhardt equally prodigious as the one and the other. Everybody who saw her as Hermione wanted to see her as Andromaque, and vice versa. These ingenious matinees made such a sensation at the time that on several occasions later, until 1912, Sarah had to revive *Andromaque* under the same circumstances.

On March 6, 1903, the evening performances of *Théroigne de Méricourt* were succeeded by one of the most lamentable plays Sarah Bernhardt had ever acted in or produced: a detestable *Werther*, by Pierre Decourcelle. This was probably the most painful failure of her entire career. She played the part of Werther, with Blanche Dufrène as Charlotte, Desjardins as Albert, and De Max as an incidental character —Gurth. It is understandable that she should have tried to incarnate the morbid but poetical romanticism of Goethe's hero. But the mere choice of the author whom she asked to adapt the German play was incomprehensible to begin with. Pierre Decourcelle was and will remain the author of *Les Deux Gosses*, a crude melodrama well constructed but of no literary value. Was it reasonable to ask him to make a French version of *Werther*, which could have been so well done by Marcel Schwob, Catulle Mendès, Jean Aicard, and so many others? It was a noble and flattering task, requiring a poet; but a writer of popular fiction undertook it. His play was a deadly bore, and Sarah Bernhardt did not give a good performance. As soon as she made her entrance, her impersonation of the character was a disappointment; her costume was not right; her conception of Werther was even more disconcerting. It would be in bad taste to dwell upon this mistake by a great artist who achieved so many triumphs. *Werther* played thirteen performances to empty houses. On March 23 she revived *L'Aiglon* with her usual success, and three days later everybody had forgotten that other sad adventure.

Sarah Bernhardt's annual season in London was longer in 1903. She remained there six weeks, from May 15 to June 30, at the Adelphi Theatre, where she played *Phèdre*, *Werther*, *Sapho*, and also *Plus que*

Reine—a historical drama by Emile Bergerat, first performed at the Porte Saint Martin in April, 1899, by Coquelin *aîné* as Napoleon I and Jane Hading as Josephine. De Max played the Emperor and Sarah the Empress in London, where the work of Bergerat was new to the English public and made a deep impression. It is, in fact, a well-written play which retraces the entire life, first, of young Bonaparte and then of Napoleon—culminating in the repudiation of Josephine, whose heart-rending despair is nobly expressed. This was another of those rather numerous roles which Sarah Bernhardt performed only on tour and never in Paris.

At the beginning of the season 1903–04 the Théâtre Sarah Bernhardt reopened with *La Dame aux Camélias*, but without Sarah Bernhardt. For the first time since 1882 she handed over the part to her usual understudy, Blanche Dufrène, who was soon to play *L'Aiglon* also while Sarah went to Brussels in *Plus que Reine*. Thanks to Sarah, the play of Dumas *fils* had acquired such a reputation that it could now be put on from time to time without any particular actress in the lead; but the receipts, of course, although sufficient, were not the same as for Sarah Bernhardt. Twenty-five years earlier no producer would ever have dared to give *La Dame aux Camélias* with an unimportant cast. But Sarah's innumerable revivals, the prodigious successes which she achieved, had conferred such prestige on the play that now its title alone was a sufficient attraction. This was perhaps one of Sarah Bernhardt's most astonishing achievements. Thirty years after its first performance, a play of hitherto moderate success was launched by her and reached a point where its commercial value remained even when she no longer played it.

On November 5, 1903, she had another failure in another German play—this time a modern one, *Jeanne Wedekind*, by Félix Filippi, adapted by Luigi Krauss. It was a rural drama devoid of interest, in which Sarah played a gray-haired mother for the first time. To this fact certain of her friends tried to attribute the failure of the play. "People don't want to see her yet as an old woman," they said. Yet Sarah Bernhardt was then fifty-nine and could undertake such a part without being accused of undue haste. The only reason for the failure was that it was a bad play, running for only eleven performances.

But her eternal lifesaver, *La Dame aux Camélias*, was still there.

On November 16 Sarah Bernhardt herself reappeared as Marguerite
Gautier, which she played alternately with *La Tosca* and *Andromaque*.
During the first two weeks of December she ventured so far as to
play the tragedy of Racine on Thursdays in the afternoon and evening, which allowed her to perform on the same day, in turn, Hermione and Andromaque.

On December 15, 1903, Sarah Bernhardt was richly consoled for
her two recent successive failures by giving the first performance of
La Sorcière, by Victorien Sardou. This was the seventh play by him
in which she performed during a period of twenty-one years, and it
was to be the last. He gave *La Piste*, with Réjane, at the Variétés in
1906, and the successful *Affaire des Poisons*, with Coquelin *aîné*, at the
Porte Saint Martin in 1907. He died in 1908 at the age of seventy-
seven.

La Sorcière, of which I spoke at the beginning of this book, was
not a play of such strength and quality as *Fédora*, *Théodora*, and *La
Tosca*, but it was very tense at intervals and gave Sarah Bernhardt
an opportunity of being wonderfully pathetic. It was undoubtedly a
success. In the order of the Sardou–Sarah Bernhardt successes it takes
fourth place. Together they had three triumphs; one great success,
La Sorcière; two semisuccesses, *Cléopâtre* and *Gismonda*; and one
failure, *Spiritisme*. The total result was greatly to be envied.

On April 23, 1904, two years after *Théroigne de Méricourt*, Sarah
gave the first performance of a new play about the French Revolution:
Varennes, by Henri Lavedan and Georges Lenôtre. She played Marie
Antoinette in admirable style. One would have thought that the
famous portrait of the Queen of France, by Madame Vigée-Lebrun,
had stepped out of its frame. But, although it was scrupulously correct down to the slightest details, the play seemed more ingenious
and full of anecdotes than really touching. It had only fifty performances. On June 15 Sarah was playing *La Sorcière* in London.

On October 1 she revived *L'Aiglon* for twenty performances; and
during the months of November and December she went on a tour of
the capitals of Europe, making only a short stay in each city.

During her absence the Théâtre Sarah Bernhardt witnessed the
debut of Maurice Bernhardt as a dramatist. Before her departure she
herself staged and directed, with exceptional care, *Par le Fer et par
le Feu*, a play in five acts which he had based on the famous novel of

Henry Sienkiewicz, in which Félix Huguenet and Desjardins performed, also the lovely Gabrielle Robinne—who was making her first appearance in the theater. By an amusing coincidence, the opening night of this play took place at the Théâtre Sarah Bernhardt on October 23, 1904, on the very day when Sarah was sixty. This was Maurice's birthday present to his mother. It was, moreover, a very fair success of which she had reason to be proud, for it ran for seventy-three performances.

On her return, on December 24, Sarah Bernhardt renewed the practice of alternating plays for six weeks, announcing simultaneously *La Sorcière, L'Aiglon, La Dame aux Camélias, Magda,* and *La Femme de Claude.* On February 7, 1905, for the first time, she played *Angelo, Tyran de Padoue,* the drama in prose by Victor Hugo first produced at the Théâtre Français in 1835. Twenty years had elapsed since the death of the great poet, but the dominating position which he had occupied in France during almost the entire nineteenth century had not been filled. Despite the triumphant successes of *Cyrano* and *L'Aiglon,* Edmond Rostand described himself as the respectful disciple of the poet of genius who wrote *Hernani.* In 1905 the name of Hugo was still one with which to conjure, and Sarah Bernhardt played the formidable character of Tisbé with marvelous artistry. With Desjardins and, particularly, De Max, who was extraordinary as Homodei, the revival of *Angelo* was a very great success.

On April 8, for the Easter holidays, the picturesque revival of *Esther* took place which was mentioned in an earlier chapter. The performance re-created an evening at the Ecole de Saint-Cyr in 1689. As the curtain rose, De Max in the costume of Louis XIV, followed by Madame de Maintenon and his Court, entered and sat down at one side of the stage. Then Racine's tragedy was supposed to be performed, in his presence, exclusively by the pupils of the school, as was the case at its first performance. All the parts were taken by women, and Sarah Bernhardt herself played Assuérus.

Some ten performances were sufficient to exhaust the success of this amusing exhibition, which was not understood. Generally speaking, people did not know that *Esther* and *Athalie,* the two last tragedies of Racine, written after a silence of twelve years, were not first performed in a theater but at the Ecole de Saint-Cyr, by a group of pupils chosen from the young girls who were studying at that institution. This re-creation escaped the general public, which wondered why

Esther's uncle, old Mardochée, and the officers of the King's palace were represented by young women. Rather than explain this, it was simpler to close the play. This ephemeral revival was merely the relaxation of an artist.

Three weeks later Sarah Bernhardt set off on a long tour of North and South America. Before leaving she put on a short revival of *L'Aiglon*, with De Max, for the first time, as Metternich, the part created by Calmettes and previously revived by Desjardins. If De Max, having played the Duc de Reichstadt, was now willing to appear as the Chancellor of Austria, it was because he was accompanying Sarah Bernhardt on her tour and was going to play the part with her in America.

Sarah Bernhardt left Paris on April 26, 1905, going first to London, where she again gave *Sapho* during the month of May and then played Maurice Maeterlinck's *Pelléas et Mélisande* for the first time. She took the part of Pelléas, and the great English actress Mrs. Patrick Campbell, who spoke perfect French, played Mélisande. She had already played the same part in English in England and the United States.

On June 5 Sarah Bernhardt embarked at Southampton for Buenos Aires. She took with her twelve plays: *La Sorcière, L'Aiglon, La Dame aux Camélias, Angelo, Sapho, Fédora, La Femme de Claude, Phèdre, Magda, Plus que Reine, La Tosca,* and a new play in six acts, *Adrienne Lecouvreur,* of which she was the author and which she was going to perform for the first time during her tour.

Because her last tour with Coquelin *aîné* had been such a brilliant success, she thought it wise this time also to place an actor of the first rank at the head of her company, but she had had some difficulty in persuading De Max to accompany her. He did not wish to leave Paris, which he adored, and he loathed traveling. It required all his veneration for Sarah, and also the attraction of a very large salary, before he resigned himself to going away for more than a year. When it came to his parts, there was further discussion. He was willing to play only those which he knew. However, when Sarah stated and proved to him that, four years previously, Coquelin had played the Gravedigger in *Hamlet* and the father of Duval in *La Dame aux Camélias,* he could not show himself to be less obliging than the distinguished creator of Cyrano. With a sigh he finally agreed to learn Loris in *Fédora,* Scarpia in *La Tosca,* and at last to play Hippolyte in *Phèdre*. Separated by the Atlantic from Mounet Sully, he was willing to make a timid attempt at this part which he had renounced forever in Europe. In *La Sorcière, Angelo,* and *Plus que Reine*, De Max resumed the parts he had already performed. In *L'Aiglon* he was a remarkable Metternich, harsh, biting, and pitiless. In Sarah Bernhardt's *Adrienne Lecouvreur* he had agreed to take the small part of her confessor, Father Dominique, who does not appear until the last act.

For a long time Sarah had been dreaming of playing another *Adrienne Lecouvreur* than that of Scribe, which she had been taking around everywhere since 1880. She thought it old-fashioned, in the first place, and not human enough. It seemed to her that the love of the famous tragedienne for Maurice de Saxe might be more poignant, more heartbreaking, than as Scribe described it. At different times she had asked several of the authors who regularly "supplied" the Théâtre Sarah Bernhardt to write a new version of the play for her. Apparently no one had decided to do so, and in the course of the summer of 1904, at Belle Isle, she had written it herself.

Her *Adrienne Lecouvreur* consisted of six acts, and it must be admitted that its superiority to Scribe's is doubtful. Summing up the opinion of the American press, Hamilton Mason writes in his interesting work *French Theater in New York*:

"Madame Bernhardt's rearrangement of Scribe and Legouvé's play was not a particularly happy one. This version was prolix and rambling, with little purpose other than to display its star in the rôle of a great actress who is so imbued with the classics that she overwhelms even her rival with a reading from Phèdre."

In 1907, when she performed her *Adrienne Lecouvreur* in Paris, the press was not very much more favorable.

Sarah Bernhardt opened in Buenos Aires on July 1, 1905, and for three months and a half she performed in Argentina, Uruguay, Chile, and Brazil. On October 10 she left Rio de Janeiro for New York. On October 9, 1905, the day of her last performance in Rio, in the theater of that city, she met with the accident to her knee which, ten years later, caused the amputation of her right leg. The following are the circumstances in which it happened.

At her farewell performance to the Brazilian public Sarah Bernhardt played *La Tosca*. The sixth and last scene of the play takes place on the terrace of the Château Saint-Ange. Floria discovers that her lover, Mario, is dead. Maddened with despair, she shouts to his guards that she has killed Scarpia. The Captain of the Guards, Spoletta, rushes at her to arrest her. She escapes from him by suicide: she jumps over the parapet and throws herself into space.

Behind the set, naturally, the ground is covered by heavy mattresses, and Floria falls backstage on a padded surface carefully prepared to receive her. What exactly happened that night? Had the mattresses been pushed out of place by the carelessness of a stagehand? The fact remains that she made a false landing and struck her right knee violently on the floor of the stage. The pain was so great that she fainted, and could not come out to greet her public. In a few moments her leg was extremely swollen, and she had to be taken to her hotel on a stretcher. They begged her to stay in Rio for a few days and be medically treated, but she would not consent. Her tour in the United States was to begin in the early days of November. It took twenty days to get from Rio de Janeiro to New York, and she had barely time to get there. What she needed most, she said, was rest. Nowhere could she be more comfortable than on the boat, where she could remain lying down, without moving, for nearly three weeks. She would certainly find a doctor on board who could give her the necessary care. The next day she was carried to the harbor and embarked.

No sooner was she settled in her stateroom than the ship's doctor came to examine her. She looked at him. He had dirty hands and black fingernails. She would never allow such a man to touch her! Without even permitting him to undo the bandage, she dismissed him. Her friends protested, swearing that they would make the doctor take a complete bath, at which they would be present if necessary, in order to make certain that he would really wash himself. She would not listen to reason. She would never look at this repulsive creature again and, moreover, his assistance did not seem to her so very necessary. After all, her injury was not very serious. Then she would be so much better treated in New York, where she could find the greatest doctors in the world. Meanwhile her leg would probably heal.

But on her arrival, her leg was far from healed. Having remained for three weeks without any attention other than bathing, her knee looked very ugly and, still very swollen, it made her suffer a great deal—to such a point that it was impossible for her to open on the date which had been arranged. Her first performances in the United States had to be postponed for a full fortnight, while the doctors did their best. About November 15 she was able to walk, and on the twentieth she began her tour in Chicago.

But those three weeks had been fatal. Subsequently all the treatments which she underwent for years could never repair the damage done by those three weeks. After that her condition grew slowly worse, little by little but implacably. As early as 1908 she could walk only with difficulty, and about 1911 she could not take a step without leaning on somebody's arm. By 1913 in every set on the stage it was necessary so to arrange the furniture that she had never more than two steps to take while acting. Everything had to be set so that she could, at any moment, lean against the back of a chair, against a table or some other property. But she was so prodigiously clever, with so much skill and grace at the same time, that nobody in the audience could suspect the incredible effort she had to make in order to seem as if she were walking in normal fashion. As soon as she got off the stage, she fell into a chair exhausted; and often it was only after two or three minutes of remaining seated that she could get back to her dressing room, with the help of the stage manager or her dresser.

Her tour of 1905–06 in the United States was the greatest financially. By agreement with her, Sam and Lee Shubert and William F. Connor, her managers, had announced her "Farewell American Tour." At this hint that, after this journey, she would never again return to America, the public rushed in greater crowds than ever. She was sixty-one years old, and it was easy to believe that this series of performances in the New World would be her last. But that was not the case; for she made three more "farewell tours," in 1910–11, 1912–13, and in 1916–17. In the end, the American press began to laugh a little at this unusual number of final farewells.

After Chicago, Sarah Bernhardt played at the Garden Theater in New York, where she remained from December 11 to December 26, 1905. Then, having made a tour of the entire United States, as usual, performing this time in sixty-two cities, she reappeared in New York on June 12, 13, and 14, 1906, at the Lyric. She gave three performances, in the course of which, on the same evening, she played the second act of *Hamlet*, the fourth of *La Sorcière*, the fourth of *L'Aiglon*, and the third of *Froufrou*. On June 15 she sailed again to France, having earned more than two million in one year! But her journey to North

America had been greatly disturbed and, at the beginning, an extraordinary incident had almost interrupted it.

During her previous tours in the United States, Sarah Bernhardt had taken in such large receipts that her visits had had disastrous results for American managers. Three or four weeks in advance, when she was advertised to arrive in a city, the public stopped going to the theater, no matter what was offered. They were waiting for Sarah Bernhardt. She arrived and performed at very high prices. Everybody rushed to see her and, in three or four days, spent all the money provided by the family budget for three months' theatergoing. When she left, the theaters were empty again for three or four weeks, because everybody was penniless! Obviously, while her performances were running, the share of the receipts due the owners of the theaters guaranteed them a nice figure. But these days of maximum receipts were far from compensating them for the two or three months with a deficit which followed. On the whole, her visit was a catastrophe so far as they were concerned.

In 1905 the managers of all the theaters in the West—Texas, Arizona, Kansas, Oklahoma, Colorado, California, etc.—made an agreement to boycott Sarah Bernhardt; that is to say, they told the brothers Shubert and William Connor that they would not book the French actress on any conditions. What could be done? Suddenly the itinerary for two or three months had become disrupted. Unperturbed, Sarah Bernhardt suggested to her impresarios to give the performances "under canvas." This was done, and a transportable theater, with room for forty-eight hundred seats and a large stage, was hastily built. It was moved from place to place like Barnum and Bailey's Circus, being taken down, transported, and set up again from city to city. Thus there was no necessity to come to any understanding with theatrical managers. Sarah Bernhardt's impresarios asked the mayors for permission to set up her tent on some spot in the city, or in a neighboring field.

This extraordinary stunt and the ingenious way in which Sarah Bernhardt got the better of the syndicate of American managers created intense publicity for this tour. She never made so much money. In cities like Austin, Salt Lake City, Houston, and Dallas the receipts were as high as eight and nine thousand dollars a performance. From the depths of the country, from the most distant ranches, thousands of people traveled for two or three days to see her. Her fame was such that all these people confidently rushed to see her because they had heard her name repeated for years, sometimes without knowing exactly who she was.

One night in Omaha, Nebraska, the curtain had been up for half an hour, the woman in the box office had left her window, and the secretary of the tour was checking up his accounts. Suddenly a cowboy arrived on horseback, attached his horse by its bridle to a tree, entered, and asked for a seat. There were no more left. Two hundred extra chairs had been added.

The man became obstinate: "I want to see Bernhardt. I have come three hundred miles to see her, and I'm going to see her."

He became threatening and drew his revolver. The cashier calmed him down, sold him a ticket, but warned him that he would be in a poor spot, at the back, in a corner where he would have to stand.

"That doesn't matter to me," said the man, now satisfied. "As long as I can see her, that is all I ask."

He raised the flap of the tent and was about to enter the auditorium. At that moment he turned to the cashier and asked: "By the way, what does this Bernhardt do—dance or sing?"

Back in France at the end of June, Sarah returned to London again for three weeks. Then, tired and suffering from her leg, she went to Belle Isle; here she remained for two full months, which she occupied by dictating her *Mémoires*. By the autumn it was time for her to return to Paris, for her theater had not prospered during her absence. Under the temporary management of the actor André Calmettes they had performed *Le Masque d'Amour*, a bad play by Madame Daniel Lesueur; and after a mediocre revival of *Pour la Couronne*, by François Coppée, they staged the first performance of *Le Frisson de l'Aigle*, which is not one of the best plays of Paul Gavault. The most successful show was the revival of *L'Aiglon*, in which Blanche Dufrène played for the first time and which had a hundred satisfactory performances.

On November 10, 1906, after an absence of eighteen months, Sarah Bernhardt made her return in *La Vierge d'Avila*, a new play by Catulle Mendès, in which she had the part of Sainte Thérèse. All Paris was eager to see Sarah Bernhardt as a nun! Moreover, the work had nobility and a certain grandeur, and the death of Sainte Thérèse was a superb spectacle. It was a successful show and ran to almost one hundred performances. As a matter of fact, that entire season was excellent.

On January 25, 1907, Sarah Bernhardt first performed a delightful comedy in verse, *Les Bouffons,* by Miguel Zamacoïs. It was a poetic, medieval fantasy, full of comedy and lyricism and extremely graceful. The day after, the author had his hour of fame. "A second Rostand has been born," people said rather prematurely. Three years later another comedy in verse by Zamacoïs, *La Fleur Merveilleuse,* was produced at the Comédie Française and failed. He will remain only as the author of *Les Bouffons.*

The story was charming. In her father's old castle young Solange is bored and wasting away. In order to entertain her he announces throughout the country that he is looking for a clown, a buffoon. A tournament takes place, and a neighboring young lord, who is in love with Solange but has never approached her, puts down his name on a list of candidates as Jacasse. He introduces himself. He is a hunchback! People cry out at the sight of this deformed clown and are on the point of giving preference to handsome Narcisse. But Jacasse is witty, gay, brave, and tender. Above all, he is so eloquent that his spirit triumphs over the elegance of Narcisse. Solange not only chooses him but marries him. Then he appears, slim and upright. His hump was false. The subject has a certain resemblance to that of *Cyrano de Bergerac.* A man's beauty is nothing if it is not combined with intellectual qualities. Lyrical and gay by turns, Sarah Bernhardt scored a great success as the clown Jacasse. The play was performed to packed houses for three months, and was very soon revived.

On April 3, 1907, Sarah Bernhardt gave a single gala performance of her own play, *Adrienne Lecouvreur,* which she had played for the first time during her last tour in America. Packed with her friends, the house registered a success which encouraged her to give a series of performances of the play. After the last night of *Les Bouffons* she advertised *Adrienne Lecouvreur* "for thirty evenings only." People had such respect for Sarah Bernhardt that only a few newspapers were cruel. The others expressed their opinions by talking only of the performer and not of the new play. The public stayed away, and it did not even run for the month advertised. By the first of June the theater had closed.

Sarah Bernhardt's *Adrienne Lecouvreur,* published by Eugène Faquelle in 1908, is dedicated "To my dear daughter-in-law, Terka

Bernhardt," in tender memory of the young mother of Simone and Lysiane whom they were to lose two years later. She died prematurely in 1910.

On June 11, 1907, another "Sarah Bernhardt Day" took place, but the program was somewhat different. A few months earlier a subscription had been opened to present the great actress with a magnificent work of art by the sculptor A. J. Hébrard. To invest the presentation with a certain solemnity, a matinee was given at the Théâtre Fémina. For this single occasion Sarah learned, produced, and acted in a play by Emile Moreau in one act, *Le Vert-Galant,* written "in the language of the period." She played Queen Margot, and a member of her company, Maury, was King Henri IV. After this, homages in verse were addressed to Sarah Bernhardt by Catulle Mendès, André Rivoire, Hélène Picard, Marie Leconte, Constance Maille, Henry Krauss, and De Max.

Reopening in the fall, Sarah Bernhardt, as manager, produced a play by her old friend and ex-manager Félix Duquesnel: *La Maîtresse de Piano,* a charming comedy which was first performed at the Théâtre Sarah Bernhardt on October 4, 1907, and was one of the first successes of Gabrielle Dorziat. After that, Sarah Bernhardt herself opened on December 24, 1907, in *La Belle au Bois Dormant,* by Jean Richepin and Henri Cain. Twenty-three years after *Nana Sahib* and *Macbeth,* Sarah and Richepin, now aged sixty-three and fifty-eight, met again for the first time and finally made a success in collaboration! The play was nothing more than Perrault's fairy tale, cleverly adapted to the stage. It was a spectacle of fairyland and almost a play for children. But it was prettily written and lavishly presented, and it was greatly liked. The curiosity of the evening was to see Sarah Bernhardt playing, not the Sleeping Princess, whose part was not greatly developed by the authors, but that of Prince Charming, who comes to awaken her and who is "as handsome as the daylight and twenty years old" in the story. This was one of the miracles of the career of Sarah Bernhardt. I was fourteen when she created the part and my memories are exact. It was impossible to imagine a more radiant, more youthful, more poetic, and more ideal apparition. She was Prince Charming himself, supernaturally handsome, a blond and striking figure out of legend. Thanks to Sarah Bernhardt, the evening was one of real enchantment.

This was followed, on April 8, 1908, by *La Courtisane de Corinthe,* a rather feeble drama by Michel Carré and Paul Bilhaud, which Sarah played with De Max. It was a failure. People persuaded Sarah that the title was frightening. Why announce in advance that she was again playing the part of "a bad woman"? At the fifth performance the bill was changed and the play was called *Cléonice*, after the leading character. This did not help matters. The only title which would really have suited this play was one which had already been used, *Le Monde ou l'On s'ennuie!*[2] This woman of easy virtue was unattractive and made few conquests. On May 15 Sarah was playing in London.

In September came the annual performances of *La Dame aux Camélias*, more popular than ever. During the entire season of 1908–09 Sarah produced only revivals. For ten months her marvelous repertory, in which Sardou still occupied the first place, enabled her to take in excellent receipts without creating any new parts. After *La Dame aux Camélias* and until the end of June, 1909, she appeared successively in *L'Aiglon, La Samaritaine, La Tosca, Fédora,* and *La Sorcière.*

On May 5, 1909, Adeline Dudlay, *Sociétaire* of the Comédie Française, gave her farewell performance. In the course of the striking program the hit of the evening was Alfred de Musset's *La Nuit de Mai,* played by Sarah Bernhardt and Julia Bartet. This was the only time that Sarah reappeared on the stage of the Comédie Française, which she had left twenty-nine years before. Having often played the part of the Muse, between 1873 and 1880, with Mounet Sully as the poet, this evening Sarah Bernhardt was the poet, looking adorable in a tight-fitting, long frock coat of 1830, with a velvet collar. With Bartet, an ideal Muse—both in *La Nuit de Mai* and in *La Nuit d'Octobre,* which she constantly played in turn at the Théâtre Français—Musset's poem had the benefit of an unparalleled interpretation. At this time Julia Bartet had achieved an important position at the Théâtre Français. In 1909 Réjane, Julia Bartet, and Jeanne Granier were undoubtedly the three leading actresses of Paris. "What about Sarah Bernhardt?" one may ask. I shall reply in the words of Robert de Flers:

"Sarah Bernhardt is no longer an actress. It would be as absurd to assign a place to her on the list of French actresses as to try to classify Molière among our dramatists. Like the author of *Le Misanthrope*, Sarah is henceforth above and beyond all classification."

[2] *The World Where One Gets Bored.* Trans.

This was true. For twelve years the fabulous glory of Sarah Bernhardt was such that one almost forgot that she was an actress by profession. It seemed much more natural to classify her with the greatest figures of French and of world history. On other occasions Sarah Bernhardt was asked several times to appear again at the Comédie Française, but she always refused. She did not have pleasant memories of the "House of Molière," whose *Sociétaires*, with a few exceptions, she considered very bad actors. Twelve years later I was driving with her past the stage door of the Théâtre Français. It was a Sunday, about six o'clock, and the matinee was just finished.

There were about a hundred people standing outside the door, and Sarah Bernhardt said to me: "Who are all those people?"

"They are waiting for the actors of the Comédie Française to come out."

Then, bursting into her silvery little laugh, she said: "In order to kill them?"

On May 28, 1909, on the death of Catulle Mendès, which had occurred a few days previously, the Théâtre Sarah Bernhardt gave a gala matinee and, in honor of the poet's memory, Sarah played two acts of his *Vierge d'Avila*, and—surprisingly—a few scenes from the first and third acts of *Cyrano de Bergerac*, in which she played Cyrano. This was the only time that she appeared in this part and it was nothing more than a picturesque effort, amusing but without artistic significance. Obviously, Cyrano, the very masculine Gascon fighter, could not be played by a woman; but Sarah Bernhardt could take any liberty she liked.

On September 25, 1909, Sarah Bernhardt played another important part, but this time not on the stage. She was present at the marriage of the elder of her granddaughters, Simone Bernhardt, who became Madame Edgar Gross. The following year Sarah Bernhardt was to become a great-grandmother. On November 25—another miracle!— she again played Jeanne d'Arc. Twenty years after the play of Jules Barbier, in which she had performed at the Porte Saint Martin, she created a new part in Emile Moreau's *Le Procès de Jeanne d'Arc*, and it was a very great success. The play was very cleverly constructed, and Sarah appeared only in two acts: the second, at the trial; and the third, in Jeanne's prison. In the last act the characters on the stage watched the torture of the Saint, whose stake was supposed to be set up in the wings out of the sight of the spectators. De Max gave a masterful performance as Bedford, the principal part in the play. I shall never forget the cross-examination scene at the beginning of the second act. Standing, alone and absolutely apart in the middle of the stage, Sarah replied to the judges who, from their lofty stalls ranged along the walls of the court, questioned her from every side.

"What is your name?"

"Jeanne."

"Your age?" . . .

Taking her time, Sarah gradually turned facing the public and, looking at the audience, gently but firmly said: "Nineteen years."

Every evening, at these words, the audience burst into applause. This piece of business, so skillful and discreet, which seemed to submit her reply to the approval of the spectators, never passed unnoticed. *Le Procès de Jeanne d'Arc* had almost a hundred performances.

Meanwhile Sarah Bernhardt made her third and last attempt as a dramatist, by giving a play in four acts, on December 22, 1909, at the Théâtre des Arts. It was called *Un Coeur d'Homme* and was played by Henry Roussell, Blanche Dufrène, and Emmy Lynn. This is what the critic of *Le Journal de Débats*, Raoul Aubry, said:

"One has to overlook many signs of inexperience and many echoes of other writers before reaching a pathetic scene at the end. The public at the Théâtre des Arts received this drama somewhat . . . smilingly, but the genius of our great Sarah will be no worse for this adventure. Was Ingres a lesser figure because he tried to play the violin? We shall call it quits by going back to the Place du Châtelet to applaud Jeanne d'Arc in the scene of the trial."

Un Coeur d'Homme had a few performances and happily disappeared from memory as well as from the playbill.

On March 2, 1910, at the Théâtre Sarah Bernhardt there was a new work by Jean Richepin, *La Beffa*, based on an Italian play by Sem Benelli, *La Cena delle Beffe*.[3] Sarah Bernhardt again played, in men's clothes, the picturesque character of Gianetto Malespini, curious, angry, ironical, and violent. "A new creation which will be remembered," people had said. But the play was not a success, although it had been in Italy. To the French public it seemed rambling and without interest. To finish the season Sarah then revived *Les Bouffons*,

[3] As *The Jest*, this was played in New York with great success by John and Lionel Barrymore in April, 1919. *Trans.*

whose run she had prematurely interrupted to play her *Adrienne Lecouvreur*. Concurrently she presented one of her most ingenious scenic inventions.

A few months earlier Edmond Rostand had published in *L'Illustration* a delightful poem, *Le Bois Sacré,* whose lyrical fantasy was positively dazzling. The author imagines a young couple motoring along the roads of Greece. The car breaks down and they fall asleep on the grass beside it. While they are sleeping all the gods of Olympus emerge from the neighboring wood and examine the car in amazement. Vulcan repairs the motor. The delighted gods take a turn in the car and then bring it back to the owners, who, on awakening, are astounded to find that the breakdown has been repaired. They will never know that, one hour before, Jupiter, Venus, Mars, and Cupid were driving around in their car.

Sarah Bernhardt conceived the idea of presenting *Le Bois Sacré* on the stage of her theater, in the form of a pantomime, while the actor Brémont, in evening dress, recited Rostand's poem from the stage box. It was ravishing. The set was marvelous and the costumes exquisite: the arrival of the large Panhard, the latest model of the day, driven by the two young people; the gods circling around the car; their flight in the car as the night falls. A prettier picture had rarely been seen. Thanks to this delightful concluding spectacle, *Les Bouffons* had a magnificent revival. Why, for thirty years, has no one ever produced again Rostand's marvelous *Bois Sacré* as staged by Sarah Bernhardt?

In September, 1910, for the first time in her life, Sarah appeared as a music-hall attraction, at the Coliseum in London. Twice a day she played the second act of *L'Aiglon* in the middle of a variety program. Thus she addressed a different public, giving an opportunity of applauding her to the masses who could not afford the high prices asked for her at the Lyric, the Adelphi, or the Gaiety.

On October 23, 1910, another birthday, when she was sixty-six years old, Sarah Bernhardt embarked again for America on her second "farewell tour." Her usual repertory was augmented by *Les Bouffons* and *Le Procès de Jeanne d'Arc*, and her company, as always, consisted of about thirty actors. At their head, in the place of a star, people were astonished to see the name of a quite unknown young actor, called Lou Tellegen. For three years, until June, 1913, both on tour and in Paris, he became Sarah's sole partner in the principal men's parts of all her plays.

I should have preferred not to mention his name in this book. The interest of Sarah Bernhardt, almost seventy years of age, in Lou Tellegen is not a memory which it is agreeable to me to recall. But have I the right to ignore Lou Tellegen's career with her, in view of the wide publicity which was given to him in the French and American newspapers? All the Paris critics discussed it and deplored it. Many even thought it necessary to tell their readers discreetly the reasons for the surprising solicitude for this mediocre actor on the part of the great artist, who ordinarily chose her partners more judiciously. In its issue of December 3, 1911, the *New York Times* announced the marriage of Sarah Bernhardt and her young employee. The event was denied the next day, but she continued to act only with him.

Lou Tellegen himself devoted a hundred pages to his relations with Sarah Bernhardt in his memoirs, published in 1931 under the title *Women Have Been Kind to Me*. In these confidential confessions, of which twenty thousand copies were printed, he emphasizes with charming discretion the fact that, during the two tours which he made in the United States with Sarah Bernhardt, in 1910–11 and 1912–13, she had such a predilection for him that she would never allow him to travel with the rest of the company. She insisted on his being "willing to accept" a stateroom in her special car, where the only other sleeping quarters were those of her private physician, Dr. Marot, and her companion, Suzanne Seylor. I shall not follow Lou Tellegen in his subsequent insinuations. Even to refer to them would be to approve of them, whereas I am astounded that a man, of whatever type he may be, could think of writing such a book. I prefer to hope and I am determined to believe that everything he gives the reader to understand is not true, and that Sarah Bernhardt never had for Tellegen anything more than a purely artistic weakness. I have reluctantly mentioned the extraordinary memoirs of this actor solely in order to make this declaration.

Born in 1883 of Dutch origin, Lou Tellegen came to France when he was very young; followed his dramatic studies at the Paris Conservatoire, in the class of Paul Mounet; and had played a few minor parts at the Odéon and the Théâtre des Arts. In the course of the season of 1907–08 he appeared in *La Tragédie de Salomé*, by Robert d'Humières, with Loie Fuller; in *Le Grand Soir*, a German play about Nihilism, by Leopold Kampf, in which Vera Sergine played the principal part; and in *La Fille de Pilate*, by René Fauchois, also with Sergine.

Le Grand Soir was a very great success, but Lou Tellegen, who then acted under the name of Lou Van Tel, was completely ignored. While continuing to act here and there, whenever he had an opportunity, he had become a model. Extraordinarily handsome, tall, thin, and clean-shaven, with a very delicate little head and blond curly hair, beautifully arranged, and the body of a young god, he was greatly in demand by sculptors, posing for Rodin—among others—who modeled his admirable "Eternal Spring" on Tellegen.

During the summer of 1910 Sarah Bernhardt insisted that De Max should leave with her in October for America, but he obstinately refused. Five years earlier he had done so to oblige her. He had gone to the United States and was desperately bored for months, far from his beloved apartment in the Rue Caumartin. He would not do it again for ten thousand francs a day.

"Well, then, tell me the name of somebody," said Sarah. "I have nobody to play the important young male leads in my repertory."

Just by accident, as he might have brought anybody else, De Max had introduced Tellegen—whose acquaintance he had just made, having played with him in some tragedy at the Roman Theater in Orange. He little suspected that, by way of thanks, the young actor would soon take his place on the billboard at the Théâtre Sarah Bernhardt and would even monopolize his parts, particularly that of Bedford in *Le Procès de Jeanne d'Arc*.

As she had done previously, in 1910, Sarah began her tour of the United States in Chicago, where she opened on November 10. While she was acting there, her impresario, William Connor, asked her to add a play to her repertory for New York. On February 5 of that year a well-known American star, Dorothy Donnelly, had played on Broadway with enormous success a play advertised under the title of *Madame X*. This was an adaptation of *La Femme X*, a French play by Alexandre Bisson, first performed at the Porte Saint Martin by Jane Hading on December 15, 1908, which had also been a success in Paris. Connor thought that the American public would like to see Sarah performing in French in the same play in which Dorothy Donnelly, in English, had attracted New York. Sarah Bernhardt was perfectly willing and, although acting every night, she learned and put on *La Femme X*.

The role is that of a woman of fifty who, having formerly been driven out by her husband, has become, after various stages of degradation, the mistress of a criminal, the leader of a gang. They are plotting a "job" against her ex-husband. In order to protect him she kills one of the bandits. She is brought into court; and the young lawyer appointed to defend her is her own son, who does not know her and believes that his mother is dead. The trial scene is tremendously effective, and Sarah Bernhardt appears to have been extraordinary in it. She acted in the play for the first time in New York, on December 12, 1910. Afterward she was asked to do it in all the large cities on her itinerary, and in London; but she never played it in Paris.

Indefatigably, a fortnight later, on December 29, 1910, in New York, she gave the first production of *Judas*, by John De Kay, an American author, translated into French by J. C. de Chassagne. She played the part of Judas, having learned and produced it for only one performance. She concluded her New York season on December 31 and then set out on her regular tour of the United States. On the road she gave a performance in the enormous open-air theater at Berkeley, near Oakland. In February, while she was in San Francisco, she played once in the San Quentin Prison, to an audience of two thousand convicts. She was never to forget the impression made upon her by these extraordinary spectators, all dressed in the same costume of broad striped canvas, some of whom were about to be executed during the following weeks. After a tour of thirty-five weeks she reappeared, as usual, in New York for three days, from June 19 to June 21, 1911, embarking for Havre on the twenty-third. In July she was playing in London.

On November 22, 1911, Sarah reopened at the Théâtre Sarah Bernhardt, playing for the first time *Lucrèce Borgia*, the magnificent drama of Victor Hugo, first performed at the Porte Saint Martin in 1833. Prolonged applause greeted her return after her long absence. Her conception of the part of Lucrèce was one of the masterpieces of the second half of her career. But, as Alphonse d'Este, Lou Tellegen performed for the first time with Sarah in Paris. There was consternation. People thought him not only a very ordinary actor but a very bad actor, lifeless, awkward, with a disagreeable and very strong Dutch accent, without any passion or authority—tolerable, in short, in minor parts but utterly impossible as a leading character.

Sarah Bernhardt's intimates tried discreetly to make her understand this; but she shrugged her shoulders and declared that he was admirable, as she had formerly done for Damala. Soon, in her yearly revival of *Phèdre*, she made him play Hippolyte—a part which he took without the least hesitation, lacking the modesty of De Max. But this self-confidence of his was not to the taste of the public, and it was a relief in the fifth act to hear Théramène describing the death of Hippolyte. So he would not be seen again! Already, in the previous act, when Tellegen declared *"Le jour n'est pas plus pur que le fond de mon coeur,"*[4] there had been bursts of ironical laughter among the audience.

Sarah was angry and interrupted the matinees of *Phèdre*. In order to create a diversion she had the strange notion of producing Molière's *Tartuffe*, playing herself the part of Dorine. Why did she choose this character of a good-natured, fat maid, comical, expansive, and enormous? A malicious wit wrote that, since her last American tour, Madame Sarah Bernhardt had evidently decided to astonish Paris, and for her next classical matinees he suggested a revival of *La Surprise de l'Amour*, by Marivaux!

On January 4, 1912, she revived *Le Procès de Jeanne d'Arc*; and Lou Tellegen played the part of Bedford, first created by De Max. In February she did not hesitate to give him Oreste in *Andromaque*. And on April 11, 1912, with him, she first performed *La Reine Elisabeth*, a new play by Emile Moreau. This time the press was so terrible to the wretched fellow that the play collapsed. All the genius of Sarah Bernhardt, who was wonderful as Elizabeth of England, could not compensate for the disastrous effect of Tellegen as Essex. The play ran for twelve performances.

In five consecutive parts he had been positively slain by the critics and the public. In his place, after the second play, any other actor would have pretended to fall ill, or would have arranged to disappear one way or another. But this did not cross the mind of Lou Tellegen. He had a good job and would take good care not to leave it. As for Sarah Bernhardt, obstinate as always, the more he was criticized, the more determined she became to act only with him. She finished her

---

[4] "The daylight is not more pure than the depths of my heart." *Trans.*

season with revivals of *La Dame aux Camélias* and *Lorenzaccio*, allowing him to play Armand Duval and Alexandre de Médicis. Apropos of this latter revival, I quote from the article of Edmond Stoullig, in *Les Annales du Théâtre et de la Musique,* these few lines:

"Never, perhaps, has the great artist reached such heights. In consequence, what applause, what curtain calls, what a triumph! How right she was to revive this *Lorenzaccio* even for so short a time. But what a pity that she is surrounded by such a bad cast! There is, particularly, an actor who has been given the part of Alexandre de Médicis, who is positively worse than mediocre. 'Work hard at your tears,' a certain teacher of diction used to say to a young pupil. 'Work hard at your laughs,' one might say to M. Lou Tellegen, whose perpetual bursts of laughter are as insufferable as they are unnatural."

As a matter of fact, the young actor had proved so inadequate that, on the opening night, a trifling but eloquent incident occurred. At the end of the performance Sarah Bernhardt came out alone to take the first two curtain calls and was loudly acclaimed. At the third, as Tellegen appeared with her, the applause stopped dead and was not resumed until Sarah, having understood, reappeared alone.

Having given him in eight months at her own theater seven principal parts, one an original creation, Sarah Bernhardt had not succeeded in imposing Tellegen on Paris. At this she conceived a sort of spite. Since Paris did not want to see her with him, it would not see her at all! Whereas she always allowed four or five years to elapse between her American tours, she signed a new contract in which she agreed to leave again at the beginning of the following season. Having left the United States in June, 1911, she appeared there again in November, 1912, less than eighteen months later. It was this which made the American press say that the public had never seen so much of Sarah Bernhardt as now that she had announced her retirement from the theater.

In the course of the season which was ending, Paris had again witnessed one of Sarah Bernhardt's now habitual "triumphs." I mention this one because it constitutes one of my earliest personal memories of her. I was eighteen and just leaving school. As a start in my theatrical life, I was the secretary of Robert Trébor, now President of the Theater Managers' Association in Paris. At that time he wrote theatrical news for the newspaper *Excelsior* and was also manager of the

Vendredis de Fémina, weekly programs which were given from five to seven.

On January 19, 1912, a "Sarah Bernhardt Gala" took place and, following the usual custom, it consisted of a long glorification of Sarah by her regular poets, who spoke their own verses or had them read by some eminent artist. Because of my position with Trébor, it was I who "conducted" the program, taking the part of the stage manager, and who had the honor of helping Sarah Bernhardt, leaning one hand on my shoulder and the other on Tellegen's arm, to come down from her dressing room to the stage of the Théâtre Fémina, where she seated herself on the customary throne before the curtain rose.

That day the poets who came in person to read their verses to Sarah Bernhardt were Edmond Rostand, the Comtesse de Noailles, Lucie Delarue-Mardrus, Jean Aicard, Henri de Régnier, Jean Richepin, and Edmond Haraucourt. The actors were Mounet Sully, Silvain, Dessonnes, Decoeur, Jeanne Delvair, Madeleine Roch, René Alexandre, Louise Silvain, and Lou Tellegen. Sixteen "homages to Sarah Bernhardt" were addressed to her in succession. To finish the matinee she played two scenes from *Phèdre*.

At this gala Edmond Rostand once again recited the celebrated "Sonnet to Sarah" which he had composed a few years before. I cannot resist the pleasure of quoting it in full. I can hear and still see the great poet, his monocle in his eye, wonderfully distinguished and elegant, wearing a long gray morning coat, reciting—and how beautifully!—this sonnet. In the wings I listened with delight; my youthful eyes were dazzled and traveled tirelessly from the author of *L'Aiglon* to his divine interpreter.

> *En ces temps sans beauté, seule encor tu nous restes,*
> *Sachant descendre, pâle, un grand escalier clair,*
> *Ceindre un bandeau, porter un lys, brandir un fer,*
> *Reine de l'attitude, et princesse des gestes.*
>
> *En ces temps sans folie, ardente, tu protestes,*
> *Tu dis des vers, tu meurs d'amour, ton vol se perd,*
> *Tu tends des bras de rêve, et puis des bras de chair,*
> *Et quand Phèdre paraît, nous sommes tous incestes.*
>
> *Avide de souffrir, tu t'ajoutes des coeurs,*
> *Nous avons vu couler, car ils coulent, tes pleurs,*
> *Toutes les larmes de nos âmes sur tes joues.*

"The play which we have had the honor of giving you for the first time is by Monsieur Tristan Bernard"—he said: "The play which has had the honor of being interpreted by Madame Sarah Bernhardt is by, etc." It had a hundred successful performances, and at the thirtieth, on January 15, 1914, Sarah Bernhardt was decorated with the Legion of Honor—at last.

On March 15, 1914, she gave a final revival of *La Dame aux Camélias*, with Romuald Joubé as Armand Duval. She played it for a month, walking with increasing difficulty. The condition of her knee had become much worse during the past year. Already, in *Jeanne Doré*, she scarcely moved. The staging of the play had been most carefully arranged in order to reduce to a minimum the number of steps she had to take in each scene.

On April 16, 1914, she opened in another new play, *Tout-à-Coup*, a strange dramatic piece by Paul and Guy de Cassagnac, which she played with Du)mény and which was a total failure, running to only six performances. On April 23 she revived *Jeanne Doré*, which she performed in Paris until May 15. These were the last occasions when Sarah Bernhardt appeared in her theater in an upright position, still having her two legs.

On May 10, at a matinee, she gave a lecture full of spirit, entitled *The Three Hamlets*, in the course of which she cleverly compared the characters which she had interpreted in *L'Aiglon*, *Lorenzaccio*, and *Hamlet*—all three both similar and different.

On May 17 she toured France with *Jeanne Doré*. The performances were interrupted at Lille, near the Belgian frontier. She returned to Paris on July 28. On August 1, 1914, general mobilization was declared. Thus ended the great career of Sarah Bernhardt, who was very nearly seventy. She was not to open in a new play in her theater until six years later. Then she was minus a leg and old and unable to walk, but she was more acclaimed than ever—at the summit of her glory, which remained intact until her dying day.

CHAPTER IX

Last Years

SARAH spent the whole month of August, 1914, in Paris, suffering greatly from her knee and almost never leaving her house in the Boulevard Péreire. Morning and evening, every day, she anxiously read the official bulletins, optimistic at first, and then noncommittal, but finally more and more disturbing. They were obliged to announce in succession the invasion of Belgium, the retreat from Charleroi, and the German advance to Saint Quentin, to Compiègne . . .

On August 1 the capital was crowded with people. The mobilized men were leaving every day by tens of thousands; but their families remained in Paris, nobody thinking of spending the summer in the country. But, when the French troops had retreated, on August 15 the exodus began. Packed trains took the Parisians to Bordeaux and Biarritz; to Toulouse, Marseilles, and Nice. As the pressure of the enemy got worse, departures very soon became more numerous. Through all the gates automobiles, carriages, trucks, and even taxis were evacuating Paris. On September 1 the President of the Republic, Raymond Poincaré, and the government also left to establish themselves provisionally in Bordeaux.

About August 25 her family advised Sarah Bernhardt to leave, but she would not listen to them. She had spent the entire war of 1870 in Paris, and this time she was not going to leave either. They insisted; they begged her; but she could not be shaken from her decision. It was Georges Clémenceau who succeeded in making her change her mind. Temporarily out of politics, he was then owner of the newspaper *L'Homme Libre* (which he soon ironically called *L'Homme Enchaîné*, as a protest against the severity of the censorship) and was not appointed Prime Minister until 1917. For years he had been a friend of Sarah Bernhardt, for whom he had unlimited admiration. Through his friends he had learned of her decision to remain. And he had been warned by the French counterespionage service that, if the Germans seized Paris, Sarah Bernhardt was on the list of hostages who would be taken immediately and sent to Berlin. At the end of August there were many who believed that the occupation of Paris was inevitable.

Clémenceau went to see Sarah Bernhardt and gave her the information which he had received from the secret police. Had she any right to risk being taken prisoner? She was one of the greatest names in France, perhaps the greatest. She had a son, two granddaughters, and also a theater, which employed two hundred persons—actors and workers. For the sake of her staff, which had no means of living without her; for her family; and, above all, for her country, it was her duty to seek safety. Clémenceau's intelligence and his arguments got the better of her obstinacy; she gave in. On August 31 she set out in her car to drive toward the south.

A few days later she rented a villa at Andernos, about twenty-five miles from Bordeaux. With her family and a few friends she settled there for an indeterminate period waiting for the turn of events. In September came the victory of the Marne, the miraculous strengthening of the front, the stopping of the German troops, Paris saved. Sarah would have liked to return about the end of October, but the state of her knee was very much worse; the slightest movement made her cry out in pain. She was almost unable to walk and could not bend her right leg at all, which had soon to be put in a cast.

After three months of complete immobility, no improvement occurred. On the contrary, when the cast was removed it was discovered with horror that the disease was no longer confined to the knee but was threatening the general condition and the very life of Sarah Bernhardt. Several consultations took place, in which Doctors Denuce and Arnozan, of Bordeaux, and her great friend Professor Pozzi took part, the latter coming especially from Paris. They hesitated for two or three days, so serious was the decision which they had to make. Then it became necessary to tell her the truth. The amputation of her leg was necessary and unavoidable. Sarah Bernhardt received the news without flinching. When Pozzi asked her what was her decision, she replied: "Since there is nothing else to be done, why ask my opinion?"

She was taken to Bordeaux, and on February 22, 1915, Dr. Denuce proceeded to amputate the right leg of Sarah Bernhardt. In the morning, when she was taken to receive the anesthetic, Maurice Bernhardt, Simone, Lysiane, Louise Abbéma, Georges Clairin, were all in a state of consternation and despair, making great efforts not to cry in her presence. But she had noticed this and, laughing and singing as she lay on the stretcher, she left them to be taken into the operating theater. At this terrible moment, when she had to renounce walking forever, this woman, with admirable energy, thought only of reassuring and comforting those whom she loved.

Her convalescence was lengthy. Obviously, at seventy-one years of age, it was difficult for her to undergo such a serious operation. It was only after two long months that they were certain she would recover. Five or six months later, resigned to not taking a step, accustomed to her "chair," she began to make plans. Undoubtedly she should have rested a little longer, but she could not allow herself to do so; as usual, Sarah Bernhardt needed money but not to meet extravagant expenses any more. At her age, during the war and since her operation, she had considerably reduced her scale of living. But she still had her house in Paris, her castle in Belle Isle, and seven or eight persons in her service. All these persons had to live and the cost had to be met. She had to work.

At Belle Isle, one morning in 1922, Sarah Bernhardt amused herself with me by making up an approximate account of what she had earned in the course of her existence. She estimated the total at more than forty-five million gold francs, or nine million dollars, and about four hundred and fifty million paper francs, at the 1939 rate of exchange!

In 1915, after her operation, she lived by the sale of her jewelry and on loans. Every month twenty or twenty-five thousand francs passed through her hands, but she had not ten thousand francs of her own. A tragic lack of foresight, but one which has also its admirable side. All her life she had had such confidence in her genius, in her capacity for work, and also in her star that she had never thought of economizing. Moreover, would she ever have succeeded? Forty years of display and prodigality and so many costly failures in her two theaters had always prevented her from troubling about the morrow.

Early in the war, after being closed for five or six months, most of the theaters in Paris reopened one by one, between December, 1914, and May, 1915. The Théâtre Sarah Bernhardt reopened on April 1, with *La Dame aux Camélias*—played by Blanche Dufrène. Then came a new "topical" play, *La Vierge de Lutèce,* by Auguste Villeroy, which had little success. Two revivals were better: *Le Bossu,* the inexhaustible play of Paul Féval, with Romuald Joubé, and *L'Aiglon,* played for the first time by Mary Marquet.

Returning to Paris in October, 1915, Sarah first wanted to devote herself to those who were fighting, within the full limits of her resources. In agreement with her son and Ullmann, who were now managers of her theater, both in name and in fact, she arranged a program, which was put on for a few matinees only, the receipts of which were to be paid over without deduction to a charitable committee. The show consisted of one act by Joseph Schwoebel, *L'Enfant Vainqueur,* with Mary Marquet; a play in one act by Maurice Donnay, *L'Impromptu du Paquetage,* played by Jeanne Granier; and a sort of tableau in rhymed dialogue, by Eugène Morand, *Les Cathédrales.* This "scenic poem" gave voice to the principal cathedrals of France: Reims, Bourges, Arles, Amiens, etc. Sarah Bernhardt represented Strasbourg; Mary Marquet, Notre Dame—the Cathedral of Paris. It was assuredly the war charity for which the receipts were destined which interested a few hundred spectators, rather than the work of Eugène Morand; its patriotism was undoubted, but its interest was dubious. Only the gravity of the times caused this rather puerile allegory to be politely received.

During the following months the Théâtre Sarah Bernhardt revived *Le Chemineau,* by Jean Richepin; *La Tour de Nesle,* by Alexandre Dumas *père;* and *La Dame aux Camélias,* which was played for the first time by Madeleine Lély in 1916. Meanwhile Sarah Bernhardt was making a topical movie, *Mères Françaises,* in which she was shown as a nurse at the front. Then, in the spring of 1916, she actually did go to the front, and appeared several times in certain programs of the *Théâtre aux Armées.* By turns in the north, Champagne, and the Vosges she recited poetry to the *poilus* and, knowing of her operation, seeing her condemned henceforth to this tragic immobility, they acclaimed her courage and unconquerable energy louder than ever.

During the war, both at the front and in Paris, one of the poems which Sarah Bernhardt recited most frequently was *La Vitre,* by Edmond Rostand, which appeared in a collection entitled *Le Vol de la Marsellaise.* It has a superb idea. A peasant is caught by mobilization in his village in the Basses Pyrénées, close to the Spanish border. He leaves grumblingly. "Why do they disturb me to go to war?" he

thinks. I am a Basque and have no desire to defend the Ardennes.
He gets into the train and, out of the window, he sees passing before
his eyes, from south to north, the whole of France described with
sublime eloquence by Rostand. Then the peasant understands why
he is going to fight. That country which he sees is worth fighting for.
As he concludes his story, he murmurs:

> *Et je vois encor le visage*
> *Qu'auprès de moi fit un dragon,*
> *Quand je baisai le paysage*
> *A la vitre de mon wagon.*[1]

Sarah Bernhardt recited this wonderful poem admirably. One could
not hear her without weeping. But, while she thus devoted herself
with all her heart, aiding innumerable charitable undertakings, Sarah
Bernhardt could not afford to confine herself to giving performances
for charity. Once her movie was finished, she had to continue to earn
a living.

At the age of seventy-two, with one leg amputated, having always
to be carried, and in more delicate health, she would clearly have
preferred not to leave Europe. But what could she do? Ten countries
were at war and one fifth of France was invaded. In the part that
was free, there were, apart from Paris, perhaps three or four towns—
Lyons, Marseilles, Nice, and Toulouse—which had a large music hall
where she could appear as "a turn," the only way in which she now
thought it was possible for her to perform on the stage.

Again she was obliged to leave for America, embarking on September 30, 1916. She remained away for a year and a half. She had
a very small company with her, only ten actors: Jean Angelo (the son
of the actor who played the principal parts in her repertory during
her first American tour in 1880), Deneubourg, Favières, Gervais, Glass,
and Hubert; Mesdames Jane Méa, Caubet, Baujault, and Pelisse. She
did not require any more to play her repertory, which consisted of
about ten "acts" each having only five or six characters. Among these
there were two by Maurice Bernhardt—*La Mort de Cléopâtre*, in collaboration with Henri Cain, and *Hécube*, in collaboration with René
Chavance—and another, *L'Holocauste*, written by Sarah Bernhardt
herself. There were also *Du Théâtre au Champ d'Honneur*, by an unknown young writer at the front; *Vitrail*, by René Fauchois; *L'Etoile*

[1] And I still see the look On the face of the dragoon beside me, When I kissed
the landscape On the window of my car. *Trans.*

dans la Nuit, by Henri Cain; and *Le Faux Modèle,* by Edouard Daurelly. She also played the third act of *Le Procès de Jeanne d'Arc,* the
fifth act of *La Dame aux Camélias,* the sixth act of *L'Aiglon,* and the
trial scene from Shakespeare's *Merchant of Venice.*

In the course of this last tour, whose manager was Charles Frohman,
as she already had done in the United States in 1912–13, Sarah Bernhardt appeared in the music halls of all the large cities in the United
States. In the space of fourteen months she played at three different
times in New York: from December 4 to 23, 1916, at the Empire
Theater; from September 1 to 13, 1917, at the Knickerbocker; and
from December 17 to 31, at the Palace. In January, 1918, in order to
say good-by, this time irrevocably, to all her American publics, she
also played in other places off Broadway, particularly Keith's Riverside Theater.

Sarah Bernhardt returned to France tired and very discouraged.
Not that this tour had been bad, for America always received her with
enthusiasm. But she fully realized how disappointed the public was
by the unfavorable conditions under which she now appeared. To
begin with, her repertory was very mediocre. These little plays in one
act, put together more or less ingeniously by authors whose good intentions were more obvious than their skill, could not satisfy the
famous interpreter of so many masterpieces and were bound to sad-
den her admirers. It probably seemed even more melancholy to her
to appear only in the last act of *La Dame aux Camélias,* knowing
that the first four acts were now forbidden to her, or the death of
L'Aiglon, a magnificent spectacle but the epilogue of a play in six
acts. When she played it alone, her regrets became more poignant at
having to renounce the rest of the part.

Admittedly, in the course of her career, she had long since acquired
the habit of playing a single act of a great play—from the opening
night of the performances of the Comédie Française in London, in
1879—but then this was merely the result of her own whim, or of the
nature of a special program. She knew that, if she wanted to, she
could play the entire performance the next day. One is willing to be
deprived of someone who is dear if one can recall him or rejoin him
at any moment. What is painful is a definite and irrevocable separation. That was approximately what she now felt. She continued to
live, while Floria Tosca, Adrienne Lecouvreur, and Fédora were dead,
as far as she was concerned. On February 22, 1915, the day when she

was operated upon at the hospital in Bordeaux, she had been separated forever from these heroines she loved so much, for whom she lived, and whom she had called to life for so long. Had she not played certain characters, such as Phèdre and Andromaque, for forty years?

It is true many other actresses have left the theater long before they died, which is also a very melancholy fact. Others, because of their age, have been obliged to change their type of work and to give up definitely roles which they had created thirty or forty years earlier. But if they had to substitute other characters, at least their importance and quality could remain the same. In 1909, when Blanche Pierson created the part of Mademoiselle de Saint-Salbi in *Sire*, by Henri Lavedan, at the Comédie Française, she shone with the same brilliance as when she created Victorien Sardou's *Dora* at the Vaudeville thirty-five years earlier. One was a young woman, the other a white-haired dowager; but both parts suited the actress equally well. In each play she was the chief character and was on the stage during the entire evening. Both her authors were equally famous. Age did not involve any falling off nor compel her to renounce anything.

What a difference with Sarah Bernhardt, who, for more than half a century, had incarnated the great heroines of the most striking works in the French repertory and who had suddenly to be content with little twenty-minute dramas signed by obscure names! Even then she was lucky to find them, for plays, even in one act, in which one character can remain strictly without moving, from beginning to end, are not plentiful. She performed in what was brought to her, what could be adapted to her physical capacities. Ah, how forgetful and ungrateful her regular authors proved to be! When she returned from America in 1918 it was three years since she had been operated on, and not one of them had thought of writing for her a play in three or four acts in which she could perform without having to walk.

In the first chapter of this book I have described how, disgusted with these little sketches so strangely unworthy of her and having nothing new especially written for her, she had been obliged to play *Athalie*, without any pleasure and without any great profit. Although she was admirable in it, this particularly austere tragedy could not run, obviously, for more than a few performances. Revived in April 1920, it was the first of the four important plays—I mean those occupying a whole evening—which Sarah played seated. These four plays— *Athalie, Daniel, La Gloire,* and *Régine Armand*—exclusively constituted her repertory during her last years. They were also the only four important plays in which she performed from the beginning of the war until her death; that is, from 1914 to 1923. Chronologically *Athalie* must be mentioned first, but it was *Daniel* which really marked her return to the theater.

As a matter of fact, since her last performances in *Jeanne Doré* in May, 1914, *Les Cathédrales* had provided only a few isolated matinees in 1915, at a time when people's minds were far from the theater; at the Alhambra, in 1919, *Vitrail* had a run of only fourteen days, and *Athalie* was given only at classical matinees.

Daniel marked the revival of her regular performances. According to custom it had first a public dress rehearsal and then a gala opening, and afterward it was played consecutively every evening and on Sunday matinees. For more than six years—seventy-nine months, to be exact—Sarah Bernhardt had not appeared before the regular Paris first-nighters. Her last dress rehearsal had been that of *Tout-à-Coup*, on April 16, 1914, and *Daniel* was first performed on November 9, 1920. That is why this opening was such a sensation. I have all the less hesitation in saying that it constituted a real event because I well know that my play had nothing whatever to do with the curiosity, the anxious expectation, aroused for some days by the announcement of Sarah Bernhardt's return.

After having seen her in *Vitrail*, when I determined to write a play for her, the question of the part immediately arose. Sarah Bernhardt not only could not walk but was seventy-six years of age. How and in what guise should I present her? She could still appear convincingly as a woman of sixty to sixty-five years, but not younger. If she played the character of a woman, I should have to write a maternal role for her—like *Jeanne Doré*. That was easy, and it is what I did in *Régine Armand*. But it would have been a pity to do so for her return.

I recalled her miraculous youth in *La Beffa*, in which she had appeared not so long ago. I also remembered how much she delighted the public in love scenes. Rather than show her as a grandmother, thus emphasizing her age and what she had sacrificed, would it not be cleverer to restore her to her admirers as they had so long applauded her; that is, always loving and passionate? In short, I was convinced that, in my play, she would have to be young and she would have to be in love. But how could that be reconciled with her age and her infirmity? Thus I realized the necessity of offering her a man's part. Speaking of the interpreters of *L'Aiglon*, I pointed out that, age for age, a man always shows his years more than a woman in the theater. She could no longer play a woman of thirty, but she could play a man of that age.

Except as Chérubin in 1873 and Werther in 1903, her appearances in men's clothes had always been great successes. From Zanetto in *Le Passant* to Prince Charming in *La Belle au Bois Dormant*, she had triumphed in *Lorenzaccio, Gringoire, Hamlet, L'Aiglon, Pelléas, Les Bouffons,* and many others. A sort of superstition made me believe that by making her act again as a man I was sure of success in advance. If this man was so ill that he could not move from his chair, I at once justified the forced immobility of Sarah and the ravages of the years on her face. And if, shivering with fever, the character constantly kept a rug over his legs, her infirmity would be definitely hidden.

I also thought that it was not possible to make the public accept a character who did not move during an entire evening. But Sarah Bernhardt's age and her health, which was now more precarious, counseled prudence. I must neither tire her nor tire the spectators by her constant immobility. I therefore decided that I should have her appear only in two of the four acts—the two last, naturally. In this way I could announce her, make people want her, in short, prepare her entrance for more than an hour, and the evening would conclude, and the public would leave the theater, after the two acts in which she was playing.

Such were the limits of the problem: to construct a play in four acts around a central character, who must be the sole hero of the story, who would be constantly mentioned from the beginning but who would not appear until the third and fourth acts and could never enter or leave; that is to say, he would have to be on the stage from the rise to the fall of the curtain in each of the two acts, which could not have any scene in which he did not participate. Subject to these imperative limitations, which did not simplify my task, the following was the subject of *Daniel*.

Two brothers, Albert and Daniel Arnault, are very devoted to each other; they are respectively forty and thirty years of age. Two years previously they together made the acquaintance of a young girl, Geneviève, and together they fell in love with her, but each without the other's knowledge. Daniel is idle and poor, while Albert is the powerful manager of an important automobile factory. Geneviève had no fortune, and had to support her mother and her sister in addition. Without a word Daniel withdrew and Albert married Geneviève. No one ever sees Daniel again. He adored the girl and his grief was such that he shut himself up at home—never going out, and smoking opium in an attempt to forget. His health grows worse, and in two years he has aged twenty.

Geneviève is not happy with Albert, who is a very good man but completely wrapped up in his business. Feeling lonely and morally abandoned, she takes refuge in the love for her long felt by Maurice Granger, a friend of the two brothers. Albert is suspicous and soon becomes certain: his wife has a lover. But is it really Granger? If he has proof of this, he will kill him. In order to find out for certain he goes to see Daniel, who often sees Granger and perhaps knows something.

As a matter of fact, Daniel has known of Geneviève's affair with Maurice; and at first he was disgusted and hurt by it. But Geneviève comes to see him, explains her lapse and justifies it. By formerly withdrawing so generously, Daniel did not make her happy. Living with Albert, she suffers—whereas she has a great love for Granger. She has resolved to devote her life to him. Daniel listens to her, deeply upset, but his mind is made up: he will sacrifice himself once more. He will save the two lovers. When Albert questions him, instead of naming Granger, as he intended to, he lies. He makes use of certain pieces of evidence which seem to confirm his admissions, certain visits which Geneviève has paid him. In short, he denounces himself and admits that he, Daniel, is Geneviève's lover. Maddened with anger, Albert is about to choke him; but he cannot. Daniel is almost dying; and he is his brother, after all. Thus Daniel sidetracks the suspicions of Albert, and Maurice and Geneviève can run away together. Some weeks later Daniel grows worse. Albert returns and forgives him for lying. Daniel asks his brother to reread aloud a letter which he has just received from Geneviève. She begs Albert's pardon and thanks Daniel. Thanks to the latter, she has at last found happiness. Daniel listens in a state of peace. Now he can die happily.

On the morning of the dress rehearsal, Georges Casella, who was then manager of *Comoedia*, a daily paper exclusively devoted to the theater, had published an article on the front page signed by himself and more or less couched in the following terms:

"To my colleagues, the journalists of Paris, to the dress-rehearsal public: We are often accused of being discourteous to authors and actors. We are reproached with arriving late and leaving before the end of the play, of not dressing for gala occasions; in short, of going solely about our business, attending the most beautiful artistic evenings just as other people go to their offices. An opportunity has arisen for us to attack this legend. After being in retirement for more than six years, and in spite of all that might have kept her from the stage, the greatest actress in the world is making her return to her own theater, and is appearing for the first time this evening in a new play. Let us all thank her for her courage and express our affectionate admiration for her. I ask you all, my colleagues and my friends, not to go to see *Daniel* tonight without bringing at least one flower for Sarah Bernhardt."

This appeal was more widely heard than might have been imagined. That night two thousand persons crowded into the Théâtre Sarah Bernhardt. There were twelve in boxes with seats for six, and thirty persons stood in each of the aisles. The first two acts, in Albert Arnault's house, first at Saint Germain and then in Paris, were applauded, but the impatience of the audience was obvious. When would they see Sarah Bernhardt? And, above all, how would she look? People knew of her operation and that she would never walk again. How would the author present her?

Finally, about a quarter to eleven, the curtain rose on the third act. The magnificent set represented the studio-drawing room, darkened with grief and feebly illuminated. Sarah Bernhardt was alone in the middle of the stage. Daniel was seated in an armchair reading by the light of a lamp on the table beside him. Sarah Bernhardt was wearing a long dressing gown of garnet-red velvet over a white shirt and a soft collar and a black satin tie. She was wearing a deep chestnut-brown wig parted at the side. In a more modern form her make-up recalled that of the poet in *La Nuit de Mai*, whom she had incarnated one night, eleven years earlier, at the Comédie Française.

On her appearance the enthusiasm was indescribable. The applause, the acclamations, the shouts of "Sarah! Sarah!" lasted more than ten minutes. Seven or eight times she had to stand up and bow. Very gracefully she took the rug resting on her knees in one hand and, holding it cleverly in front of her, stood up on her one leg, leaning her right hand on the table and her left on the arm of the chair. The gesture was so natural and her movement so simple, her smile so radiant, that no one, even in the first row, could suspect that she was making a tremendous effort by balancing herself in this way on one leg and propping herself up by stiffening her two arms.

When the applause finally died down, she was able to begin the third act. At the first word she uttered, when at last Paris again heard the golden voice after such a long interval, a thrill ran through the house. There was a religious silence; the audience seemed to be fascinated. Twice, in the course of the act, she repeated the first line of a song which Daniel had formerly composed:

Et puis, par un beau soir, une femme a passé.[2]

It was nothing, but she put so much intensity and grief into it that her desperate love for Geneviève, the destruction of her life from the day of their meeting, the heartbreaking resignation of Daniel, could all be felt in these twelve banal syllables. Both times the house burst into applause. Twenty or thirty of her lines were applauded. The act, which was timed for three quarters of an hour, lasted nearly one hour, so frequent and prolonged were her effects. Then, when Geneviève left for the last time, Daniel remained alone, and the curtain fell only to rise immediately.

From every part of the house, from the front row of the orchestra to the last row in the galleries, a veritable rain of bouquets and bunches of flowers fell on the stage. In three minutes Daniel's drawing room looked like an enormous flower bed. All around Sarah were mountains of flowers. Meanwhile, stamping and shouting, the whole house stood up and acclaimed Sarah Bernhardt, recalling her again and again and again. When the curtain calls stopped, it took ten minutes to clear the stage and remove the bouquets. All the stagehands had to help. Behind the scenes the pile of flowers was larger and taller than a haystack.

The fourth act lasted fifteen minutes. Sarah Bernhardt played the death of Daniel miraculously. At the end of the play, for another fifteen minutes, the ovations were interminable. Nobody thought of leaving. From 1904 to 1922 I was present at many unforgettable performances by Sarah Bernhardt. I do not believe that many of them

---

[2] And then, one lovely evening, a woman passed by. *Trans.*

could be compared to the triumph achieved, not by *Daniel*, but by Sarah as Daniel. The rest of the company, moreover, played remarkably. Arquillière represented Albert Arnault exactly as I had conceived him: big, robust, violent, and kind; Yonnel gave a good impersonation of the gentle and romantic Granger. Mauloy was definitely first-rate in the part of the doctor, an ironical and indulgent confidant; and Marcelle Géniat was a sensitive, sad, passionate, and very beautiful Geneviève, who justified the love which three men had for her.

Sarah Bernhardt was very fond of Marcelle Géniat, both as an actress and as a woman. She called her "my little flower." Her affection enabled me to smooth out an incident which occurred a few days after the opening of *Daniel*.

One morning, about the tenth performance, Marcelle Géniat telephoned to me. She had caught cold, was very feverish and, having almost lost her voice, she could not play that night. I immediately called Ullmann, who told me that the understudy did not yet know the part and would not be ready until the following week. Eighteen thousand francs' worth of tickets had been sold. (The prices of the seats having been increased since the war, the maximum receipts of the Théâtre Sarah Bernhardt were then twenty thousand francs.) To close the theater and reimburse the money, so soon after the return of Sarah Bernhardt, would have been a catastrophe.

Fortunately the play had been produced at the Théâtre du Parc in Brussels, two days after the opening in Paris. I seemed to remember that it was to run for one week. I made inquiries. It turned out that, after the run was arranged, the actors who had gone to play *Daniel* in Brussels had just returned to Paris, among them the actress who had the part of Geneviève—the very beautiful and talented Nelly Cormon. In agreement with Ullmann I hastened to her and begged her to play that night, making her own terms.

Very graciously she replied: "In principle my position in the theater would not permit me to understudy my comrade Géniat. But here it is a question of Madame Sarah Bernhardt. You can count on me. I will give the performance until the original actress in the part is better. Doing this as a service, I do not wish to be paid. What I should like is a photograph signed by Madame Sarah Bernhardt."

I thanked Nelly Cormon effusively, and promised that she would have her photograph, telephoning to the theater that everything was all right. In the afternoon I made her rehearse her part, dwelling with particular care on the third act. I showed her in detail everything that Sarah Bernhardt did, the "timing" and the slightest pieces of business. She had only one long scene with her and another very short one. She knew her lines perfectly and everything promised to go well.

In the evening, however, doubtless greatly excited at playing with Sarah Bernhardt for the first time in her life, Nelly Cormon became somewhat disturbed. During her big scene Geneviève knelt in front of Daniel, begging him to save her, and clasped his hands in her grief, covering them with tears and kisses. Having badly judged her distance, Nelly Cormon fell on her knees precisely on the foot of Sarah Bernhardt, who made a grimace of pain. Then, being excessively nervous, she squeezed her hand so hard that Sarah could not help uttering a slight cry. From the fireman's box where I was watching the act I saw what was happening, and Sarah's irritated look. I guessed that there would be a storm during the intermission!

It was a tempest. Beside herself, Sarah shouted: "What on earth have you given me here to act with? She's not a woman, but a torturer! An executioner! She has crushed my hands and reduced my foot to pulp! I don't want to see her again; I never want to hear of her any more. So long as Géniat is not available, I will not play again!"

Fortunately Geneviève Arnault did not appear in the fourth act, and the evening ended without further trouble. Next day Géniat, having taken great care of herself, was able to resume her role. But there was still the problem of the photograph, the signed photograph of Sarah Bernhardt, which I had promised to Nelly Cormon and which I had to give her. With extremely good grace and refusing all payment, she had saved us twenty thousand francs in receipts. I had to keep my promise. On the other hand, I knew very well that, if I asked Sarah to sign one of her photographs for her, she would launch into a stream of invectives and tell me to go to the devil.

I gave Géniat a photograph of Sarah Bernhardt in the part of Daniel, and told her what to do. After all, it was her indisposition, involuntary but most unfortunate, which had got us into this dilemma. She might well help me to settle the matter. Géniat was a most exquisite friend, and agreed to do so.

That night, before the performance, she went to see Sarah Bernhardt in her dressing room and said: "Madame, I already have several photographs of you, but I should like to have a souvenir of this play in which I am so proud of having performed with you. Would you be so kind as to sign this portrait? But don't inscribe it in my own name. I want the name which you call me so tenderly on the stage every night —the Geneviève whom you love in the play when you are Daniel, as shown in this portrait."

The trick was rather crude, but it succeeded. Delighted to see Géniat back again, Sarah Bernhardt took her fountain pen and, thinking angrily of the brutal substitute that one night, she wrote in a rage: "To the perfect, the sweet and irreplaceable, Geneviève Arnault. In affectionate memory of Sarah Bernhardt."

As agreed, Géniat brought me the signed photograph; but she sighed: "What a dedication! It breaks my heart to give it away!"

However, she gave it to me and I took it to Nelly Cormon.

She read what Sarah Bernhardt had written and, blushing with confusion, exclaimed: "I knew that I had pleased Madame Sarah Bernhardt in the part, but I did not believe it to such an extent. What she has written is too nice for me. Indeed, it is not very pleasant for the woman who created the part. I shall see that Géniat never discovers this photo; that would hurt her!"

Three weeks after the opening of *Daniel*, Sarah Bernhardt created another role, or more exactly a scene, in a little play in two acts, which was staged only once at the Théâtre Sarah Bernhardt, on the afternoon of December 4, 1920, at the benefit performance for Georges Noblet, a delightful boulevard actor who had been out of the theater for several years. For this matinee Sacha Guitry had written specially a two-act comedy, entitled *Comment on écrit l'Histoire*, which was performed by Sarah Bernhardt, Lucien Guitry, Sacha Guitry, Yvonne Printemps, and Noblet.

Later on, the author turned this little play into an operetta in four acts, with music by Oscar Straus, entitled *Mariette*, which was first produced at the Théâtre Edouard VII in October, 1928. The first act of *Comment on écrit l'Histoire* takes place in 1851, Yvonne Printemps playing the part of Mariette as a young woman. In the second act, which takes place in our own time, Sarah Bernhardt was the same Mariette seventy years later. In the operetta Yvonne Printemps appeared in both stages of the character.

On April 4, having played *Daniel* for three months in Paris, Sarah

Bernhardt went to London and gave it for two weeks at the Princes Theatre. During her stay the English Dramatic Artists' Club organized a demonstration in her honor. It was not exactly the usual "Sarah Bernhardt Day" but something like it. One afternoon all the personalities in the theater, literature, politics, and "society" were invited to come and present personally their respects and the homage of their admiration. The point of this celebration was to bring together the greatest number of celebrities with the greatest celebrity in the world. It was difficult, in effect, to imagine a more brilliant crowd. All the best-known names in the United Kingdom were announced in succession. Sarah Bernhardt had counted on seeing five hundred persons, but there were two thousand.

About half past two she was seated in a large armchair in the center of the stage of the Princes. Those who had come to greet her were standing in the orchestra awaiting their turn. The stage was connected with the house by two small stairways. By the one on the extreme right the procession went up onto the stage, and by that at the extreme left it returned. It looked like the line of people in a sacristy, or a presentation at court. The President of the Club—Gerald du Maurier, I believe—stood beside Sarah and gave her the names, one by one, of those who bowed to her. Arquillière, Marcelle Géniat, and I stood behind her chair. All went well for an hour. At the rate of four or five persons a minute, the celebrities of London marched past. Sarah smiled: "Delighted! You are charming! Thank you!"

After an hour and a half she whispered to me: "I have had enough of this! Send for my chair." I begged her to stay a little while longer. After two hours she murmured: "My chair! I'm having an attack of nerves!" I then approached one of the organizers and told him that Madame Sarah Bernhardt felt tired and wanted to retire. "Impossible!" he said with a start. "Barely half the people have been introduced." Sarah heard this reply and simply said: "Very well." Two minutes later she fainted, so perfectly that it was impossible to suspect that she was pretending. There was nothing for it but to take her back to her hotel, and in the car she said to me: "I could not stand any more. They are delightful, all of them, and I adore them; but I would have bitten them!"

For thirty years, in every part of the world, so much official homage had been paid to her, so many matinees, banquets, various galas, and other different glorifications had been organized in her honor, that it would be an understatement to say that she was bored by them. These celebrations had become to her positively unbearable. But what never left her untouched was popular demonstrations. Regimented and pompous homage left her cold, but to the end of her days the naïve and spontaneous adoration of crowds touched her profoundly. In this connection, it was in Madrid that I witnessed the most astonishing of all the manifestations of enthusiasm of which I had seen Sarah Bernhardt the object.

It was in May, 1921. With six plays in my repertory I was making a tour of Spain. I had first played for four days in San Sebastián, and then one week in Madrid—at the end of which Sarah Bernhardt was coming to perform in *Daniel*. Beginning May 21, she played it twice in Madrid and three times in Barcelona. She was supported by my company and I myself played the part of Granger, created by Yonnel.

On May 19, about nine o'clock in the evening, she arrived by train at the central station in Madrid—coming from Paris, which she had left the night before with Dr. Marot; Jeanne de Gournay, her companion; and her butler, Emile. Performances begin very late in Spain: matinees begin at half past five, and evening performances at half past ten. I was therefore able to go to meet Sarah Bernhardt at the station before acting. Five thousand persons were waiting for her. A large force of police had been requisitioned to maintain order. The crowd was restless and buzzed with comments on her arrival. Finally the train appeared. I entered her compartment and, when she was seated in her chair, Emile and I carried her. Since her train had entered the station, the anxious curiosity of the crowd had increased tenfold. How would they find her after such a long interval? Now there was dead silence. She would be visible any moment.

When she appeared in her chair at the door of the train, smiling, a thunder of shouts and acclamations arose. Below her the crowd was like a human sea moved by long, rolling waves. There were people everywhere: on the platforms, on the tracks, on the roofs of neighboring trains, on the luggage trucks. Some men were clinging to the lampposts. Very carefully Emile and I lifted her down onto the platform.

Then something happened which I shall never forget. As if they had just at that moment received some tacit order, all the men present took off their coats and spread them on the ground, forming a kind of carpet which seemed to have been unrolled in an instant from the train to the car waiting for her in the street in front of the station. The

distance to be traversed was at least six hundred feet. We had to cross
the platform, the large waiting room, and the huge hall of the station.
Consequently, a thousand coats perhaps were simultaneously spread
on the ground. Yet Sarah was not walking; she was being carried. It
was, therefore, not in order to keep her from stepping on the ground
that all these people had made this gesture. It was in order to provide
a triumphal passage for those who had the honor of carrying her!

That day I saw that Sarah Bernhardt was really deeply touched. She
murmured: "Ah, how nice they are! Ah, what fine people!"

The first performance of *Daniel* in Madrid was exciting, at least in
the wings. According to my contract, my Spanish impresario, Mr. B.,
was supposed to hand over to me every evening a total amount which
included my salary, the expenses of the company, and of traveling. He
had paid me for the first two evenings at San Sebastián, but the third
day, pretending that it was Sunday and that the banks were closed, he
had postponed settling until the next day. Then he had only given me
something on account. In short, by the end of the week he had come
to owe me some fifty thousand francs. Tired of applying to him, I had
ceased to remind him of his debt. I was so certain that he would
pay me!

The name of Sarah Bernhardt was glowing in lights over the door,
and the Comoedia Theatre was packed to overflowing. For ten days
not even a folding seat remained. King Alfonso XIII, the Queen, and
the Queen Mother were in their box. We played the first act and then
the second. At last, Sarah Bernhardt was about to appear. It was
almost one o'clock in the morning.

"Hurry up that change of scenery," Mr. B. shouted to the stagehands.

But I went up to him and said very quietly: "My dear sir, you owe
me fifty-two thousand francs which, according to our contract, must
be paid to me in installments every night before the last act. I have
waited long enough. I must insist that you be kind enough to settle
this amount immediately. The performance will not continue until
you have paid me the entire amount."

The manager was panic-stricken and tried at first to argue. Seeing
that I was quite decided, he rushed to Sarah Bernhardt's dressing room
and told her indignantly, with a strong Madrid accent, about the
"blackmail" which I had just attempted, adding that he had no doubt
that she would play the third act as soon as the scenery was set up.
Sarah Bernhardt would never allow anyone to interfere with those

whom she loved. Since I had become her "grandson-in-law," nobody was allowed to utter the slightest criticism of me in her presence.

She replied dryly to the impresario: "For these few performances, sir, I am engaged, not by you, but by Louis Verneuil. I shall play the third act whenever he asks me to."

There was nothing for him to do but to pay up. He had not fifty-two thousand francs on him. At the time it was a relatively important sum; and I would not take a check, needless to say. He had to run all over the theater and, in order to procure the amount of his debt, he had to borrow from the treasurer, the box office, the superintendent, and the owner of the neighboring café. At the end of twenty minutes a chamberlain came on behalf of the King to ask why the intermission was so long. I quietly replied that there had been a slight accident to the scenery, and I begged His Majesty to be so kind as to excuse us: the performance would continue as soon as possible. Finally, foaming with rage, Mr. B. brought me a pile of bank notes of every denomination and of every shape, silver coins, and even nickels! The amount was correct.

I said to the stage manager: "Now you can ring up the curtain." Having thanked her tenderly, I begged Sarah Bernhardt to be so good as to go on the stage.

The next day and until the end of the tour, Mr. B. paid me very punctually. But Sarah Bernhardt had taken an even greater dislike to him than I had and, from that day on, as soon as she saw him she would say as loudly as possible: "By the way, does Mr. B. owe you any money at this time? Tell me, because I will then arrive a little late at the theater this evening. These long intervals which he forces on us bore me."

Blushing to his ears, Mr. B. would bow low to Sarah and pass on, worthy and pained.

The following month Sarah Bernhardt toured the south of France in a series of lectures on Edmond Rostand. Her program consisted of, first, an hour's talk, after which she recited parts of the plays and some poems by the author of *Cyrano*. All by herself she occupied the stage for two hours and a half, moving from town to town every day—and she was almost seventy-seven years of age.

About the same time I was engaged by C. B. Cochran to do a four weeks' season at the Garrick Theatre, London, from June 15 to July 15, 1921. I had a company of about fifteen, of whom the most important were Marcelle Géniat, Arquilière, Madeleine Lambert, Marcelle Praince, and Jacques de Féraudy; and I was to give eight plays, at the rate of two each week, each show running for three nights and one matinee. In advance I had sent the printed text or manuscripts of the eight plays to Cochran so that he might submit them to the British Censor's Office, which was then headed by Lord Cromer.

Ten days before the date of my opening Cochran telephoned me from London to Paris, saying: "The Censor has rejected three of your plays. We could not do good business in four weeks with only five shows. It is absolutely necessary for us to get his authorization to play the repertory as announced. As each play will be given only four times, and in French, I believe it will be not too difficult to make the Censor revise his decision. But you will have to help me in this. Please come over at once and see Lord Cromer, state your own case, and try to get a couple of letters of recommendation from influential French people."

That same day I paid several visits. Directly or indirectly I intruded on all the most powerful people I knew in Paris. When I took the train to London, I had a letter from Aristide Briand, the Prime Minister, in his own handwriting; a letter from Louis Barthou, who was then, if I am not mistaken, Minister of Justice; and a particularly emphatic letter signed by Paul Painlevé, who was not a member of the Cabinet at the time but was still one of the most important potential candidates for ministerial office. I think I could hardly have done better. All three warmly recommended me to the British authorities, pointing out the French propaganda purpose of my performances and thanking in advance those who were kind enough to facilitate my task.

The day after my arrival I was received in the most friendly way at Saint James's Palace by Lord Cromer, who carefully examined the letters I handed to him, shook his head, with a smile, and said: "I see, sir, that you have highly placed protectors, and I need hardly say how happy I should be to do them a favor. But I am not alone in my decisions. I have a reading committee to whom I must submit the question. I may add that it is more delicate than you might imagine. If I authorize your plays, I shall create a precedent. I shall have to authorize others of the same kind, which I wish to suppress. In short, please let me have your address and I will call you as soon as I have consulted my colleagues."

I thanked him and told him that I was stopping at the Savoy, where I returned full of confidence and waited. One day, two days, three days passed. No reply. I returned to Saint James's Palace. The matter was still "under consideration." Cochran was beginning to be uneasy, and so was I. In Paris all my actors were ready to leave, awaiting only a telegram from me to set out. We were to open the following Monday, and it was already Wednesday. Would it be possible to open?

All of a sudden it occurred to me to ask Sarah Bernhardt's advice. I had, of course, her itinerary with me, and I looked to see where she was playing that Wednesday. She was at the Théâtre Caton in Tarbes. I sent her a long telegram, telling her of my dilemma and asking her to give me the name of some influential English person to whom I could apply on her behalf and whose intercession with Lord Cromer would be decisive. She had been in London so often that she knew everybody.

A few hours later, Sarah Bernhardt replied: "Don't worry. I'll arrange everything."

At the same time she sent Queen Mary—the King of England was then George V—the following telegram:

"MY DEAR FRIEND: THE PLAYS OF MY GRANDSON ARE PARISIAN BUT NOT IMMORAL. I SHALL BE INFINITELY GRATEFUL TO YOU IF YOU WILL INTERVENE PERSONALLY, SO THAT THE CENSOR DOES NOT BAN ANY OF THEM. A THOUSAND AFFECTIONATE THANKS. SARAH BERNHARDT."

At nine o'clock the next morning Lord Cromer telephoned to me himself that my eight plays had been passed. What the Prime Minister and two of the most important French statesmen had failed to accomplish was granted to me on a telegram of a few words from Sarah Bernhardt!

Sarah Bernhardt's cable to Queen Mary became known and was published in all the papers. The exact wording will be found in the English newspapers of that date.

I could relate twenty or thirty other anecdotes of this kind. But I have to keep some of them private for my friends. If I publish them all here, this volume will be twice as long. Moreover, in future, when I am again asked to speak about Sarah Bernhardt—which often happens—as soon as I begin to tell a story someone will interrupt me by saying: "I know that. I read it in your book."

In writing this book I had no intention of making a collection of anecdotes, but wanted to relate faithfully the seventy-eight years of Sarah Bernhardt's life. Numbers of often remarkable works of every kind, and in every tone, have been published about Sarah Bernhardt, but I do not know one which is a complete and accurate history of her life and her career. That is why I undertook this task, feeling that I was filling a gap. Someday, perhaps, I shall write another book—*Sarah Bernhardt: An Intimate Portrait*—and this will consist of three hundred pages of anecdotes.

Among all those proving her popularity and her influence, I think that her intercession by telegram in favor of my performances in London is one of the most eloquent. Ignoring censors, ministers, ambassadors, and everybody else, she addressed herself directly to the royal family, treating them as one equal to another. And it was the same all over the world: a wish expressed by her became an order. What other actress ever had or will ever have such extraordinary authority?

Immediately after my season in London came the summer at Belle Isle, about which I have spoken at length. Then, on October 19, 1921, Sarah Bernhardt gave the first performance of *La Gloire*, by Maurice Rostand. Those who have seen or read this play must immediately have guessed that it was certainly not the enthusiasm which it inspired in her which decided Sarah Bernhardt to act it, but solely her affectionate gratitude to the author's father—the wonderful poet of *La Princesse Lointaine, La Samaritaine,* and *L'Aiglon.* His son had the advantage of Sarah Bernhardt's indulgent friendship, because his name was Rostand and because, twenty-five years earlier, she had known him as a little child.

In this play he had had the strange idea of having Sarah Bernhardt act the part of a . . . picture ("an ancient picture," the little intellectual reviews of the time immediately called it, an inevitable joke, which Maurice Rostand alone had not foreseen.) On the backdrop, facing the public, hung a huge framed canvas, a life-size picture of a woman, seated, in a red and gold gown, surrounded by laurel leaves: Glory. This portrait was painted on metallic canvas which became transparent when lit from behind. Behind the set, dressed like the picture, Sarah Bernhardt was seated on a level with the picture, and remained there, silent and motionless, from one end of the performance to the other, enclosed in a sort of dark cabinet where she was invisible. Then, once in every act—that is to say, three times during the evening—Glory spoke. The dark cabinet was lit up; Sarah Bernhardt appeared, recited some thirty lines to one of the characters of the play, and then disappeared in the darkness behind the picture—in which the painted Glory again hid her from the sight of the spectators.

That is what Maurice Rostand, having the extreme honor of writing a play for Sarah Bernhardt, invented to bring out the qualities of the greatest artist in the world! As for the subject of the play, it can be here summed up accurately in three lines: Clarence is a young painter who is certain that he has enormous talent, but Glory will never come to him because he has the terrible misfortune to be the son of a famous and universally admired painter. He goes mad and dies of despair.

The three acts of *La Gloire* were conceived and written solely to describe the tortures of the life of a man whose father occupies a dominating position in the same profession as himself. And this play was the work of Edmond Rostand's son. I think that all commentary would be superfluous. Writing of another play by this author, Lucien Dubech, the critic of *L'Action Française* and of *Candide*, said: "Monsieur Maurice Rostand has received from heaven a glorious name, but he has none of the necessary qualities to bear it nobly."

For my part, I have never been a dramatic critic; and I do not wish to become one, even occasionally. What I cannot refrain from expressing is the sadness which I felt, and which was shared by all of Sarah Bernhardt's friends and admirers, at the manner in which Maurice Rostand presented her in his play.

To have Sarah Bernhardt as an interpreter, only too ready to act a part—a real part—to have the unhoped-for opportunity of conceiving and writing down for her a character, a thinking and active human being, weeping, loving, and suffering—a character, in brief, who lives as only she could—and then merely to give her about a hundred lines to recite (the whole part was not much more), and shut her up in a frame attached to the wall—this was really to exceed the limits of consciencelessness. It must have been the general opinion, since, as early as the middle of December, the Théâtre Sarah Bernhardt had to announce the closing of *La Gloire*.

Early in her performances, about the end of October, 1921, toward ten o'clock one morning, Sarah Bernhardt's companion telephoned me that she was very ill. A quarter of an hour later I was at her house. She was having an attack of uremia. Cold and with her teeth chattering, her eyes half-closed, and incapable of moving, she received me with a wan smile. Dr. Marot seemed anxious. Her temperature had dropped below ninety-three degrees, and she was undoubtedly in danger. Gradually Maurice Bernhardt, Marcelle, Lysiane, and Simone had arrived, greatly upset. Sarah Bernhardt was in a stupor, and she remained for a long time motionless, silent, and shivering under ten blankets in a room where the heat was suffocating. About half past four she opened her eyes, looked at the clock, and murmured: "All right, I'll leave in an hour."

She wanted to act that night! The doctor intervened and we all begged her not to move. She let us talk, but about half past five, raising herself with an effort, she asked us to leave her bedroom and called Jeanne de Gournay to help her to dress. And she did dress! Wrapped in furs from head to foot and clasping a hot-water bottle against her body, she had herself carried to her car and, on arriving at the theater, she slept for another hour. At half past seven she began to make up. The lipstick shook in her hand and she had to make three attempts to redden the outline of her lips. When the bell for the curtain rang, she was ready.

Over her costume as Glory she wrapped woolen shawls and was carried onto the stage. During the entire performance, for three hours, she had to remain in her dark cabinet behind the picture, waiting for her moment to appear. Electric radiators had been placed all around her. Slumped in her chair and crumpled up, she remained prostrate during the whole first act. She had only to say the very last lines. Feeling that her cue was coming, she slowly sat up again and signaled to us. She took off and handed us her shawls, arranged her make-up, stiffened herself, smiled. . . . And, with a superhuman effort, she recited her entire speech in a weak but almost normal voice.

Back in the dark, she collapsed again in her chair, exhausted. We rushed to her, but it was just a momentary weakness. Similarly she was able to make her speech in the second and then in the third act. Finally she was carried to her dressing room. The show had gone on!

That night I saw the actors, the stage managers, and even the stage-hands at the Théâtre Sarah Bernhardt weeping freely. They had known her well and for a long time; but none had ever seen her make such an effort before, and display such incredible valiance at her age. We were all moved, overcome with respect and admiration. The next day she was still weak, but two days later no one would have believed that she had been on the brink of death.

For the Christmas holidays and New Year's day, 1922, she played *Athalie, La Gloire*, and *Daniel* in succession at Brussels, four or five performances of each play. She then created the chief part in *Régine Armand*, the second play which I wrote for her and which was her last creation. The first performance took place in Brussels at the Théâtre des Galeries-Saint-Hubert, on January 12, 1922. It was a dramatic play in four acts, in which Sarah Bernhardt had the part of a great actress at the end of her career. The character was obviously none other than herself, and her part had a great number of lines about the theater, art, the mission of the actor, and professional courage. When she said them, it was Sarah Bernhardt who was talking rather than Régine Armand. A short episode in the second act made a great impression. Feeling old and tired, an actor in her company wishes to retire and asks her not to renew his contract. Régine Armand refuses. Leave the theater? As long as an actor has the strength to play and feels that the public likes him, he has no right to retire. That would be deserting.

"Rest!" Sarah Bernhardt cried indignantly. "Do I think of such a thing? Do you believe that I shall ever rest?" And every evening the house thanked her loudly for this promise.

The character of Régine Armand did not appear in the first act, but in the three others. The second took place in her dressing room at the theater, during a performance of *Cléopâtre*, which permitted Sarah Bernhardt to appear in a costume which she had worn thirty-two years earlier in Sardou's play. The third act took us to her house, and the set was more or less a reproduction of the living room of her home in the Boulevard Péreire. The fourth act was again in her dressing room, during a performance of *Adrienne Lecouvreur*. Although very ill, Régine Armand had insisted on playing; but her strength failed. She fell on the stage out of sight of the public, and was carried to her dressing room in the arms of a stagehand. (In this way I had succeeded in arranging her "entrance.") But the effort she had made killed her: she was dying.

The principal parts in the supporting cast in Brussels were played by Arquillière, Gaston Dubosc, Jacques de Féraudy, Andrée Pascal, Marie Montbazon, and by myself—who played the part of her son, Michel. During almost the entire year of 1922 Sarah Bernhardt played *Régine Armand* and *Daniel* exclusively. First, from January to the beginning of April, she went on a long tour of Belgium, Holland, Switzerland, and France. In most of the towns on her itinerary she remained two days, playing each play once. Although they were pitched in very much the same key, these two dramas had the advantage of showing Sarah Bernhardt in two totally different aspects. In the one, she was a young man; in the other, a great actress of more than sixty years. She played *Régine Armand* in Paris, at the Théâtre Sarah Bernhardt, from April 20 to the end of June, 1922. Then, having spent her last summer at Belle Isle, she performed my two plays again in the south of France and in Italy, from the end of October to the end of November, 1922.

Early in April I had to undergo a throat operation, and I had the disappointment of not being able to play my part in Paris. Roger Puylagarde was Michel Armand at the Théâtre Sarah Bernhardt. The two other most important parts also had a change of cast. Jacques Grétillat followed Arquillière, and Simone Frévalles was delightful and touching as the young heroine.

I am happy to be able to write that the prodigious career of Sarah Bernhardt ended with the double success of *Daniel* and *Régine Armand*. From November, 1920, to November, 1922, she played *Daniel* more than two hundred and fifty times, and from January to November, 1922, *Régine Armand* more than one hundred and fifty times. Of course, these figures include all the performances which she gave in Paris, France, and all the foreign countries which were fortunate enough to see her during her last years: England, Belgium, Holland, Spain, Switzerland, and Italy.

These two plays were certainly quite unworthy of her genius, and I am the first to admit it. The material factors with which I had to contend also limited my possibilities greatly. At least I achieved the object which I had set for myself. In spite of her infirmity Sarah Bernhardt had finally been able to give up music halls and short sketches, which were her only repertory since 1915. She had reappeared in real plays, in which her character was either the hero or the heroine, without having to be carried on and off the stage as in *Athalie*, which demanded a very great concession from the public. Above all, and in conclusion, until her dying day she had been able to earn her living successfully.

In the first chapter of this book I have related in detail the last months of her life and the death of Sarah Bernhardt. I adopted this rather unusual procedure for two reasons. First, because this final period covered the facts which I entitled "How I Met Sarah Bernhardt." Secondly, because I thought that, by learning of the glorious and touching apotheosis of her final years, to begin with, the reader would perhaps be more tempted to find out by what series of successes and events she had achieved this fabulous renown. In the sixty years of her career, from 1862 to 1922, Sarah Bernhardt had actually moved the world. It would be even more correct to say in only forty-five years, for it was not until about 1877 that her greatest fame began.

She played everything. From the blind old Roman woman in *Rome Vaincue* to the roguish little page boy in *Le Passant*, from the cynical spy in *La Femme de Claude* to the pure Sainte Thérèse in *La Vierge d'Avila*, from Hamlet and Lady Macbeth to *Les Précieuses Ridicules* and Dorine in *Tartufe*, from poor Gringoire to the magnificent Empress Théodora, from the haughty Marie Antoinette in *Varennes* to the humble and modest Jeanne Doré. The gallery of Sarah Bernhardt's parts is the most complete, the most diverse, and the most extensive in existence. The greater part of the characters which she created are indissolubly connected with her name. One could not imagine them in any other guise.

I have occasionally mentioned the fact that people regretted that she was not more strict in the selection of her plays and her authors, attaching more importance to the immediate success which she could achieve in a part than to the quality of the work which she was interpreting. On consideration, this reproach was unjust. If one examines carefully the long list of her roles at the end of this volume, it will be seen that, with the single exception of Corneille—only one of whose plays, *Le Cid,* she performed, at her debuts at the Théâtre Français—it is precisely the most famous French authors whom she most frequently

Last Years

Last Years

Last Years

interpreted—more especially Racine, of whom she performed ten parts and seven plays. She was Aricie and Phèdre in *Phèdre*, Zacharie and Athalie in *Athalie*, and Hermione and Andromaque in *Andromaque*.

Although she was, first and foremost, a tragedienne, she performed in five plays and six parts by Molière, likewise five plays and six parts by Shakespeare, and five plays by Victor Hugo. Then came seven plays by Sardou, five by Dumas *fils*, and Rostand. These statistics are undeniable. They show that, despite the legend which describes Sarah Bernhardt as having, like Frédérick Lemaître, achieved her greatest successes in mediocre plays, her seven favorite authors were Racine, Molière, Shakespeare, Victor Hugo, Victorien Sardou, Alexandre Dumas *fils*, and Edmond Rostand. It would be difficult to conceive of a better choice.

Furthermore, Sarah Bernhardt would not have maintained her glory intact if the contents of her repertory had not been worthy of her genius. The masterpieces rendered the sensational plays acceptable. In order to surpass the greatest actresses, an actress must first serve the greatest dramatists. It was in *Phèdre, Hamlet, Lorenzaccio,* and *Andromaque* that she surpassed herself. And it is for that reason, first of all, that she created such a position for herself that no other name in the history of the theater can even be compared with hers. From Burbage and Champmeslé to Duse and Réjane, including Adrienne Lecouvreur, Garrick, Mademoiselle Mars, Rachel, Talma, Coquelin, Irving, Novelli, Ellen Terry, Mounet Sully, Lucien Guitry, is there one of them, man or woman, whose name will be remembered in the future like that of Sarah Bernhardt?

For half a century, and all over the world, she caused French writers and French art, the language and culture of France, to be acclaimed, loved, and understood. For half a century the entire world was obliged to recognize and proclaim that the greatest living actress was a Frenchwoman. And, since her death, no one in any country has taken her place.

Thus Sarah Bernhardt has done as much for the prestige of her country as its most glorious conquerors and most illustrious thinkers. One day a little girl who was graduating from school was asked to name the three greatest French people that ever lived. "Jeanne d'Arc, Napoléon, and Sarah Bernhardt," she replied. The examiner smiled. I do not think that I should have found this reply so childish. In its naïveté the wisdom of the people is often greater than we imagine. A name which has grown, which has impressed itself, and which survives to this extent can only be that of a great Frenchwoman.

It is because she has seen the birth of geniuses like Sarah Bernhardt that we can believe in the future of France, and maintain our belief that this great country will always be among the first in the world.

Roles Played by Sarah Bernhardt

1862 IPHIGÉNIE (Jean Racine) role of Iphigénie.
VALÉRIE (Scribe and Mélesville) role of Valérie.
LES FEMMES SAVANTES (Molière) role of Henriette.
L'ETOURDI (Molière) role of Hippolyte.

1864 LA MAISON SANS ENFANTS (Dumanoir).
*LE DEMON DU JEU (Théodore Barrière and Crisafulli).
*UN MARI QUI LANCE SA FEMME (Eugène Labiche and Raymond Deslandes).

1865 LA BICHE AU BOIS (Cogniard Brothers) role of the Princesse Désirée.

1866 LE JEU DE L'AMOUR ET DU HASARD (Marivaux) role of Silvia.

1867 LES FEMMES SAVANTES (Molière) role of Armande.
LE ROI LEAR (Shakespeare) role of Cordelia.
ATHALIE (Racine) role of Zacharie.
LE TESTAMENT DE CÉSAR GIRODOT (Belot and Villetard) role of Hortense.
FRANCOIS-LE-CHAMPI (George Sand) role of Mariette.
LE MARQUIS DE VILLEMER (George Sand) role of the Baronne d'Arglade.
LE DRAME DE LA RUE DE LA PAIX (Adolphe Belot) role of Julia.

1868 KEAN (Alexandre Dumas *père*) role of Anna Damby.
*LA LOTERIE DU MARIAGE

1869 *LE PASSANT (François Coppée) role of Zanetto (one-act play).
*LE BÂTARD (Alfred Touroude).

1870 *L'AFFRANCHI (Latour de Saint Ybars).
*L'AUTRE (George Sand).

1871 *JEAN-MARIE (André Theuriet) role of Thérèse (one-act play).

1872 *MADEMOISELLE AÏSSÉ (Louis Bouilhet) role of Mlle. Aïssé.
RUY BLAS (Victor Hugo) role of the Queen.
MADEMOISELLE DE BELLE-ISLE (Alexandre Dumas *père*) role of Mlle de Belle Isle.
BRITANNICUS (Racine) role of Junie.
LE CID (Corneille) role of Chimène.

1873   LE MARIAGE DE FIGARO (Beaumarchais) role of Chérubin.
      DALILA (Octave Feuillet) role of the Princesse Léonora Falconieri.
      *L'ABSENT (Eugène Manuel) (one-act play).
      *CHEZ L'AVOCAT (Paul Ferrier) role of Marthe (one-act play).
      ANDROMAQUE (Racine) role of Andromaque.
      PHÈDRE (Racine) role of Aricie.

1874   *LE SPHINX (Octave Feuillet) role of Berthe de Savigny.
      *LA BELLE PAULE (Louis Denayrousse) (one-act play).
      ZAÏRE (Voltaire) role of Zaïre.
      PHÈDRE (Racine) role of Phèdre.

1875   *LA FILLE DE ROLAND (Henri de Bornier) role of Berthe.
      GABRIELLE (Emile Augier) role of Gabrielle.

1876   *L'ETRANGÈRE (Alexandre Dumas *fils*) role of Mrs. Clarkson.
      LA NUIT DE MAI (Alfred de Musset) role of the Muse (one-act play).
      *ROME VAINCUE (Alexandre Parodi) role of Posthumia.

1877   *HERNANI (Victor Hugo) role of Doña Sol.

1878   *OTHELLO (Shakespeare–Jean Aircard) role of Desdemona (selections).
      AMPHYTRION (Molière) role of Alcmène.

1879   MITHRIDATE (Racine) role of Monime.

1880   L'AVENTURIÈRE (Emile Augier) role of Doña Clorinde.
      LE SPHINX (Octave Feuillet) role of Blanche de Chelles.
      ADRIENNE LECOUVREUR (Scribe and Legouvé) role of Adrienne.
      FROUFROU (Meilhac and Halévy) role of Gilberte.
      LA DAME AUX CAMÉLIAS (Alexandre Dumas *fils*) role of Marguerite Gautier.

1881   LA PRINCESSE GEORGES (Alexandre Dumas *fils*) role of Séverine.

1882   *FÉDORA (Victorien Sardou) role of Fédora.

1883   *NANA-SAHIB (Jean Richepin) role of Djamma.

1884   *MACBETH (Shakespeare–Jean Richepin) role of Lady Macbeth.
      *THÉODORA (Victorien Sardou) role of Théodora.

1885   MARION DELORME (Victor Hugo) role of Marion.

1886   *HAMLET (Shakespeare–Cressonnois and Samson) role of Ophelia.
      LE MAÎTRE DE FORGES (Georges Ohnet) role of Claire de Beaulieu.
      *L'AVEU (Sarah Bernhardt) role of Marthe (one-act play).

1887   *LA TOSCA (Victorien Sardou) role of Floria Tosca.

1888   FRANCILLON (Alexandre Dumas *fils*) role of Francine de Riverolles.

1889   *LÉNA (Pierre Berton–F. C. Philipps) role of Léna.

1890   *JEANNE D'ARC (Jules Barbier) role of Jeanne d'Arc.
      *CLÉOPÂTRE (Victorien Sardou) role of Cléopâtre.

1891 GRINGOIRE (Théodore de Banville) role of Gringoire (one-act play).

1893 *LES ROIS (Jules Lemaître) role of the Princesse Wilhemine.

1894 *IZÉÏL (Eugène Morand and Armand Silvestre) role of Izéïl.
LA FEMME DE CLAUDE (Alexandre Dumas *fils*) role of Césarine.
*GISMONDA (Victorien Sardou) role of Gismonda.

1895 *MAGDA (Hermann Sudermann) role of Magda.
*LA PRINCESSE LOINTAINE (Edmond Rostand) role of Mélissinde.

1896 *LORENZACCIO (Alfred de Musset) role of Lorenzaccio.

1897 *SPIRITISME (Victorien Sardou) role of Simone.
*LA SAMARITAINE (Edmond Rostand) role of Photine.
*LES MAUVAIS BERGERS (Octave Mirbeau) role of Madeleine.

1898 *LA VILLE MORTE (Gabriele d'Annunzio) role of Anne.
*LYSIANE (Romain Coolus) role of Lysiane.
*MÉDÉE (Catulle Mendès) role of Médée.

1899 *HAMLET (Shakespeare–Schwob and Morand) role of Hamlet.

1900 *L'AIGLON (Edmond Rostand) role of the Duc de Reichstadt.
CYRANO DE BERGERAC (Edmond Rostand) role of Roxane.

1901 LA PLUIE ET LE BEAU TEMPS (Léon Gozlan) role of the Baronne (one-act play).
LES PRÉCIEUSES RIDICULES (Molière) role of Madelon (one-act play).

1902 *FRANCESCA DA RIMINI (M. Crawford and M. Schwob) role of Francesca.
SAPHO (Alphonse Daudet) role of Fanny Legrand.
*THÉROIGNE DE MÉRICOURT (Paul Hervieu) role of Théroigne.

1903 ANDROMAQUE (Racine) role of Hermione.
*WERTHER (Goethe–Pierre Decourcelle) role of Werther.
PLUS QUE REINE (Emile Bergerat) role of Joséphine.
*JEANNE WEDEKIND (Filippi–Krauss) role of Jeanne Wedekind.
LA SORCIÈRE (Victorien Sardou) role of Zoraya.

1904 *VARENNES (Lavedan and Lenôtre) role of Marie Antoinette.

1905 ANGELO (Victor Hugo) role of La Tisbé.
ESTHER (Racine) role of Assuérus.
PELLÉAS ET MÉLISANDE (Maurice Maeterlinck) role of Pelléas.
*ADRIENNE LECOUVREUR (Sarah Bernhardt) role of Adrienne.

1906 *LA VIERGE D'AVILA (Catulle Mendès) role of Sainte Thérèse.

1907 *LES BOUFFONS (Miguel Zamacoïs) role of Jacasse.
*LE VERT-GALANT (Emile Moreau) role of La Reine Margot (one-act play).
*LA BELLE AU BOIS DORMANT (Jean Richepin) role of the Prince Charmant.

1908 *La courtisane de corinthe (Michel Carré and P. Bilhaud) role of Cléonice.

1909 La nuit de mai (Alfred de Musset) role of the Poète (one-act play).

Cyrano de bergerac (Edmond Rostand) role of Cyrano (selections).

*Le procès de jeanne d'arc (Emile Moreau) role of Jeanne d'Arc.

1910 *La beffa (Jean Richepin–Sam Benelli) role of Gianetto Malespini.

La femme x (Alexandre Bisson) role of Jacqueline.

*Judas (John De Kay–Chassagne) role of Judas.

1911 Lucrèce borgia (Victor Hugo) role of Lucrèce Borgia.

1912 La reine elisabeth (Emile Moreau) role of Elizabeth of England.

*Une nuit de noël sous la terreur (M. Bernhardt and H. Cain) role of Marion (one-act play).

1913 *Jeanne doré (Tristan Bernard) role of Jeanne Doré.

1914 *Tout-à-coup (Paul and Guy de Cassagnac) role of La Marquise de Chalonne.

1915 *Les cathédrales (Eugène Morand) role of Strasbourg (one-act play).

1916 *La mort de cléopâtre (M. Bernhardt and H. Cain) role of Cléopâtre (one-act play).

*L'holocauste (Sarah Bernhardt) role of La Duchesse (one-act play).

*Du théâtre au champ d'honneur role of Marc Bertrand (one-act play).

*Vitrail (René Fauchois) role of Violaine (one-act play).

*Hecube (Maurice Bernhardt and R. Chavance) role of Hécube (one-act play).

*Le faux modèle (Edouard Daurelly) role of Madeleine (one-act play).

Le marchand de venise (Shakespeare) role of Portia (fragments).

*L'etoile dans la nuit (Henri Cain) role of Jane de Mauduit (one-act play).

1920 Athalie (Racine) role of Athalie.

*Daniel (Louis Verneuil) role of Daniel Arnault.

*Comment on ecrit l'histoire (Sacha Guitry) role of Mariette (one-act play).

1921 *La gloire (Maurice Rostand) role of la Gloire.

*Régine armand (Louis Verneuil) role of Régine Armand.

Note: The present list may omit certain roles played
by Sarah Bernhardt on tour.

Important Dates in the Life of Sarah Bernhardt

1844........Born in Paris.
1856........First Communion in the Convent of Grandchamps.
1860........Enters the Conservatoire.
1861........Takes second prize in tragedy.
1862........Debut at the Comédie Française.
1863........Leaves the Comédie Française.
1864........Small roles at the Gymnase.
1865........Birth of her only son, Maurice Bernhardt.
    Plays in operetta at the Porte Saint Martin.
1866........Engaged at the Odéon.
1869........Her first success: *Le Passant*.
1870–71.....Nurse at the Odéon, transformed into a military hospital.
1872........Her first great success: *Ruy Blas*.
    Leaves the Odéon and returns to the Comédie Française.
1874........Her first triumph: *Phèdre*.
1875........Named *Sociétaire* of the Comédie Française.
1877........Important revival of *Hernani* with Mounet Sully.
1880........Resigns from the Comédie Française. First American tour.
    Plays, for the first time, *La Dame aux Camélias*.
1881........First grand tour of Europe.
1882........Marries Jacques Damala.
    Becomes manager of the Théâtre de l'Ambigu.
    First great boulevard success: *Fédora*.
1883........Legal separation from Damala.
    Relinquishes the management of the Ambigu.
1884........Her apotheosis: *Théodora* at the Porte Saint Martin.
1886–87.....Grand tour in North and South America.
1889........Becomes a grandmother and creates the principal role
    in *Jeanne d'Arc*.
    Death of Damala.
1891–92–93..Her greatest tour (in the four quarters of the globe).
1893–98.....Manager of the Renaissance.
1899........Leaves the Renaissance and takes the Théâtre Sarah
    Bernhardt.
1900........First performance of *L'Aiglon*.

1905........Accident to her knee.
1915........Her right leg is amputated.
1916–17–18..Last tour in America.
1922........Her last play: *Régine Armand.*
1923........Death in Paris.

Index

Abbé Jules (L'), 212

Abbéma (Louise), 17, 19, 21, 100-101, 108, 126, 141, 194, 230, 269

Abbesse de Jouarre (L'), 215

Abbey (Henry), 120, 121, 128, 129, 130, 133, 134, 137

Absent (L'), 93

Adrienne Lecouvreur, 54 n., 122, 130, 133, 136, 140, 159, 162, 210, 247-248, 253

Aeschylus, 14

Affaire des Poisons (L'), 245

Affaires sont les Affaires (Les), 99, 212

Affranchi (L'), 72, 90

Affranchie (L'), 224

Agar, 68, 69, 145-146, 147, 149, 168, 171

Aicard (Jean), 99, 109, 243, 264

Aigle du Casque (L'), 147

Aiglon (L'), 191, 226, 228, 231-232, 234-236, 237, 238, 239, 240-241, 243, 245, 246, 247, 248, 250, 252, 255, 258, 267, 271, 273, 276

Alexander III (Czar), 159-160

Alexandre (René), 264

Alfonso XII, 158

Alfonso XIII, 285, 286

Alix, 129

Amants, 203, 210, 223, 235

Ambre (Emilie), 139

Amphytrion, 110, 208, 235

Andromaque, 91, 94, 115, 217, 242-243, 245, 262, 295

Angèle, 163

Angelo, 127, 139, 161, 175, 201

Angelo (Jean), 272

Angelo, Tyran de Padoue, 246, 247, 248

Annunzio (Gabriele d'), 12, 214, 215-216, 218-219, 223

Antonine, 168, 175

Antony, 123, 124

Arène (Emmanuel), 235

Arlésienne (L'), 10

Arnozan (Doctor), 269

Arquillière, 280, 283, 287, 293

Artois (Armand d'), 211

As de Trèfle (L'), 172

As in a Looking Glass, 195

Assommoir (L'), 119, 221

Athalie, 14-16, 63, 246, 274-275, 292, 295

Auber, 41, 42

Aubry (Raoul), 257

Aucoc (Monsieur), 26

Augier (Emile), 105-106, 119, 162

Autre (L'), 72

Aventurière (L'), 105-106, 119, 121, 150, 162

Aveu (L'), 193-194, 239

Banville (Théodore de), 87, 201

Barber of Seville (The), 36

Barbier (Jules), 198, 199

Baretta (Blanche), 101, 116, 191.

Baretta (Rose), 101

Baring (Maurice), 189, 229

Barrès (Maurice), 207

Barrière (Théodore), 48, 129

Bartet (Julia), 12, 99, 121, 143, 191, 192, 255

Barthou (Louis), 287

Bâtard (Le), 72, 90

Bauer (Henry), 212

Baujault (Mlle.), 272

Beaumarchais, 93

Beauvallet, 41, 42, 109

Beck (Martin), 266

Beffa (La), 257, 275

Belle au Bois Dormant (La), 191, 254, 276

Belle Hélène (La), 142

Belle Paule (La), 98

Belot (Adolphe), 64

Benelli (Sem), 257

Bérénice, 99, 217

Bergerat (Emile), 191, 244

Bernard (Raymond), 266

Bernard (Tristan), 4, 106, 266
Bernhardt (Edouard), 29, 30-31, 34, 35, 36
Bernhardt (Jacqueline), 21
Bernhardt (Jeanne), 102, 122, 126, 134-135, 138, 153-154, 162, 163, 179; *see also* Van Hard, Jeanne
Bernhardt (Lysiane), 18, 25, 28, 210, 269, 291
Bernhardt (Marcelle), 20, 25, 291
Bernhardt (Maurice), 9-10, 11, 13, 19, 20, 25, 26 n., 27, 50, 54, 55, 67, 70, 72, 90, 126, 141, 166-167, 171, 172, 186-187, 188, 192-193, 194, 199, 220, 223, 226-227, 245, 266, 269, 271, 272, 291
Bernhardt (Simone), 18, 20, 198, 199, 210, 256, 269, 291
Bernhardt (Terka), 192, 194, 198, 253-254
Bernstein (Henry), 99
Berr (Georges), 18
Berton (Charles), 65, 66
Berton (Pierre), 65, 100, 122, 124, 153, 169, 180, 183, 184, 185, 192, 195, 197, 203
Biche au Bois (La), 54, 175
Bilhaud (Paul), 255
Billot (General), 221
Bisson (Alexandre), 260
Bois Sacré (Le), 258
Boisdeffre (General de), 220
Booth, 128
Bornier (Henri de), 105, 106
Bossu (Le), 271
Bouffons (Les), 253, 257-258, 276
Bouilhet (Louis), 79
Boulenger (Marcel), 21
Bouquetière des Innocents (La), 172
Bourdet (Edouard), 82
Bourgeois (Anicet), 172
Bourgeois (Léon), 233
Brandès (Marthe), 191
Brémont (Louis), 223, 258
Bressant, 41, 65, 86, 91, 109
Briand (Aristide), 12, 287
Britannicus, 14, 92, 203
Brohan (Augustine), 41
Brohan (Madeleine), 100, 107, 116
Broisat (Emilie), 86, 116
Burbage, 295
Busnach (William), 126, 221

Cain (Henri), 254, 266, 272, 273
Calmettes (André), 227, 247, 252, 265

Calvaire (Le), 220
Campbell (Mrs. Patrick), 247
Carlisle (Alexandra), 17
Carré (Albert), 82
Carré (Michel), 255
Cartouche, 167
Casanova, 154
Casella (Georges), 277-278
Cassagnac (Guy de), 267
Cassagnac (Paul de), 267
Cassive (Armande), 94, 200
Cathédrales (Les), 271, 275
Caubet (Mlle.), 272
Cavalleria Rusticana, 214, **217**
Cena delle Beffe (La), 257
Chabrillat, 166, 167
Champmeslé, 295
Chantecler, 235
Charrette Anglaise (La), 9
Chassagne (J. C. de), 261
Châtiments (Les), 66
Chavance (René), 272
Chemineau (Le), 172, 271
Chéret, 163
Chèvrefeuille (Le), 218
Chez l'Avocat, 93-94, 193
Chilly (de), 58, 60, 63, 64, 65, 67, 74, 79, 83-85
Christian IX, 159
Cid (Le), 41, 92, 294
Città Morta (La), 218-219
Clairin (Georges), 17, 19, 101, 103, 108, 110-111, 126, 141, 194, 230, 269
Claretie (Jules), 82, 178, 190, 191
Clémenceau (Georges), 12, 268-269
Cléonice, 255
Cléopâtre, 1, 199-200, 245
Cléry (Julia de), 163
Cochran (C. B.), 286-288
Coeur d'Homme (Un), 257
Cogniard (the Brothers), 54
Colombey, 175
Colombier (Marie), 127, 134
Comédiens et Comédiennes, 96
Comment on écrit l'Histoire, 282
Comtesse de Sommerive (La), 129
Connor (William F.), 250, 251, 260
Contemporains (Les), 189
Coolus (Romain), 224
Cooper, 163, 167, 200
Coppée (François), 68, 100, 145, **212**, 220, 252

Coquelin *aîné*, 94, 99, 105, 107, 114, 116, 119, 123, 201, 207-208, 216, 234-239, 244, 245, 247, 295

Coquelin *cadet*, 114, 116, 208

Coquelin (Jean), 208

Cormon (Nelly), 280-282

Corneille (Pierre), 26, 92, 204

Course du Flambeau (La), 242

Courtisane de Corinthe (La), 254-255

Crawford (Marion), 239

Cressonnois (Lucien), 184

Crisafulli, 48

Croizette (Sophie), 86, 93, 95, 96-97, 100, 101, 107, 116, 121

Cromer (Lord), 287, 288

Crosby (Dr.), 131

Cross, 118

Curel (François de), 210

Cyrano de Bergerac, 99, 231, 235, 237, 238, 256, 286

Dalila, 93, 227

Damala (Jacques), 153-157, 160-174, 176-178, 194-195, 197-198, 240, 262

Dame aux Camélias (La), 7, 57, 99, 123-124, 133, 134, 135, 136, 137, 139, 140, 144, 156, 163, 178-179, 180, 197-198, 206, 209, 210-211, 214, 215, 217, 218, 224, 228, 235, 237, 238, 244, 246, 247, 255, 263, 265, 267, 270, 271, 273

Daniel, 10-14, 16-17, 18, 25, 98, 274-282, 284, 285, 292, 293

Daniel Rochat, 143

Daudet (Alphonse), 178, 240

Daudet (Léon), 207

Daurelly (Edouard), 273

Debay (Mademoiselle), 55, 175

Decoeur, 264

Decori, 171

Decourcelle (Pierre), 172, 219, 243

Delarue-Mardrus (Lucie), 264

Delaunay, 65, 106, 116, 123, 143

Delavigne (Casimir), 43

Delpit (Albert), 191

Delvair (Jeanne), 264

Demange (Maître), 219

De Max (Edouard), 1, 203, 205, 206, 209, 235, 240-241, 242, 243, 244, 246, 247-248, 254, 257, 260, 262

Demi-Monde (Le), 96, 215

Démon du Jeu (Le), 48

Denayrousse (Louis), 98

Deneubourg, 272

Denise, 215

Denuce (Doctor), 269

Dépit Amoureux (Le), 106

Depoix, 163

Derembourg, 175, 176, 178, 179, 180

Desclée (Aimée), 122, 123, 175, 206

Deshayes (Paul), 167, 168

Desjardins, 239, 242, 243, 246, 247

Deslandes (Raymond), 48, 142-143, 151-152

Dessonnes, 264

Deux Gosses (Les), 243

Deval (Abel), 203, 204, 206, 208, 213, 219, 222, 223, 224

Deval (Jacques), 204

Diaz de Mendoza, 224

Dieudonné, 122, 163

Divorçons, 143, 215

Doche (Madame), 123, 163

Dolls' House (A), 215

Domino Noir (Le), 41

Don Pietro Caruso, 224

Donnay (Maurice), 203, 210, 223, 271

Donnelly (Dorothy), 260

Dora, 143, 274

Dorval (Marie), 109

Dorziat (Gabrielle), 254

Doucet (Camille), 44, 50, 57-58, 69

Drame de la Rue de la Paix (Le), 64

Dreyfus (Captain Alfred), 207, 219-223

Dreyfus (Mathieu), 219, 221

Dubech (Lucien), 290

Dubois (Paul), 68

Dubosc (Gaston), 293

Duchesne (Dr.), 74

Dudlay (Adeline), 191, 255

Dufrène (Alice), 21

Dufrène (Blanche), 223, 243, 244, 252, 257, 270

Dugué (Fernand), 172

Dumaine, 163, 183

Dumanoir, 48

Dumas *fils* (Alexandre), 107, 123, 163, 178, 192, 206, 214, 215, 217, 295

Dumas *père* (Alexandre), 65-66, 86, 123, 180, 228, 271

Du-mény (Camille), 192, 267

Dupuis (Adolphe), 153

Duquesne, 201

Duquesnel (Félix), 58, 60, 62, 63, 64, 65, 67, 68, 69, 71, 72, 73, 74, 79, 80, 83-86, 122, 126, 180-181, 184, 199, 200, 254
Duse (Eleonora), 214-219, 295

Ecole des Femmes (L'), 42
Ecole des Vieillards (L'), 43
Edison (Thomas), 133-134
Edward VII, 118
Enfant Vainqueur (L'), 271
Enigme (L'), 242
Ennery (d'), 56, 167, 179
Escalier (Félix), 101
Esterházy, 221, 222, 223
Esther, 14, 246-247
Eté de la Saint Martin (L'), 96
Etoile dans la Nuit (L'), 272-273
Etourdi (L'), 45
Etrangère (L'), 107, 115, 122, 124, 133, 140
Eugénie (Empress), 50
Euripides, 14

Fabre (Emile), 82
Faguet (Emile), 217
Famille Benoîton (La), 143
Fasquelle (Eugène), 253
Farrère (Madame Claude), 25
Fauchois (René), 8, 260, 272
Faure (Félicien), 32, 36, 126
Faure (Félix), 230
Faure (Henriette), 31, 36, 126
Fausse Agnès (La), 43
Faust, 234
Faux Modèle (Le), 273
Favart (Maria), 65, 93, 100, 116
Favières, 272
Fabvre (Frédéric), 107, 114, 116, 119
Fechter (Armand), 123
Fédora, 1, 151, 153, 164-165, 168, 169, 170, 171, 174, 180, 181, 184, 185, 206, 210, 235, 241, 242, 247, 255
Félix (Dinah), 99
Femme de Claude (La), 206-207, 210, 214, 215, 217, 235, 239, 246, 247, 294
Femme Idéale (La), 215
Femme X (La), 260-261
Femmes Fortes (Les), 143
Femmes Savantes (Les), 45, 63
Féraudy (Jacques de), 287, 293
Féraudy (Maurice de), 99, 177, 179

Fernande, 215
Ferrier (Paul), 94, 193
Ferry (Jules), 145
Feuilles d'Automne (Les), 52
Feuillet (Octave), 93, 95, 226
Féval (Paul), 271
Fiaccola sotto il Moggio (La), 215
Figlia di Jorio (La), 215
Figurante (La), 210
Filippi (Félix), 244
Fille de Pilate (La), 260
Fille de Roland (La), 105, 106, 115
Fille du Cid (La), 43
Fils de Coralie (Le), 191
Firmin, 109
Flers (Robert de), 18, 255
Fleur Merveilleuse (La), 253
Fleuriot (Zénaïde), 193
Fleury (the actor), 201
Fleury (the painter), 36
Foch (Ferdinand), 12, 75-77
Fourberies de Scapin (Les), 216
Fra Diavolo, 41
France (Anatole), 12
Francesca da Rimini, 239-240
Francillon, 192
François le Champi, 64
Franz Josef (Emperor), 158
French Theater in New York, 248
Fressard (Madame), 33
Frévalles (Simone), 293
Friedrich (Archduke), 158-159
Frisson de l'Aigle (Le), 252
Frohman (Charles), 273
Froufrou, 122, 132, 133, 136, 140, 160, 175, 178, 179, 180, 209, 210, 250
Fuller, Loie, 260

Gabrielle, 105, 106
Gambetta, 148
Garnier (Philippe), 150, 157, 160, 181, 182-185, 188, 192, 198, 199, 203
Garrick, 295
Gavault (Paul), 252
Geffroy, 81
Gendre de M. Poirier (Le), 96, 105
Géniat (Marcelle), 280-282, 283, 287
George V, 288
Gerbois (Monsieur de), 48
Germinal, 221
Gervais, 272

Ghosts, 224
Giffard (Pierre), 111
Gillette (William), 219
Gioconda (La), 215
Gismonda, 1, 202, 207, 208, 210, 225, 235, 245
Gladstone, 118
Glass, 272
Gloire (La), 22, 274, 289-292
Gloria (La), 215
Glu (La), 171, 180
Goethe, 243
Goldoni, 214, 215, 217
Gonse (General), 220
Got (Edmond), 106, 107, 116, 123
Gounod (Charles), 199
Gournay (Jeanne de), 11, 20, 21, 284, 291
Gozlan (Léon), 238
Grand Soir (Le), 260
Granier (Jeanne), 94, 200, 210, 255, 271
Grant (General), 133
Grau (Maurice), 188, 202, 206, 236
Grétillat (Jacques), 293
Grévy (Jules), 145, 148
Gringoire, 201, 276
Grivot (Madame Laurence), 163
Gross (Edgar), 27
Gross (Simone), 18, 20, 256
Guérard (Madame), 19, 37, 39, 41, 42, 47, 54, 60, 74, 127, 138, 171, 172, 194
Guerrero (Maria), 224
Guitry (Lucien), 25, 99, 203, 206, 207, 208, 209, 210, 219, 222, 224, 225, 234-235, 238, 266, 282, 295
Guitry (Sacha), 25, 282
Guyon (Emilie), 109
Guyot (Yves), 221

Hading (Jane), 176, 178, 188, 236, 240, 244, 260
Hahn (Reynaldo), 21
Halévy (Ludovic), 96, 122, 175
Hamlet, 184-185, 228-231, 237, 247, 250, 267, 276, 295
Haraucourt (Edmond), 212, 264
Harding (Lyn), 17
Harris (Sybil), 17
Hébrard (A. J.), 254
Hécube, 272
Hedda Gabler, 215

Hellmann (Denise), 21
Henry (Colonel), 220, 223
Hérelle (G.), 218-219
Hermant (Abel), 210
Hernani, 65, 70, 108-109, 115, 118, 122, 133, 134, 140, 142
Hervé, 200
Hervieu (Paul), 242
Hollingshead, 115, 121
Holocauste (L'), 272
Homer, 30
Hortense, 70, 145-146, 149
Houssaye (Arsène), 125
Hubert, 272
Hugo (Victor), 51, 52, 65-66, 70, 80-81, 85, 108, 109, 118-119, 147, 183, 233, 246, 261, 295
Huguenet (Félix), 195, 246
Humières (Robert d'), 259-260

Ibsen, 215
Impromptu du Paquetage (L'), 271
Infidèle (L'), 208
Iphigénie, 44, 55
Irving, 295
Izéil, 202, 206, 209, 210, 228, 235

Jablonovska (Terka), 192, 194, 198, 253-254
Jarrett (Edward), 117, 120, 128, 129, 130, 132, 133, 134, 135, 138, 139, 188
Jean-Marie, 79, 208, 239
Jeanne d'Arc, 198-199
Jeanne Doré, 4, 265, 266-267, 275, 294
Jeanne Wedekind, 244
Jeu de l'Amour et du Hasard (Le), 60, 63
Joubé (Romuald), 267, 271
Joumard, 163
Journal d'une Femme de Chambre (Le), 220
Judas, 261
Juif Polonais (Le), 235
Julius Caesar, 204
Jullien (Mary), 122

Kalb (Marie), 122, 175
Kampf (Leopold), 260
Kay (John De), 261
Kean, 65-66
Kératry (Comte de), 74
Kerly (Jeanne), 193

King Lear, 63, 90
Kismet, 266
Knoblock (Edward), 266
Krauss (Henry), 254
Krauss (Luigi), 244

Labiche (Eugène), 48
Lacressonnière, 171
Lady from the Sea (The), 215
Lafontaine, 81, 114
Lamartine, 87
Lambert (Madeleine), 287
Lambquin (Madame), 74
Lara, 110
Laroche, 98, 103
Larrey (Baron), 31, 32, 33, 36, 74
Latour de Saint-Ybars, 72
Laudi (Le), 215
Laurent (Marie), 206
Lavedan (Henri), 18, 99, 245, 266, 274
Lavolée (Régis), 36, 40, 42
Lazare (Bernard), 219, 220
Le Bargy (Charles), 99, 218, 233
Leconte (Marie), 254
Lecouvreur (Adrienne), 53n., 130-131, 295
Legault (Maria), 153
Lély (Madeleine), 271
Lemaître (Frédérick), 65, 295
Lemaître (Jules), 189, 196, 204-205, 216, 220, 266
Léna, 195-196, 197, 202
Lenôtre (Georges), 245
Lesueur (Madame Daniel), 252
Ligne (General de), 57
Ligne (Prince Eugène de), 57
Ligne (Prince Henri de), 52-54, 55, 56-60, 72, 185-187
Lincoln (Mrs. Abraham), 128
Lloyd (Marie), 100, 108
Locandiera (La), 214, 217
Lorenzaccio, 202, 211-212, 228, 263, 267, 276, 295
Lorsque l'Enfant paraît, 52
Loterie du Mariage (La), 66
Loubet (Emile), 230
Louis XIV, 246
Lovelace, 154
Lucrèce Borgia, 261, 266
Lynn (Emmy), 257
Lysiane, 224

Macbeth, 179, 180, 227

MacMahon (Marshal de), 106-107
Madame Sans-Gêne, 99, 201
Madame X, 260
Mademoiselle Aïssé, 79
Mademoiselle de Belle-Isle, 86, 87, 92
Mademoiselle ma Mère, 16
Maeterlinck (Maurice), 247
Magda, 209, 210, 214, 215, 217, 246, 247
Magnier (Pierre), 224, 227, 238, 239, 242
Maille (Constance), 254
Maintenon (Madame de), 246
Maison sans Enfants (La), 48
Maître de Forges (Le), 176-178
Maîtresse de Piano (La), 254
Mallefille (Félicien), 178
Manuel (Eugène), 93
Marais, 175, 176, 179, 180, 183, 203
Mari qui lance sa Femme (Un), 48, 142
Mariage de Figaro (Le), 93
Marie-Jeanne, or La Femme du Peuple, 179
Mariette, 282
Marion Delorme, 183, 185
Mariquita, 55
Marivaux, 60, 262
Marot (Dr.), 21, 259, 284, 291
Marquet (Marcel), 193
Marquet (Mary), 26, 271
Marquis de Priola (Le), 99
Marquis de Villemer (Le), 64
Mars (Mademoiselle), 191, 295
Martel, 119
Martyre de Saint Sébastien (Le), 218
Mary (Queen), 288
Mason (Hamilton), 248
Masque d'Amour (Le), 252
Massenet, 12
Maubant, 65, 84, 92, 105, 109, 114
Mauloy (Georges), 280
Maurier (Gerald du), 283
Maury, 254
Mauvais Bergers (Les), 219, 222, 223, 235
Mayer, 115, 121
Méa (Jeanne), 201, 272
Médecin malgré Lui (Le), 208
Médée, 224
Meilhac (Henri), 96, 122, 175
Mélesville, 44
Mélingue, 81, 114
Mendelssohn, 63
Mendès (Catulle), 5, 165, 212, 224, 229, 243, 252, 254, 256

Mercanton (Louis), 26
Merchant of Venice (The), 273
Mercier (General), 220
Mères Ennemies (Les), 165, 168, 169, 177
Mères Françaises, 265, 271
Mères Repenties (Les), 178
Meurice (Paul), 80, 228
Meute (La), 210
Meydieu (Adolphe), 36, 40, 41, 42
Meyer (Arthur), 18, 101
Meyerbeer, 145
Michel Perrin, 224
Millaud (Albert), 112-113
Miller (Gilbert), 17
Mirbeau (Octave), 99, 219, 220, 221, 222
Misanthrope (Le), 96, 115, 235
Misérables (Les), 183
Mithridate, 114
Moglie Ideale (La), 215
Molière, 42, 45, 106, 110, 208, 239, 262, 295
Monde où l'On s'ennuie (Le), 255
Monod (Doctor), 36
Monsieur Beverley, 9
Montaland (Céline), 51
Montbazon (Marie), 293
Montigny (the actor), 171
Montigny (director of the Gymnase), 48-49, 50-51
Morand (Eugène), 206, 228, 271
Moreau (Emile), 254, 256, 262, 265
Morlay (Gaby), 16
Morny (Duc de), 36, 39-40, 41, 42, 44, 47, 57, 67
Morris (Clara), 129-130
Mort de Cléopâtre (La), 272
Morte Civile (La), 224
Mounet (Paul), 193
Mounet Sully (Jean), 12, 90-92, 94, 98, 99, 105, 107, 108, 109, 110, 114, 116, 123, 147, 205, 216, 229-230, 243, 255, 264, 295
Mucha, 230
Munte (Lina), 176
Musset (Alfred de), 64, 107, 211, 255

Nana, 221
Nana Sahib, 176, 178, 179, 180
Napoléon I, 128
Napoléon III, 50-52, 69-70, 73, 109
Napoléon le Petit, 51
Nathalie, 46, 50, 82, 107, 190

Nicholas II (Czar), 211
Nilsson, 188
Noailles (Comtesse de), 264
Noblet (Georges), 282
Noé (Lily), 136
Novelli (Ermete), 224, 295
Nuit de Mai (La), 107, 255
Nuit de Noël sous la Terreur (Une), 266
Nuit d'Octobre (La), 255

Oceano Nox, 51
Odette, 153, 215
Oedipe roi, 99
Ohnet (Georges), 176, 178
On ne badine pas avec l'Amour, 96
Oncle Sam (L'), 143
Othello, 109-110

Painlevé (Paul), 287
Par le Fer et par le Feu, 245-246
Parfouru (Paul), 75
Parodi (Alexandre), 108, 212
Pascal (Andrée), 293
Passant (Le), 68-69, 70, 71, 93, 145, 159, 193, 220, 276, 294
Pasteur (Louis), 213
Patti (Adelina), 71, 188
Paty de Clam (Lt. Colonel du), 220
Pedro II (Dom), 188
Pelisse (Mlle.), 272
Pelléas et Mélisande, 247, 276
Père Lebonnard (Le), 99, 224
Perrin (Emile), 82, 83, 86, 91, 92, 93, 95, 98, 105, 106, 107, 108, 110, 112, 115, 119, 123, 190
Perrault, 254
Perronnet (Maurice), 21
Petit Faust (Le), 200
Petite Idole, 193
Phèdre, 14, 94, 98-99, 106, 108, 115, 116, 122, 133, 134, 140, 142, 159, 161, 193, 205, 206, 210, 212, 228, 235, 237, 239, 242, 243, 247, 262, 264, 266, 295
Philips (F. C.), 195
Picard (Hélène), 254
Picquart (Lieutenant Colonel), 220, 222, 223
Pierné (Gabriel), 212
Pierson (Blanche), 51, 124, 153, 163, 274
Pisanelle (La), 218
Piste (La), 245
Più che l'Amore, 215

Pius IX, 132
Pluie et le Beau Temps (La), **238**
Plus que Reine, 243-244, 247, 248
Poincaré (Raymond), 12, 268
Polhes (General de), 36
Polyeucte, 216
Porché (François), 53n.
Porel (Paul), 75, 79, 193, 208
Porto-Riche (Georges de), 12, 208
Pot-Bouille, 221
Pour la Couronne, 252
Pozzi (Professor), 269
Praga (Marco), 215
Praince (Marcelle), 287
Précieuses Ridicules (Les), 115, **239**, 294
Prière des Naufragés (La), 56
Prince of Wales (Edward), 118
Prince Zilah (Le), 178
Princesse Georges (La), 123, 124, 133, 140, 144
Princesse Lointaine (La), 209, 223, **231**, 235
Printemps (Yvonne), 282
Procès de Jeanne d'Arc (Le), 7, **256**-257, 258, 260, 262, 273
Provost, 41, 43
Puccini (Giacomo), 192
Puylagarde (Roger), 293

Quarante ans de Théâtre, 206
Quo Vadis, 203

Rabagas, 143
Rachel, 39, 43, 99, 117-118, 122, 125, 295
Racine (Jean), 14, 44, 63, 92, 94, 98, 99, 114, 145, 242, 246, 295
Rains (Claude), 17
Rayons et les Ombres (Les), 51
Régine Armand, 22, 23, 25, 98, 274, 275, 292-293
Régnier, 41
Régnier (Henry de), 264
Reichemberg (Suzanne), 100, 191
Reine Elizabeth (La), 262, 265
Réjane, 12, 75, 99, 153, 171, 195, **216**, 240, 245, 255, 295
Rémon (Maurice), 209
Rémusat (Paul de), 72-73, 77
Renan (Ernest), 215
Renard (Jules), 5-6
Richelieu (Duc de), 154

Richepin (Jean), 171, **172**, 173, 174, 175, 176, 177, 179, 254, 257, **264**, **271**
Rivoire (André), 254
Robert le Diable, 145
Robinne (Gabrielle), 246
Roch (Madeleine), 264
Rochefort (Henri), 207
Rodays (Ferdinand de), 207
Rodin, 12, 260
Rodogune, 26
Roggers (Henriette), 25
Rois (Les), 204, 206
Romain, 163
Romanesques (Les), 209, 231
Rome Vaincue, 108, 115, 212, 294
Rosmersholm, 215
Rossini, 36
Rostand (Edmond), 9, 12, 99, 209, 212, 213-214, 231-234, 238, 239, 240, 246, 258, 264, 271, 286, 289, 295
Rostand (Maurice), 22, 289-290
Roussell (Henry), 257
Rubenstein (Ida), 218
Ruy Blas, 65, 66, 80-81, 86, 109, 114, 115, 118, 121, 142, 233

Sade (Marquis de), 154
Saint-Germain, 163, 176
Saint-Saëns (Camille), 12
Saint-Victor (Paul de), 99
Sainte-Sophie (Mother), 34
Samaritaine (La), 213-214, 228, **231**, **239**, 255
Samary (Jeanne), 116
Samary (Marie), 193
Samson (Charles), 184
Samson (Joseph), 41, 43
Samson, 99
Sand (George), 64, 72
Sapho, 178, 240, 243, 247
Sarah Barnum, 127
Sarcey (Francisque), 44, 45, 87-90, **96**-97, 99, 123, 162, 206, 209
Sardou (Victorien), 1, 9, 48-49, 55, 99, 103, 143, 151-153, 164-165, 166, 168, 175, 180-181, 184, 191-192, 196, 199, 200, 207, 208, 212, 213, 215, 220, 245, 255, 274, 295
Saxe (Maurice de), 53n., 54n., 131, 248
Scheurer-Kestner, 220, 221

Scholl (Aurélien), 104
Schurmann (Joseph), 214, 215
Schwob (Marcel), 228, 239, 243
Schwoebel (Joseph), 271
Scribe (Eugène), 44, 53n., 54n., 122, 136
Sébastien Roch, 220
Secret Service, 219, 223
Segond-Weber (Madame), 16
Serge Panine, 178
Sergine (Vera), 260
Servir, 266
Sexe Faible (Le), 106
Saylor (Suzanne), 201, 259
Shakespeare (William), 179, 273, 295
Shubert (Lee), 250, 251
Shubert (Sam), 250, 251
Sienkiewicz (Henry), 246
Silvain, 99, 264
Silvain (Louise), 264
Silvestre (Armand), 206, 212
Simon (Auguste), 167, 172
Sire, 274
Sisos (Raphaèle), 193
Smith (Aubrey), 17
Smith (Henry), 135-136, 137
Sogno d'un Mattino di Primavera, 214, 215, 217
Sophocles, 14, 99
Sorcière (La), 1-3, 245, 246, 247, 248, 250, 255
Sphinx (Le), 95, 96, 97, 100, 115, 122, 133, 140
Spiritisme, 213, 223, 245
Stevens (Alfred), 100
Stoullig (Edmond), 164, 197, 263
Straus (Oscar), 282
Sudermann (Hermann), 209, 214
Sujet de Roman (Uu), 25
Sulbac, 200
Surprise de l'Amour (La), 262
Sydney, 163

Talbot, 122
Talien, 80
Talma, 295
Tartuffe, 262, 294
Tellegen, Lou, 258-260, 261-263, 264, 265, 266
Tenailles (Les), 242
Terry (Ellen), 295
Tessandier (Aimée), 163

Testa (Gherardi de), 215
Testament de César Girodot (Le), 64
Théâtre au Champ d'Honneur (Du), 7, 272
Théodora, 1, 175, 180-182, 198, 239, 266
Thermidor, 208
Théroigne de Méricourt, 242
Theuriet (André), 79, 208, 212
Thierry (Edouard), 44, 46, 81-82
Thiers (Adolphe), 72, 77
Thiron, 107, 116
Tillet (Jules de), 211
Topaze, 106
Tosca (La), 1, 65, 191-192, 194, 197-198, 200, 204, 213, 214, 227, 237, 245, 247, 248-249, 255
Tour de Nesle (La), 180, 271
Touroude (Alfred), 72
Tout-à-Coup, 267, 275
Tovaritch, 204
Tragédie de Salomé (La), 259
Train, 122
Traité d'Auteuil (Le), 9
Traviata (La), 139
Trébor (Robert), 263
Turquet (Edmond), 112

Ugalde (Jeanne), 54
Ullmann (Victor), 10, 11, 13, 21, 206, 226-227, 271, 280
Umberto (King), 158

Vacquerie (Auguste), 80
Valérie, 44
Van Hard (Gustave), 30
Van Hard (Henriette), 31, 36, 126
Van Hard (Jeanne), 33, 35, 36, 37, 38, 50, 68, 102; see also Bernhardt, Jeanne
Van Hard (Julie), 29, 30-39, 44, 46, 47, 48, 50, 67-68, 71, 102, 107, 126
Van Hard (Lisa), 30, 34, 67, 70, 126
Van Hard (Mathilde), 31, 78
Van Hard (Régina), 35, 46, 50, 72, 101, 126
Van Hard (Rosine), 31, 32-33, 36, 67, 68, 126
Van Hard van Bruck (Anna), 31, 35
Varennes, 245, 294
Verga, 214
Verlaine (Paul), 53n.
Verlaine tel qu'il fut, 53n.

Vert-Calant (Le), 254
Vierge d'Avila (La), 252, 256, 294
Vierge de Lutèce (La), 271
Vigée-Lebrun (Madame), 245
Ville Morte (La), 219, 223
Villeroy (Auguste), 271
Villetard, 64
Violaine, 21
Vitrail, 8, 272, 275
Vitre (La), 271-272
Vitu (Auguste), 119
Vol de la Marseillaise (Le), 271
Voltaire, 43, 98
Voyante (La), 26

Weiss (J. J.), 141
Werther, 243
Wilhelm I, 79
Wilhelm II, 241
Willy, 242
Worms, 101, 109, 116

Yonnel (Jean), 280, 284

Zaïre, 43, 98, 112
Zamacoïs (Miguel), 253
Zaza, 195
Zola (Emile), 119, 221-223
Zukor (Adolph), 265

171 P